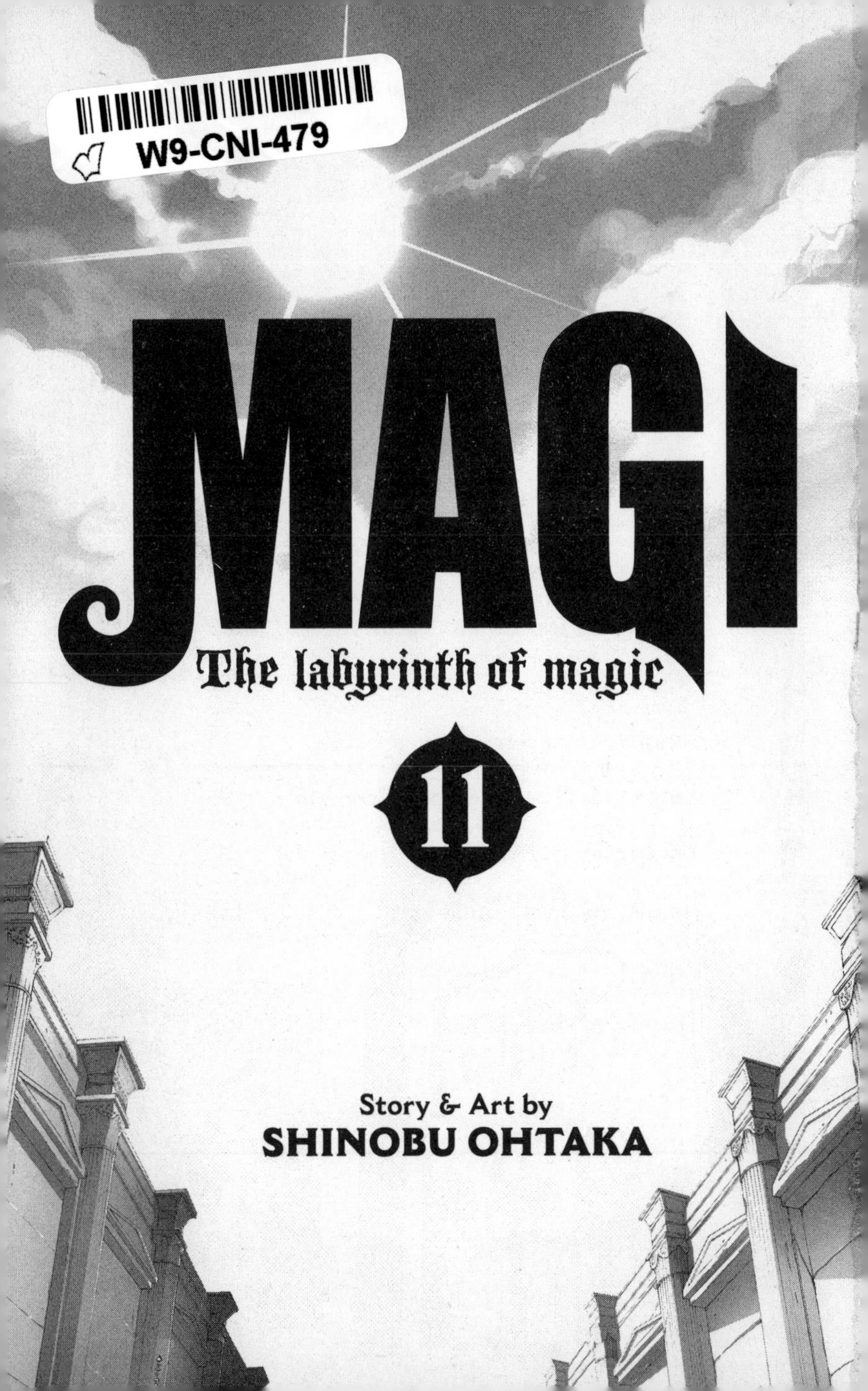

MAGI

The labyrinth of magic

11

Story & Art by

SHINOBU OHTAKA

MAGI
The labyrinth of magic

11

CONTENTS

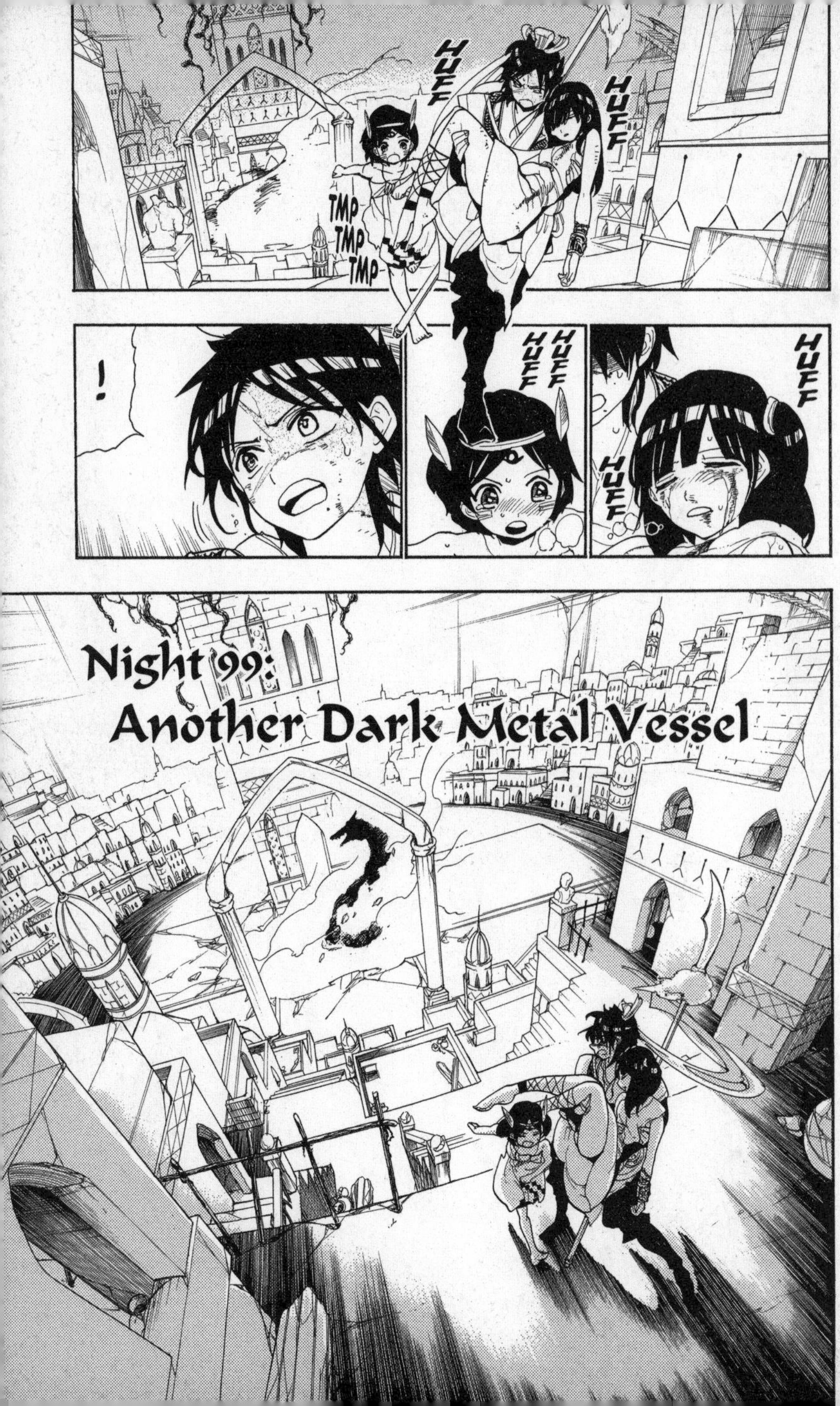
HUFF
HUFF
TMP TMP TMP
HUFF
HUFF
HUFF HUFF
!
Night 99: Another Dark Metal Vessel

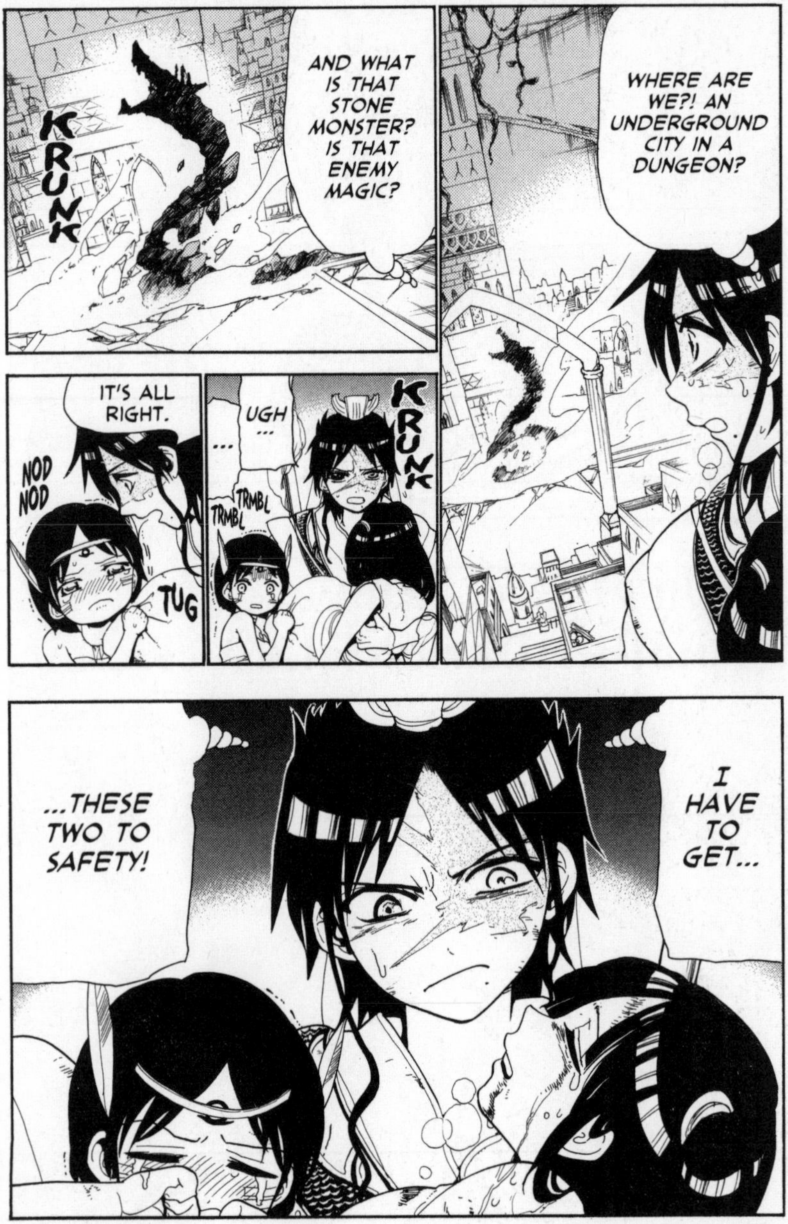
WHERE ARE WE?! AN UNDERGROUND CITY IN A DUNGEON?
AND WHAT IS THAT STONE MONSTER? IS THAT ENEMY MAGIC?
KRUNK
KRUNK
UGH ...
...
TRMBL TRMBL
IT'S ALL RIGHT.
NOD NOD
TUG
I HAVE TO GET...
...THESE TWO TO SAFETY!

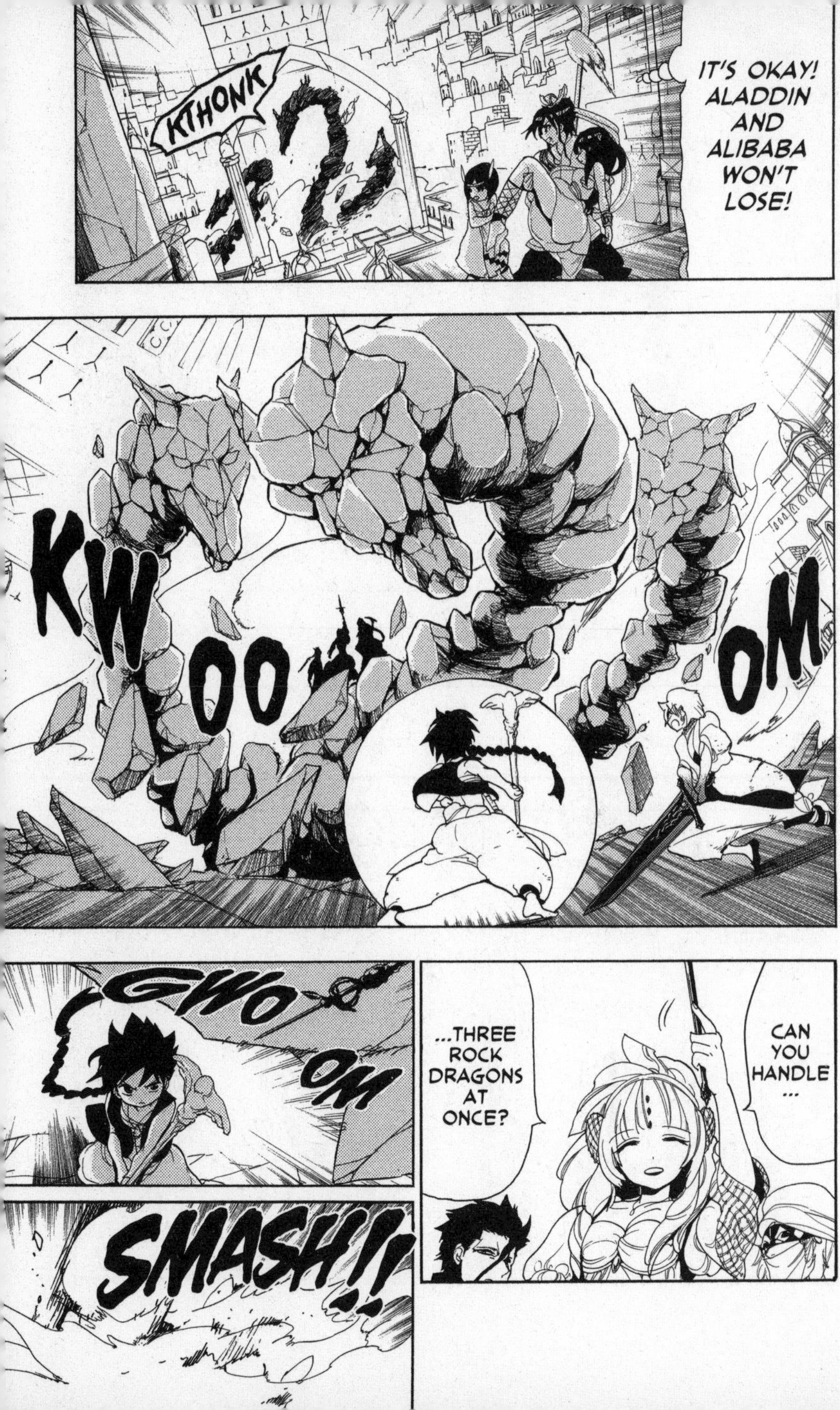
IT'S OKAY! ALADDIN AND ALIBABA WON'T LOSE!
KTHONK
KWOOOM
CAN YOU HANDLE ...
...THREE ROCK DRAGONS AT ONCE?
GWOOOM
SMASH!!

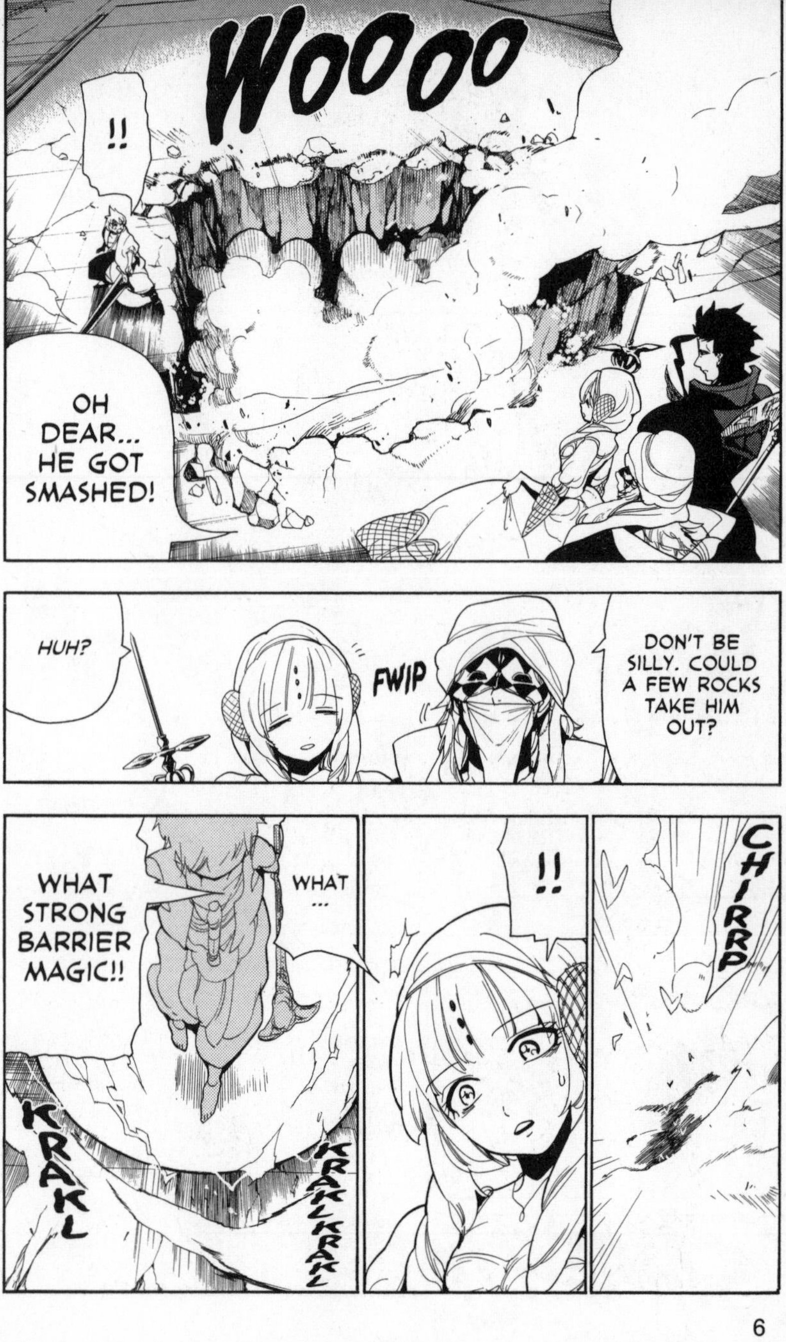
WOOOO
!!
OH DEAR... HE GOT SMASHED!
DON'T BE SILLY. COULD A FEW ROCKS TAKE HIM OUT?
FWIP
HUH?
CHIRRP
!!
WHAT ...
WHAT STRONG BARRIER MAGIC!!
KRAKLKRAKL
KRAKL

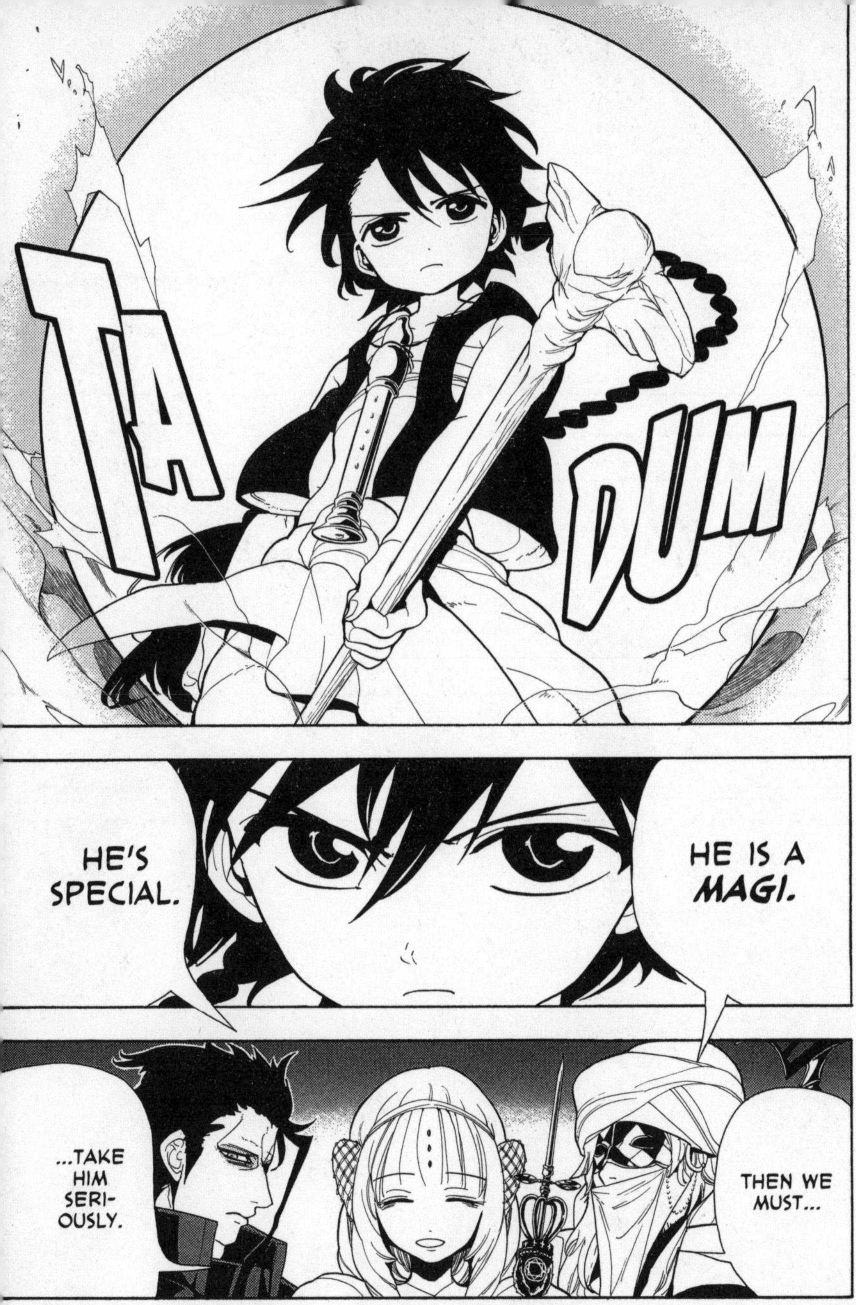
TA
DUM
HE IS A MAGI.
HE'S SPECIAL.
THEN WE MUST...
...TAKE HIM SERIOUSLY.

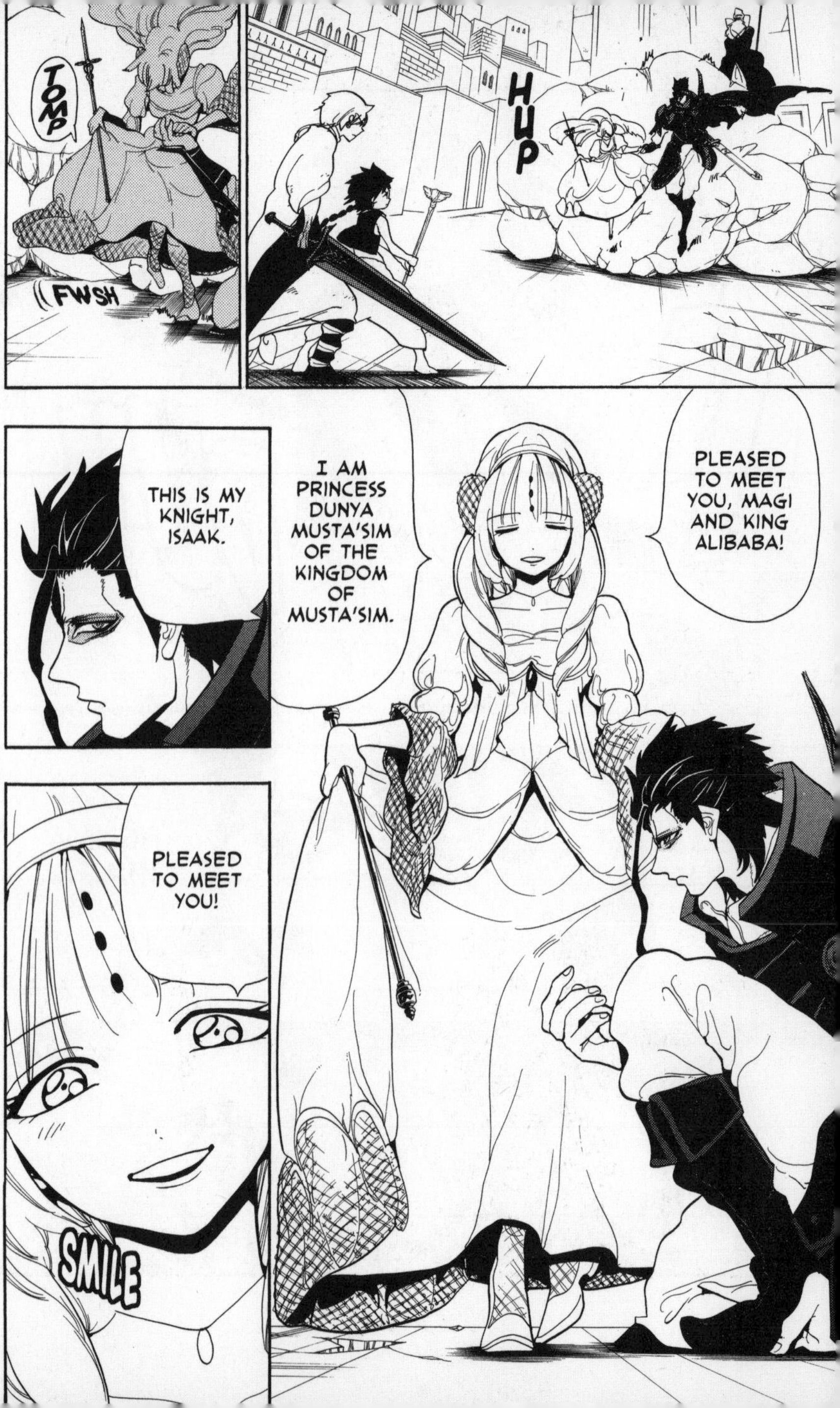
HUP
TOMP
FWSH
PLEASED TO MEET YOU, MAGI AND KING ALIBABA!
I AM PRINCESS DUNYA MUSTA'SIM OF THE KINGDOM OF MUSTA'SIM.
THIS IS MY KNIGHT, ISAAK.
PLEASED TO MEET YOU!
SMILE

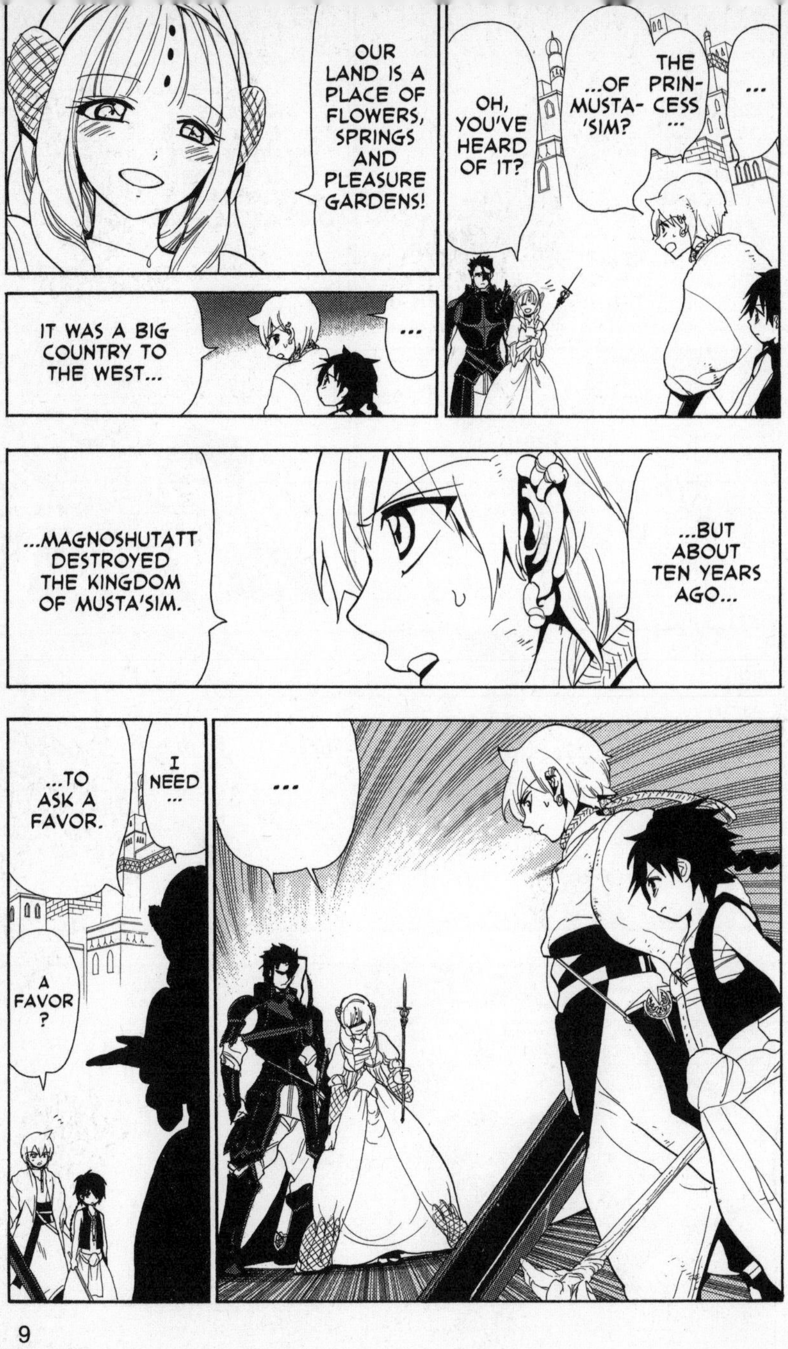
...
THE PRINCESS...
...OF MUSTA'SIM?
OH, YOU'VE HEARD OF IT?
OUR LAND IS A PLACE OF FLOWERS, SPRINGS AND PLEASURE GARDENS!
...
IT WAS A BIG COUNTRY TO THE WEST...
...BUT ABOUT TEN YEARS AGO...
...MAGNOSHUTATT DESTROYED THE KINGDOM OF MUSTA'SIM.
...
I NEED...
...TO ASK A FAVOR.
A FAVOR?

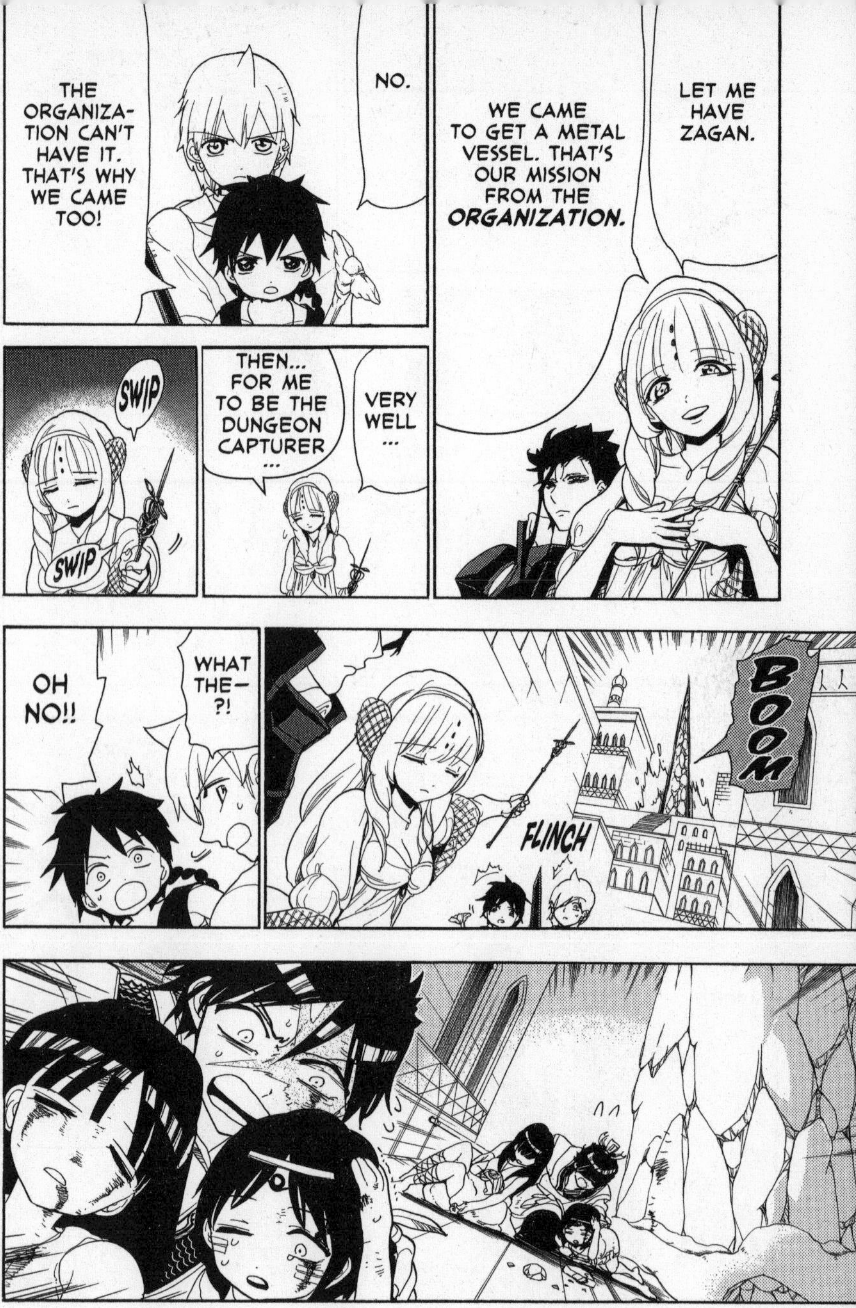
LET ME HAVE ZAGAN.
WE CAME TO GET A METAL VESSEL. THAT'S OUR MISSION FROM THE ORGANIZATION.
NO.
THE ORGANIZATION CAN'T HAVE IT. THAT'S WHY WE CAME TOO!
VERY WELL ...
THEN... FOR ME TO BE THE DUNGEON CAPTURER ...
SWIP
SWIP
BOOM
FLINCH
WHAT THE—?!
OH NO!!

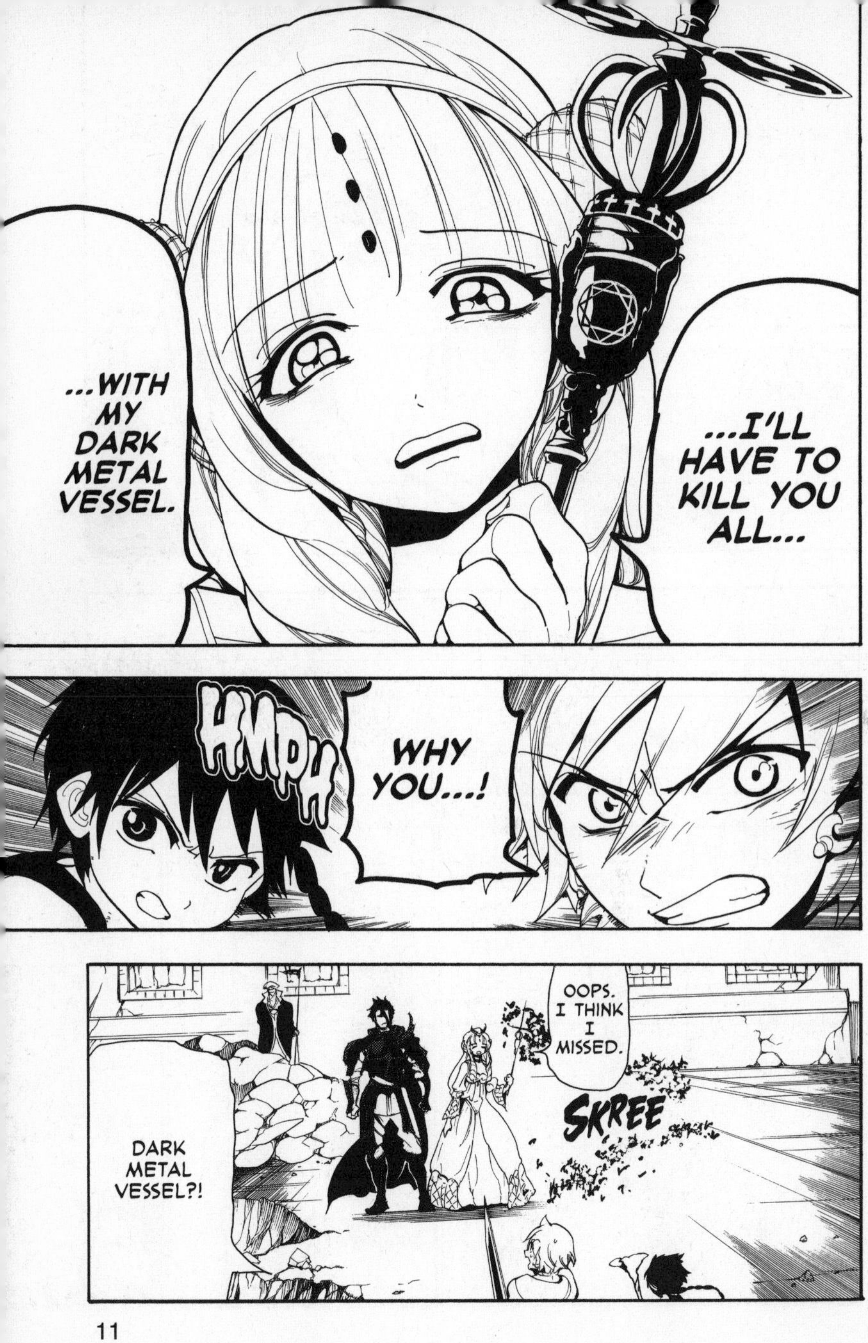
...I'LL HAVE TO KILL YOU ALL...
...WITH MY DARK METAL VESSEL.
WHY YOU...!
HMPH
OOPS. I THINK I MISSED.
SKREE
DARK METAL VESSEL?!

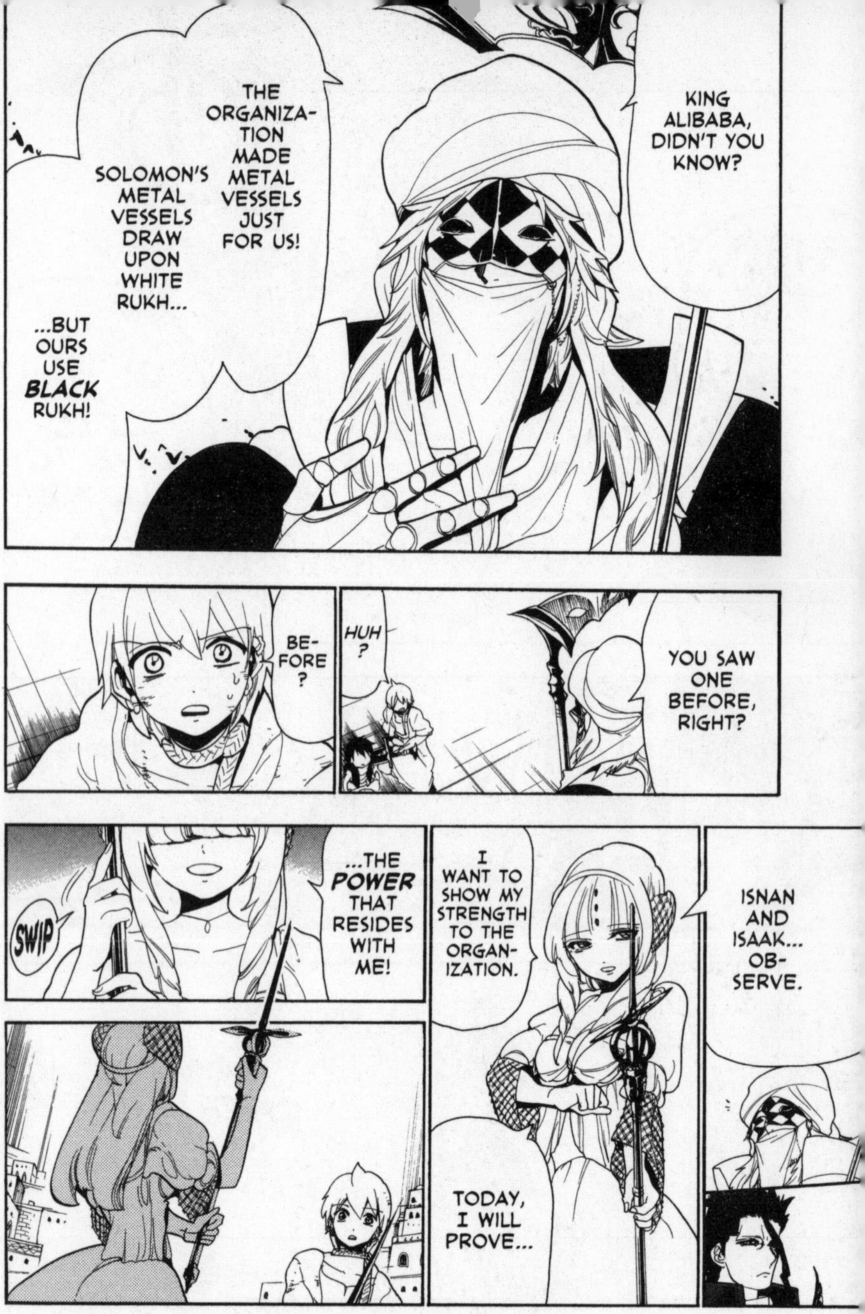
KING ALIBABA, DIDN'T YOU KNOW?
THE ORGANIZATION MADE METAL VESSELS JUST FOR US!
SOLOMON'S METAL VESSELS DRAW UPON WHITE RUKH...
...BUT OURS USE BLACK RUKH!
YOU SAW ONE BEFORE, RIGHT?
HUH?
BEFORE?
ISNAN AND ISAAK... OBSERVE.
I WANT TO SHOW MY STRENGTH TO THE ORGANIZATION.
TODAY, I WILL PROVE...
...THE POWER THAT RESIDES WITH ME!
SWIP

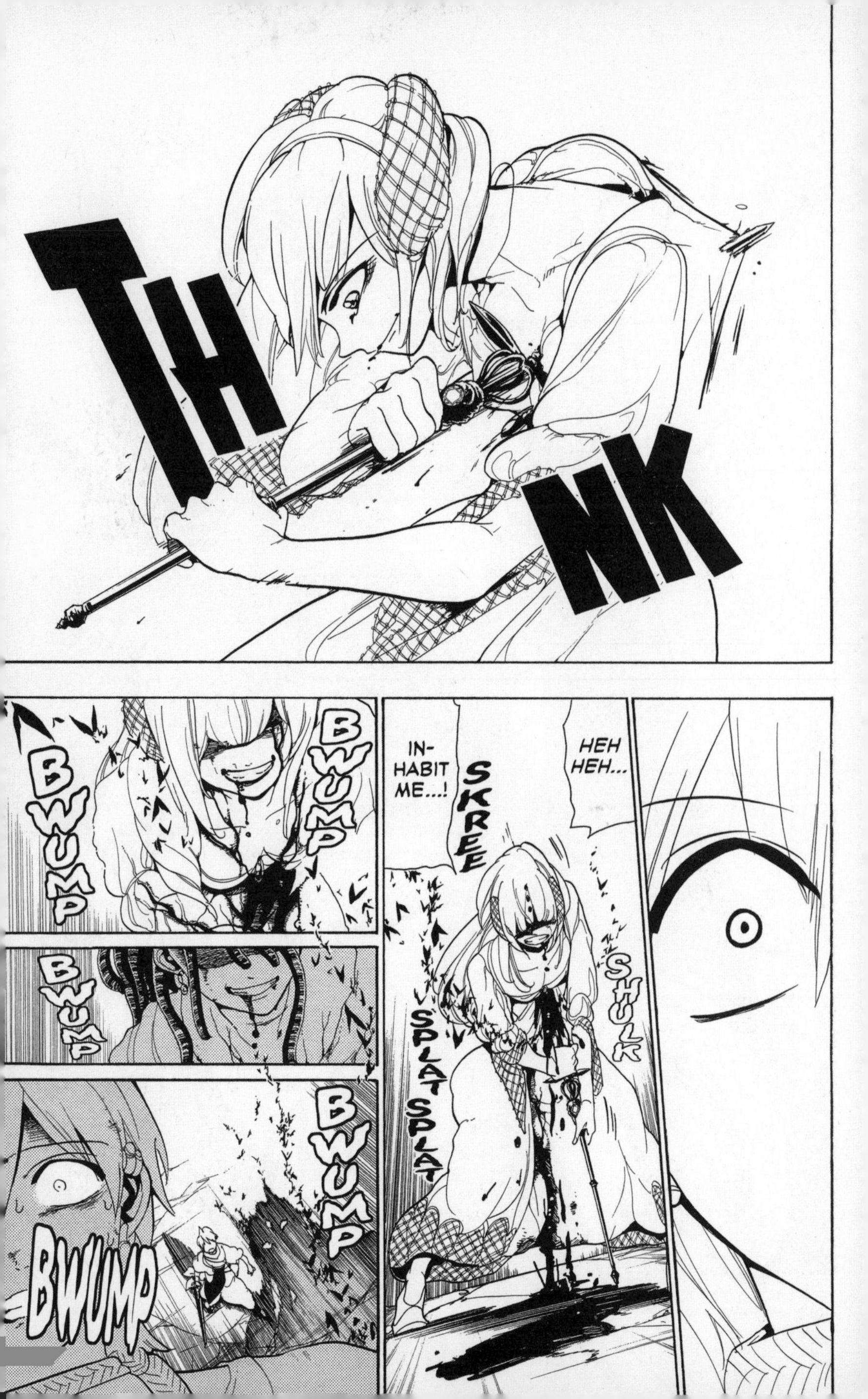
TH
NK
HEH HEH...
IN-HABIT ME...!
SKREE
SHULK
SPLAT SPLAT
BWUMP
BWUMP
BWUMP
BWUMP
BWUMP

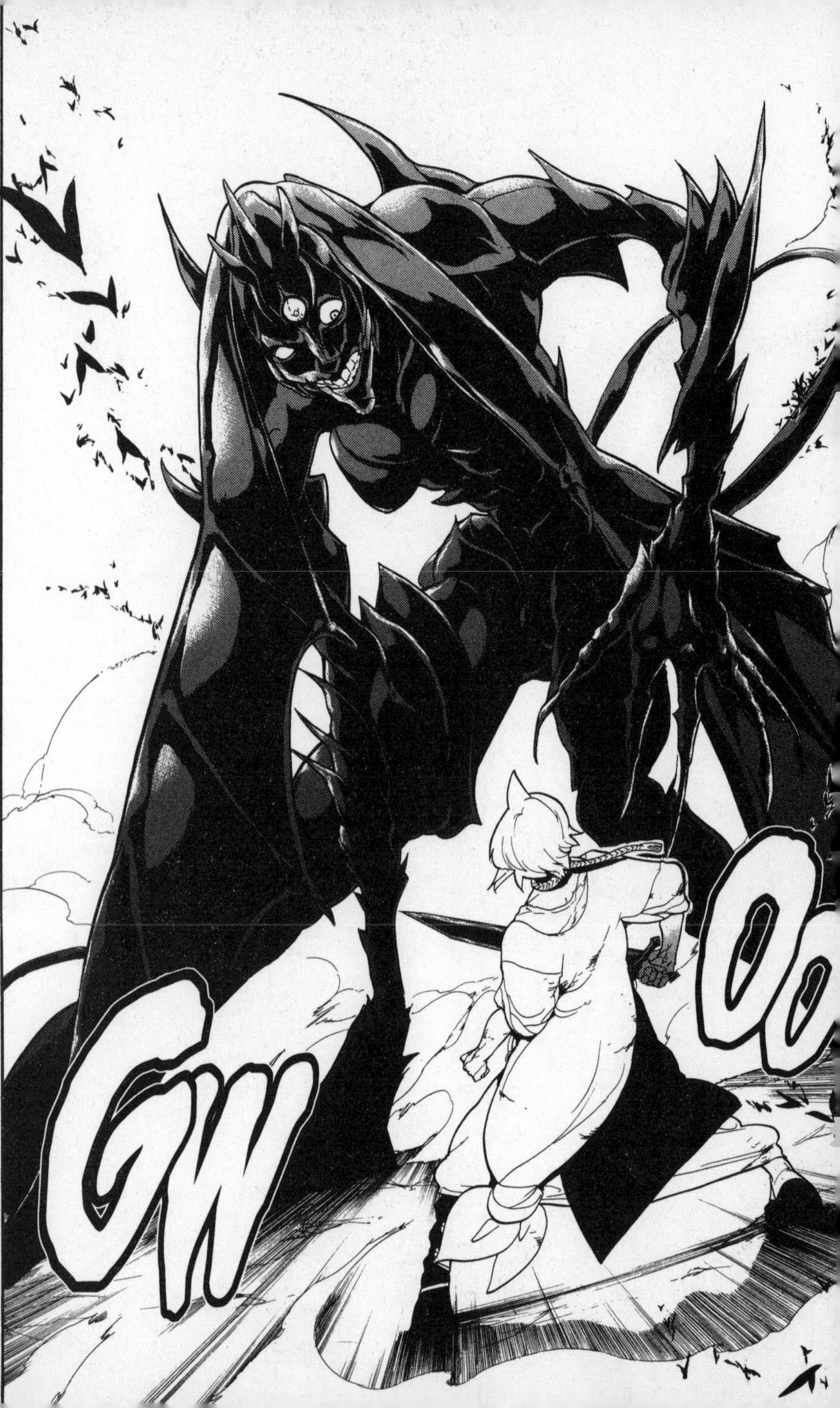
GW
OO

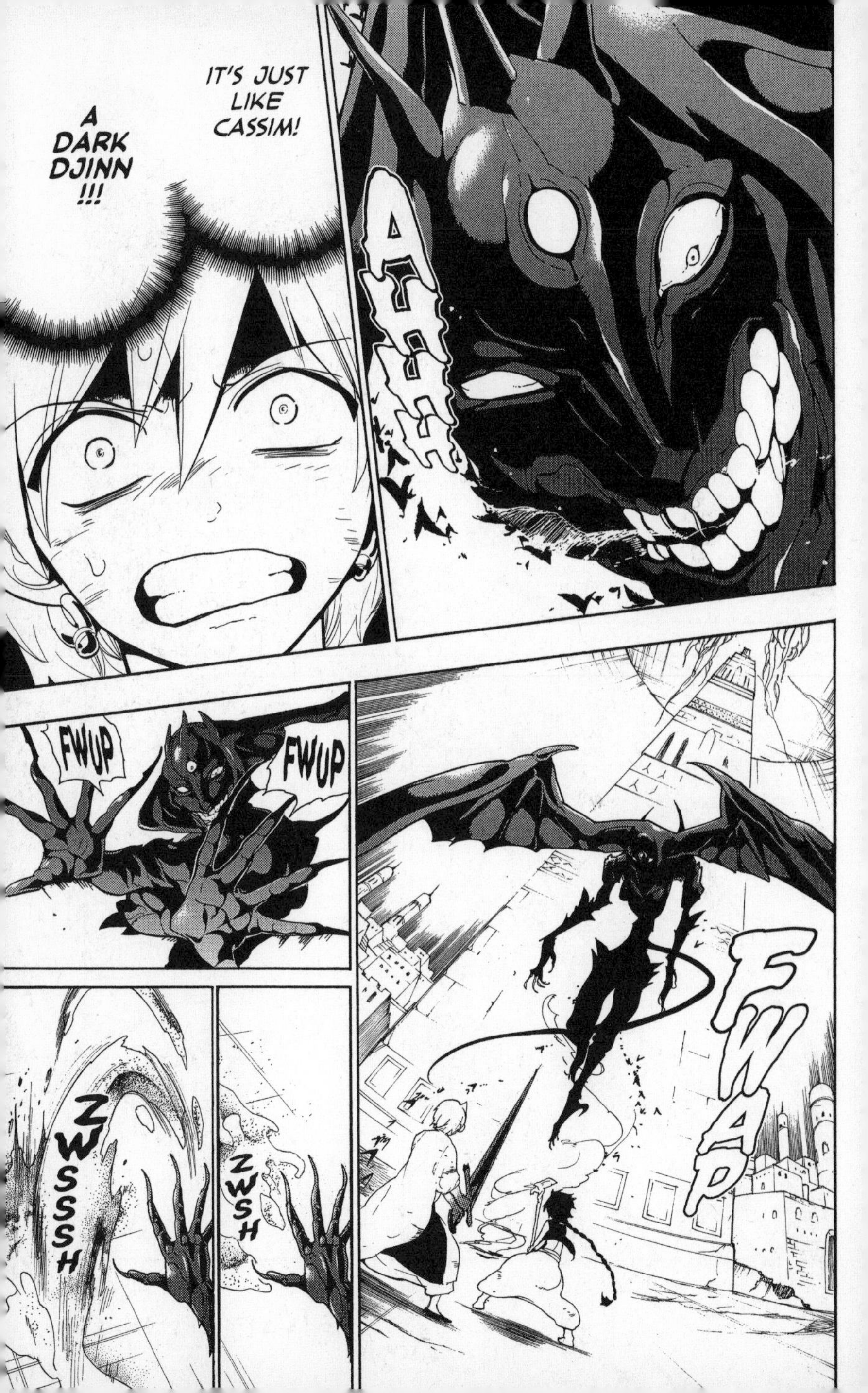
AH
IT'S JUST LIKE CASSIM!
A DARK DJINN!!!
FWAP
FWUP
FWUP
ZWSH
ZWSSSH

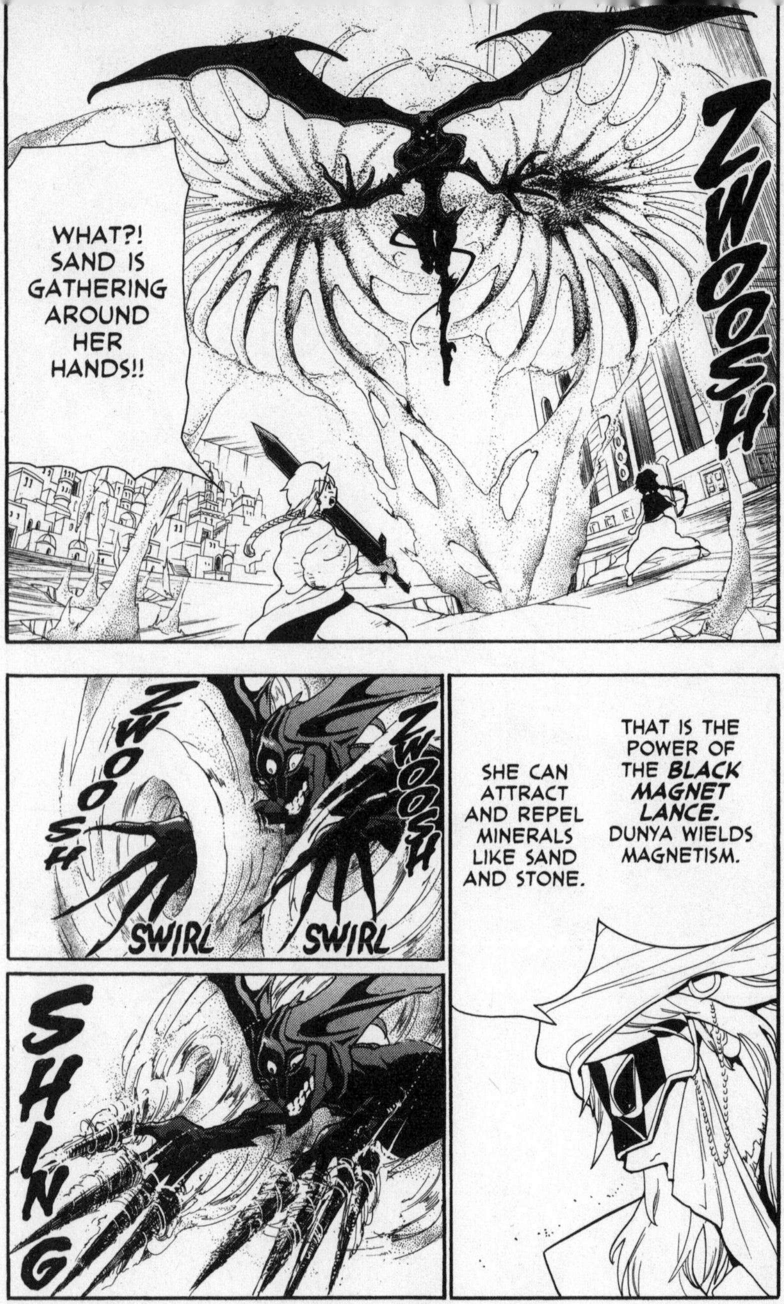
ZWOOSH
WHAT?! SAND IS GATHERING AROUND HER HANDS!!
THAT IS THE POWER OF THE *BLACK MAGNET LANCE.* DUNYA WIELDS MAGNETISM.
SHE CAN ATTRACT AND REPEL MINERALS LIKE SAND AND STONE.
ZWOOSH
ZWOOSH
SWIRL
SWIRL
SHING

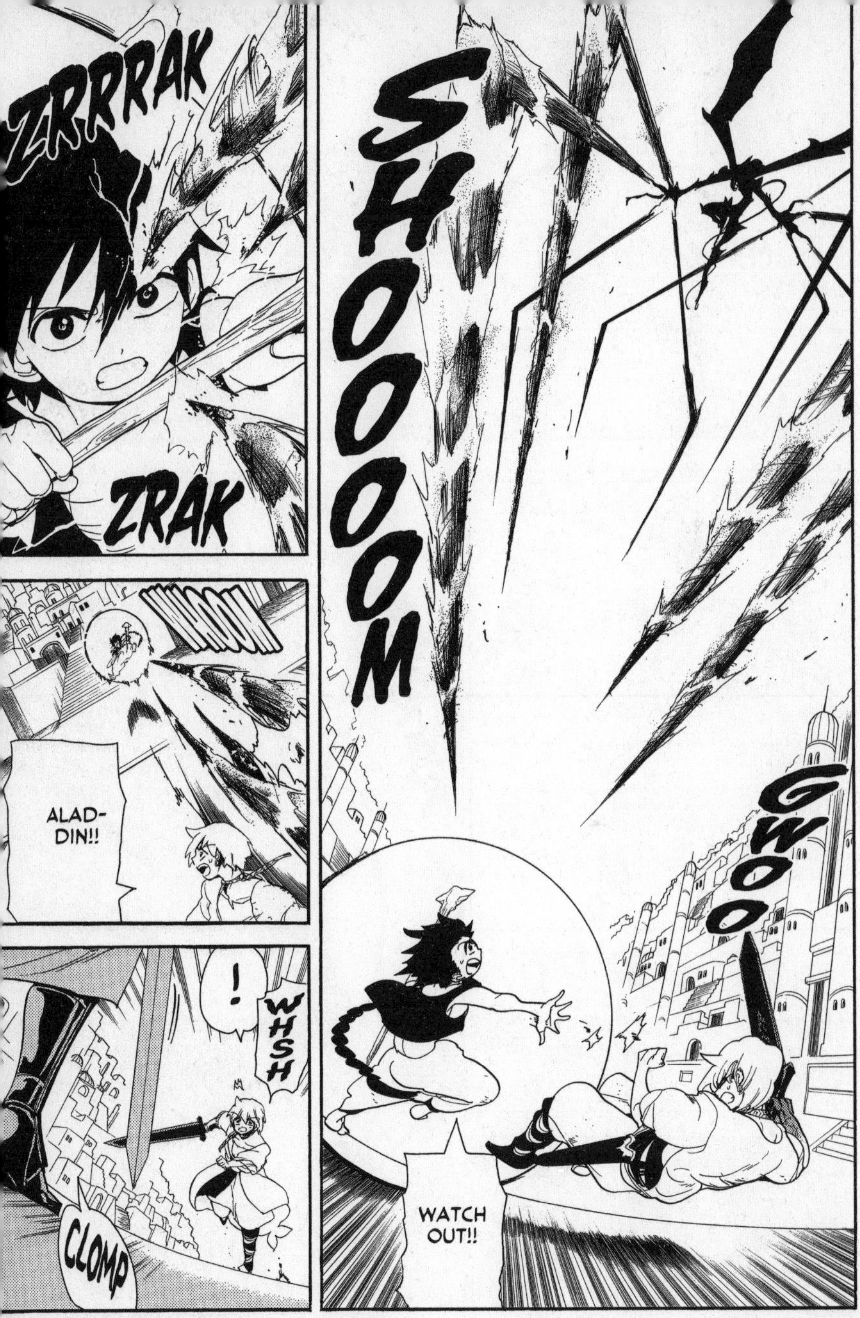
SHOOOOOM
GWOOO
WATCH OUT!!
ZRRRAK
ZRAK
ALAD-DIN!!
!
WHSH
CLOMP

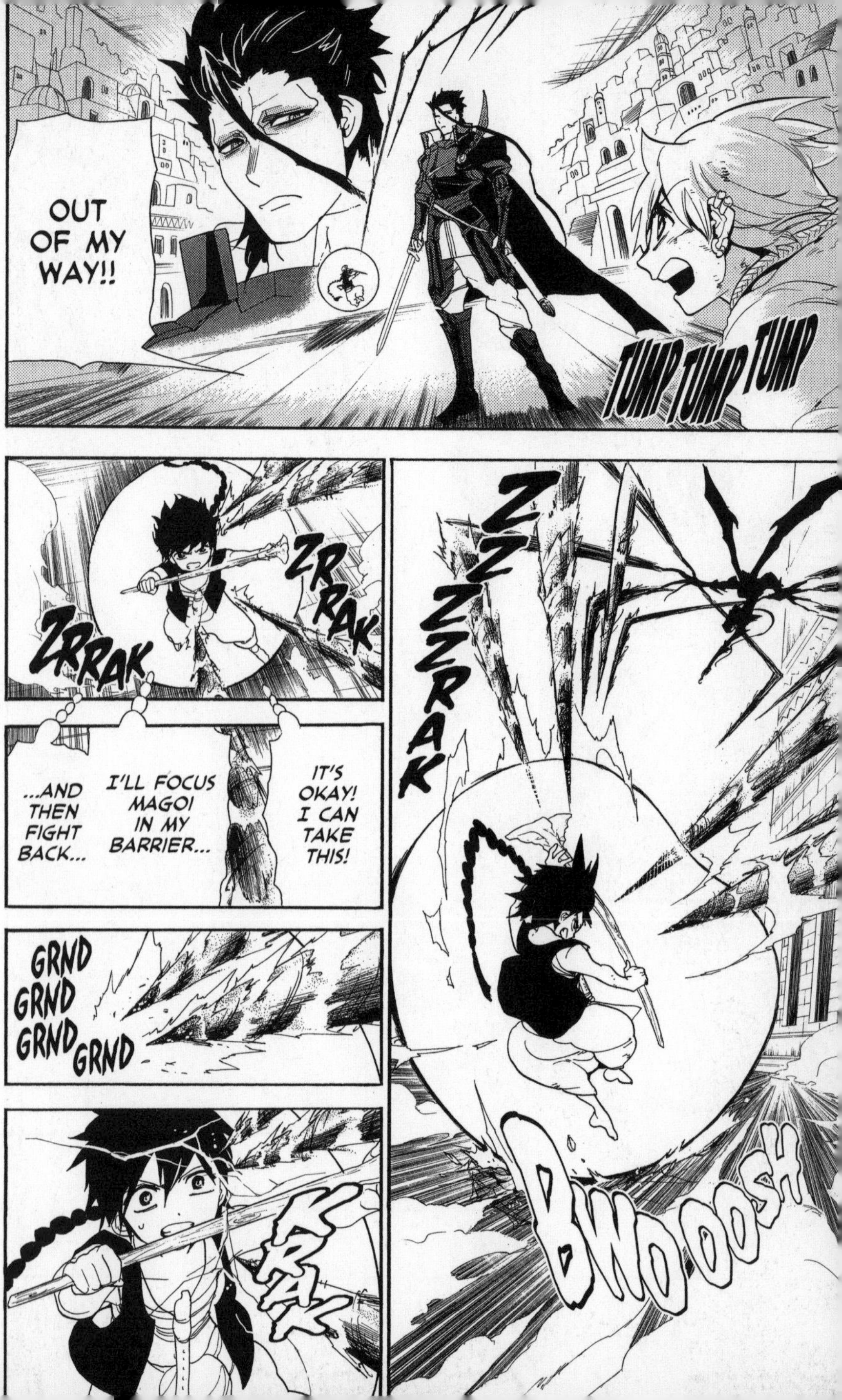
OUT OF MY WAY!!
TUMP TUMP TUMP
ZZZZRAK
BWOOOSH
ZRRAK
ZRRAK
IT'S OKAY! I CAN TAKE THIS!
I'LL FOCUS MAGOI IN MY BARRIER...
...AND THEN FIGHT BACK...
GRND GRND GRND GRND
KRAK

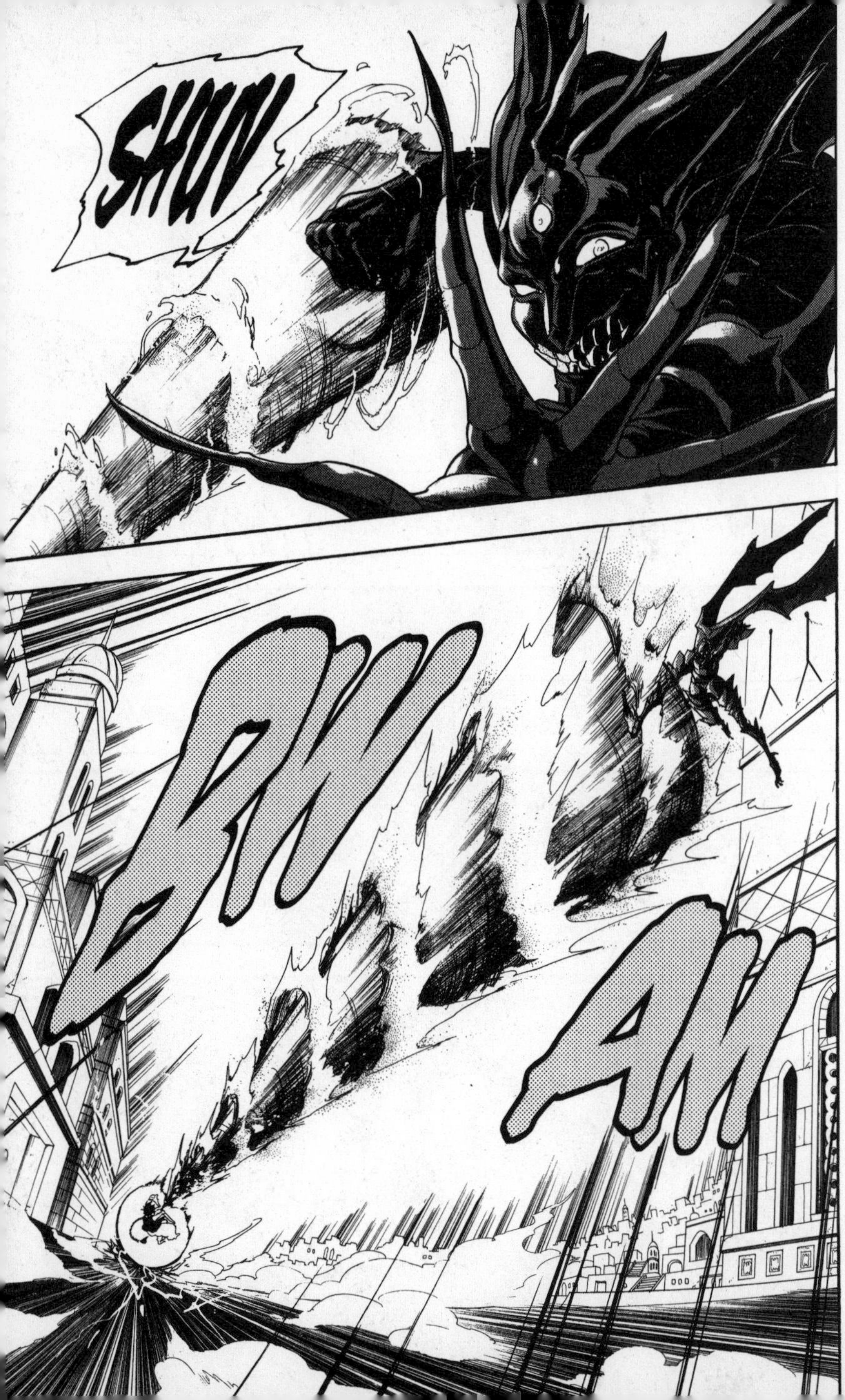
SHUN
BWAM

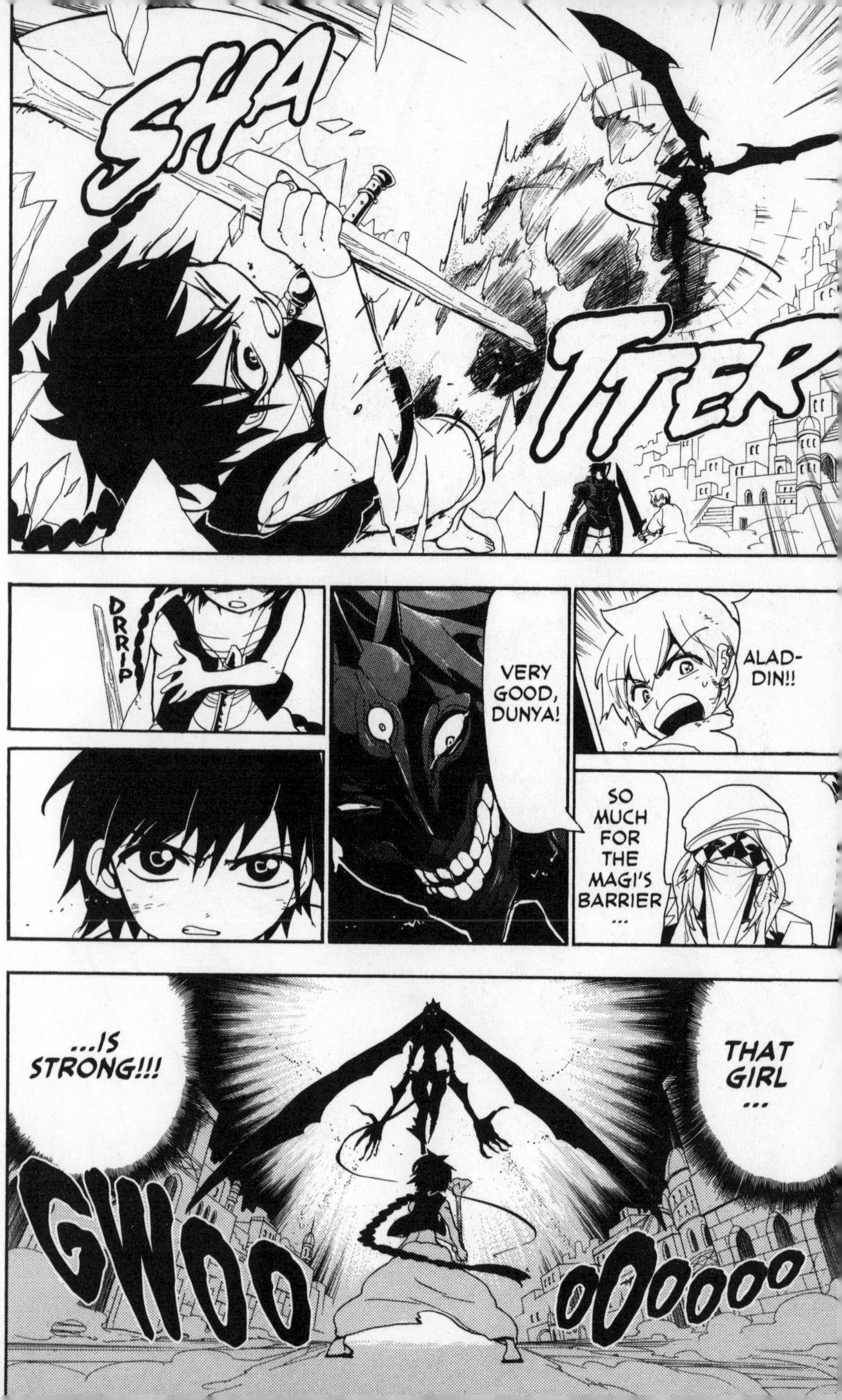
SHA
TTER
ALAD-DIN!!
SO MUCH FOR THE MAGI'S BARRIER ...
VERY GOOD, DUNYA!
DRRRIP
THAT GIRL ...
...IS STRONG!!!
GWOO
OOOOOO

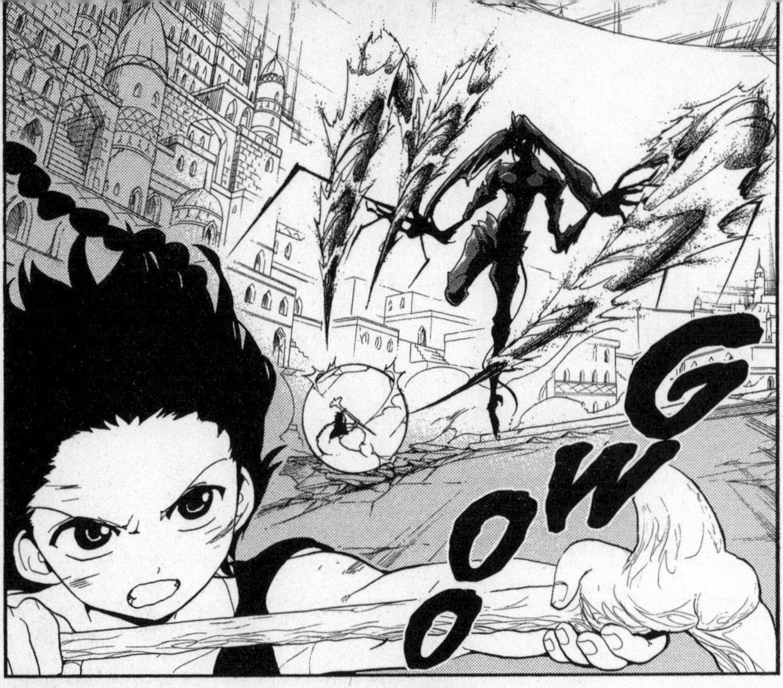

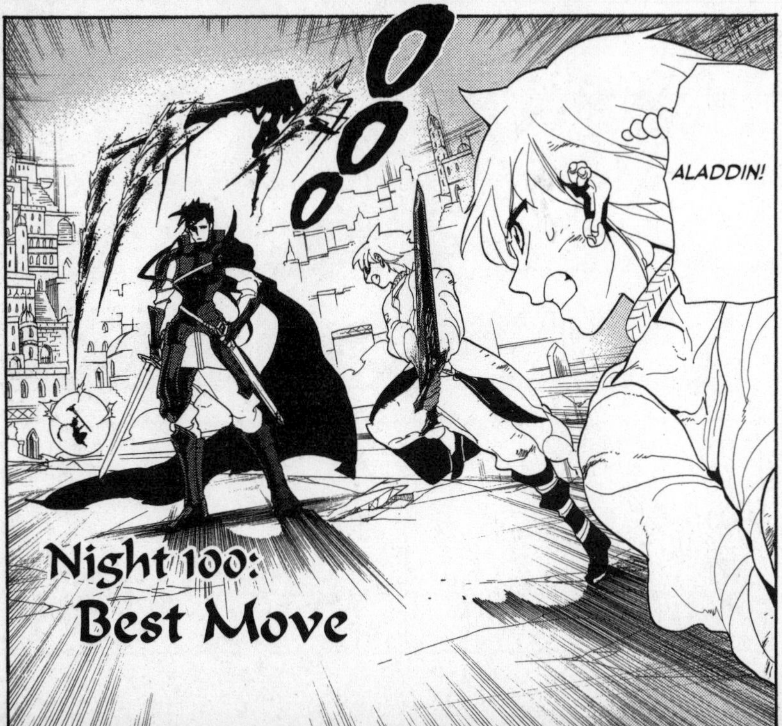
ALADDIN!

Night 100: Best Move

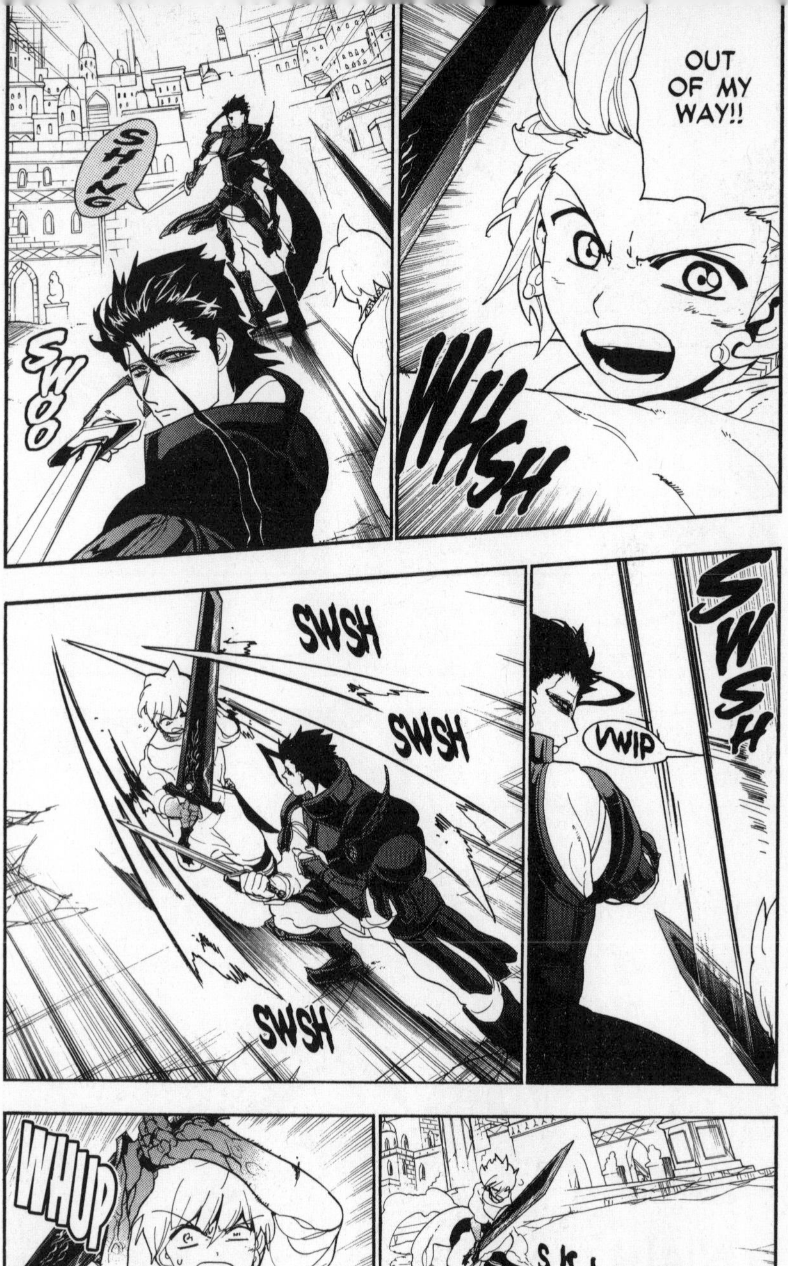
OUT OF MY WAY!!
WHSH
SHING
SWOO
SWSH
VWIP
SWSH
SWSH
SWSH
SKIDDD
WHUP

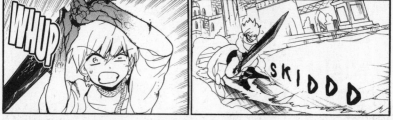

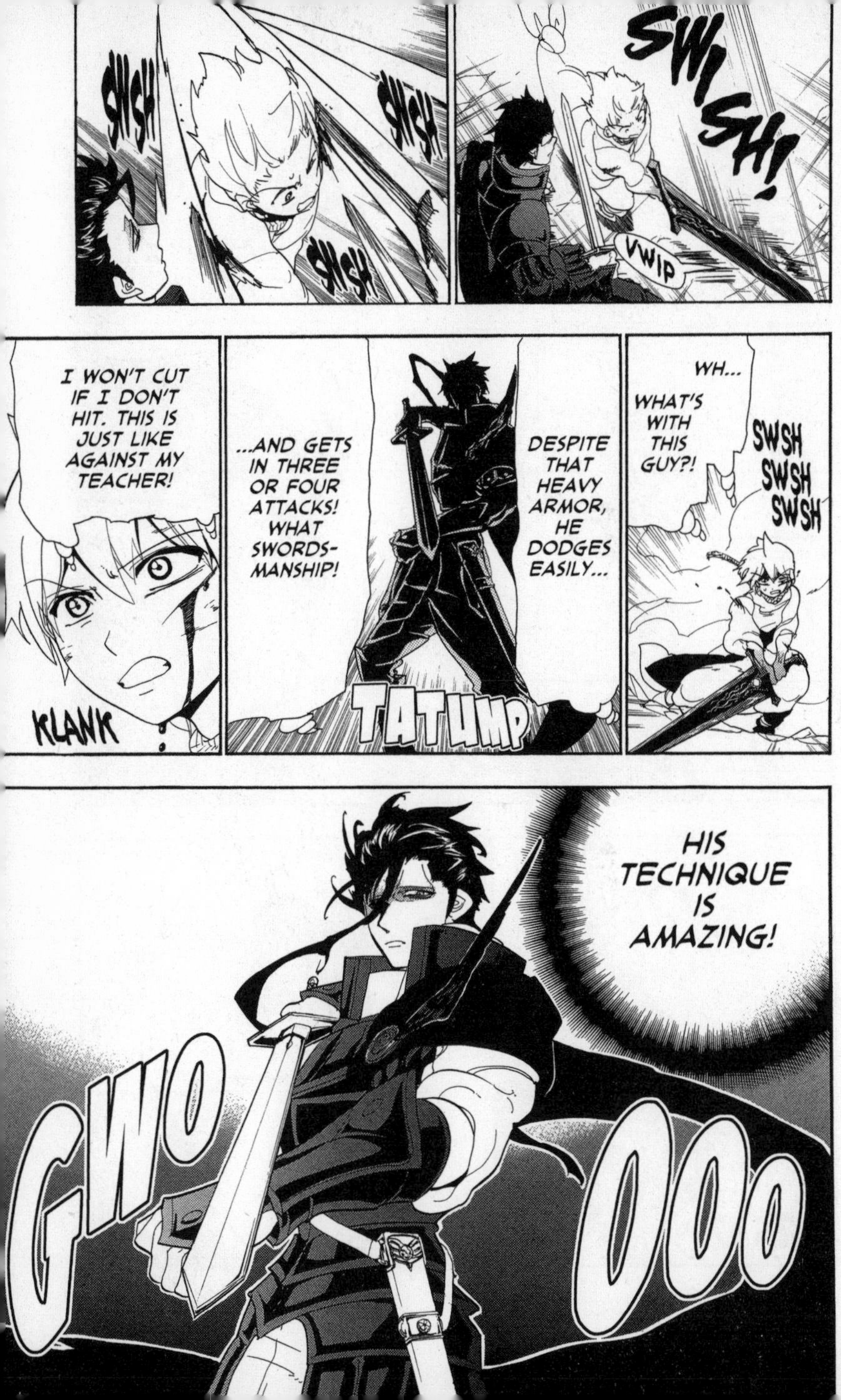
SWISH!
VWIP
SWSH
SWSH
SWSH
WH...
WHAT'S WITH THIS GUY?!
SWSH SWSH SWSH
DESPITE THAT HEAVY ARMOR, HE DODGES EASILY...
...AND GETS IN THREE OR FOUR ATTACKS! WHAT SWORDS-MANSHIP!
TATUMP
I WON'T CUT IF I DON'T HIT. THIS IS JUST LIKE AGAINST MY TEACHER!
KLANK
HIS TECHNIQUE IS AMAZING!
GWO
OOO

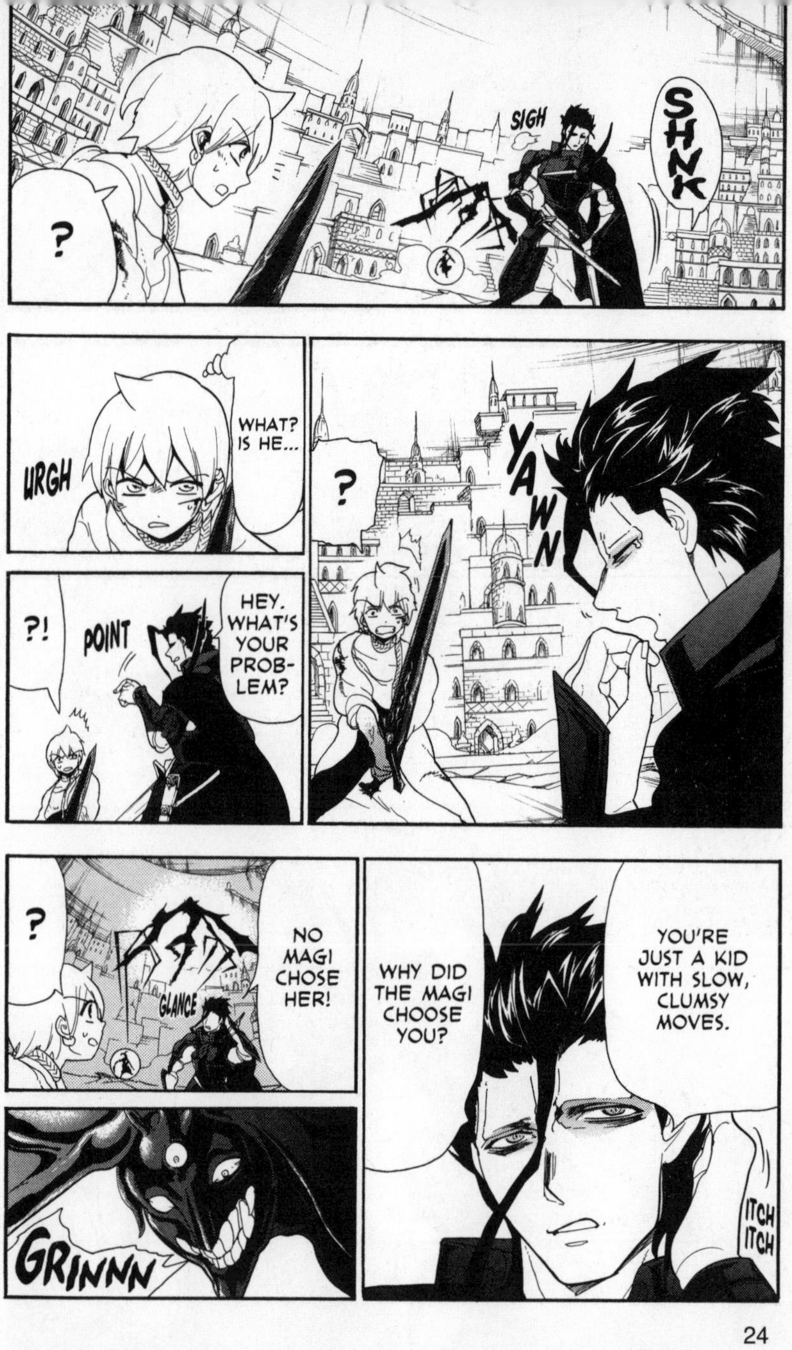
SHNK
SIGH
?
YAWN
?
WHAT? IS HE...
URGH
HEY. WHAT'S YOUR PROB-LEM?
POINT
?!
YOU'RE JUST A KID WITH SLOW, CLUMSY MOVES.
WHY DID THE MAGI CHOOSE YOU?
ITCH ITCH
NO MAGI CHOSE HER!
?
GLANCE
GRINNN

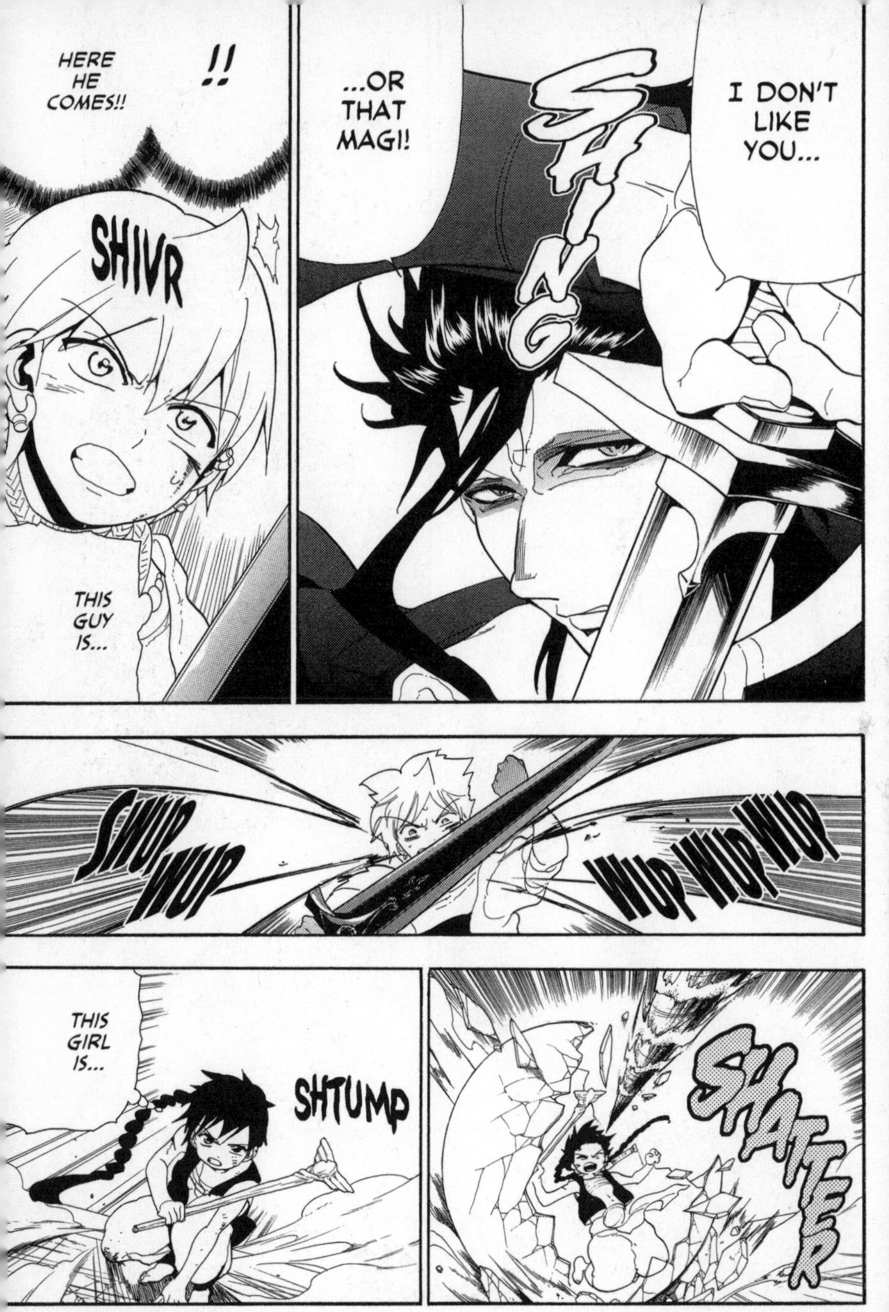
I DON'T LIKE YOU...
...OR THAT MAGI!
SHING
!!
HERE HE COMES!!
SHIVR
THIS GUY IS...
WUP WUP WUP
SWUP WUP
SHATTER
SHTUMP
THIS GIRL IS...

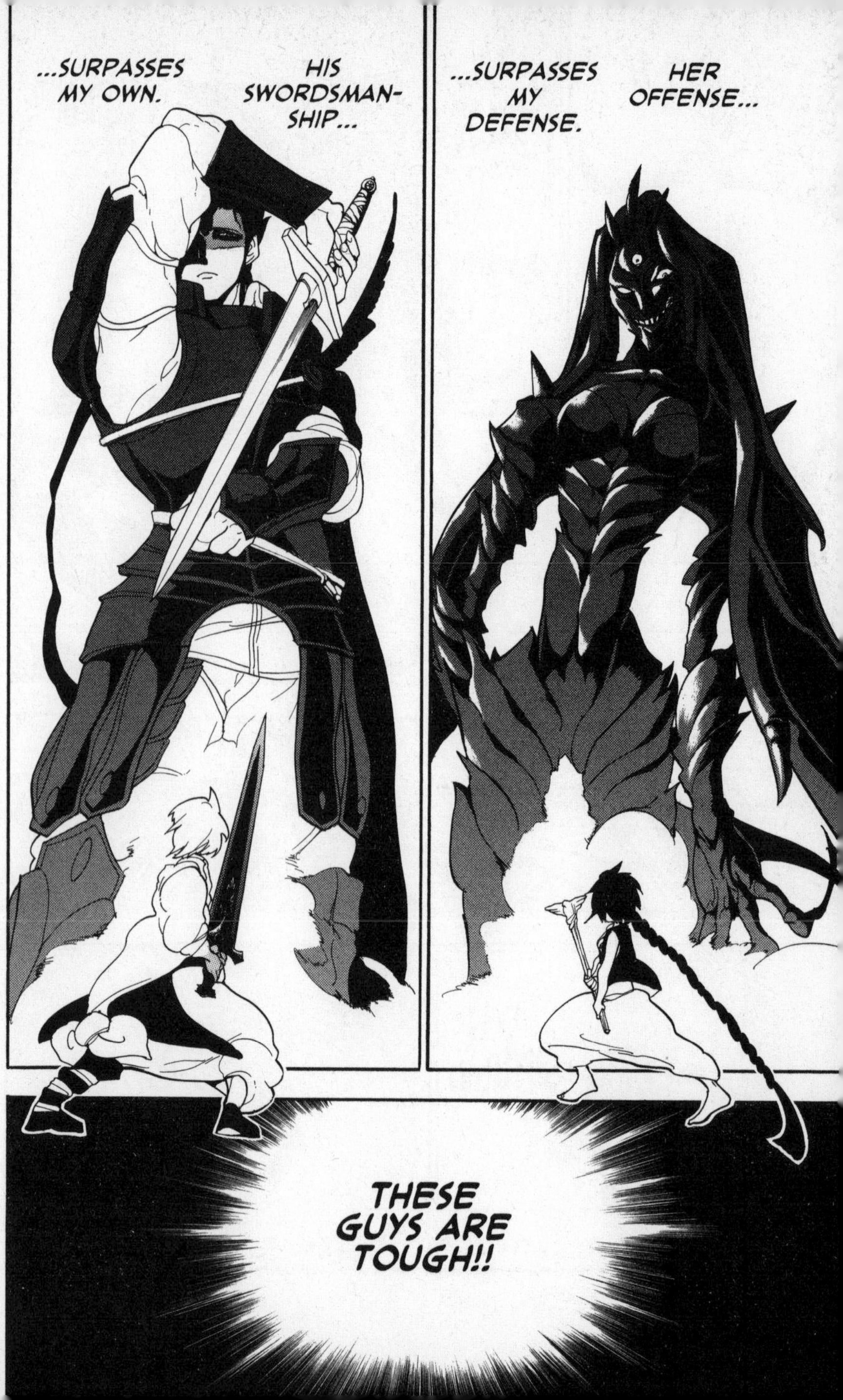
HER OFFENSE...
...SURPASSES MY DEFENSE.
HIS SWORDSMAN-SHIP...
...SURPASSES MY OWN.
THESE GUYS ARE TOUGH!!

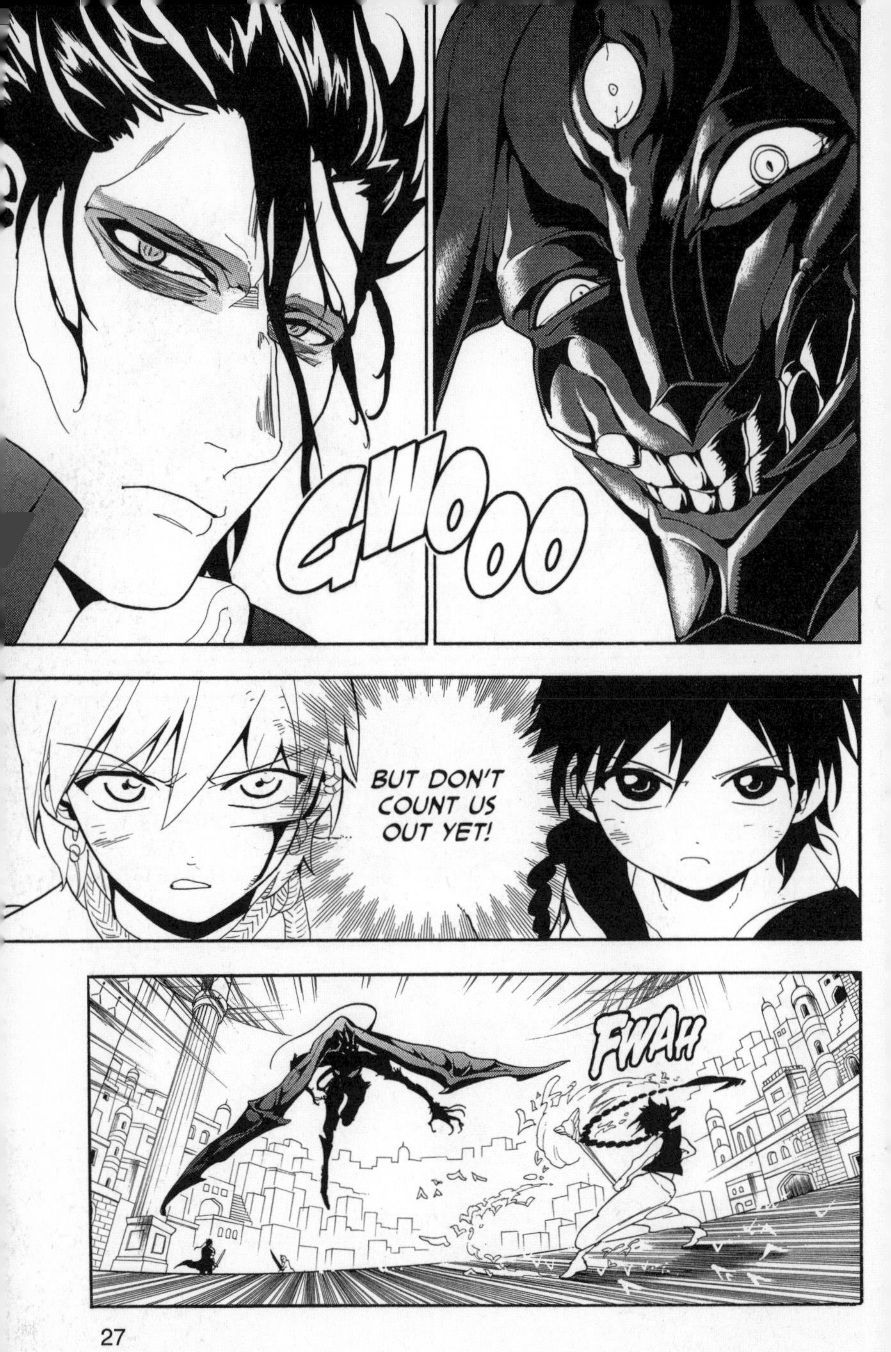
GWOOOO
BUT DON'T COUNT US OUT YET!
FWAH

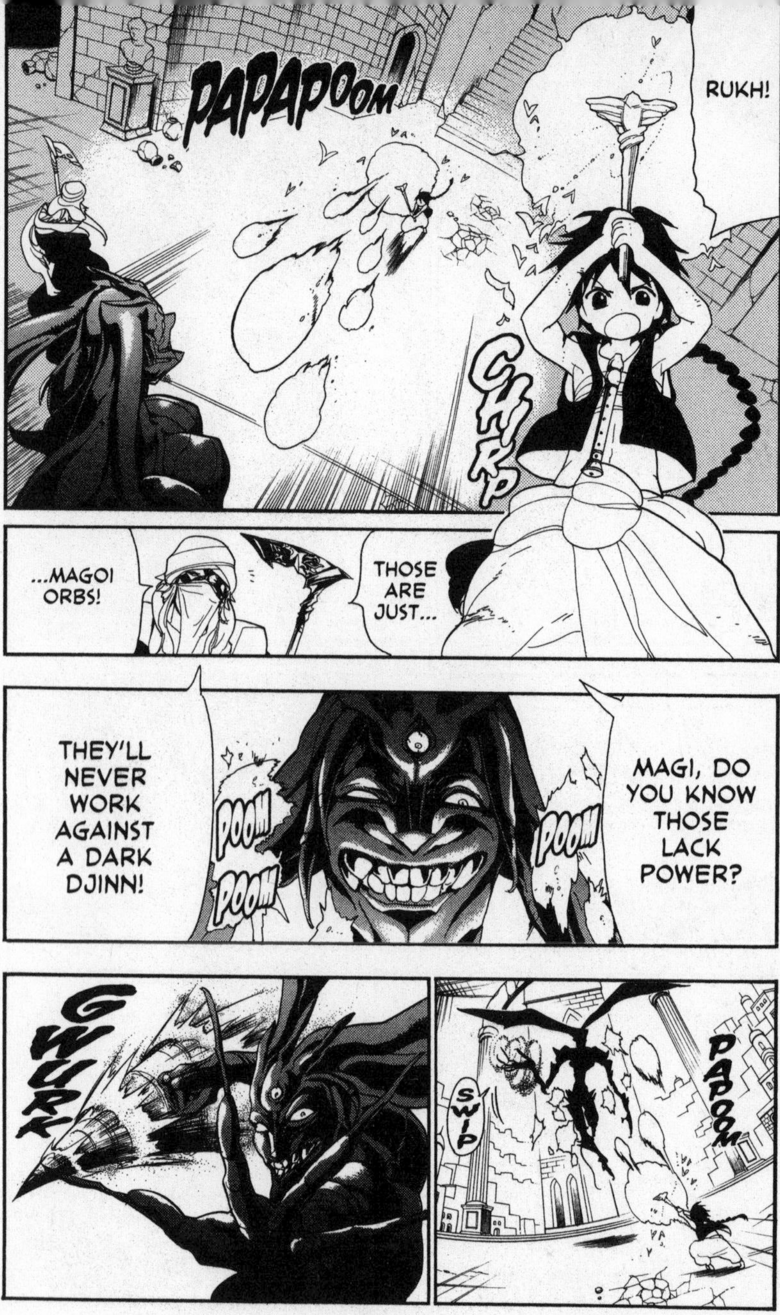
RUKH!
PAPAPOOM
CHIRP
THOSE ARE JUST...
...MAGOI ORBS!
MAGI, DO YOU KNOW THOSE LACK POWER?
POOM
THEY'LL NEVER WORK AGAINST A DARK DJINN!
POOM
POOM
PAPOOM
SWIP
GWURK

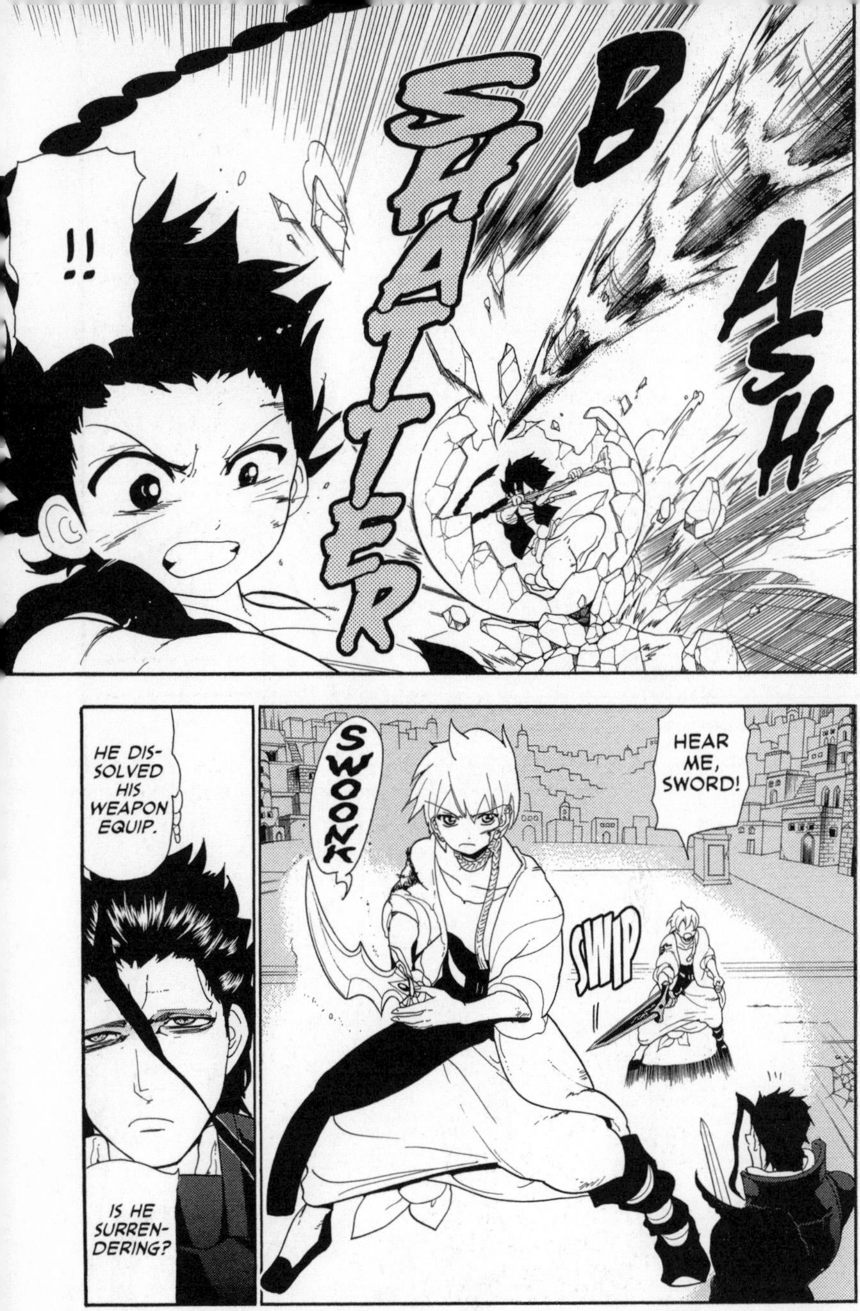
BASH
SHATTER
!!
HEAR ME, SWORD!
SWOONK
SWIP
HE DIS-SOLVED HIS WEAPON EQUIP.
IS HE SURREN-DERING?

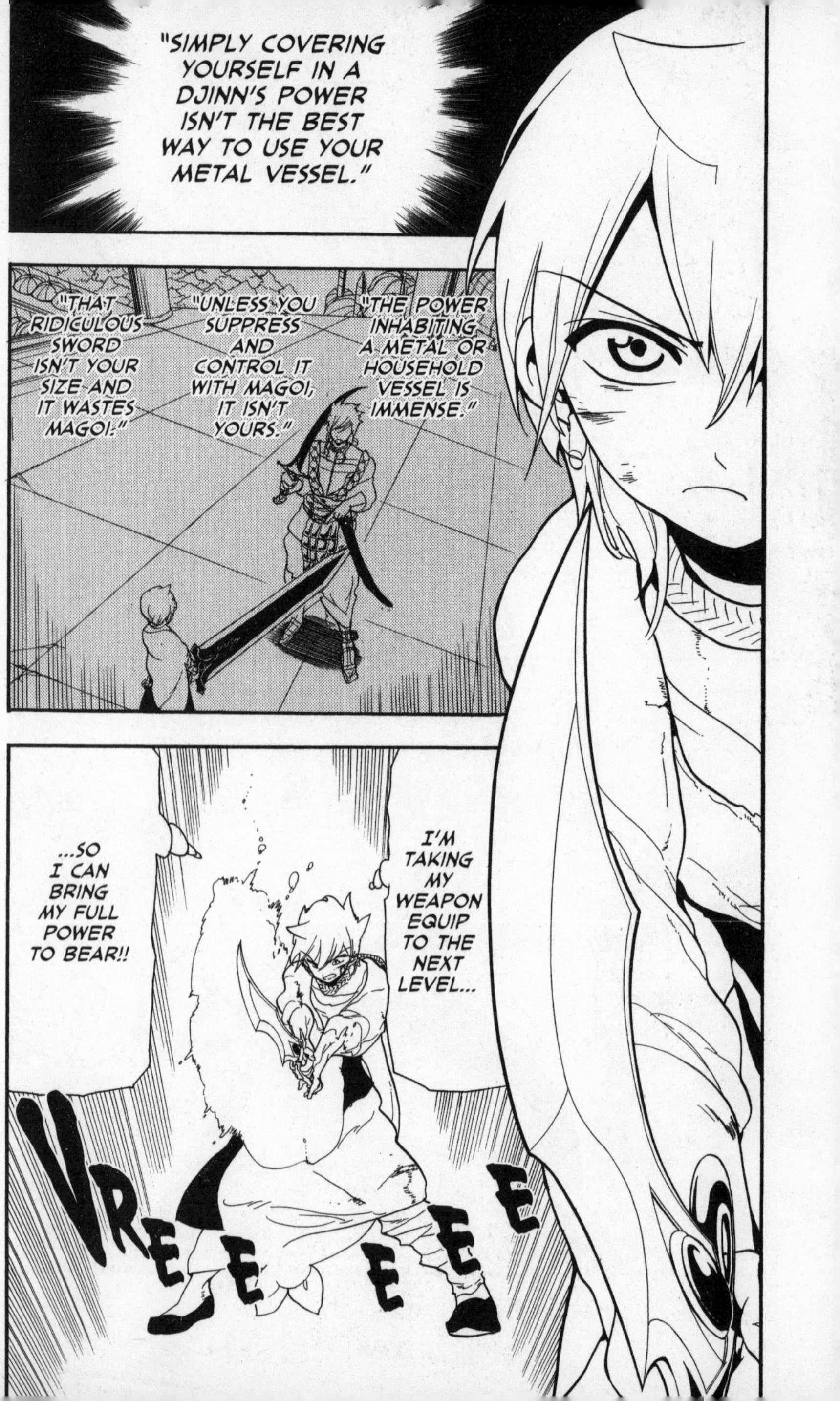
"SIMPLY COVERING YOURSELF IN A DJINN'S POWER ISN'T THE BEST WAY TO USE YOUR METAL VESSEL."
"THE POWER INHABITING A METAL OR HOUSEHOLD VESSEL IS IMMENSE."
"UNLESS YOU SUPPRESS AND CONTROL IT WITH MAGOI, IT ISN'T YOURS."
"THAT RIDICULOUS SWORD ISN'T YOUR SIZE AND IT WASTES MAGOI."
I'M TAKING MY WEAPON EQUIP TO THE NEXT LEVEL...
...SO I CAN BRING MY FULL POWER TO BEAR!!
VREEEEEE

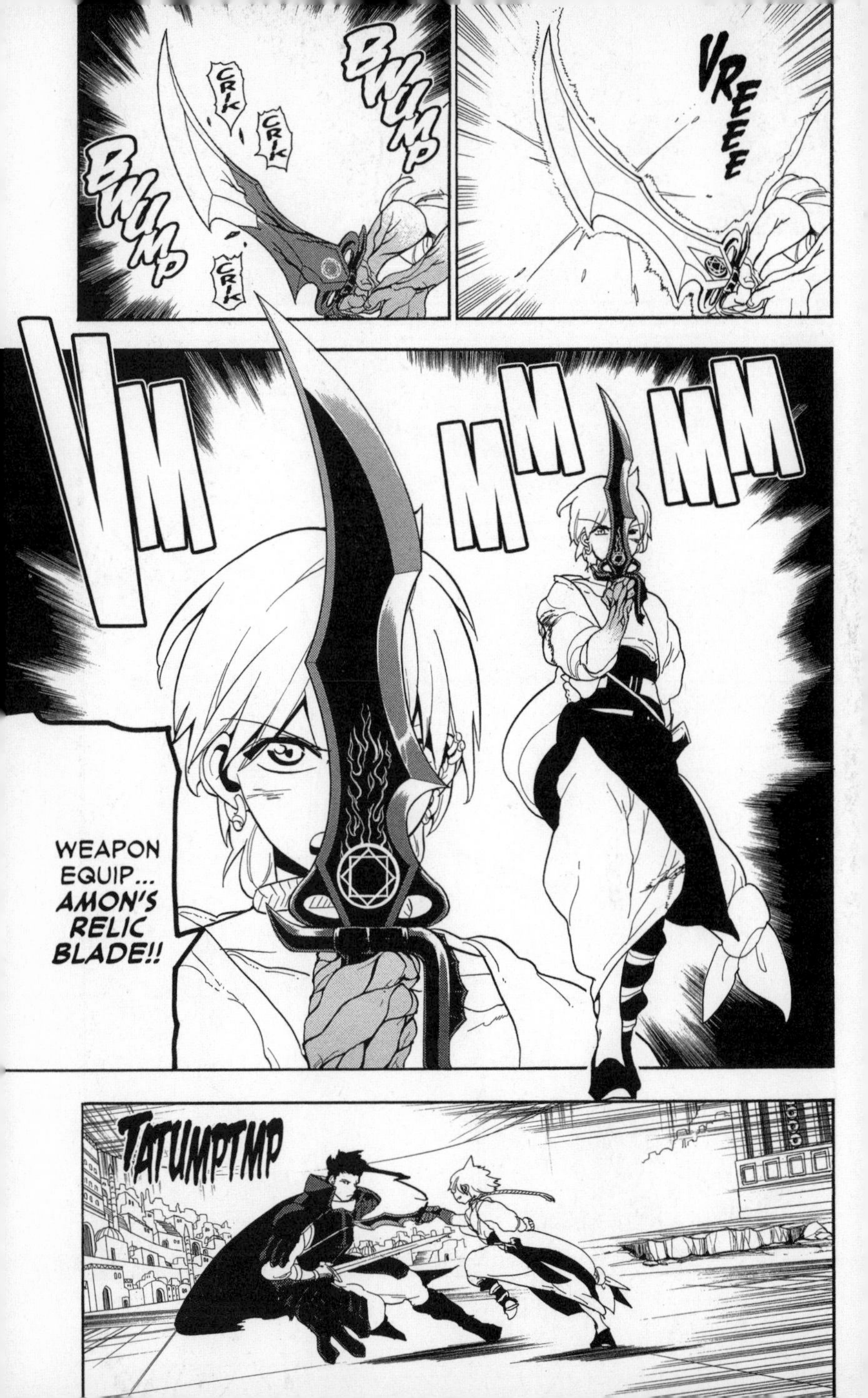
VREEEE
BWUMP
CRIK
CRIK
BWUMP
CRIK
VM MMM MMM
WEAPON EQUIP... AMON'S RELIC BLADE!!
TATUMPTMP

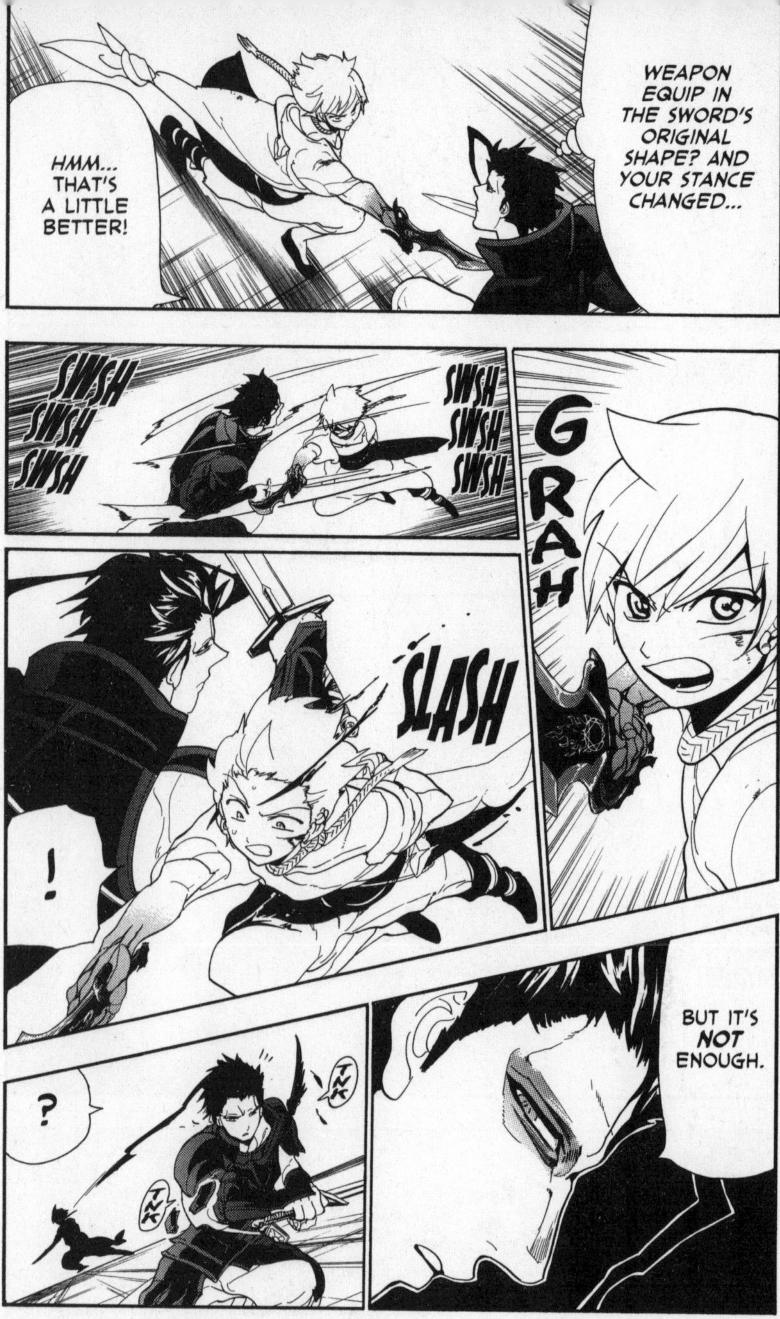
WEAPON EQUIP IN THE SWORD'S ORIGINAL SHAPE? AND YOUR STANCE CHANGED...
HMM... THAT'S A LITTLE BETTER!
GRAH
SWSH SWSH SWSH
SWSH SWSH SWSH
SLASH
!
BUT IT'S *NOT* ENOUGH.
TNK
?
TNK

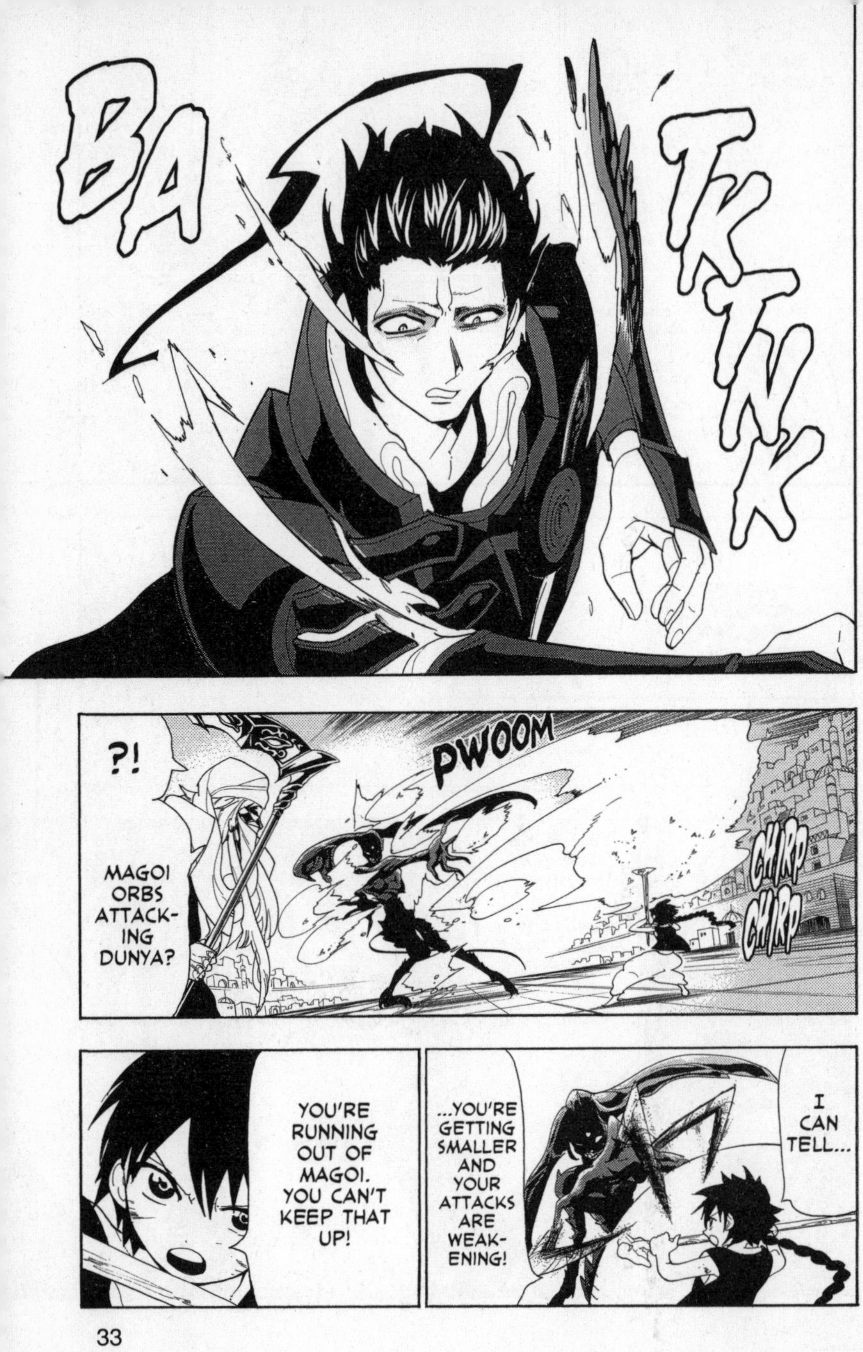

BA
TKTNK
PWOOM
CHIRP CHIRP
?!
MAGOI ORBS ATTACKING DUNYA?
I CAN TELL...
...YOU'RE GETTING SMALLER AND YOUR ATTACKS ARE WEAKENING!
YOU'RE RUNNING OUT OF MAGOI. YOU CAN'T KEEP THAT UP!

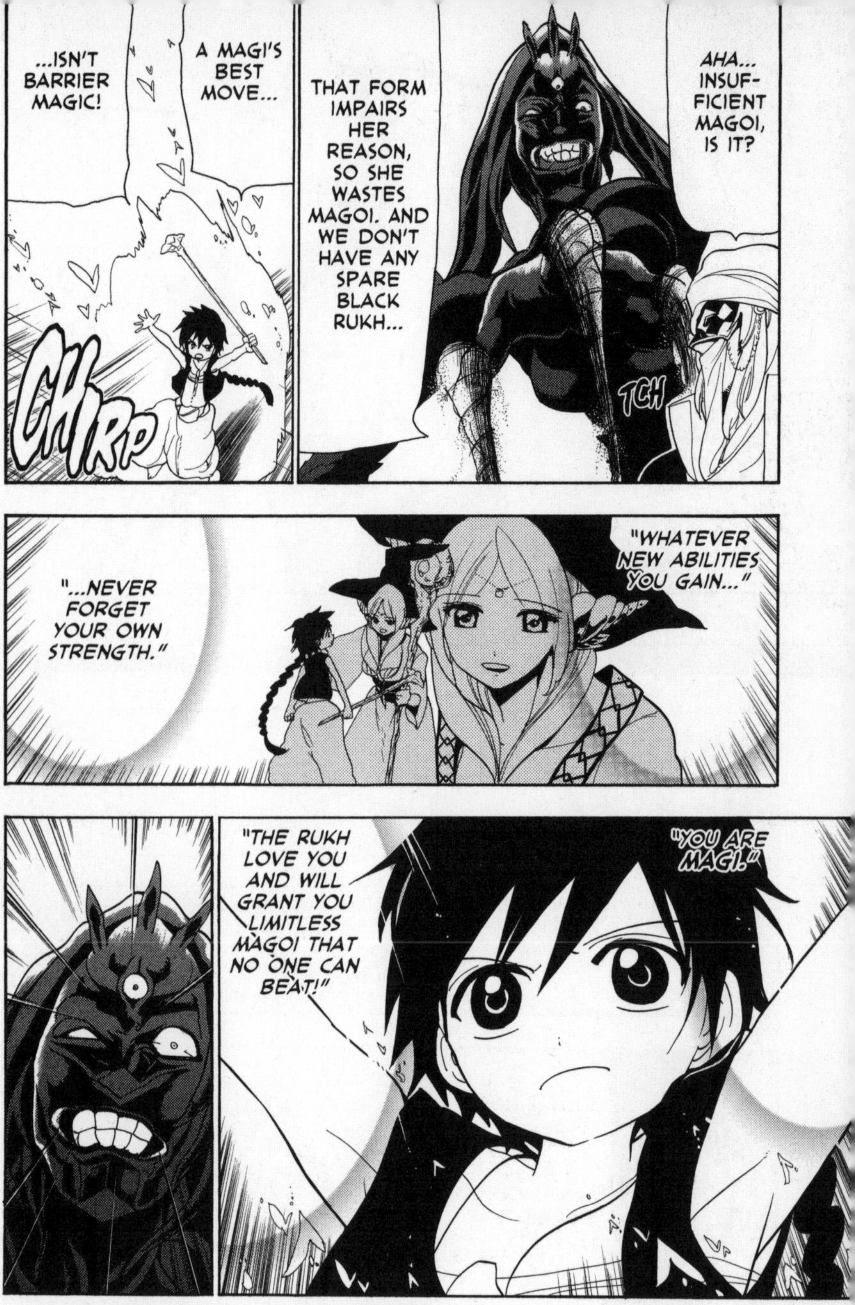
AHA... INSUF-FICIENT MAGOI, IS IT?
THAT FORM IMPAIRS HER REASON, SO SHE WASTES MAGOI. AND WE DON'T HAVE ANY SPARE BLACK RUKH...
TCH
A MAGI'S BEST MOVE...
...ISN'T BARRIER MAGIC!
CHIRP
"WHATEVER NEW ABILITIES YOU GAIN..."
"...NEVER FORGET YOUR OWN STRENGTH."
"YOU ARE MAGI."
"THE RUKH LOVE YOU AND WILL GRANT YOU LIMITLESS MAGOI THAT NO ONE CAN BEAT!"

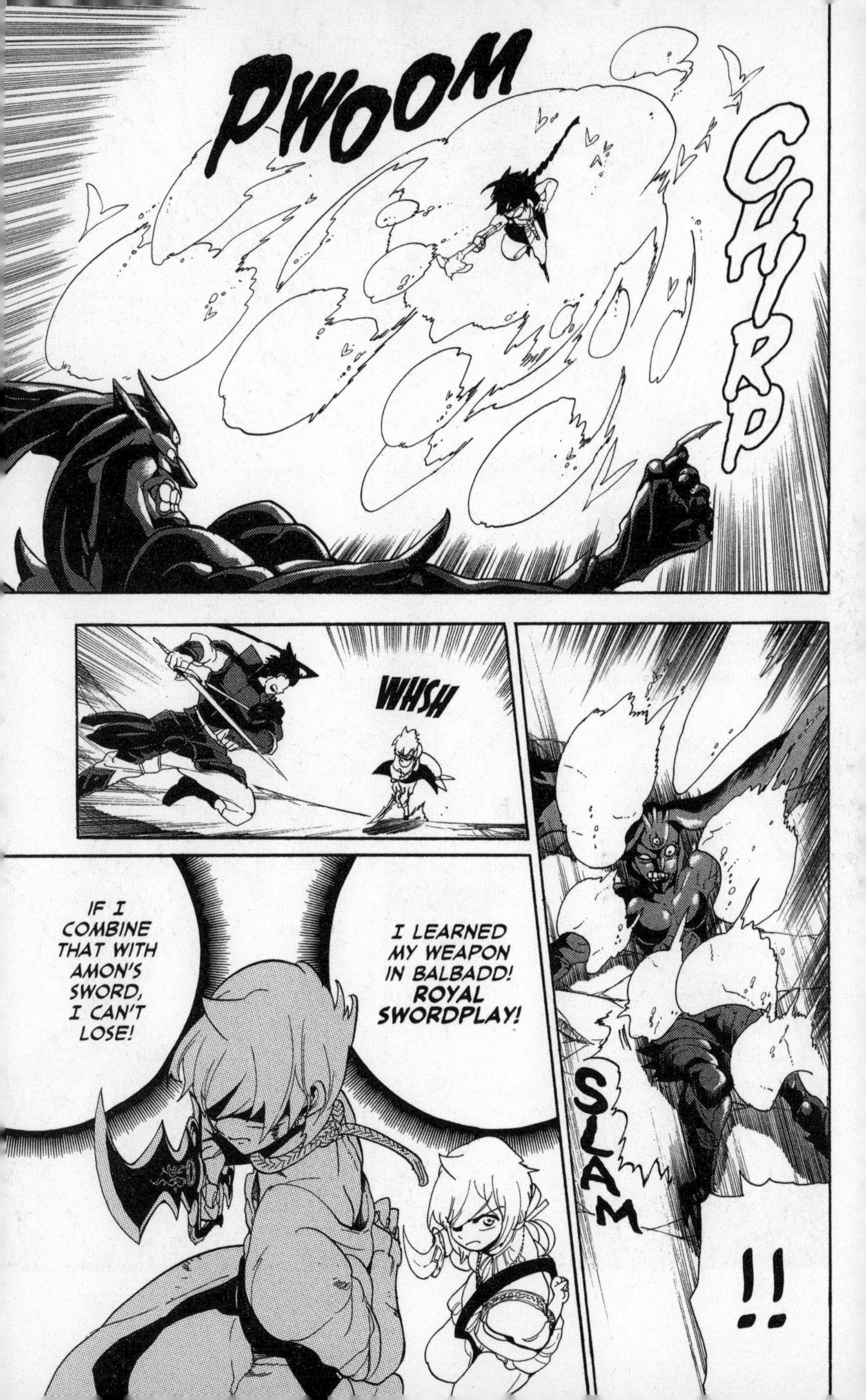
CHIRP
PWOOM
SLAM
!!
WHSH
I LEARNED MY WEAPON IN BALBADD! ROYAL SWORDPLAY!
IF I COMBINE THAT WITH AMON'S SWORD, I CAN'T LOSE!

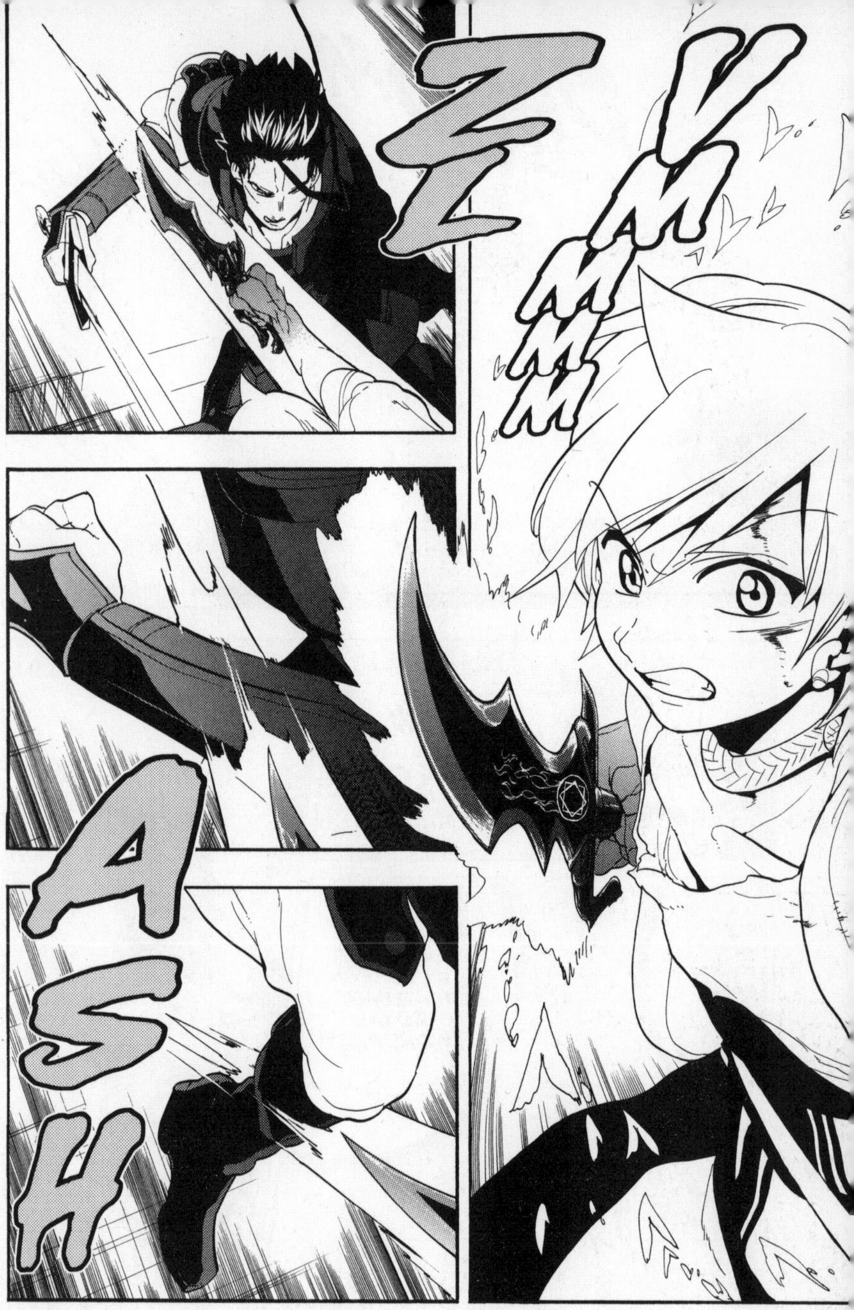
ASH

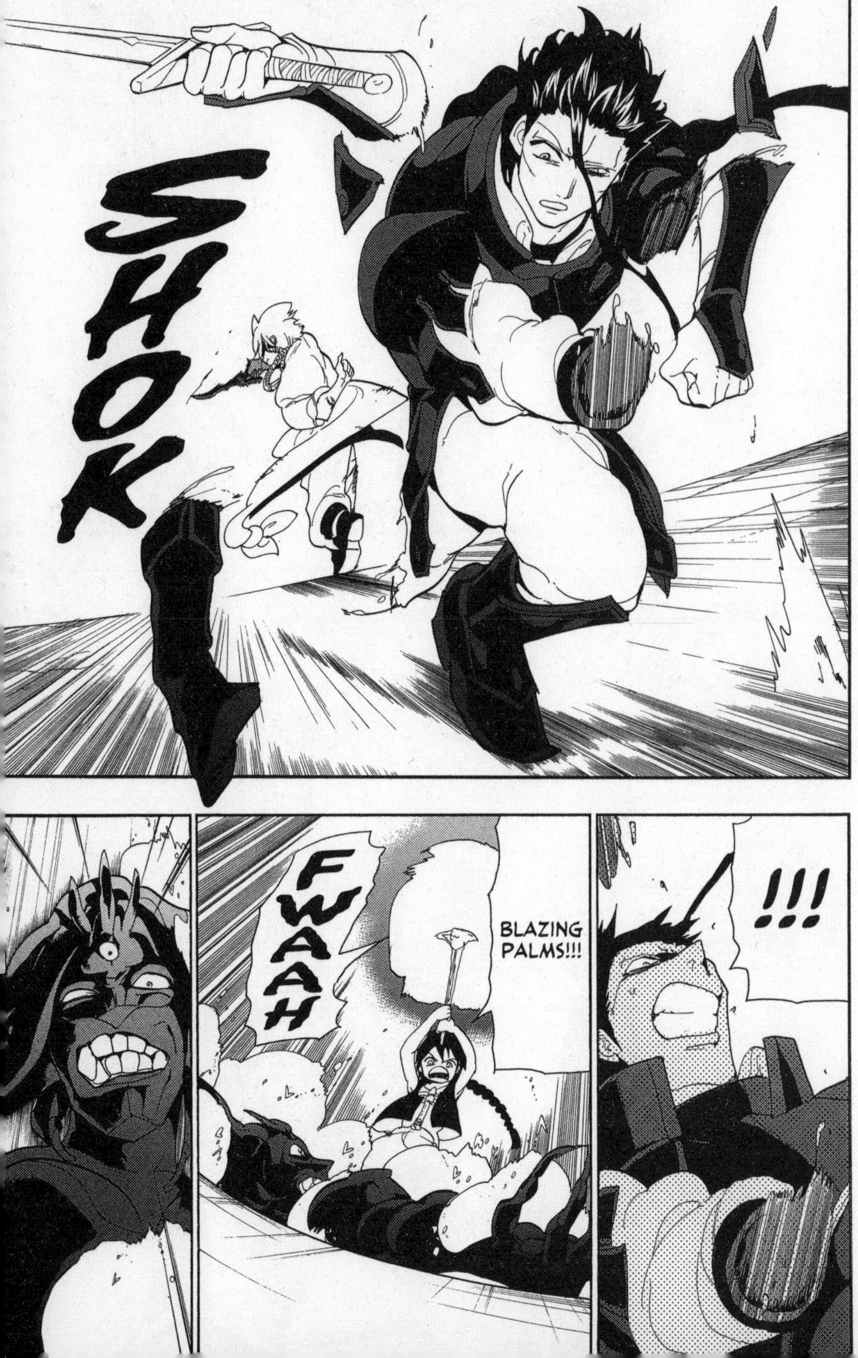
SHOK
!!!
BLAZING PALMS!!!
FWAAH

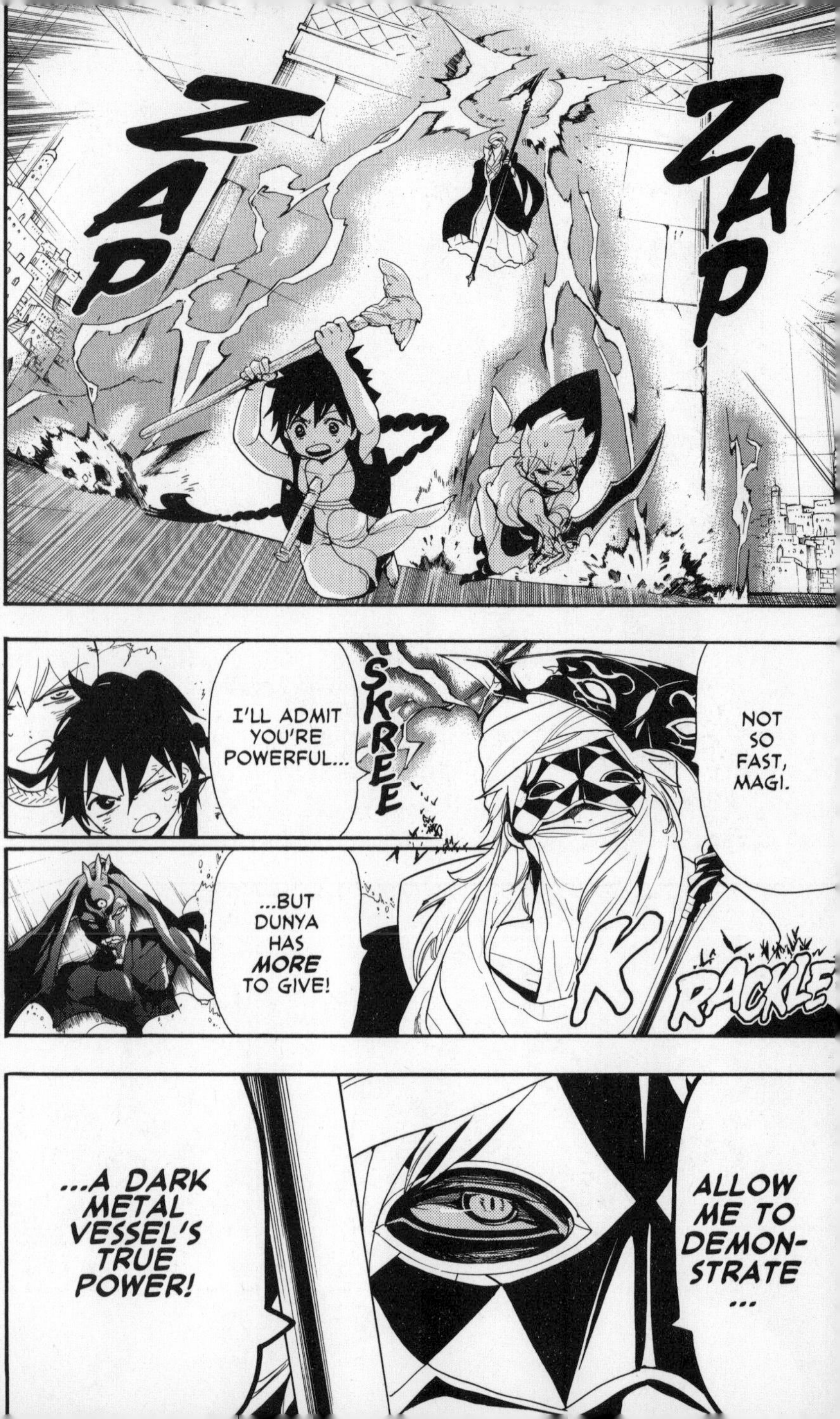
ZAP
ZAP
NOT SO FAST, MAGI.
SKREE
K
RACKLE
I'LL ADMIT YOU'RE POWERFUL...
...BUT DUNYA HAS MORE TO GIVE!
ALLOW ME TO DEMON-STRATE...
...A DARK METAL VESSEL'S TRUE POWER!

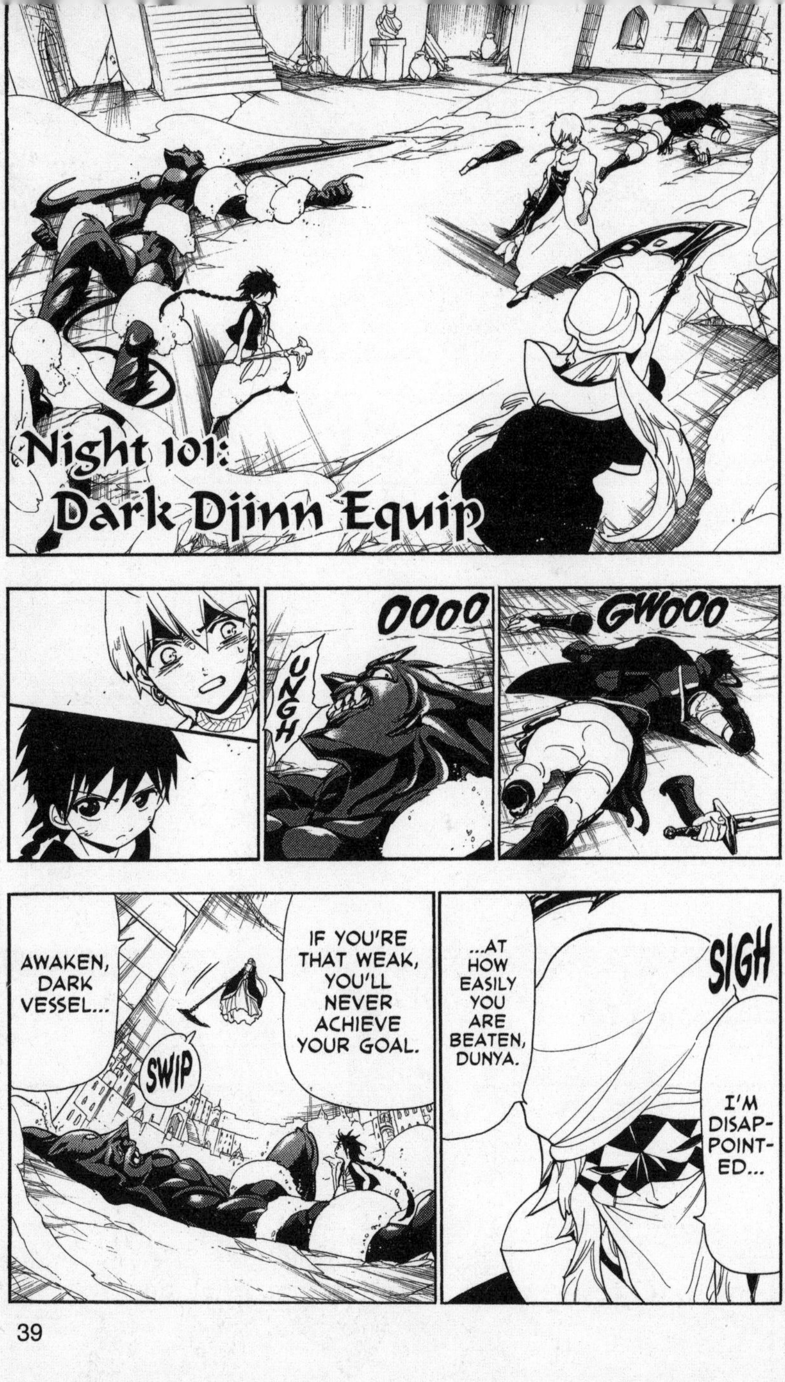
Night 101: Dark Djinn Equip
GWOOO
OOOO
UNGH
SIGH
I'M DISAPPOINTED...
...AT HOW EASILY YOU ARE BEATEN, DUNYA.
IF YOU'RE THAT WEAK, YOU'LL NEVER ACHIEVE YOUR GOAL.
AWAKEN, DARK VESSEL...
SWIP

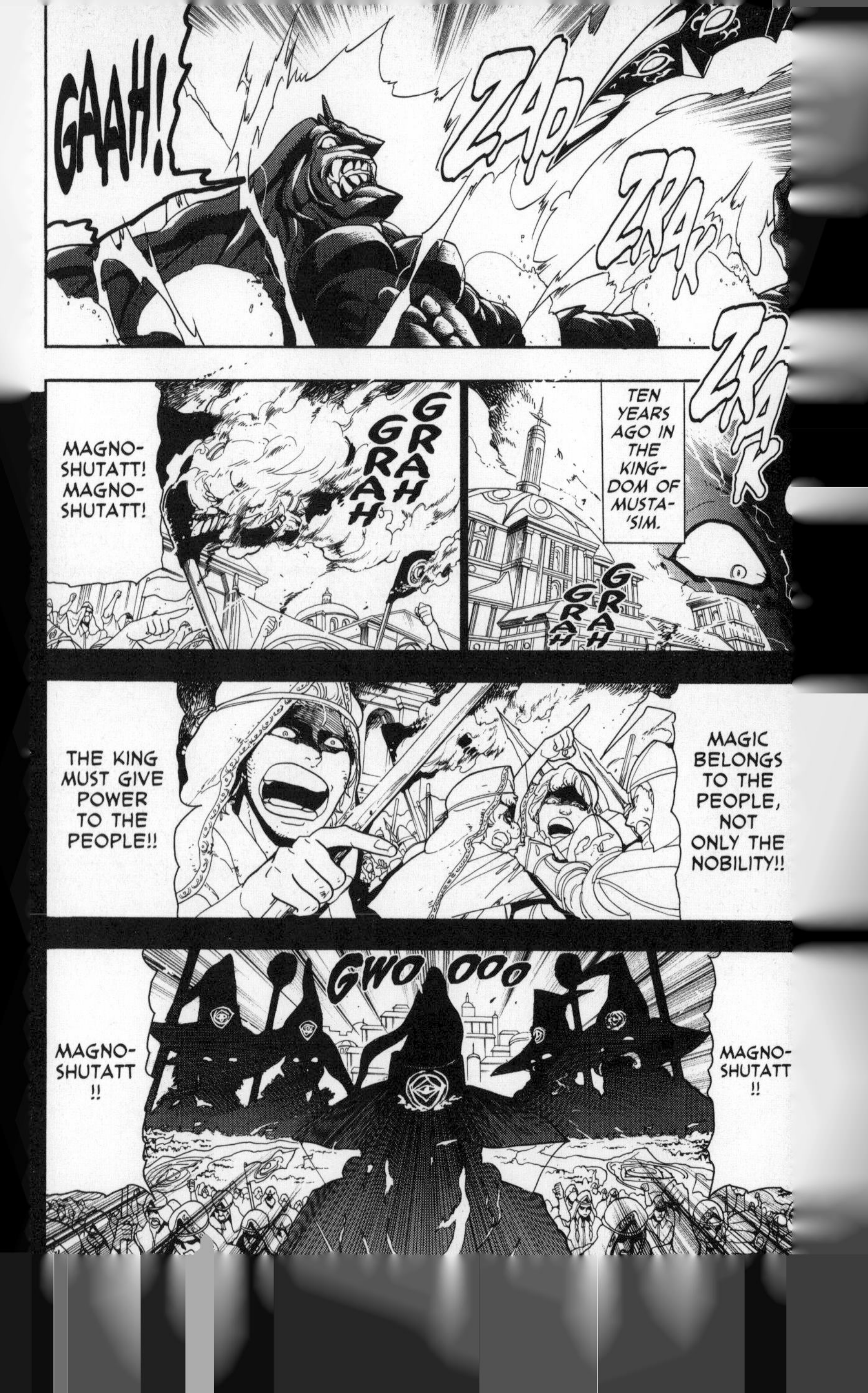
ZAP
GAAH!!
ZRAK
ZRAK
TEN YEARS AGO IN THE KINGDOM OF MUSTA'SIM.
GGRAH GRAH
GGRAH GRAH
MAGNO-SHUTATT! MAGNO-SHUTATT!
MAGIC BELONGS TO THE PEOPLE, NOT ONLY THE NOBILITY!!
THE KING MUST GIVE POWER TO THE PEOPLE!!
GWOOOO
MAGNO-SHUTATT!!
MAGNO-SHUTATT!!

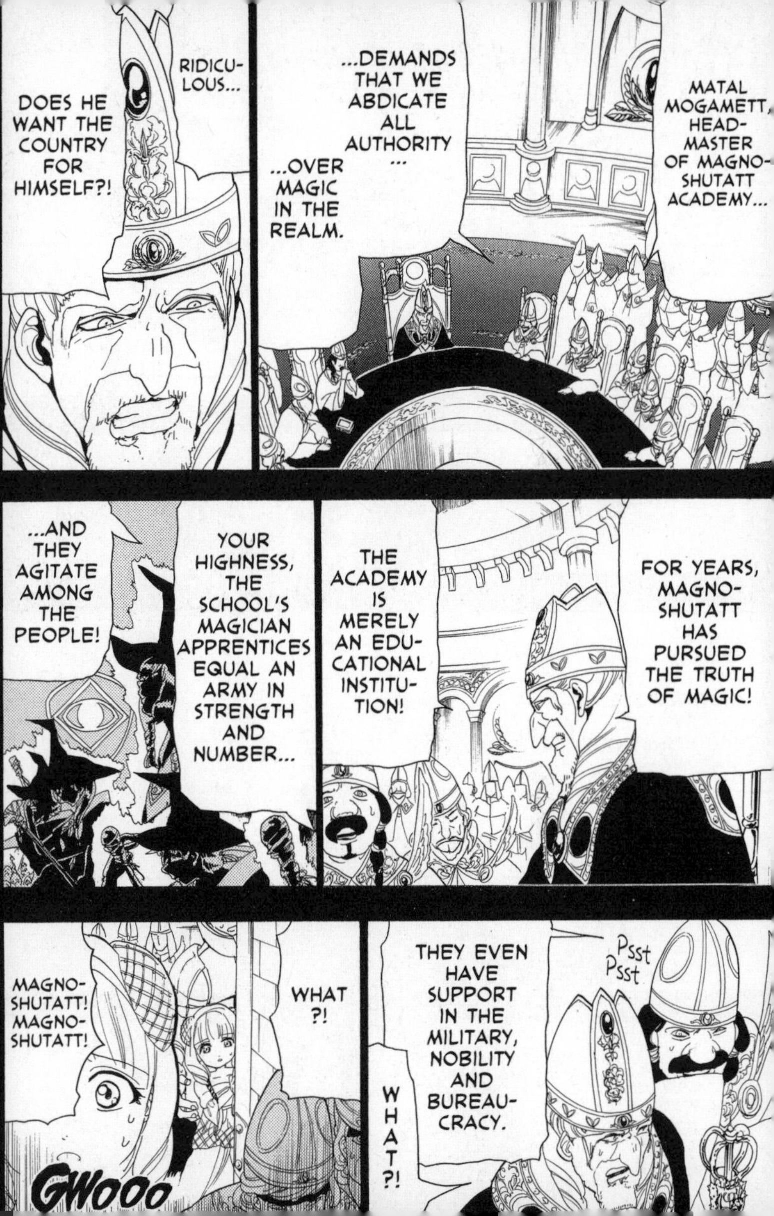

MATAL MOGAMETT, HEADMASTER OF MAGNOSHUTATT ACADEMY...
...DEMANDS THAT WE ABDICATE ALL AUTHORITY...
...OVER MAGIC IN THE REALM.
RIDICULOUS...
DOES HE WANT THE COUNTRY FOR HIMSELF?!
FOR YEARS, MAGNOSHUTATT HAS PURSUED THE TRUTH OF MAGIC!
THE ACADEMY IS MERELY AN EDUCATIONAL INSTITUTION!
YOUR HIGHNESS, THE SCHOOL'S MAGICIAN APPRENTICES EQUAL AN ARMY IN STRENGTH AND NUMBER...
...AND THEY AGITATE AMONG THE PEOPLE!
Psst Psst
THEY EVEN HAVE SUPPORT IN THE MILITARY, NOBILITY AND BUREAUCRACY.
WHAT?!
WHAT?!
MAGNOSHUTATT! MAGNOSHUTATT!
GWOOO

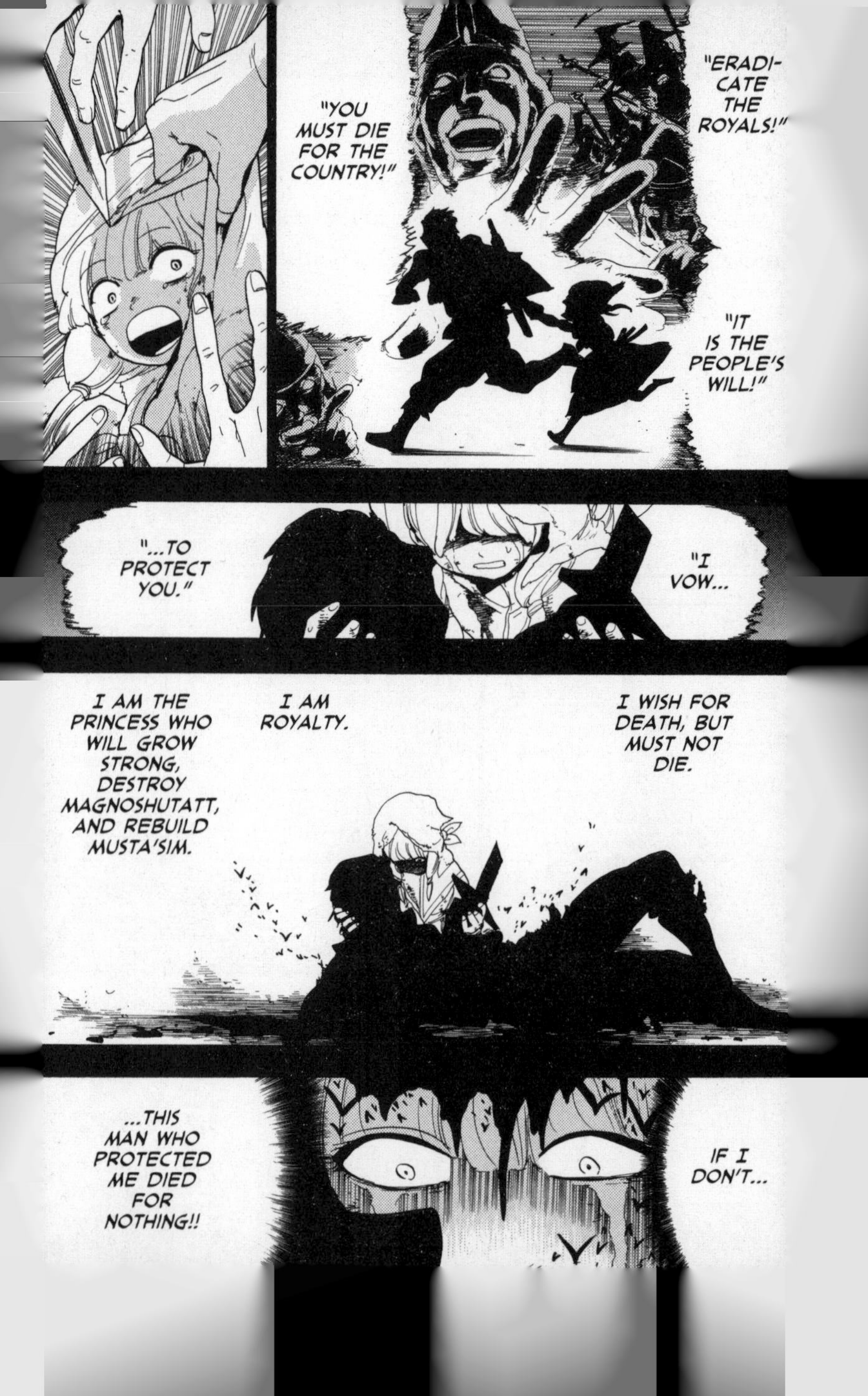
"ERADI-CATE THE ROYALS!"
"YOU MUST DIE FOR THE COUNTRY!"
"IT IS THE PEOPLE'S WILL!"
"I VOW...
"...TO PROTECT YOU."
I WISH FOR DEATH, BUT MUST NOT DIE.
I AM ROYALTY.
I AM THE PRINCESS WHO WILL GROW STRONG, DESTROY MAGNOSHUTATT, AND REBUILD MUSTA'SIM.
IF I DON'T...
...THIS MAN WHO PROTECTED ME DIED FOR NOTHING!!

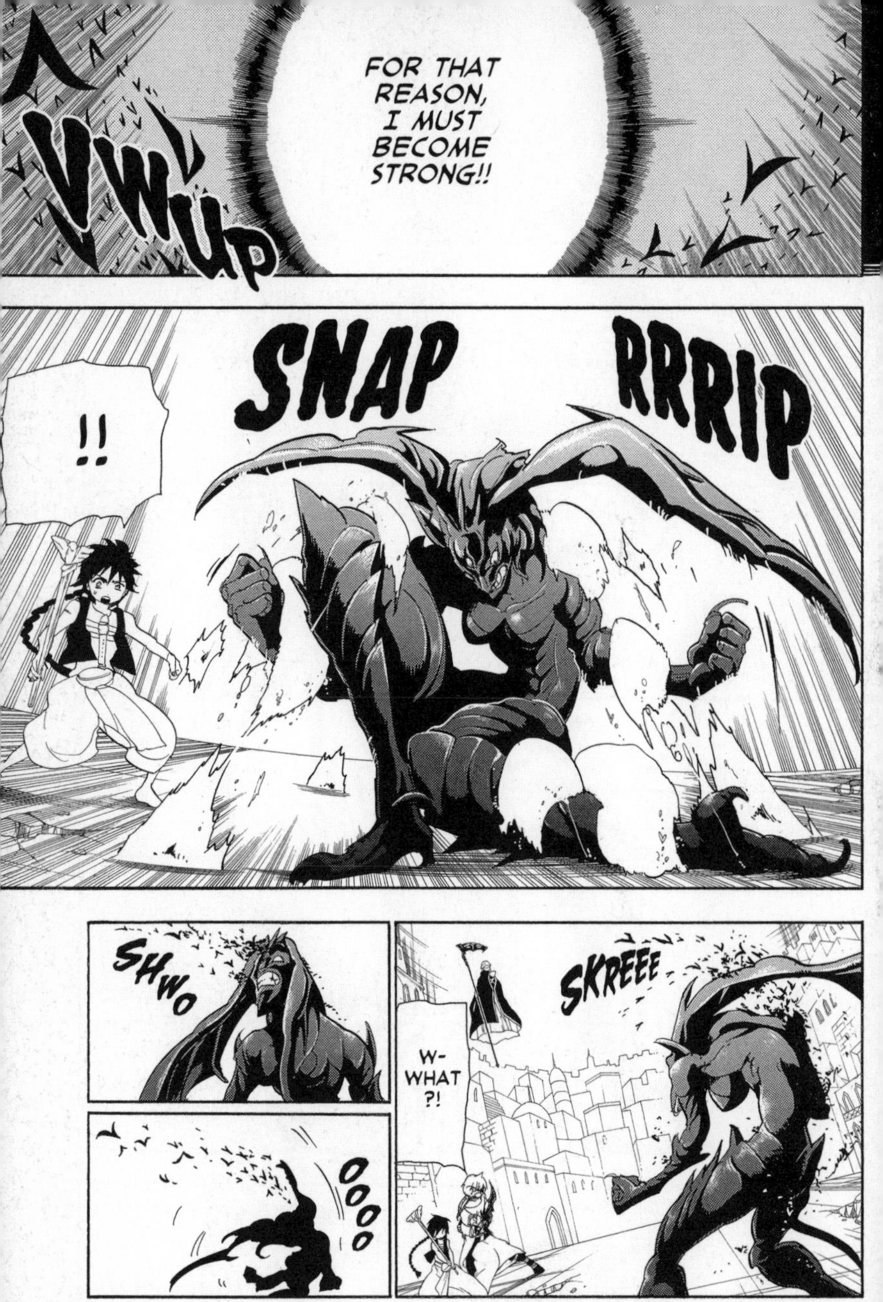
FOR THAT REASON, I MUST BECOME STRONG!!
VWUP
RRRIP
SNAP
!!
SKREEE
W-WHAT?!
SHWO
OOOO

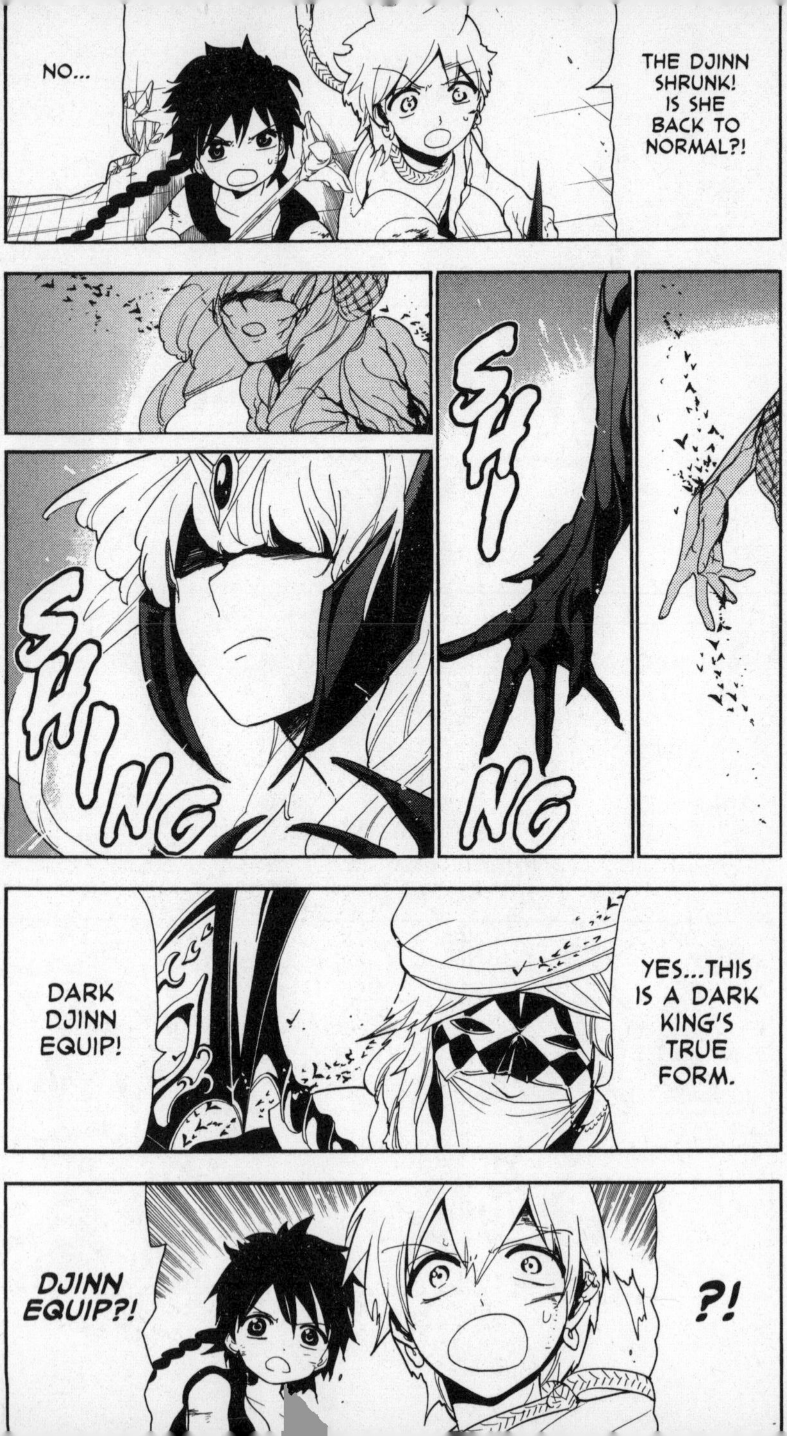
THE DJINN SHRUNK! IS SHE BACK TO NORMAL?!
NO...
SHING
SHING
YES...THIS IS A DARK KING'S TRUE FORM.
DARK DJINN EQUIP!
?!
DJINN EQUIP?!

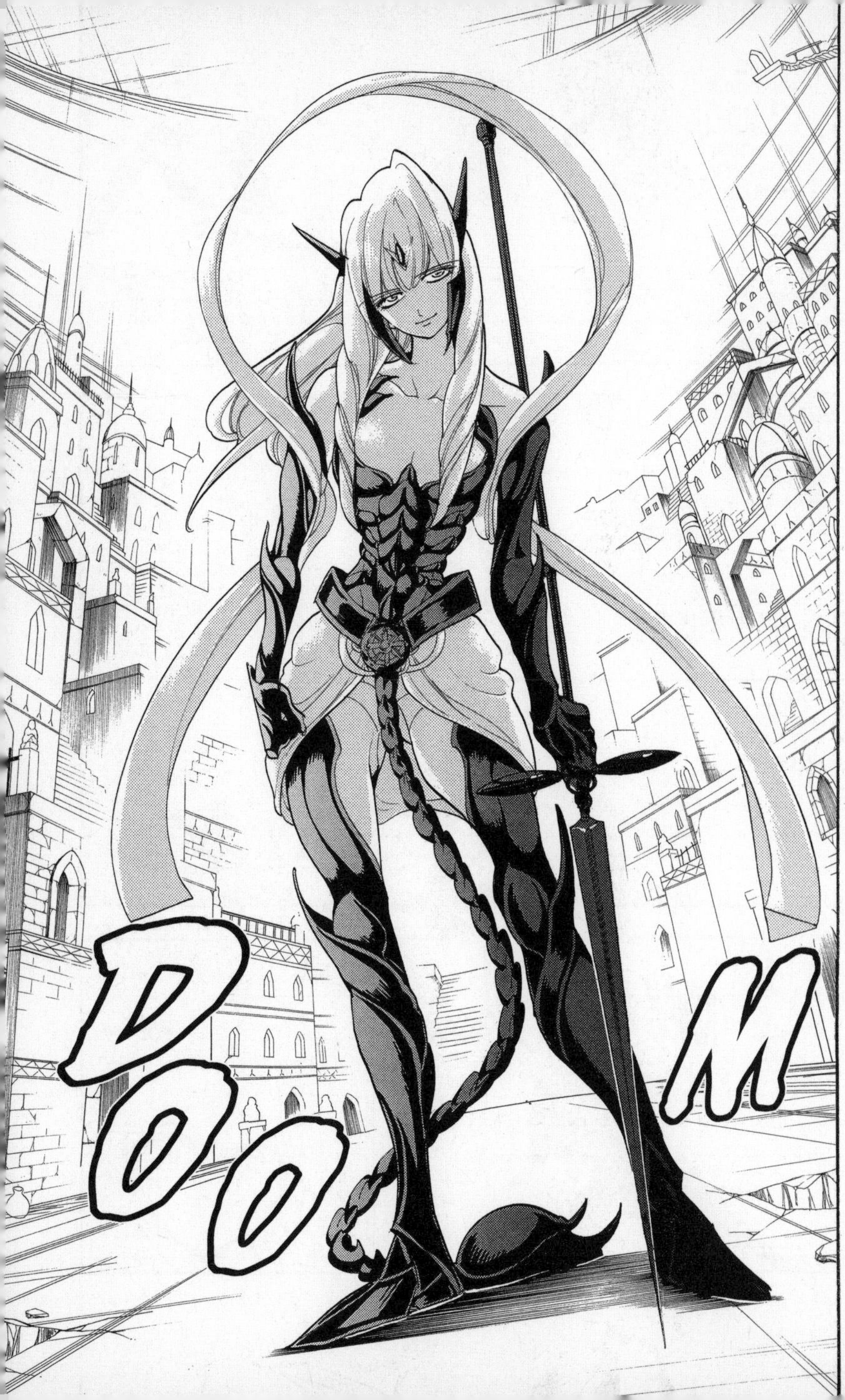
DOOM

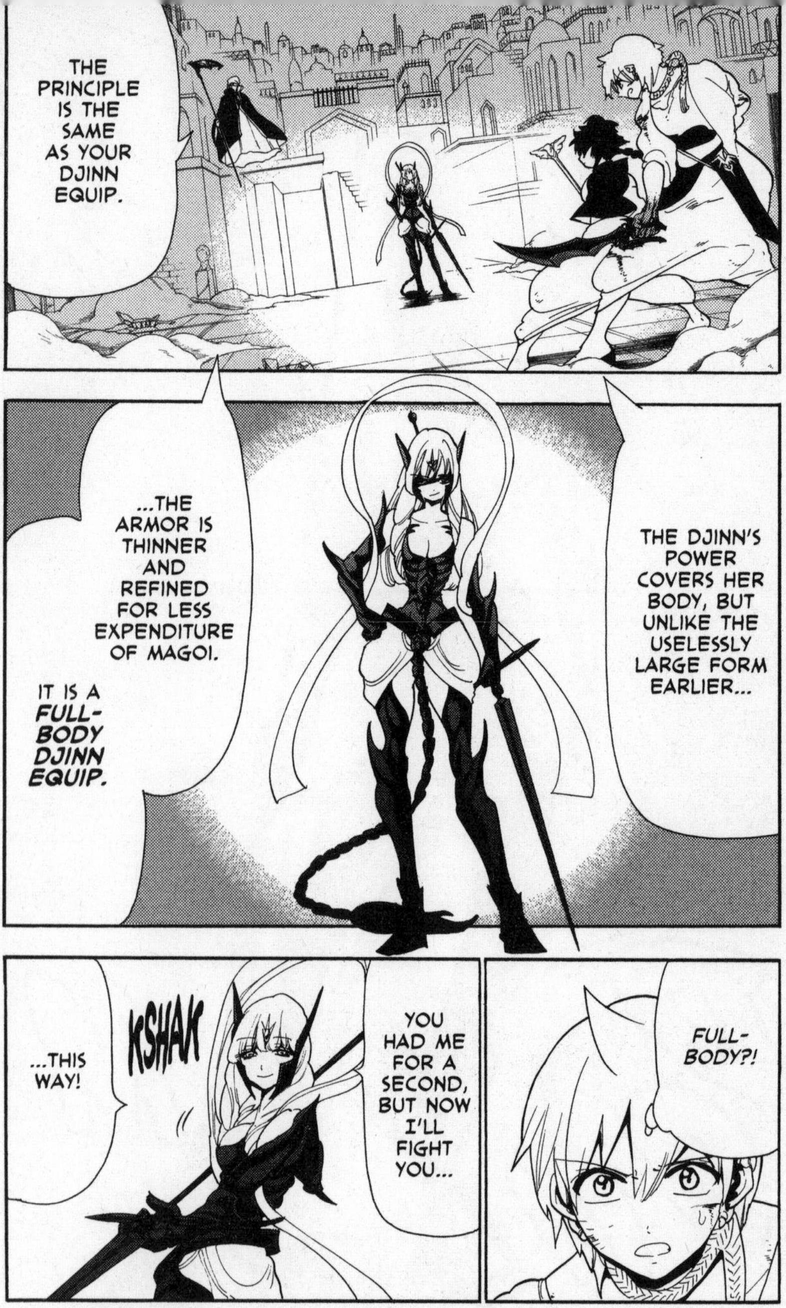
THE PRINCIPLE IS THE SAME AS YOUR DJINN EQUIP.
THE DJINN'S POWER COVERS HER BODY, BUT UNLIKE THE USELESSLY LARGE FORM EARLIER...
...THE ARMOR IS THINNER AND REFINED FOR LESS EXPENDITURE OF MAGOI.
IT IS A *FULL-BODY DJINN EQUIP.*
FULL-BODY?!
YOU HAD ME FOR A SECOND, BUT NOW I'LL FIGHT YOU...
KSHAK
...THIS WAY!

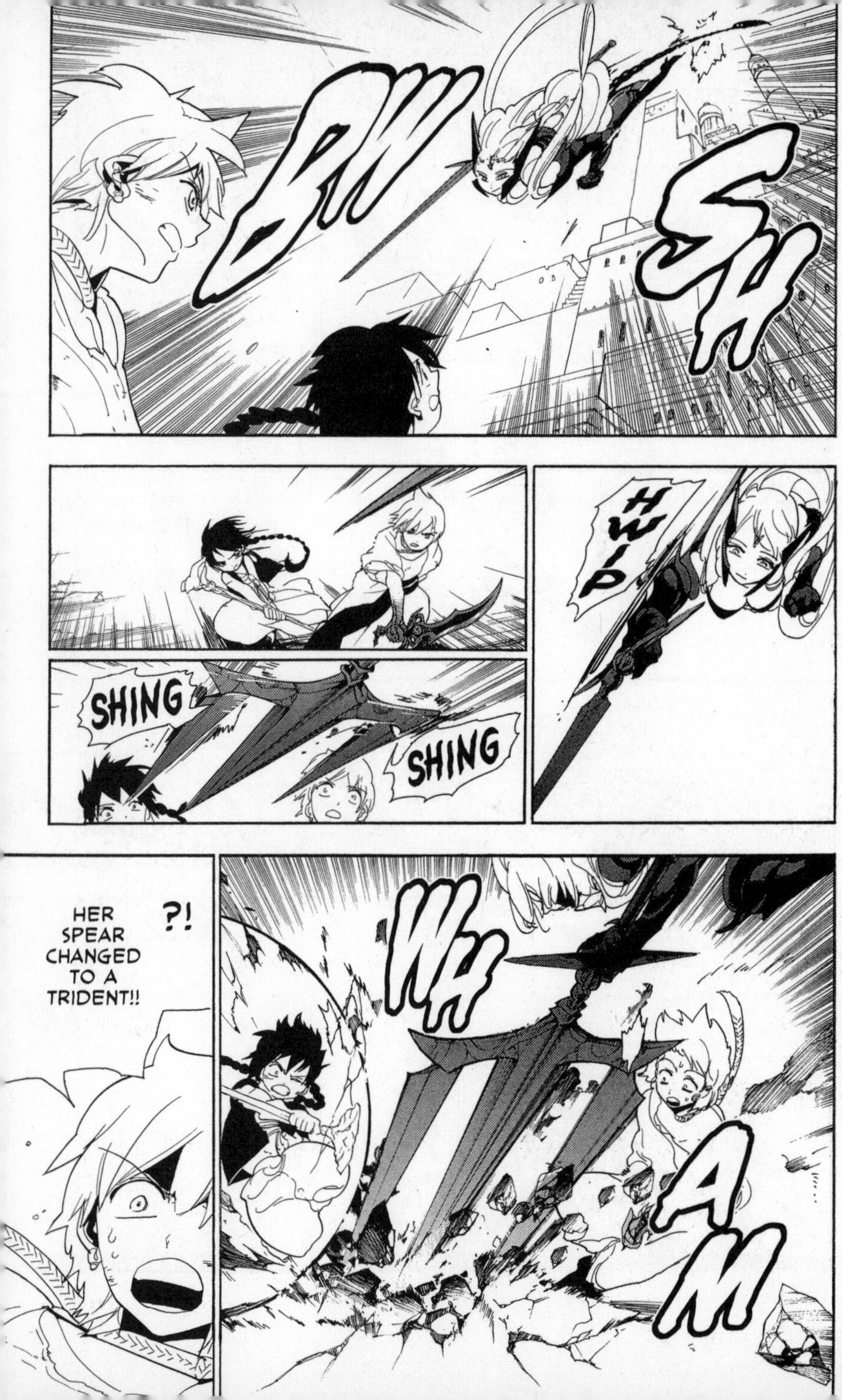
SH
HWIP
SHING
SHING
WH
AM
?!
HER SPEAR CHANGED TO A TRIDENT!!

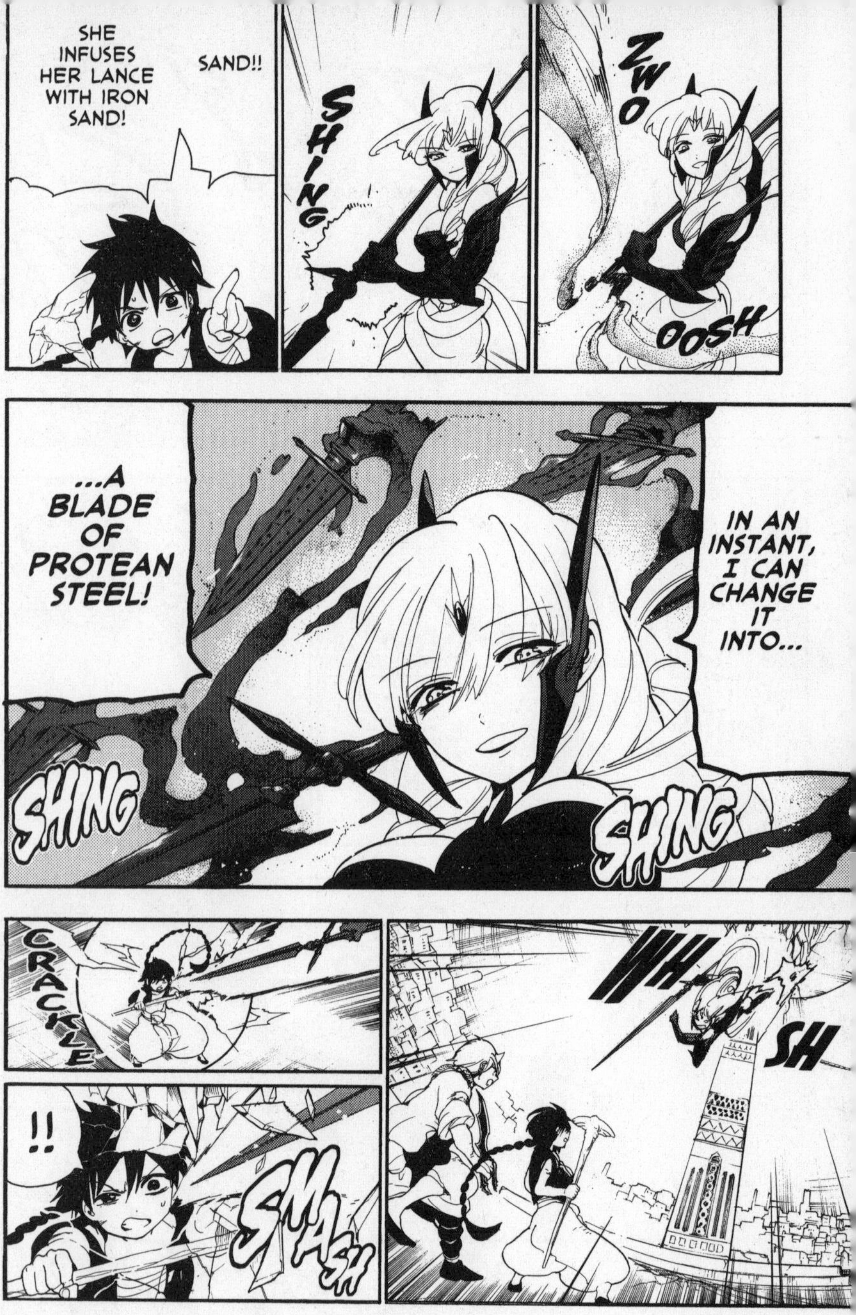
ZWO
OOSH
SHING
SAND!!
SHE INFUSES HER LANCE WITH IRON SAND!
IN AN INSTANT, I CAN CHANGE IT INTO...
...A BLADE OF PROTEAN STEEL!
SHING
SHING
WH-
SH
CRACKLE
!!
SMASH

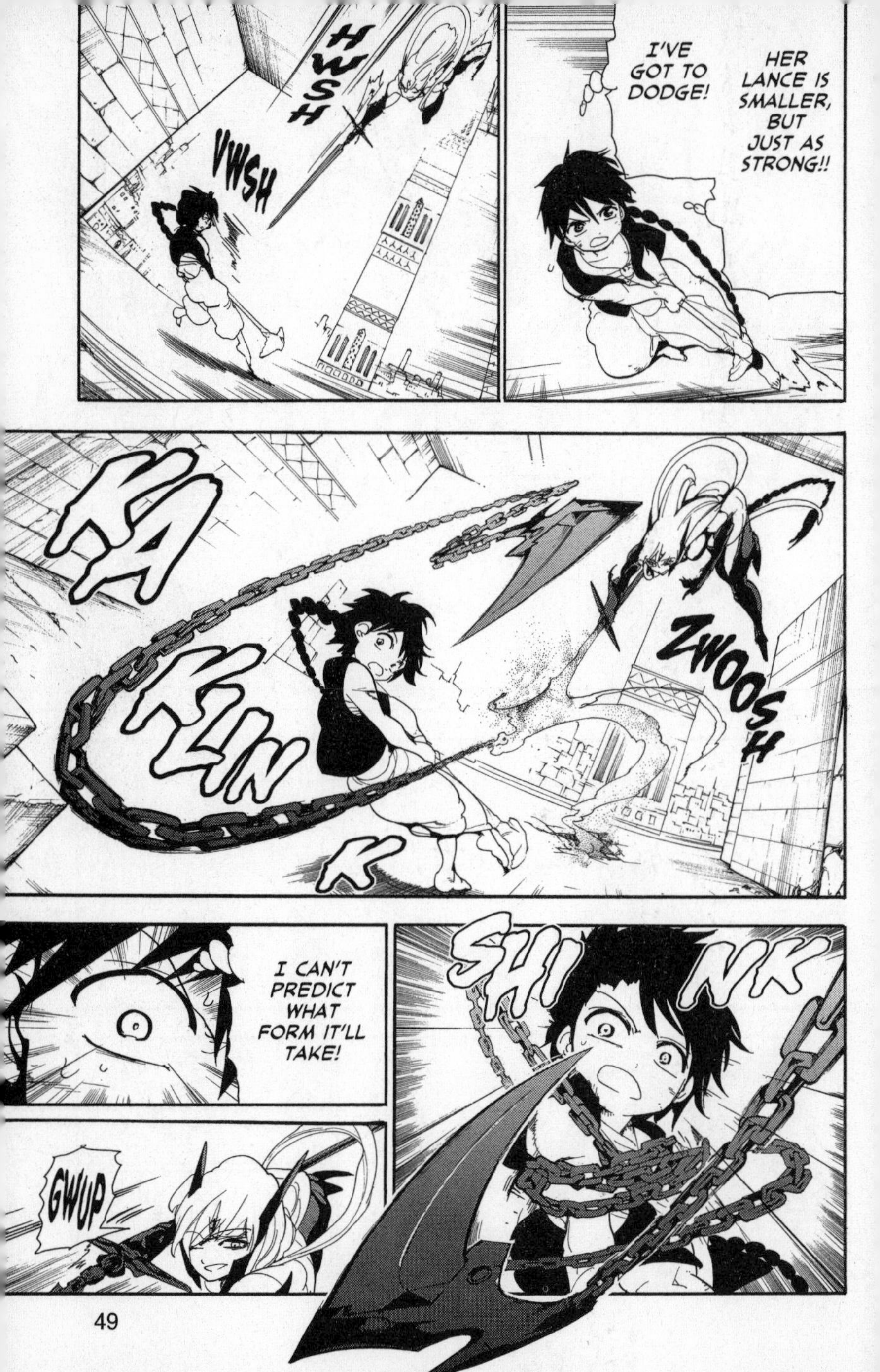

HER LANCE IS SMALLER, BUT JUST AS STRONG!!
I'VE GOT TO DODGE!
HWSH
VWSH
ZWOOSH
KA
KLINK
SHINK
I CAN'T PREDICT WHAT FORM IT'LL TAKE!
GWUP

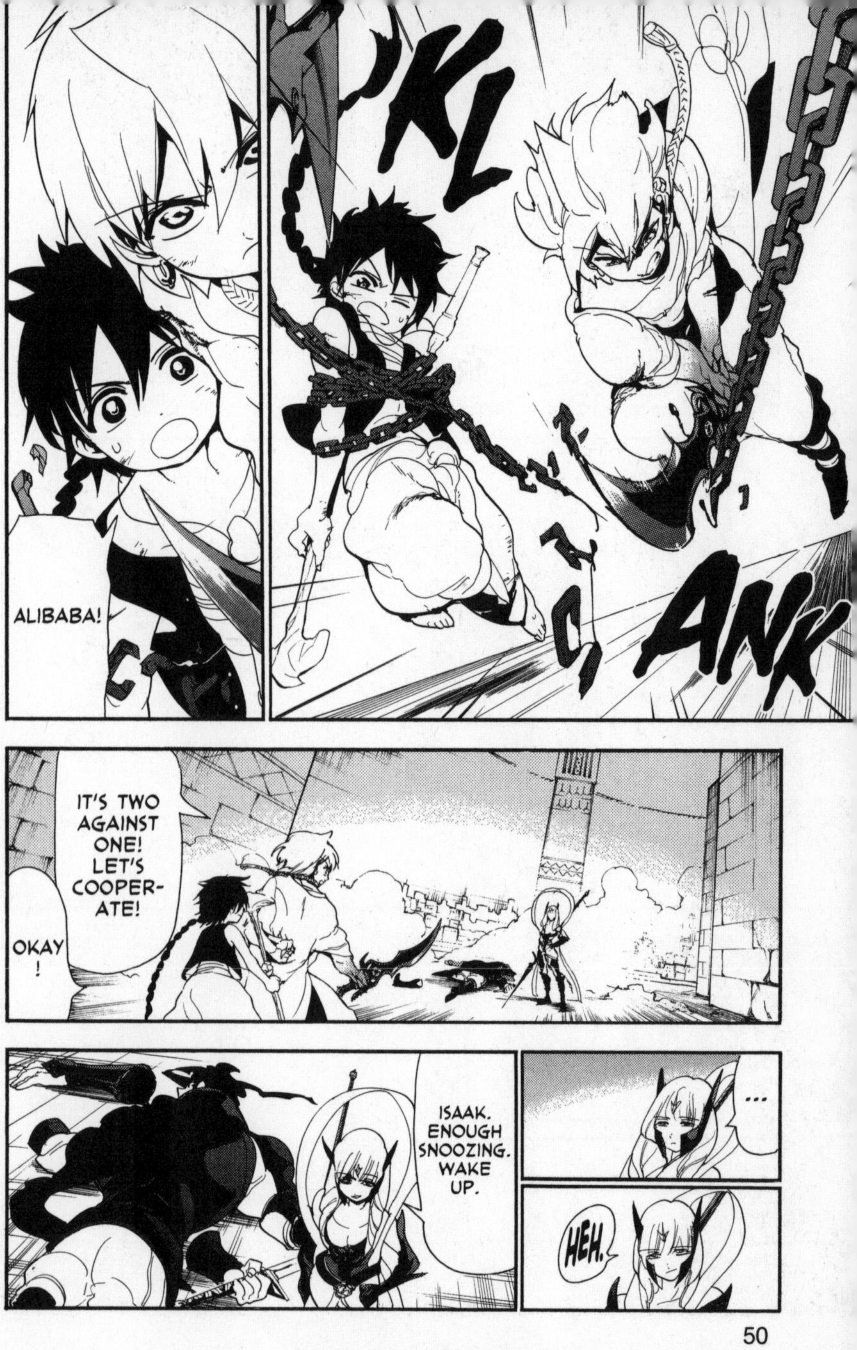
KL
ANK
ALIBABA!
IT'S TWO AGAINST ONE! LET'S COOPER-ATE!
OKAY!
...
HEH.
ISAAK. ENOUGH SNOOZING. WAKE UP.

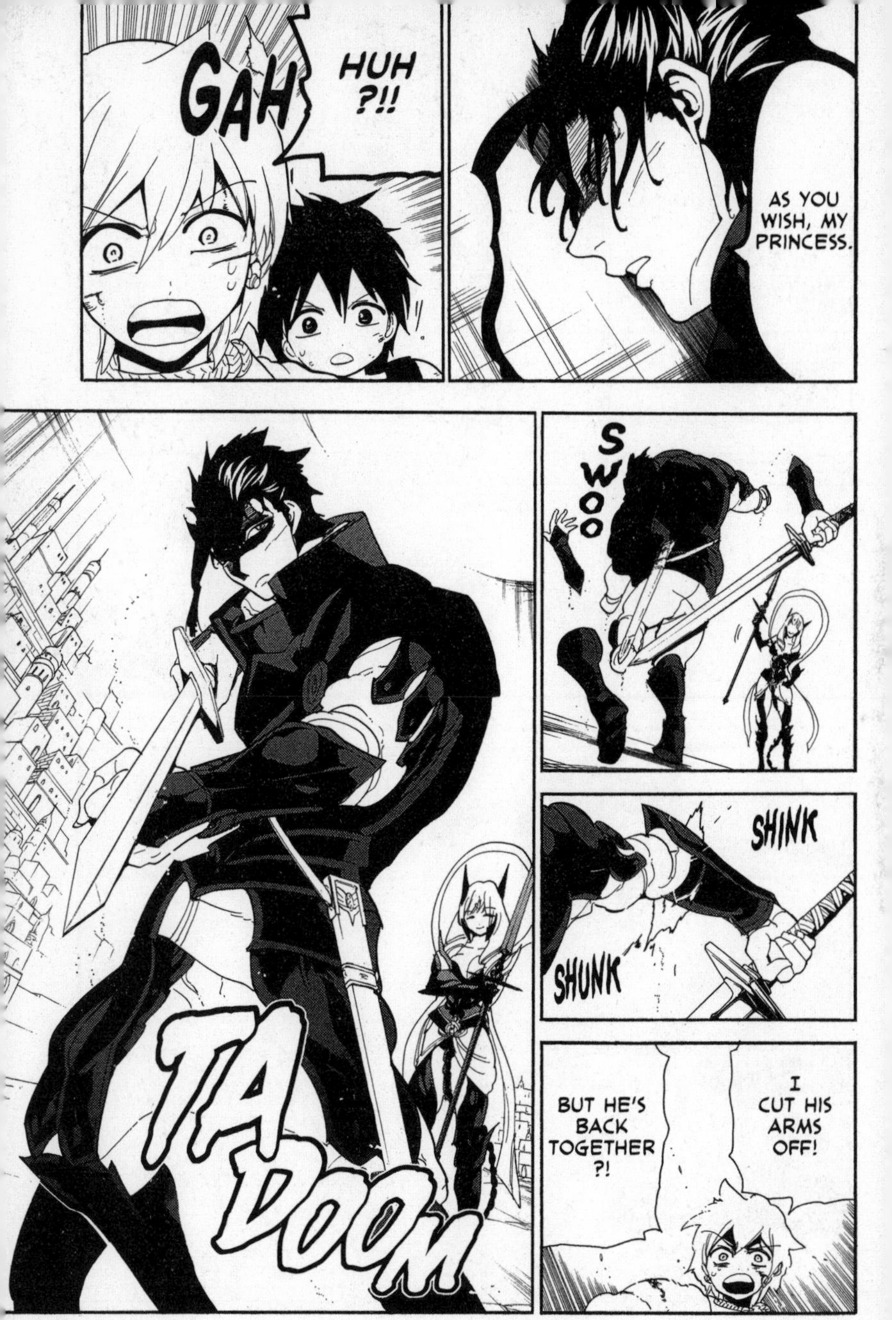
AS YOU WISH, MY PRINCESS.
HUH ?!!
GAH
SWOOO
SHINK
SHUNK
I CUT HIS ARMS OFF!
BUT HE'S BACK TOGETHER ?!
TA DOOM

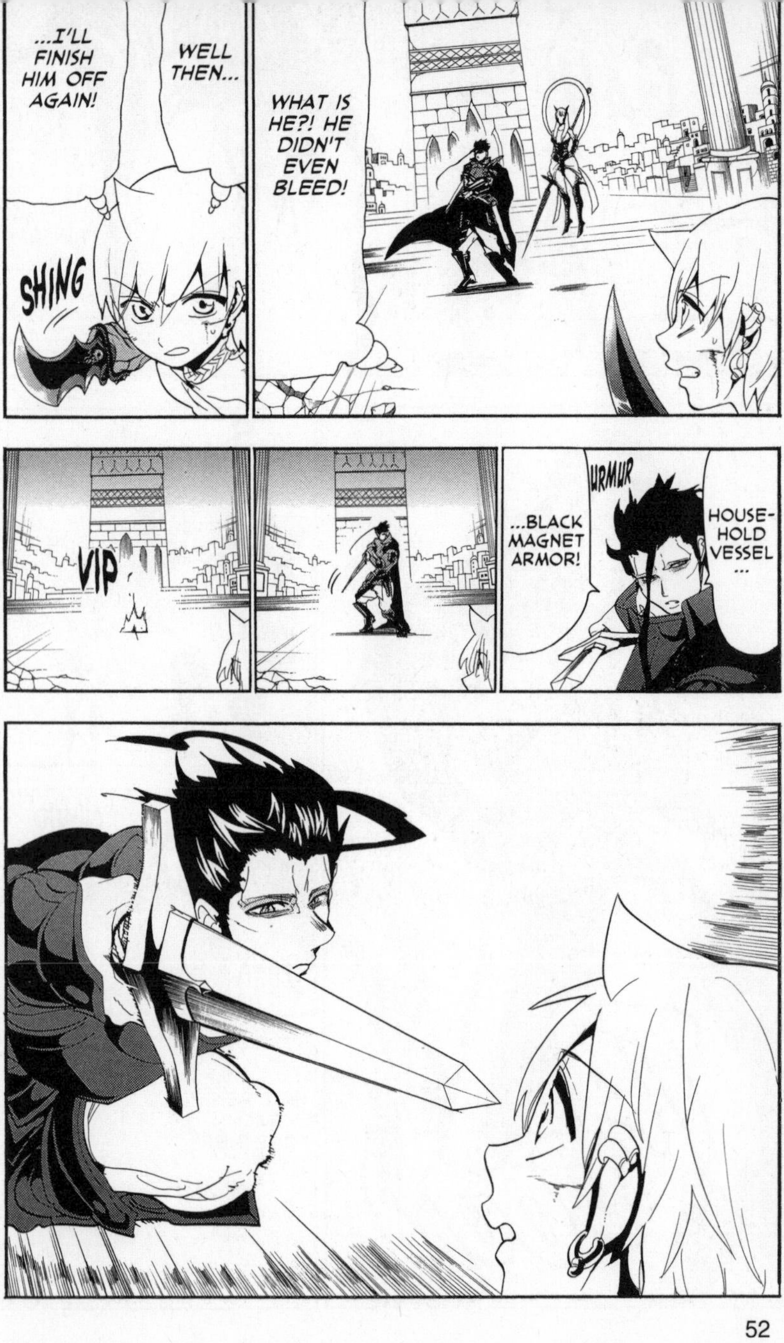
WHAT IS HE?! HE DIDN'T EVEN BLEED!
WELL THEN...
...I'LL FINISH HIM OFF AGAIN!
SHING
HOUSE-HOLD VESSEL ...
URMUR
...BLACK MAGNET ARMOR!
VIP

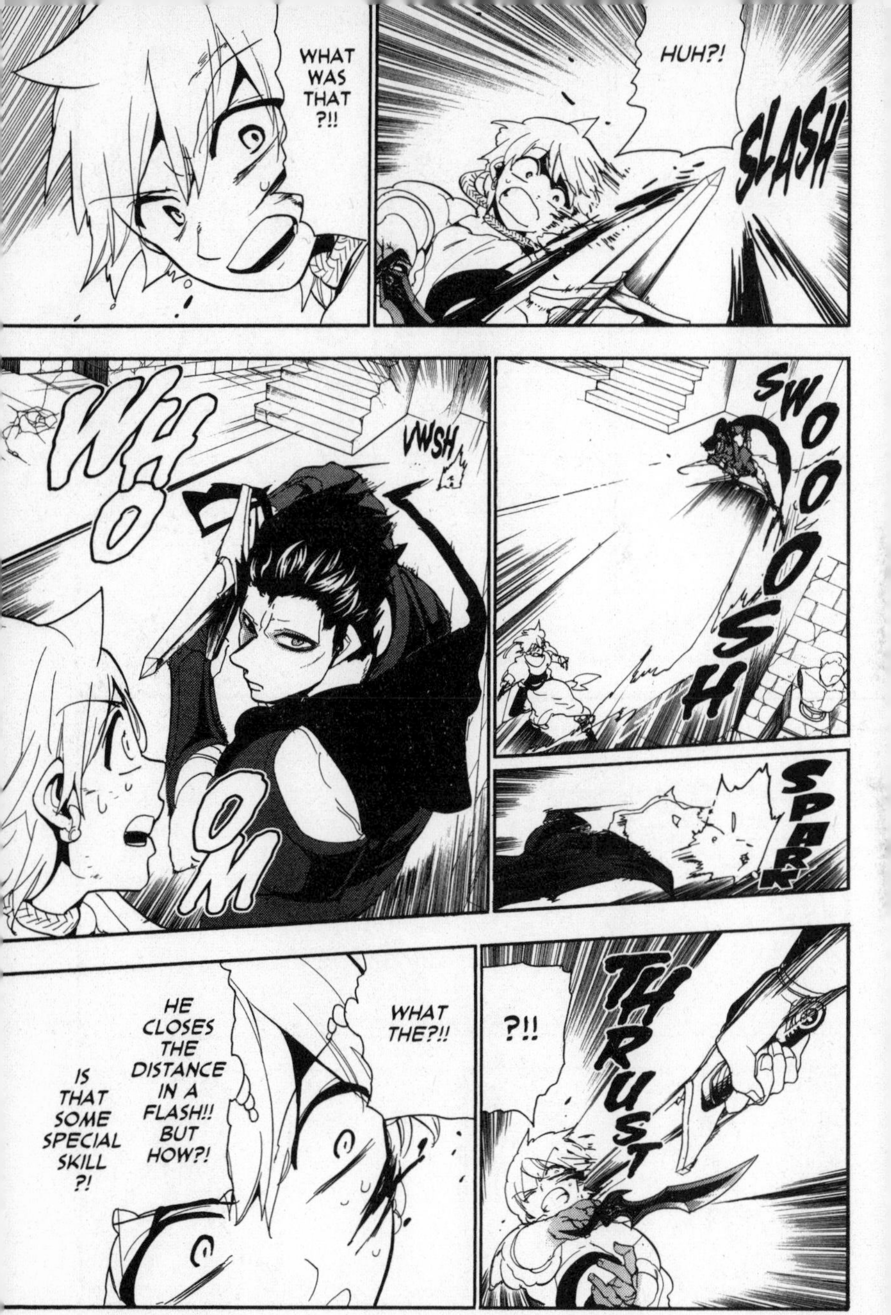
HUH?!
SLASH
WHAT WAS THAT ?!!
SWOOOOSH
SPARK
VWSH
WHOOOM
THRUST
?!!
WHAT THE?!!
HE CLOSES THE DISTANCE IN A FLASH!! BUT HOW?!
IS THAT SOME SPECIAL SKILL ?!

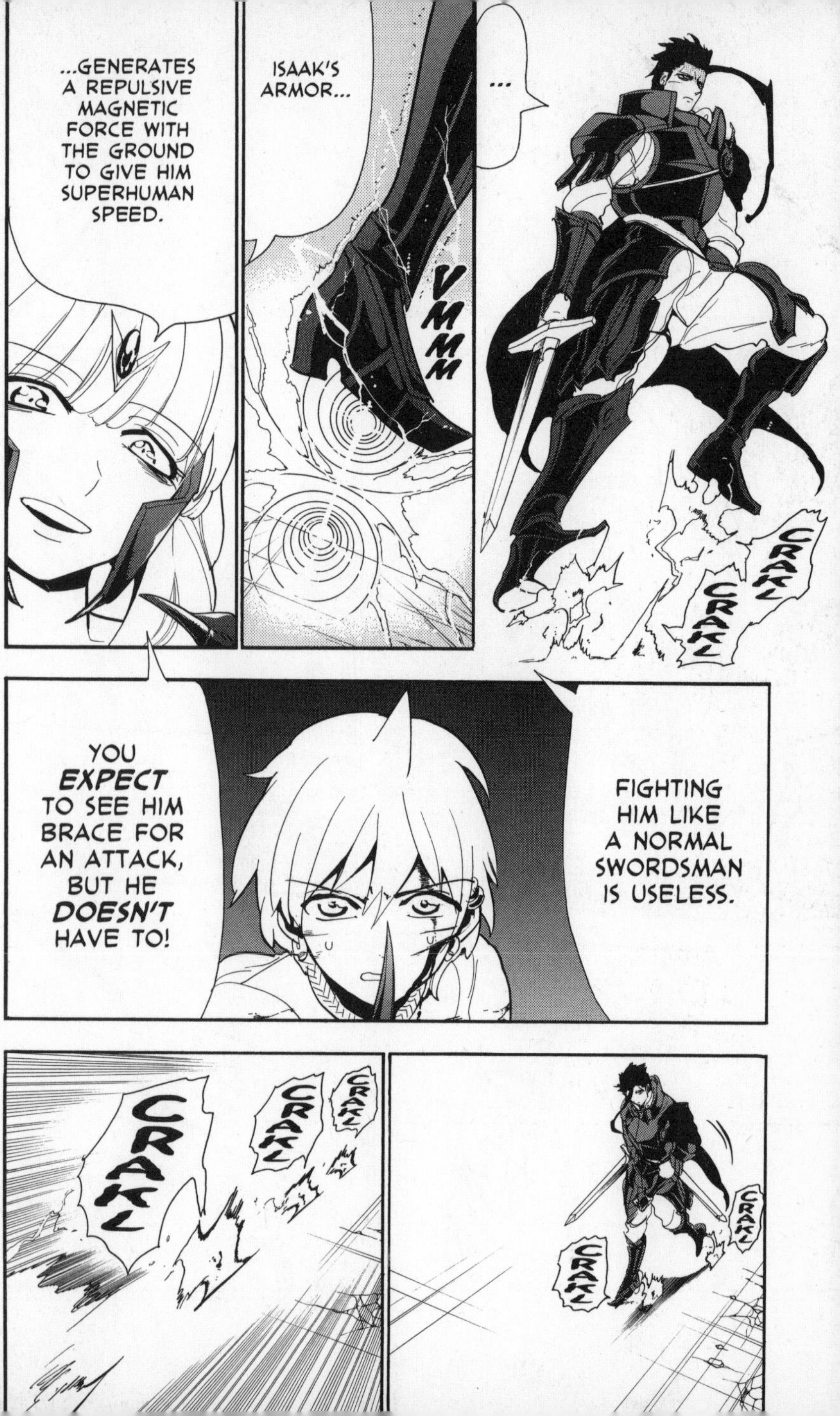
...
CRAKL
CRAKL
ISAAK'S ARMOR...
VMMM
...GENERATES A REPULSIVE MAGNETIC FORCE WITH THE GROUND TO GIVE HIM SUPERHUMAN SPEED.
FIGHTING HIM LIKE A NORMAL SWORDSMAN IS USELESS.
YOU EXPECT TO SEE HIM BRACE FOR AN ATTACK, BUT HE DOESN'T HAVE TO!
CRAKL
CRAKL
CRAKL
CRAKL
CRAKL

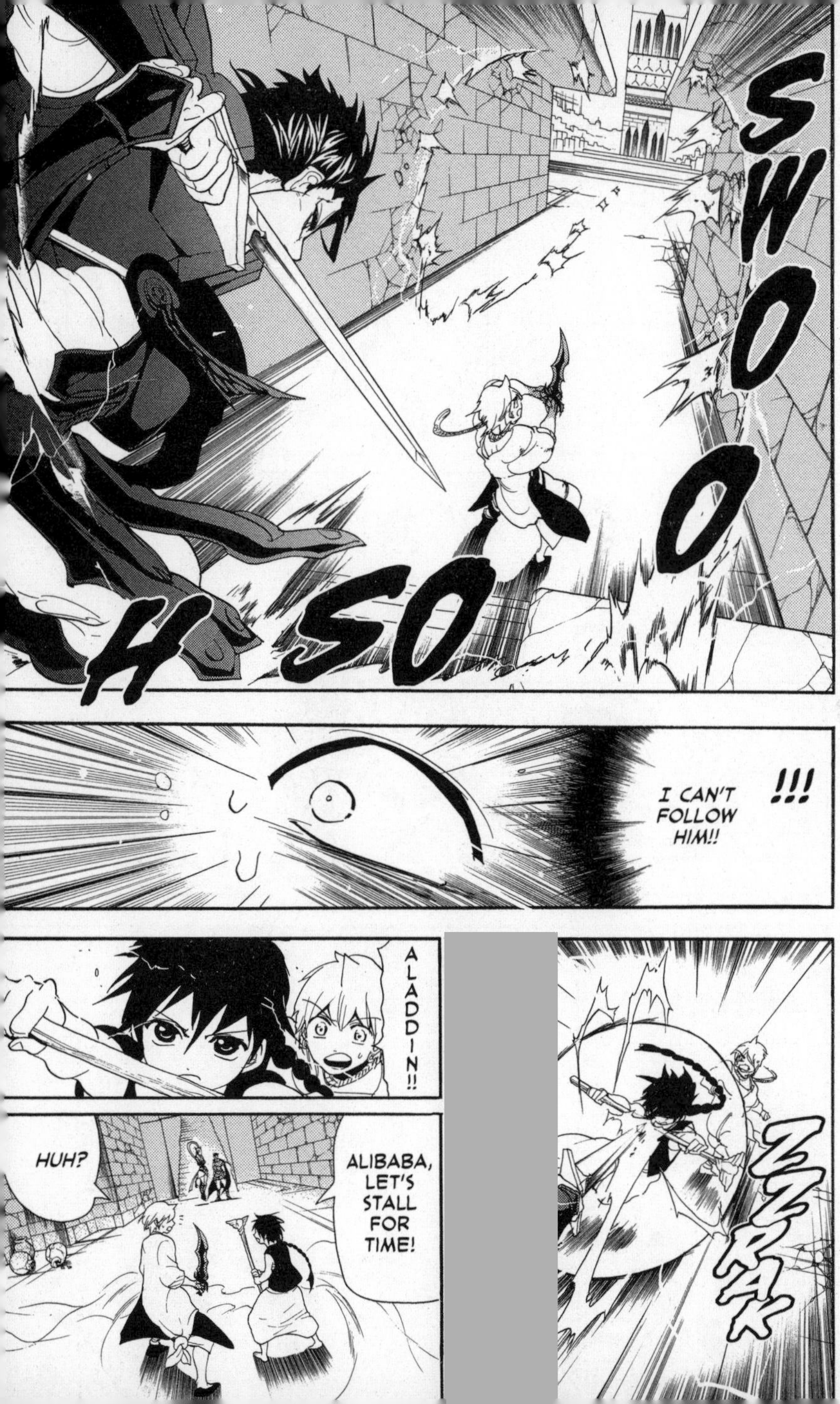
SWOOOOSH
!!!
I CAN'T FOLLOW HIM!!
SWRAK
ALADDIN!!
ALIBABA, LET'S STALL FOR TIME!
HUH?

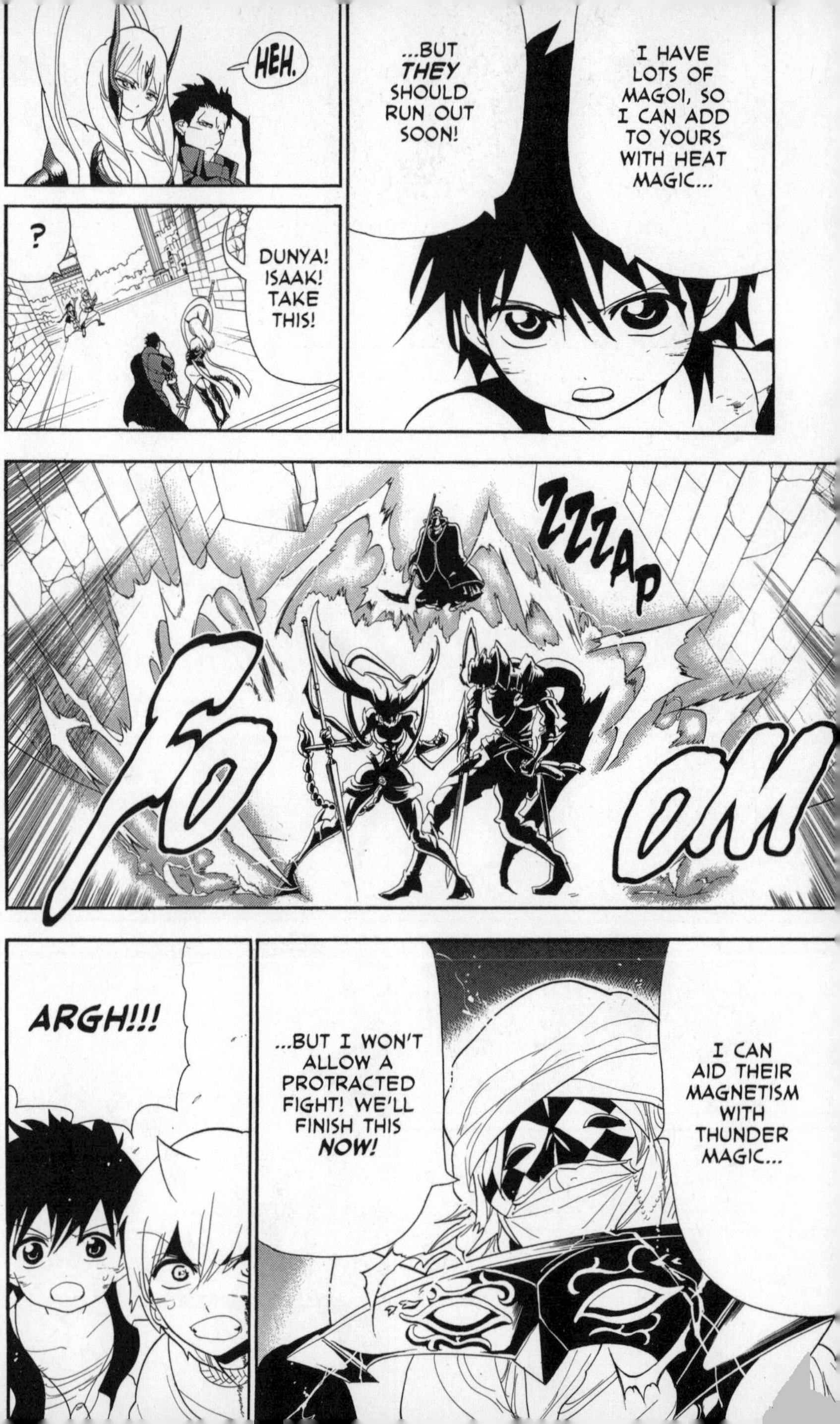
I HAVE LOTS OF MAGOI, SO I CAN ADD TO YOURS WITH HEAT MAGIC...
...BUT THEY SHOULD RUN OUT SOON!
HEH.
?
DUNYA! ISAAK! TAKE THIS!
ZZZAP
FOOM
I CAN AID THEIR MAGNETISM WITH THUNDER MAGIC...
...BUT I WON'T ALLOW A PROTRACTED FIGHT! WE'LL FINISH THIS NOW!
ARGH!!!

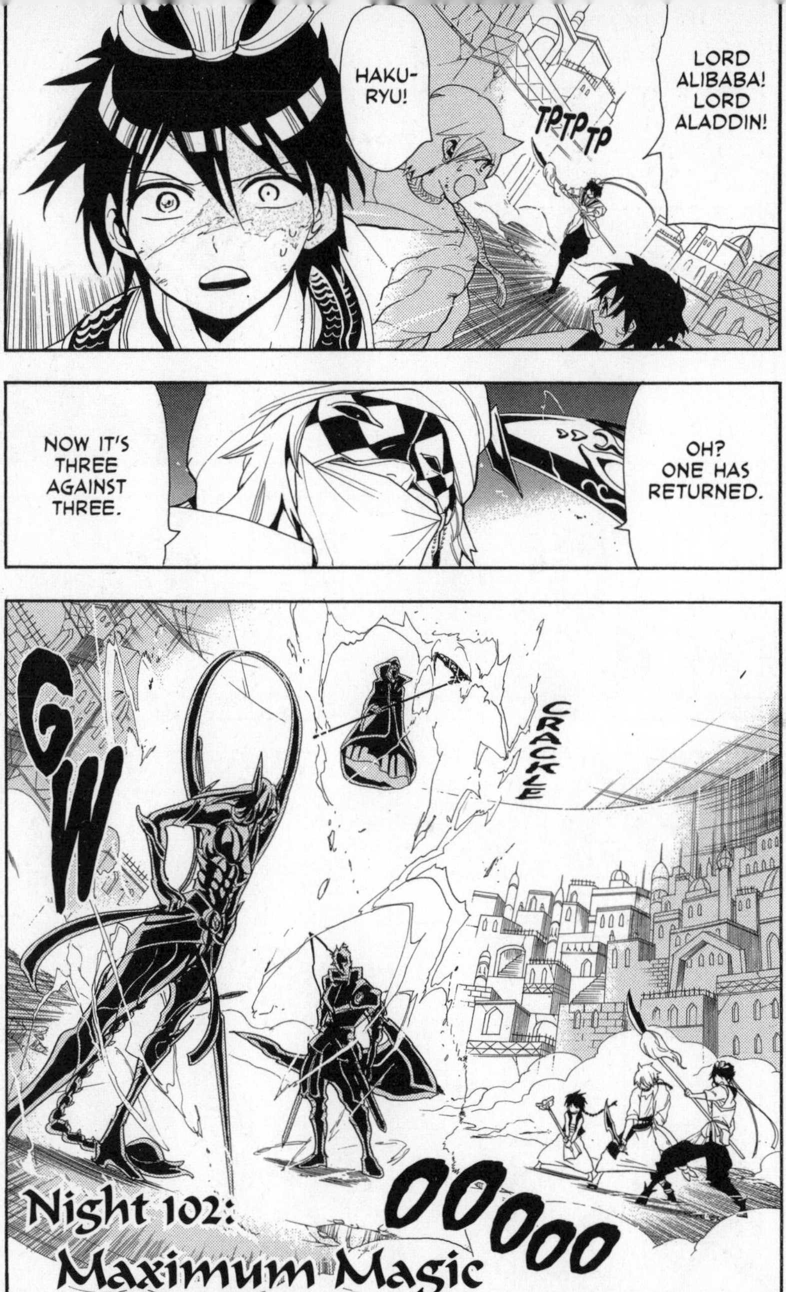
LORD ALIBABA! LORD ALADDIN!
TPTPTP
HAKU-RYU!
OH? ONE HAS RETURNED.
NOW IT'S THREE AGAINST THREE.
CRACKLE
GW
OOOOO
Night 102: Maximum Magic

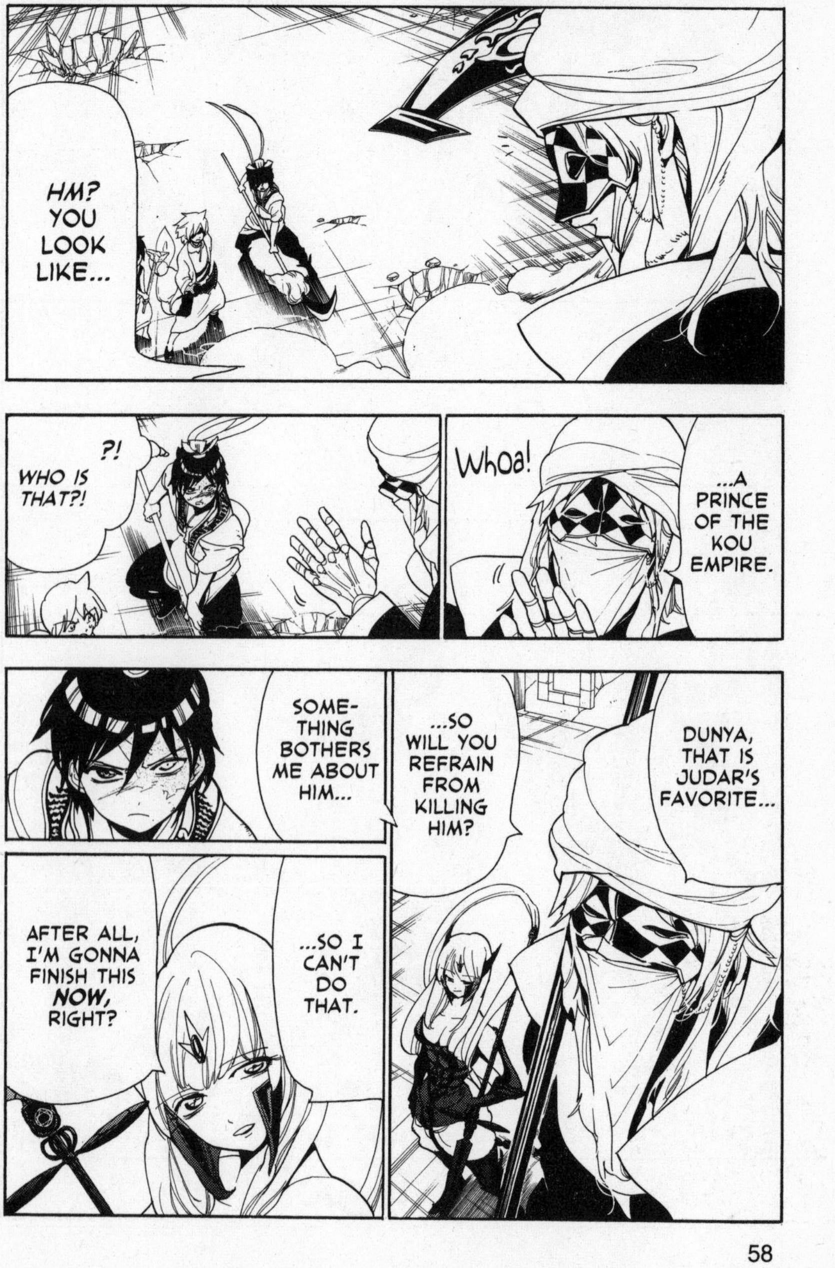
HM? YOU LOOK LIKE...
Whoa!
...A PRINCE OF THE KOU EMPIRE.
?!
WHO IS THAT?!
DUNYA, THAT IS JUDAR'S FAVORITE...
...SO WILL YOU REFRAIN FROM KILLING HIM?
SOME-THING BOTHERS ME ABOUT HIM...
...SO I CAN'T DO THAT.
AFTER ALL, I'M GONNA FINISH THIS *NOW*, RIGHT?

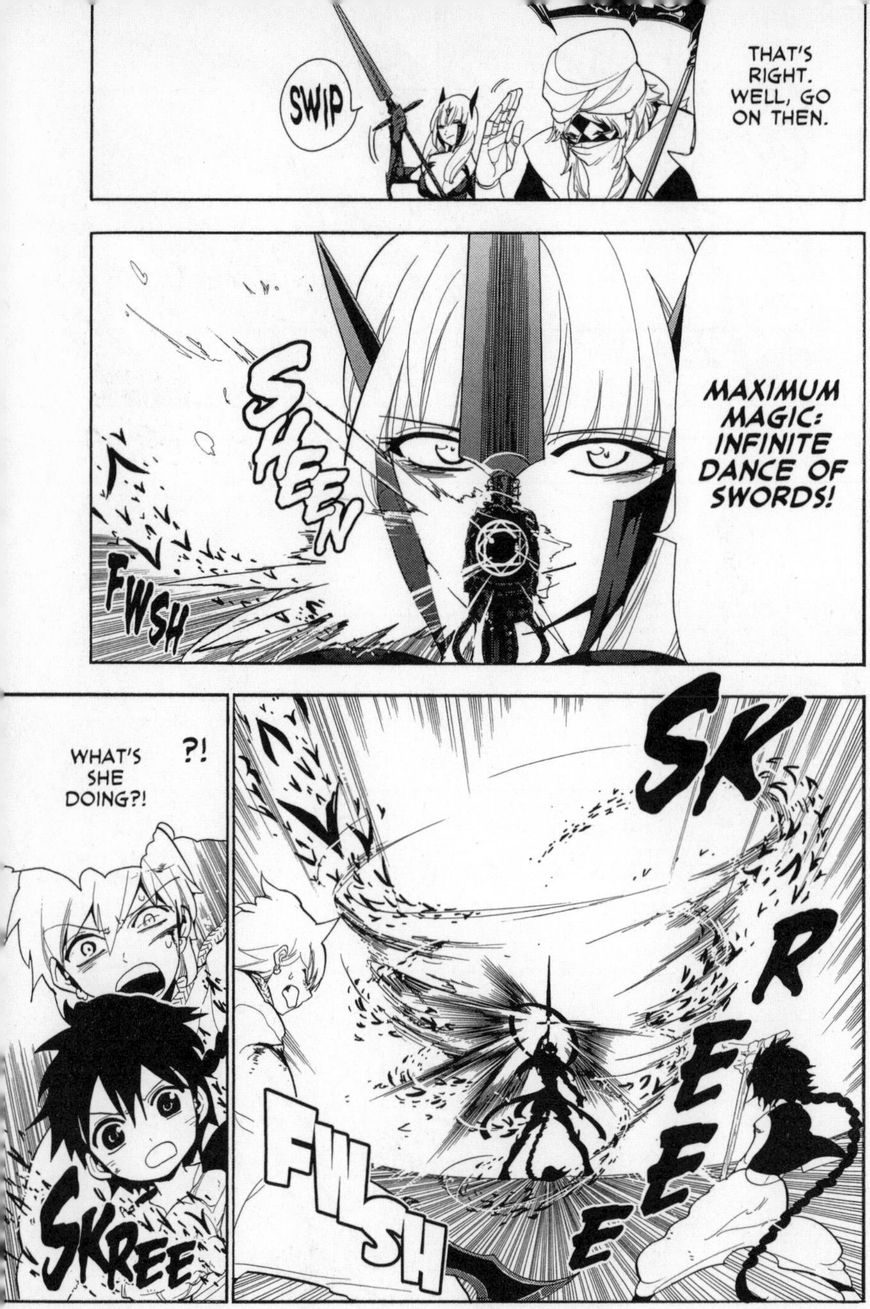
THAT'S RIGHT. WELL, GO ON THEN.
SWIP
MAXIMUM MAGIC: INFINITE DANCE OF SWORDS!
SHEEN
FWSH
SKREEEE
FWSH
?!
WHAT'S SHE DOING?!
SKREE

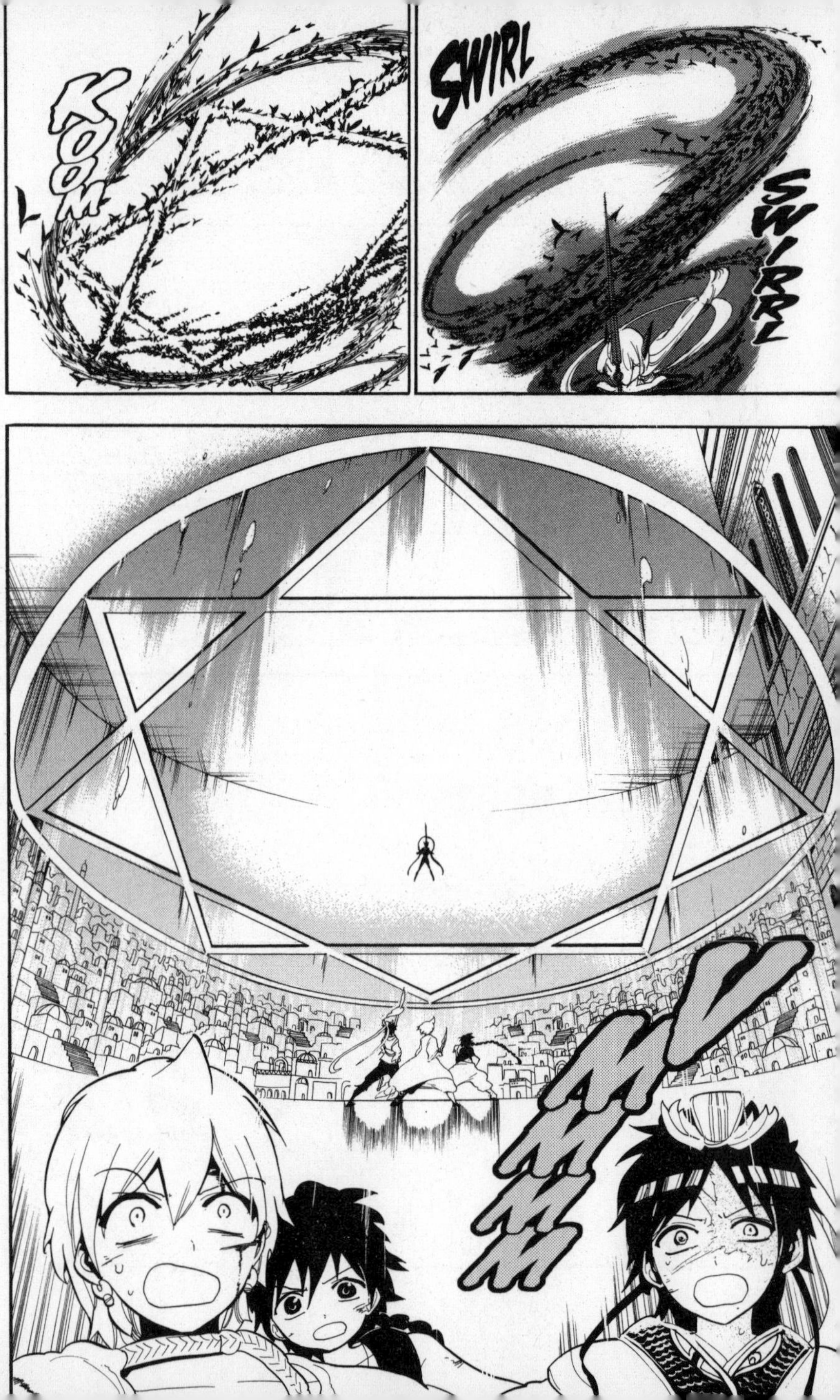
SWIRL
SWIRRL
KOOM
VMMMM

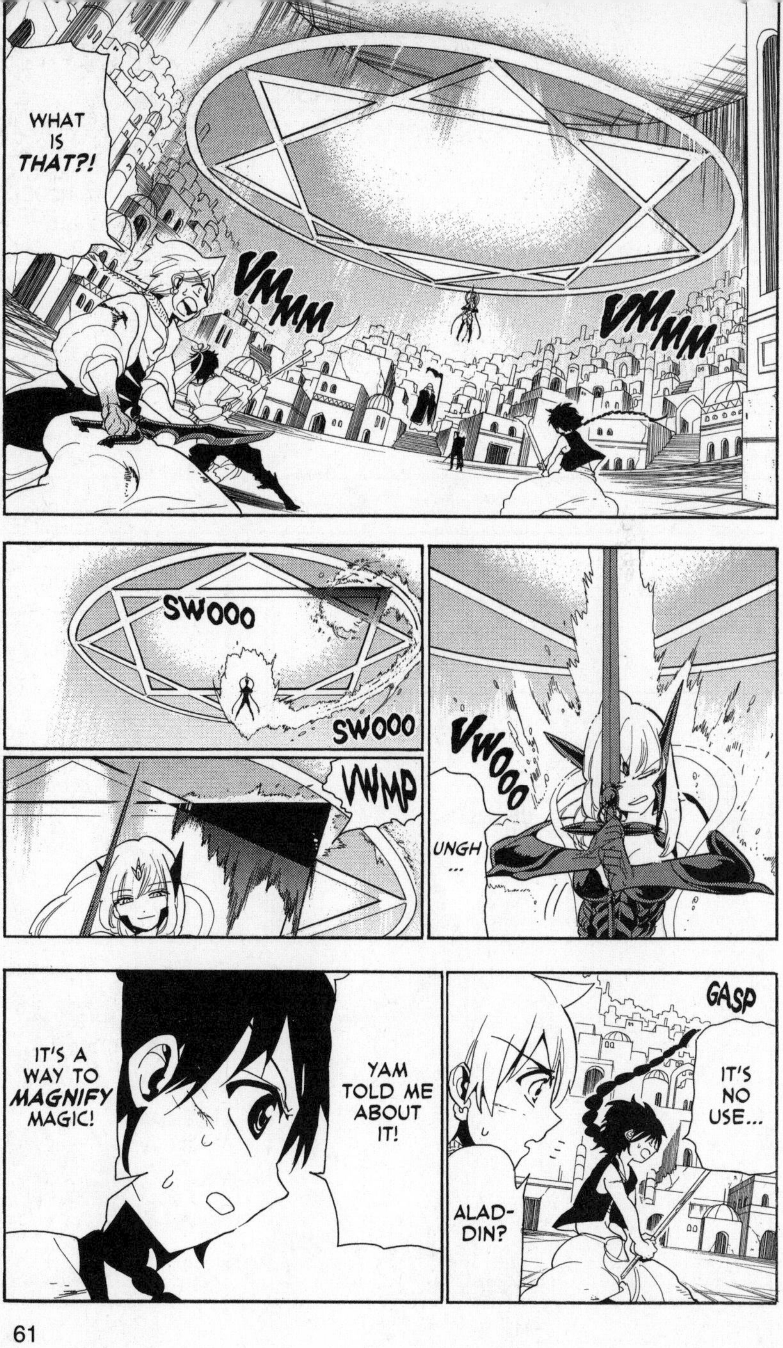
WHAT IS THAT?!
VMMM
VMMM
VWOOO
UNGH...
SWOOO
SWOOO
VWMP
GASP
IT'S NO USE...
ALAD-DIN?
YAM TOLD ME ABOUT IT!
IT'S A WAY TO MAGNIFY MAGIC!

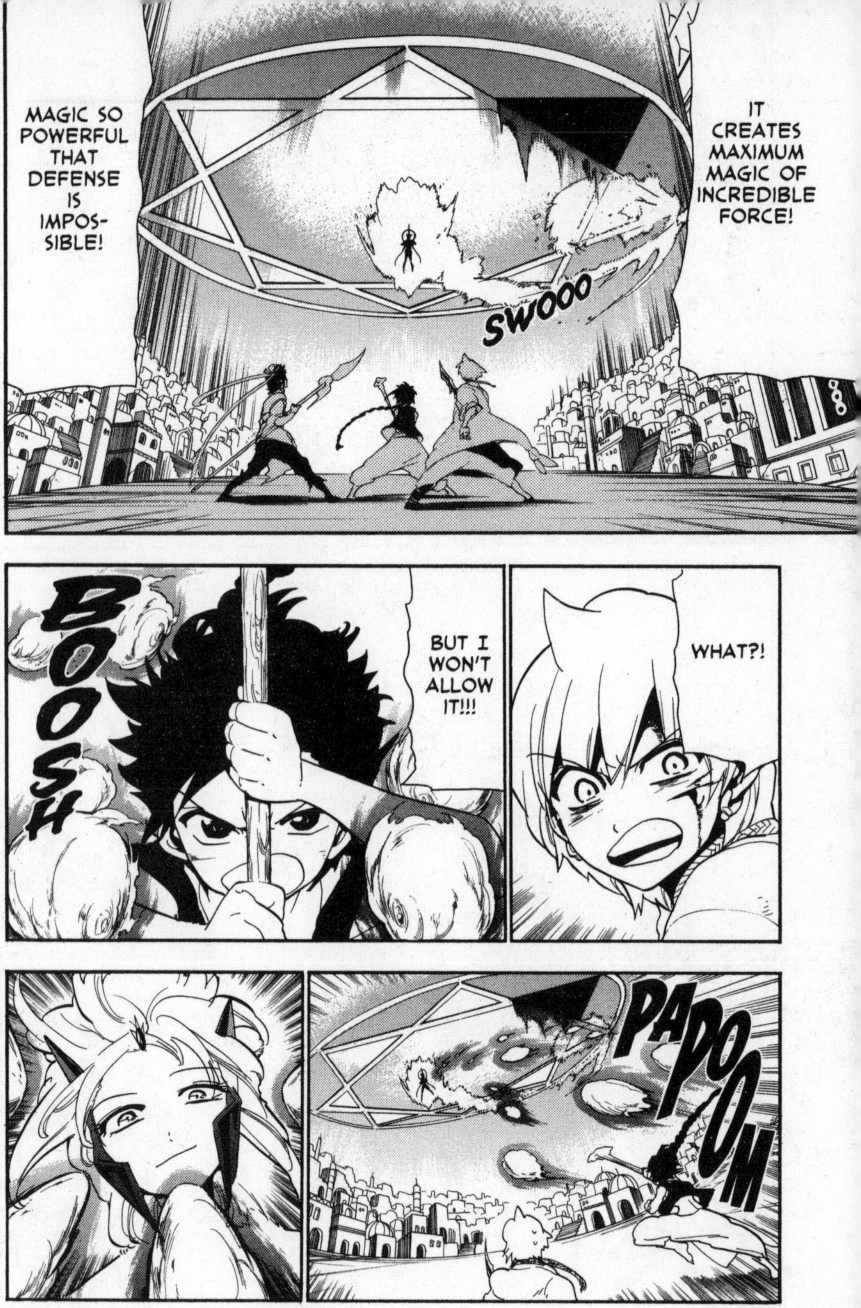
IT CREATES MAXIMUM MAGIC OF INCREDIBLE FORCE!
MAGIC SO POWERFUL THAT DEFENSE IS IMPOS-SIBLE!
SWOOO
WHAT?!
BUT I WON'T ALLOW IT!!!
BOOSH
PAPOOM

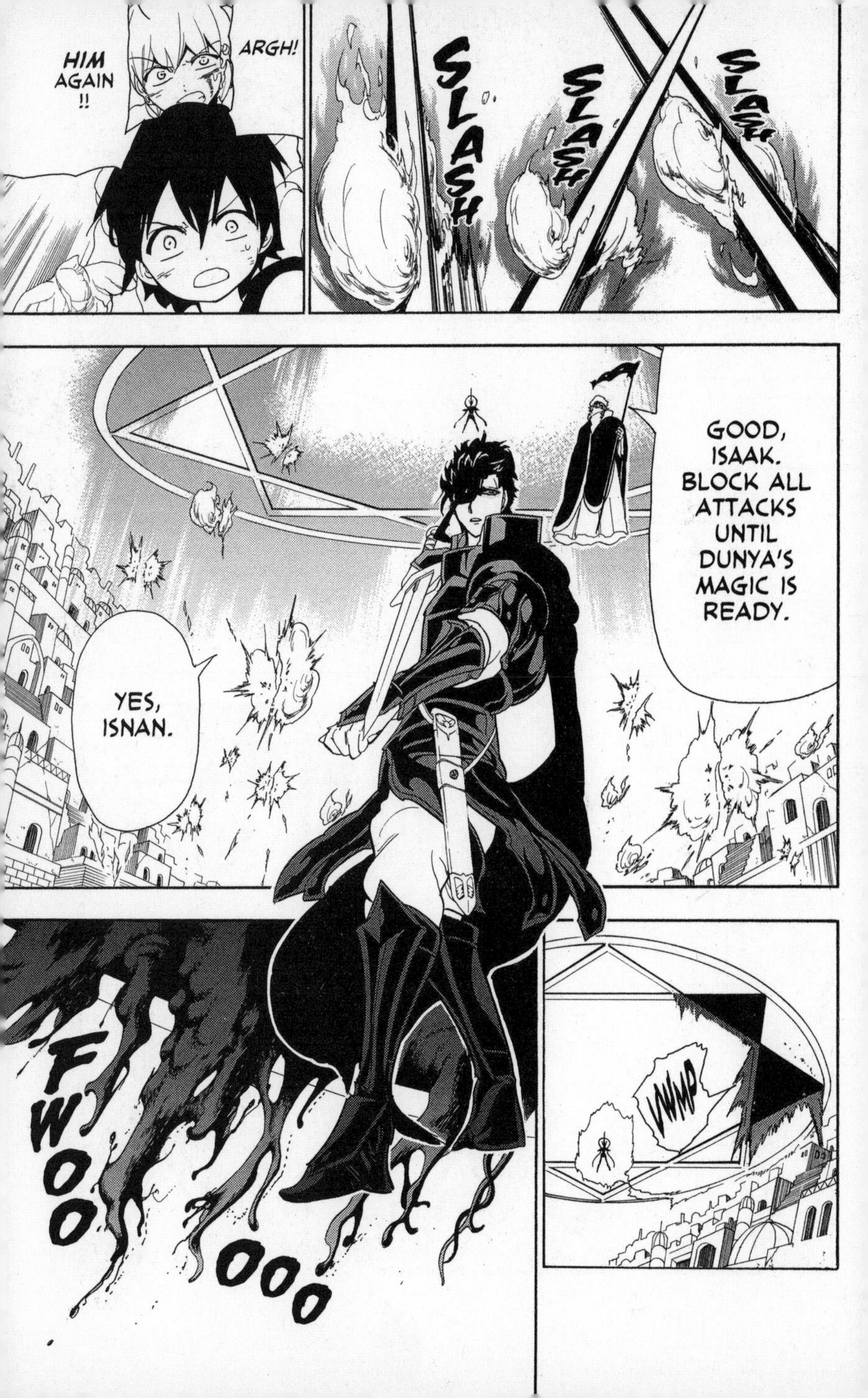
SLASH
SLASH
SLASH
ARGH!
HIM AGAIN!!
GOOD, ISAAK. BLOCK ALL ATTACKS UNTIL DUNYA'S MAGIC IS READY.
YES, ISNAN.
VWMP
FWOOOOOO

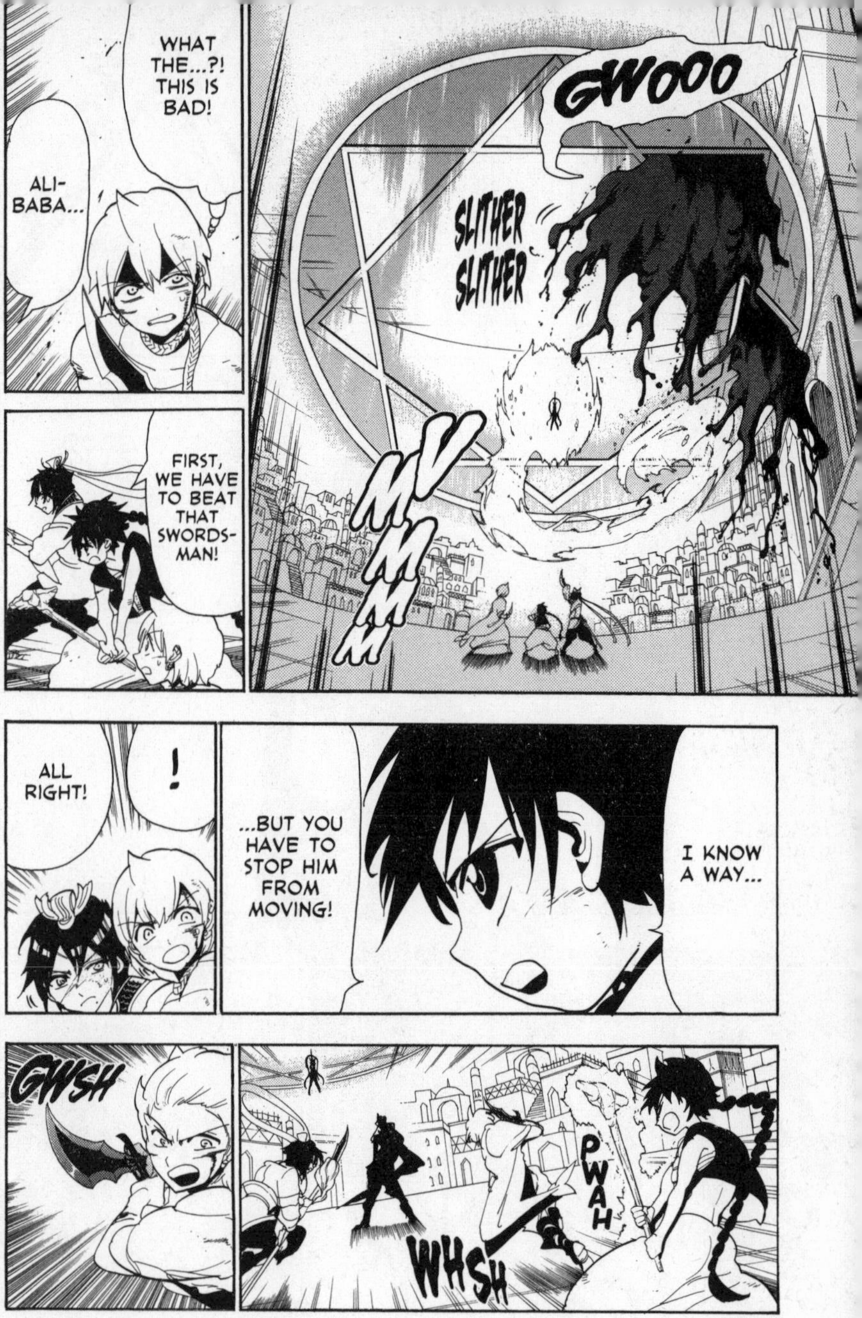
GWOOO
SLITHER SLITHER
MVMMMM
WHAT THE...?! THIS IS BAD!
ALI-BABA...
FIRST, WE HAVE TO BEAT THAT SWORDSMAN!
I KNOW A WAY...
...BUT YOU HAVE TO STOP HIM FROM MOVING!
!
ALL RIGHT!
PWAH
WHSH
GWSH

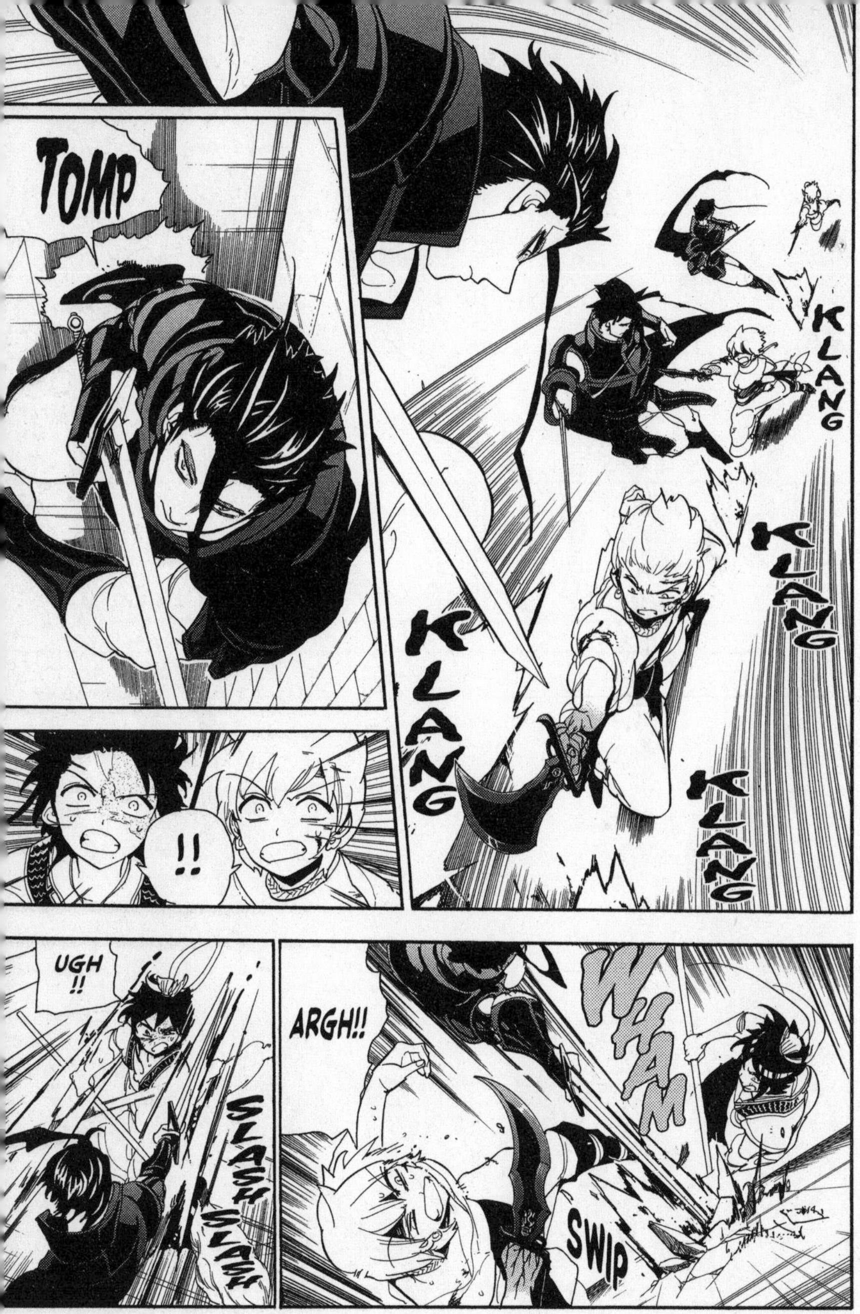
KLANG
KLANG
KLANG
KLANG
TOMP
!!
WHAM
ARGH!!
SWIP
UGH !!
SLASH
SLASH

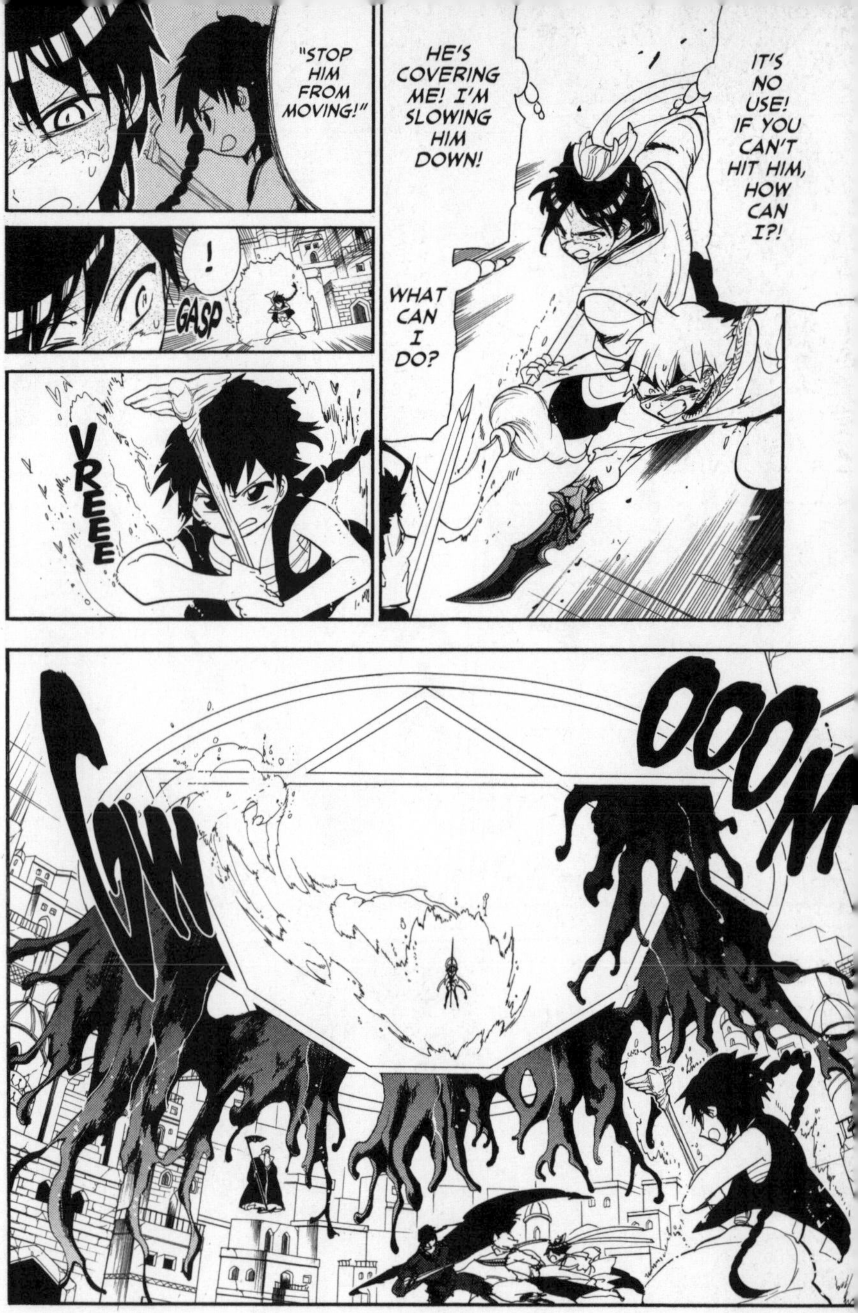
IT'S NO USE! IF YOU CAN'T HIT HIM, HOW CAN I?!
HE'S COVERING ME! I'M SLOWING HIM DOWN!
WHAT CAN I DO?
"STOP HIM FROM MOVING!"
!
GASP
VREEE
OOOM

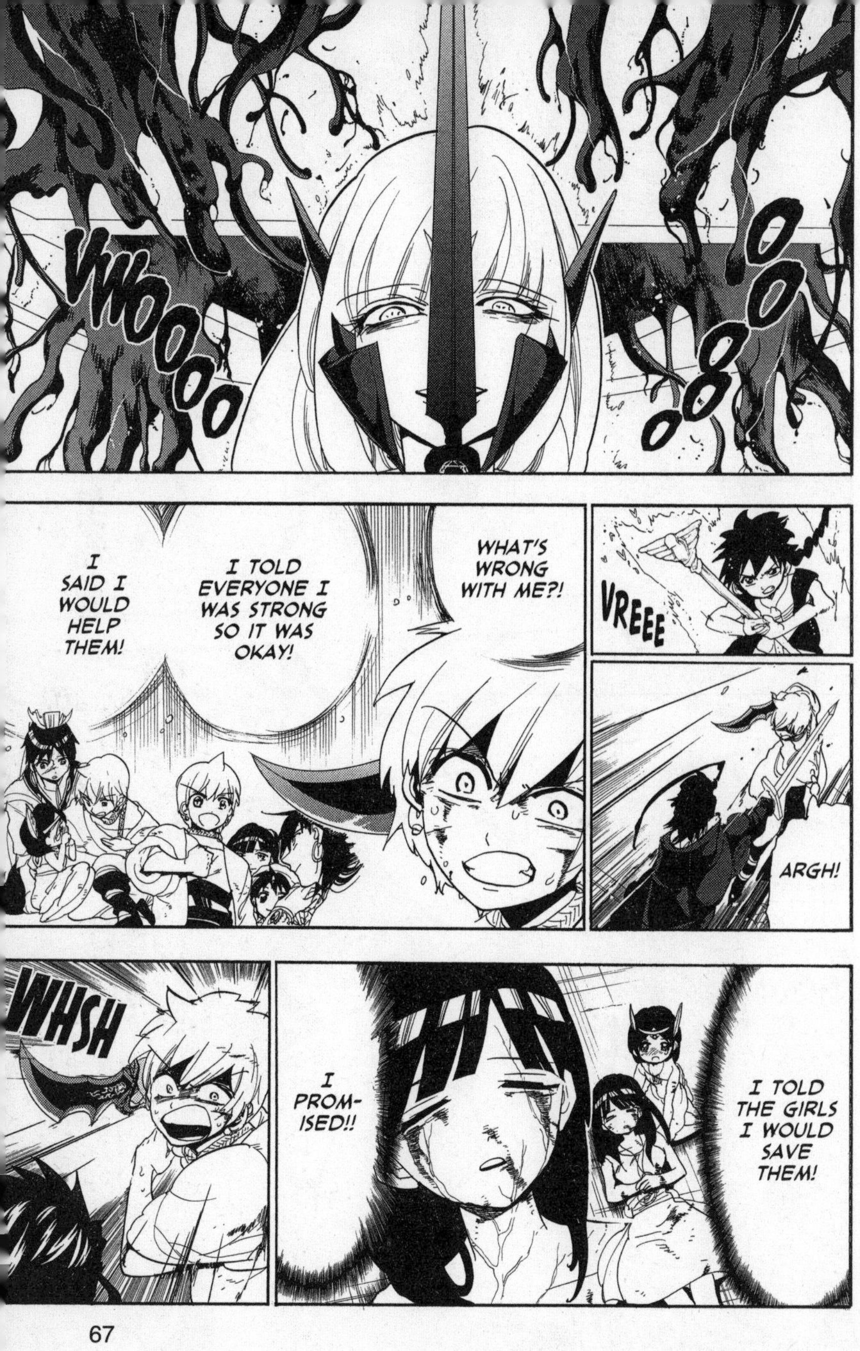
VWOOOOO
OOOOOOO
VREEE
ARGH!
WHAT'S WRONG WITH ME?!
I TOLD EVERYONE I WAS STRONG SO IT WAS OKAY!
I SAID I WOULD HELP THEM!
I TOLD THE GIRLS I WOULD SAVE THEM!
I PROMISED!!
WHSH

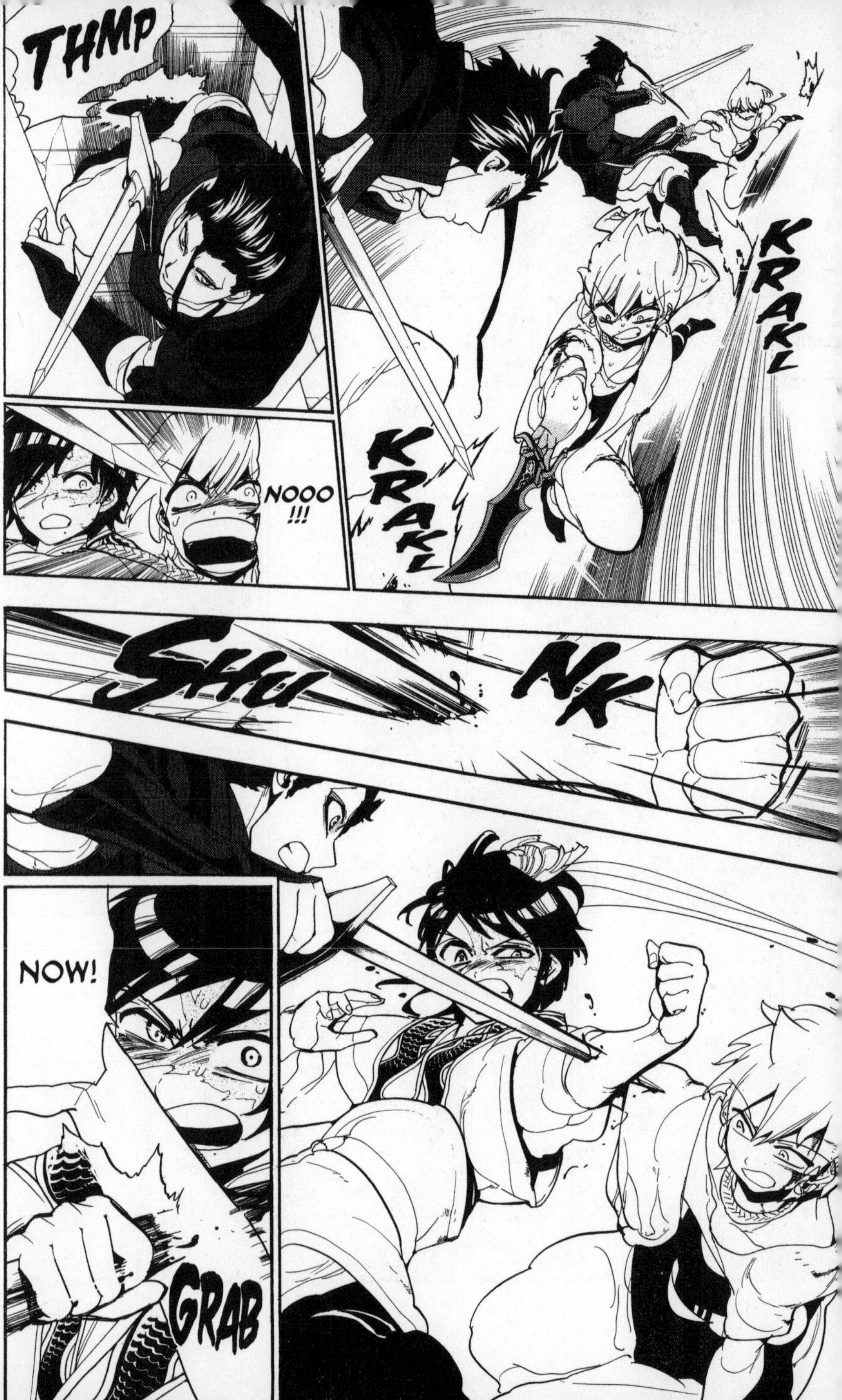
KRAKL
KRAKL
THMP
NOOO !!!
SHU NK
NOW!
GRAB

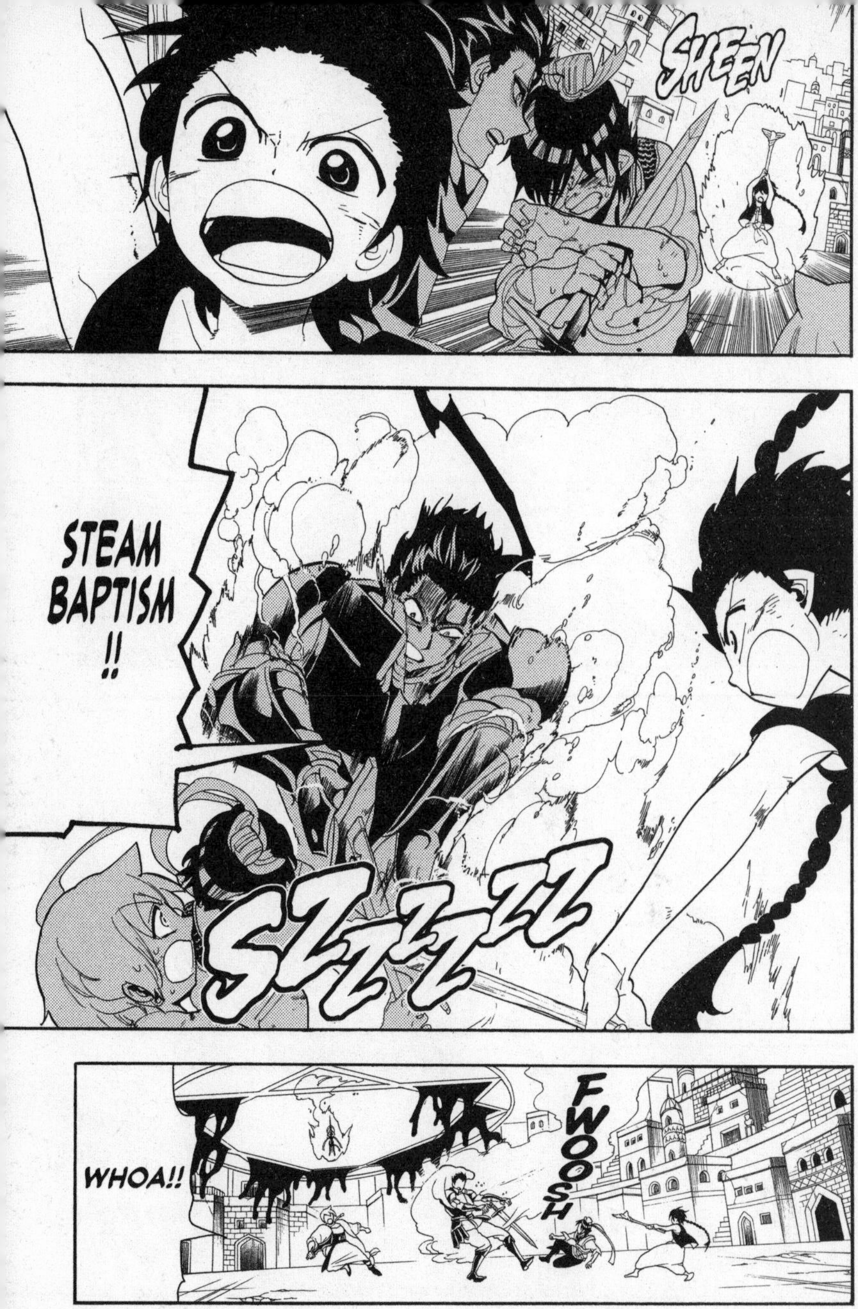
SHEEN
STEAM BAPTISM !!
SIZZZZZZ
FWOOSH
WHOA!!

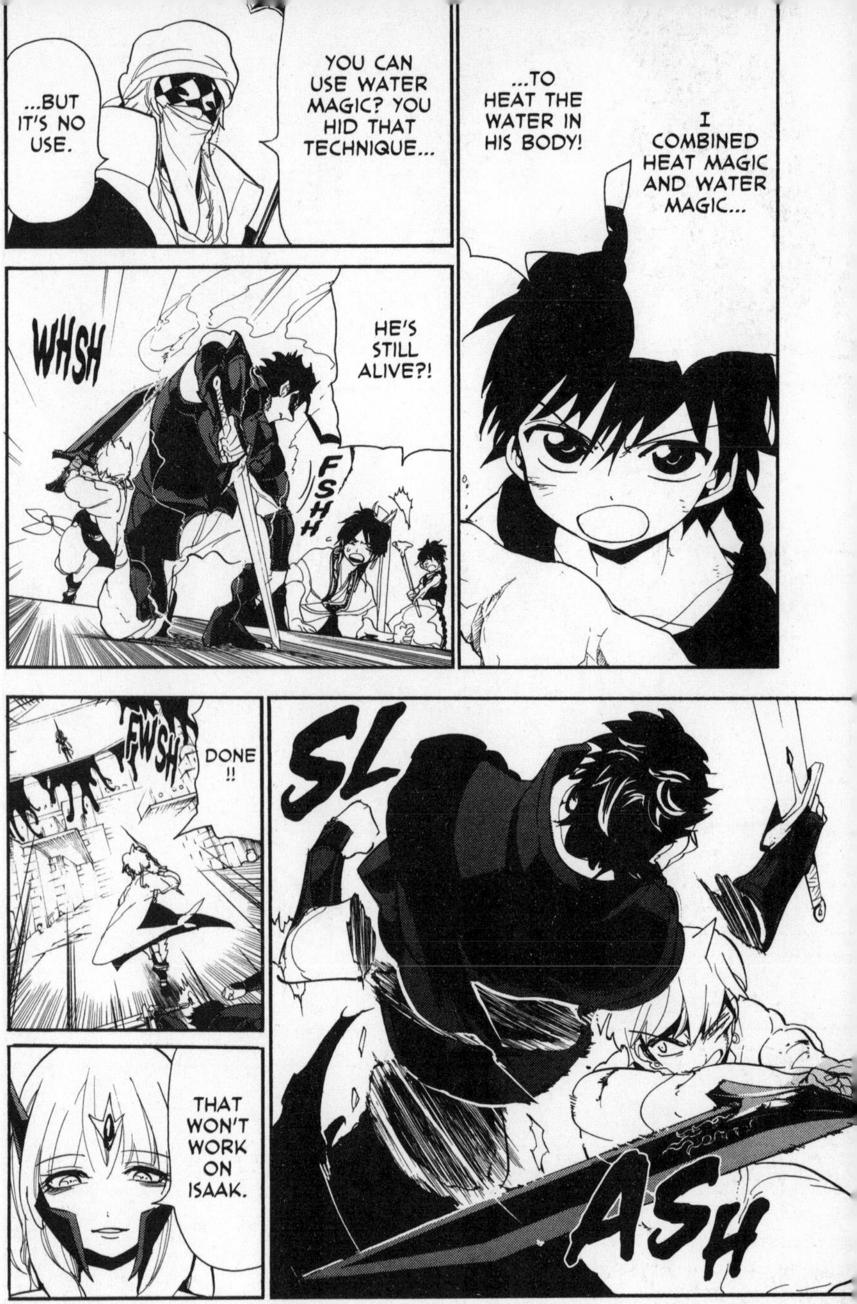
I COMBINED HEAT MAGIC AND WATER MAGIC...
...TO HEAT THE WATER IN HIS BODY!
YOU CAN USE WATER MAGIC? YOU HID THAT TECHNIQUE...
...BUT IT'S NO USE.
HE'S STILL ALIVE?!
WHSH
FSHH
SL
ASH
FWSH
DONE !!
THAT WON'T WORK ON ISAAK.

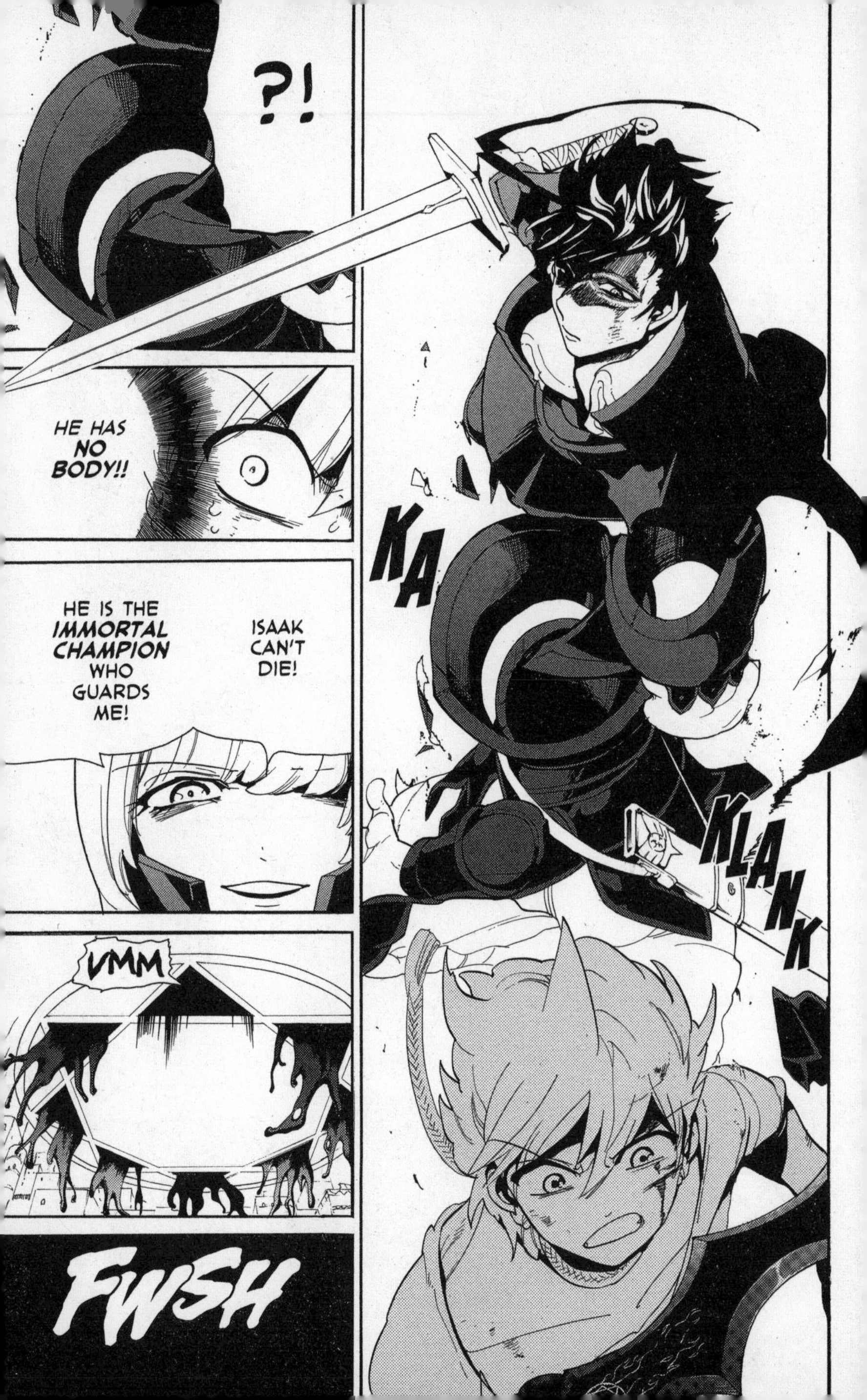
KA
KLANK
?!
HE HAS NO BODY!!
ISAAK CAN'T DIE!
HE IS THE IMMORTAL CHAMPION WHO GUARDS ME!
VMM
FWSH

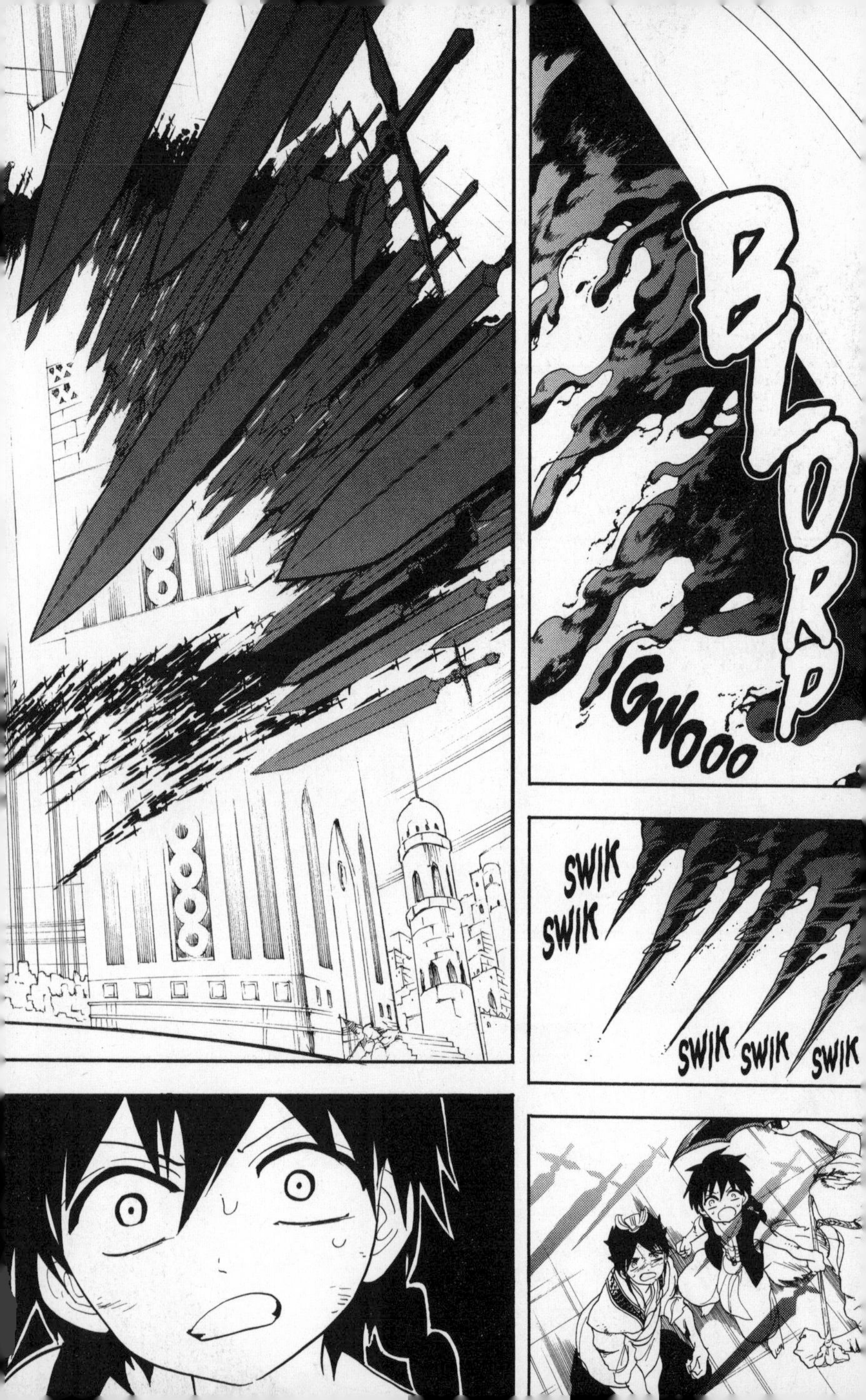
BLORP
GWOOO
SWIK SWIK
SWIK SWIK SWIK

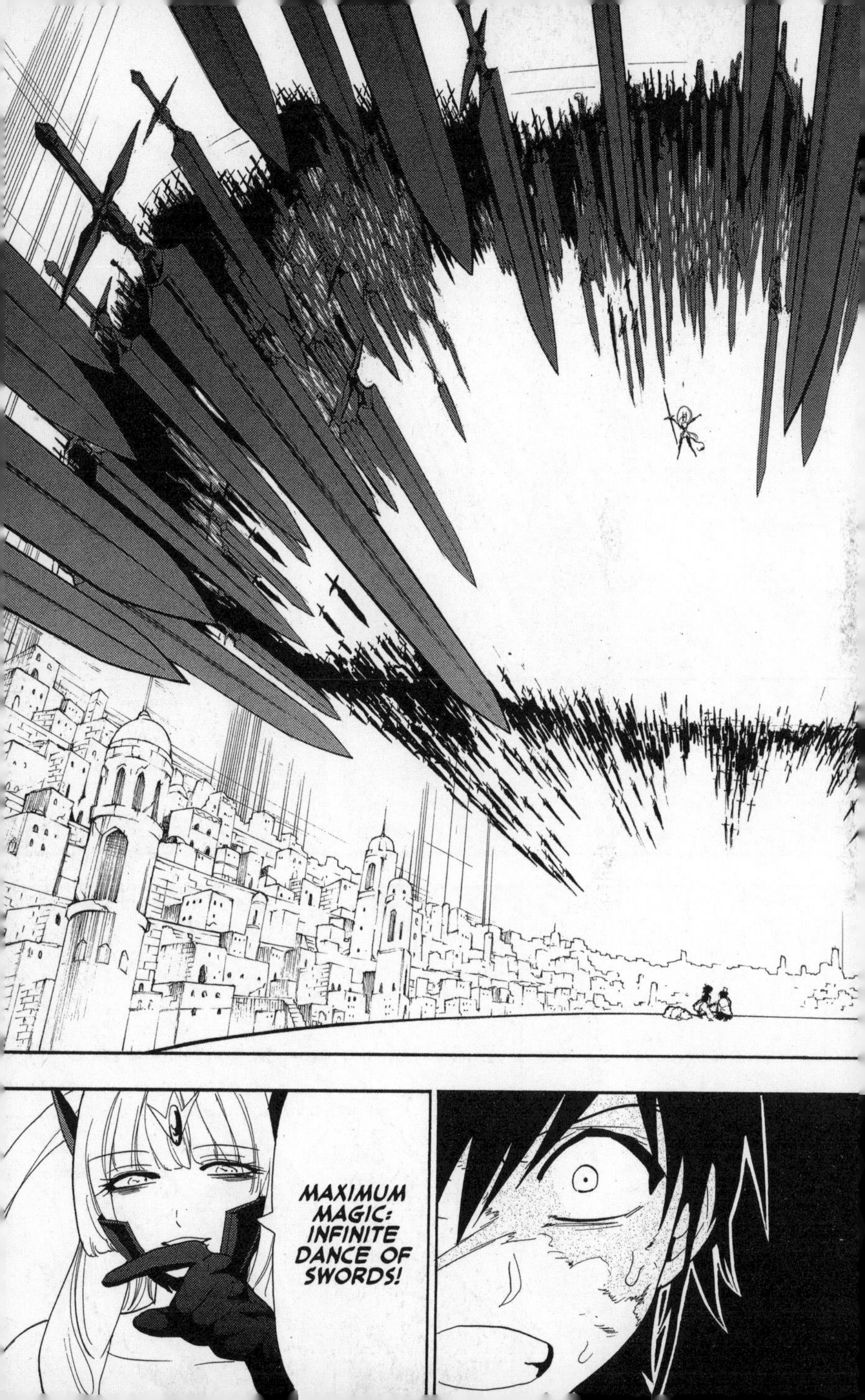
MAXIMUM MAGIC: INFINITE DANCE OF SWORDS!

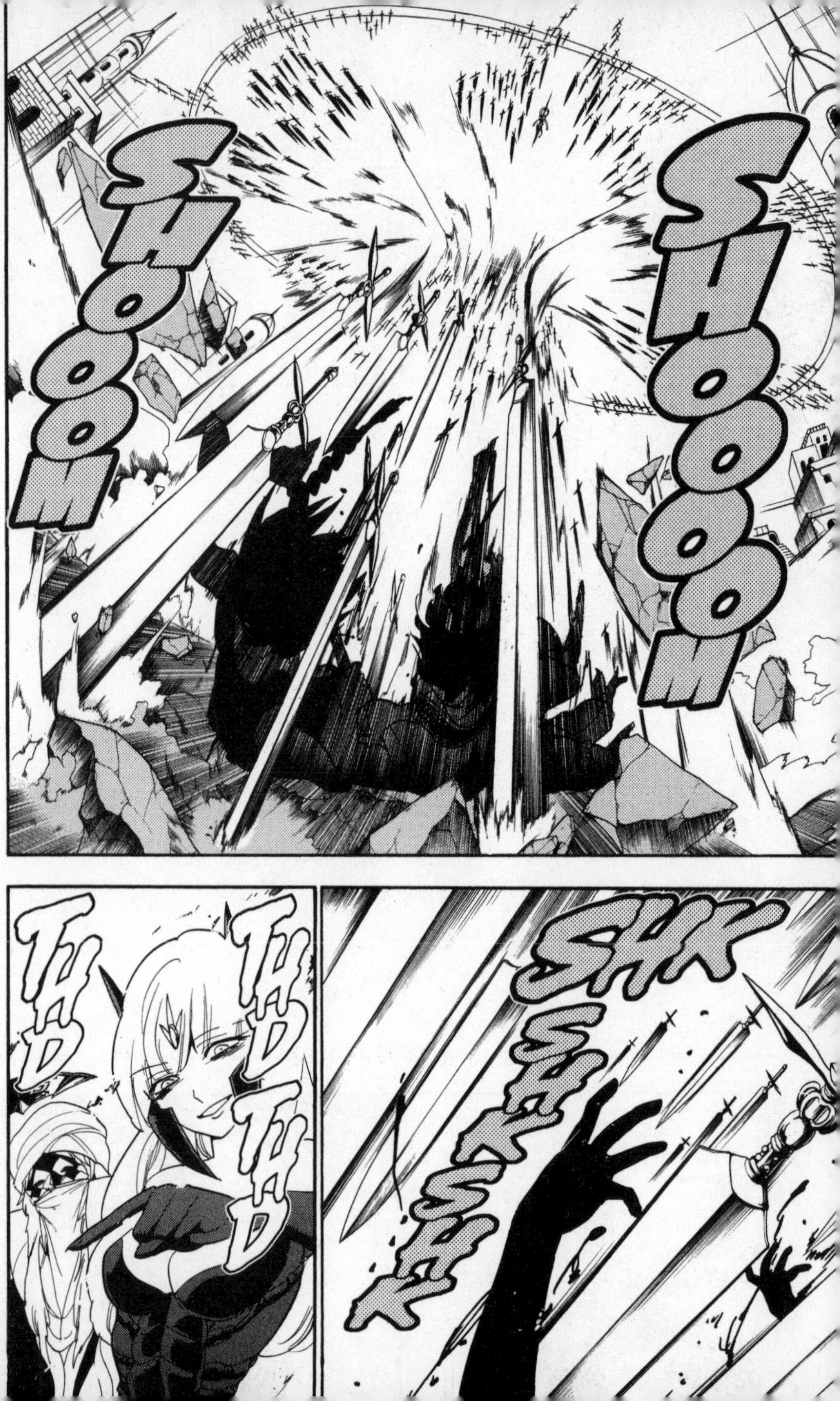
SHOOOOM
SHOOOM
SHK SHAK SHAK
THUD THUD
THUD

Night 103: Reverse Flow of Fate

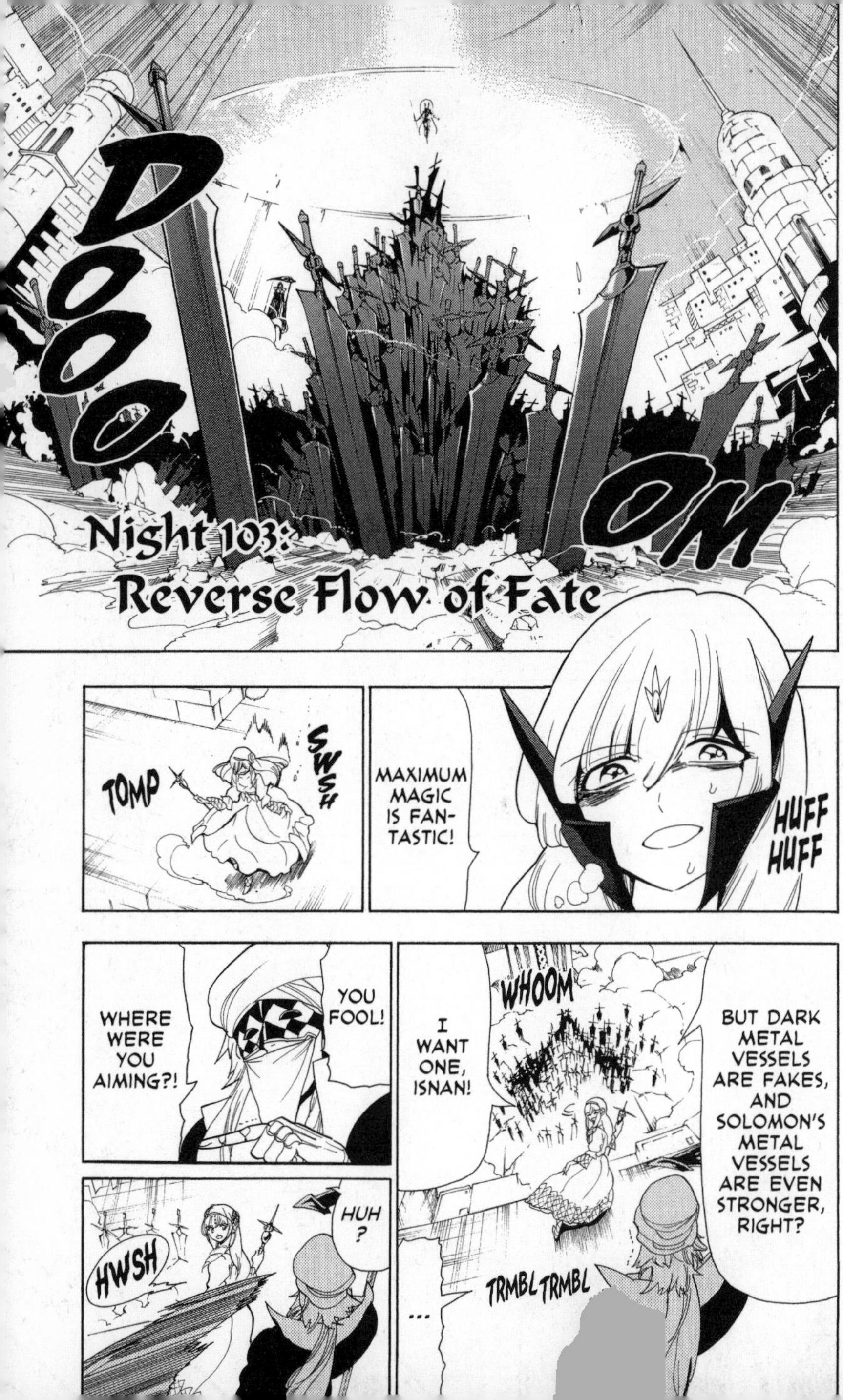
DOOOOOM
Night 103: Reverse Flow of Fate
MAXIMUM MAGIC IS FAN-TASTIC!
HUFF HUFF
SWSH
TOMP
BUT DARK METAL VESSELS ARE FAKES, AND SOLOMON'S METAL VESSELS ARE EVEN STRONGER, RIGHT?
WHOOM
I WANT ONE, ISNAN!
TRMBL TRMBL
...
YOU FOOL!
WHERE WERE YOU AIMING?!
HUH?
HWSH

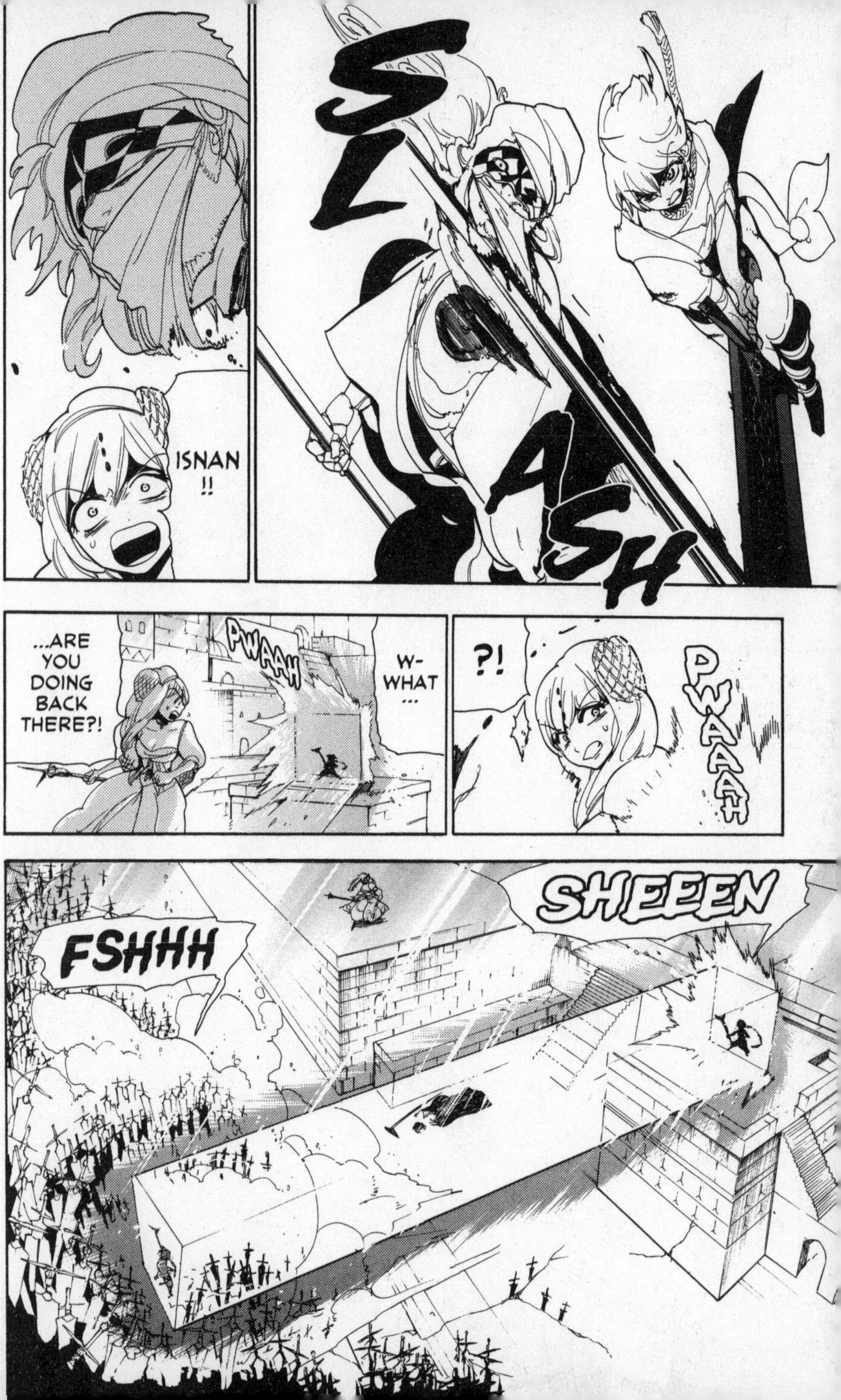
SLASH
ISNAN !!
?!
PWAAAH
W-WHAT ...
...ARE YOU DOING BACK THERE?!
PWAAAH
SHEEEN
FSHHH

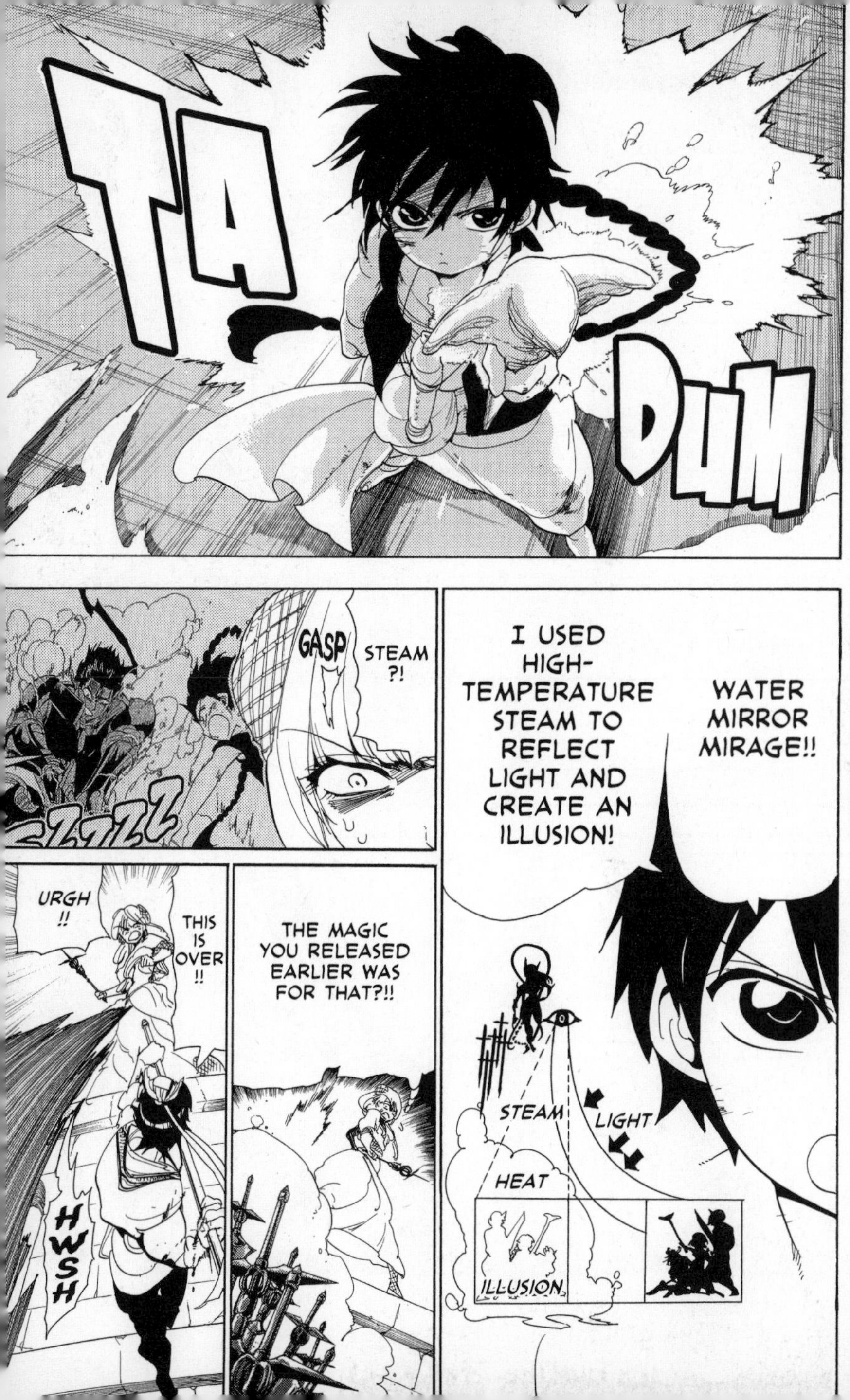
TA
DUM
WATER MIRROR MIRAGE!!
I USED HIGH-TEMPERATURE STEAM TO REFLECT LIGHT AND CREATE AN ILLUSION!
STEAM
LIGHT
HEAT
ILLUSION
STEAM?!
GASP
THE MAGIC YOU RELEASED EARLIER WAS FOR THAT?!!
THIS IS OVER!!
URGH!!
HWSH

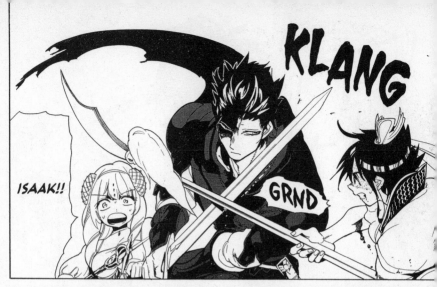

KLANG
GRND
ISAAK!!
YEAH! GET THEM, ISAAK!
YES... MY... PRIN... CESS...
SWIP
WHSH
CRACKLE
?!
HE HAS SLOWED DOWN!!
OH NO! ISAAK'S MAGOI IS RUNNING OUT!

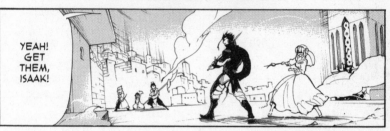

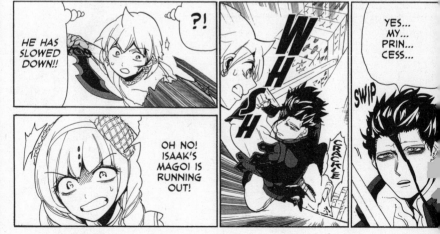

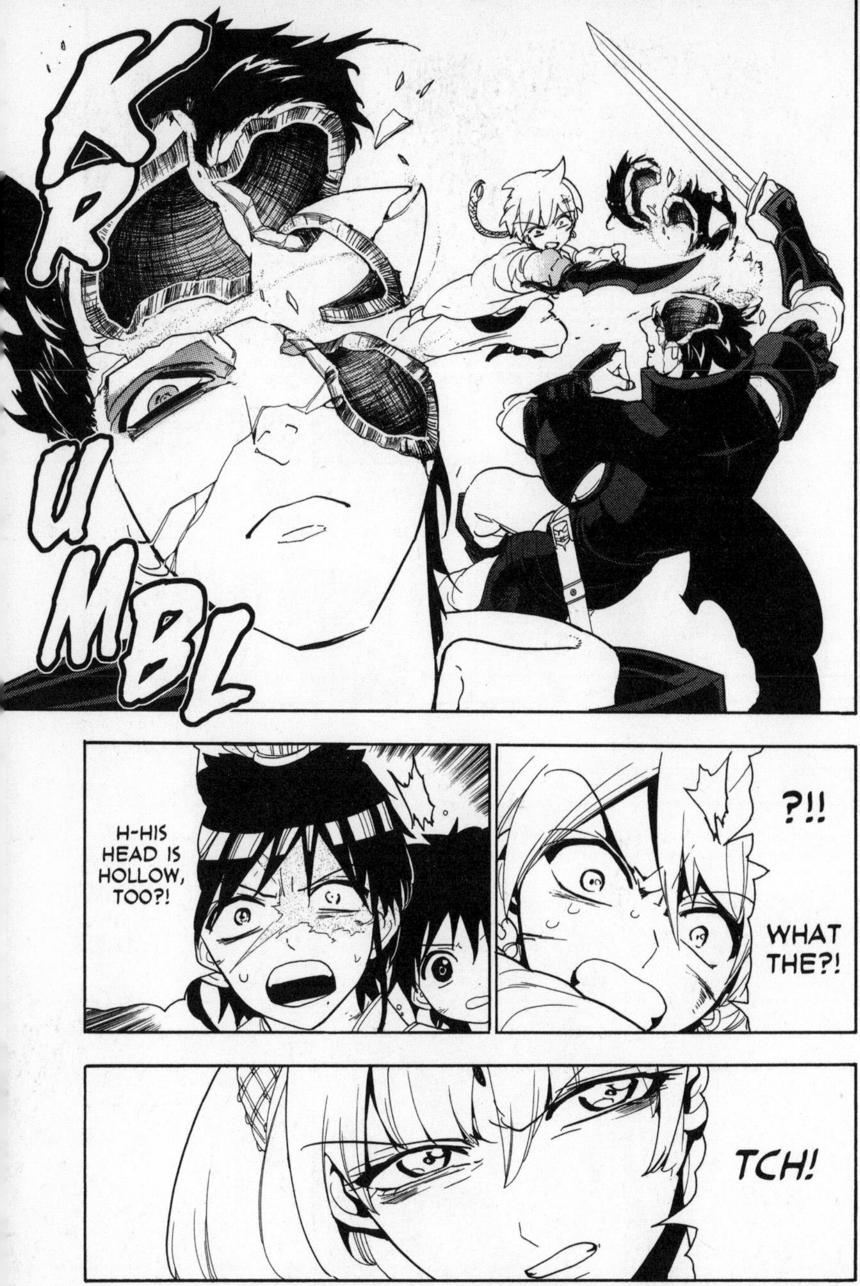
KRUMBL
?!!
WHAT THE?!
H-HIS HEAD IS HOLLOW, TOO?!
TCH!

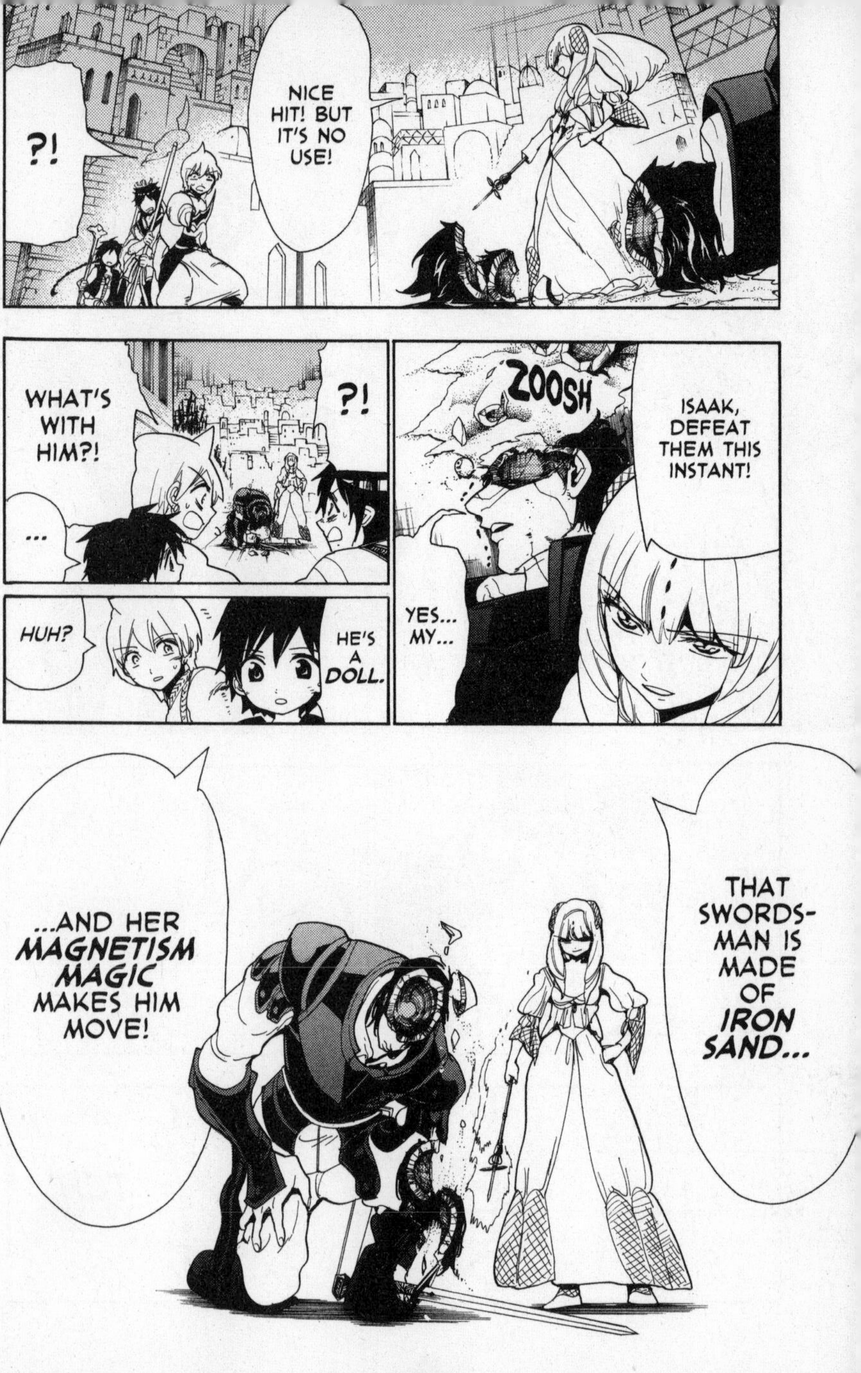
NICE HIT! BUT IT'S NO USE!
?!
ISAAK, DEFEAT THEM THIS INSTANT!
ZOOSH
YES... MY...
?!
WHAT'S WITH HIM?!
...
HE'S A DOLL.
HUH?
THAT SWORDS-MAN IS MADE OF IRON SAND...
...AND HER MAGNETISM MAGIC MAKES HIM MOVE!

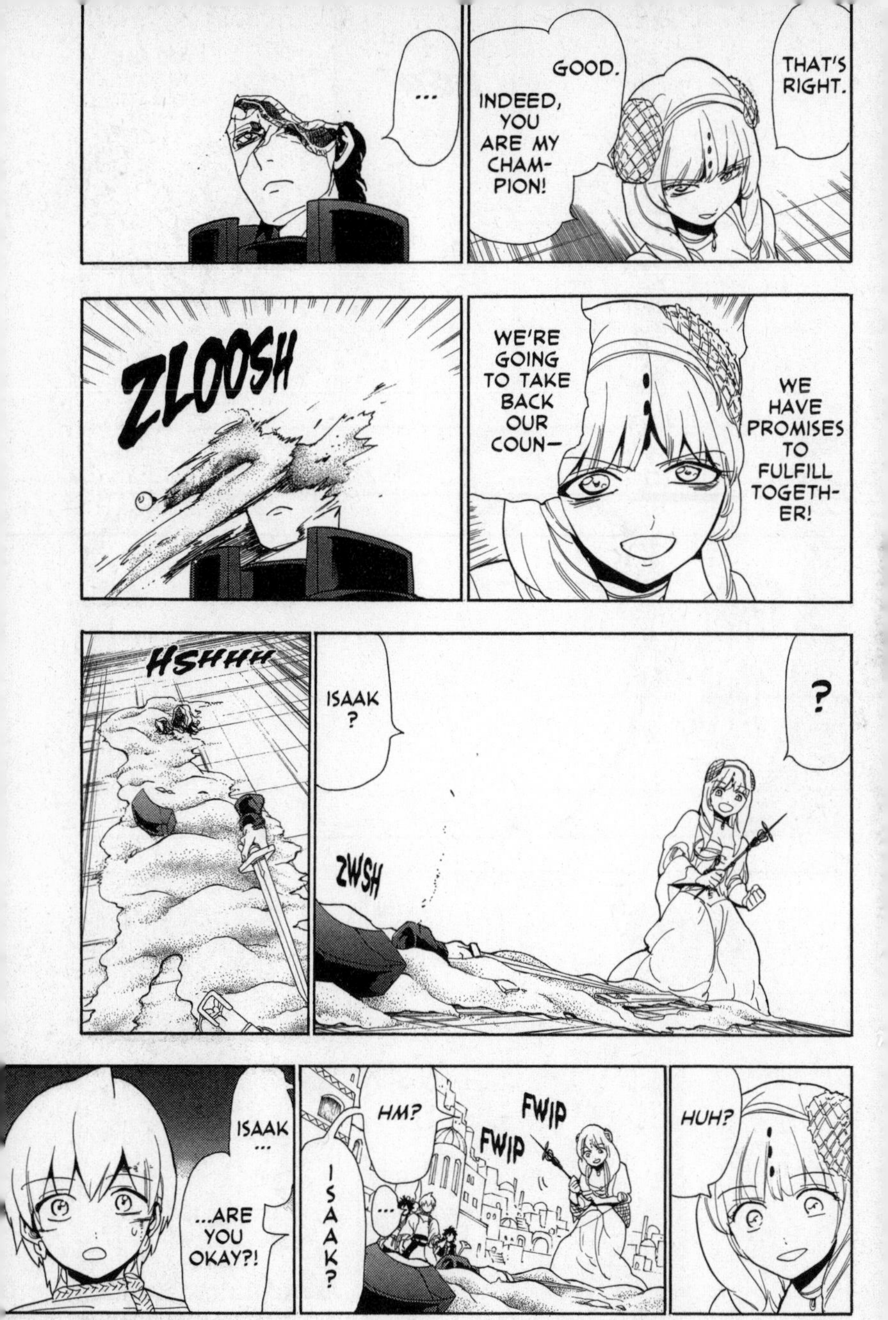
THAT'S RIGHT.
GOOD.
INDEED, YOU ARE MY CHAMPION!
...
WE HAVE PROMISES TO FULFILL TOGETHER!
WE'RE GOING TO TAKE BACK OUR COUN—
ZLOOSH
?
ISAAK ?
ZWSH
HSHHH
HUH?
FWIP
FWIP
HM?
ISAAK?
...
ISAAK ...
...ARE YOU OKAY?!

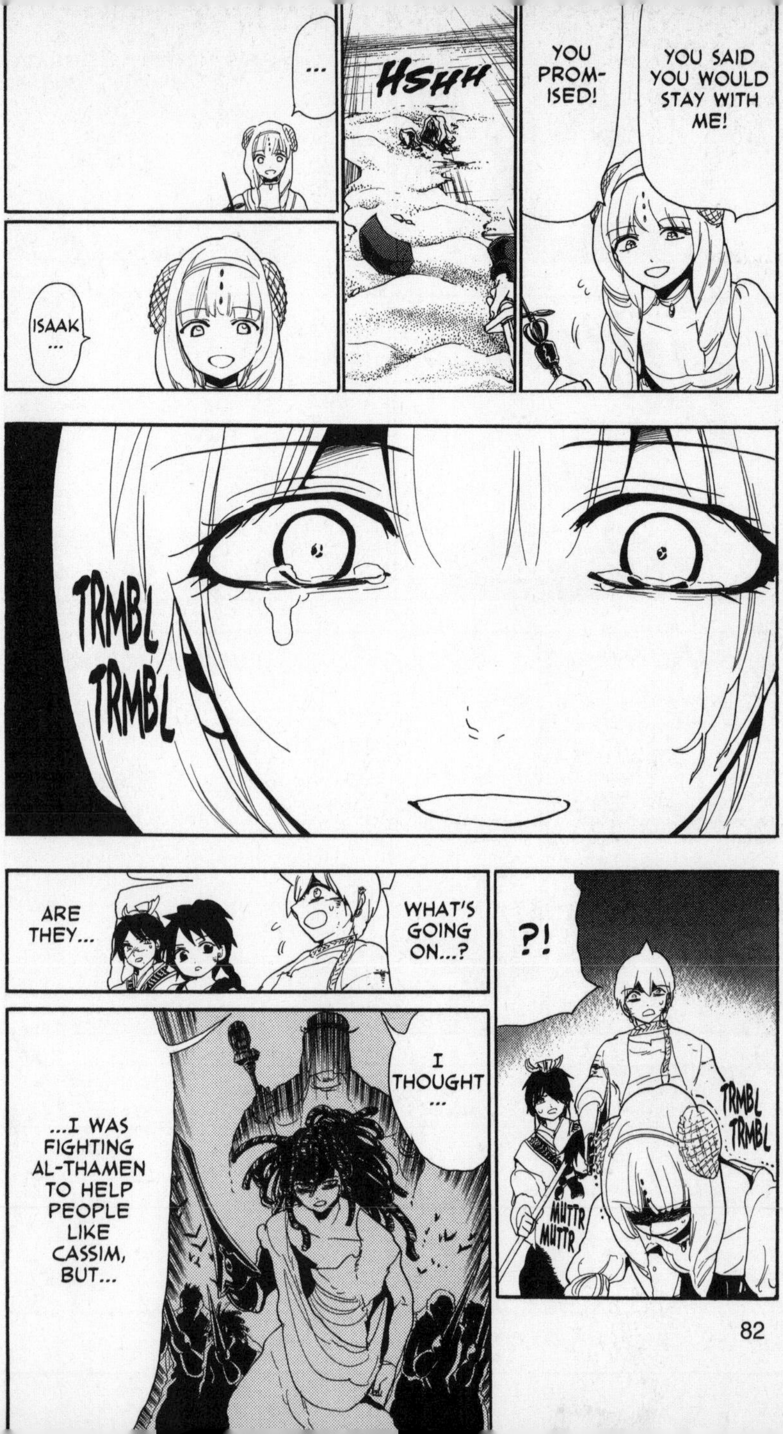
YOU SAID YOU WOULD STAY WITH ME!
YOU PROMISED!
HSHH
...
ISAAK ...
TRMBL TRMBL
?!
TRMBL TRMBL
MUTTR MUTTR
WHAT'S GOING ON...?
ARE THEY...
I THOUGHT ...
...I WAS FIGHTING AL-THAMEN TO HELP PEOPLE LIKE CASSIM, BUT...

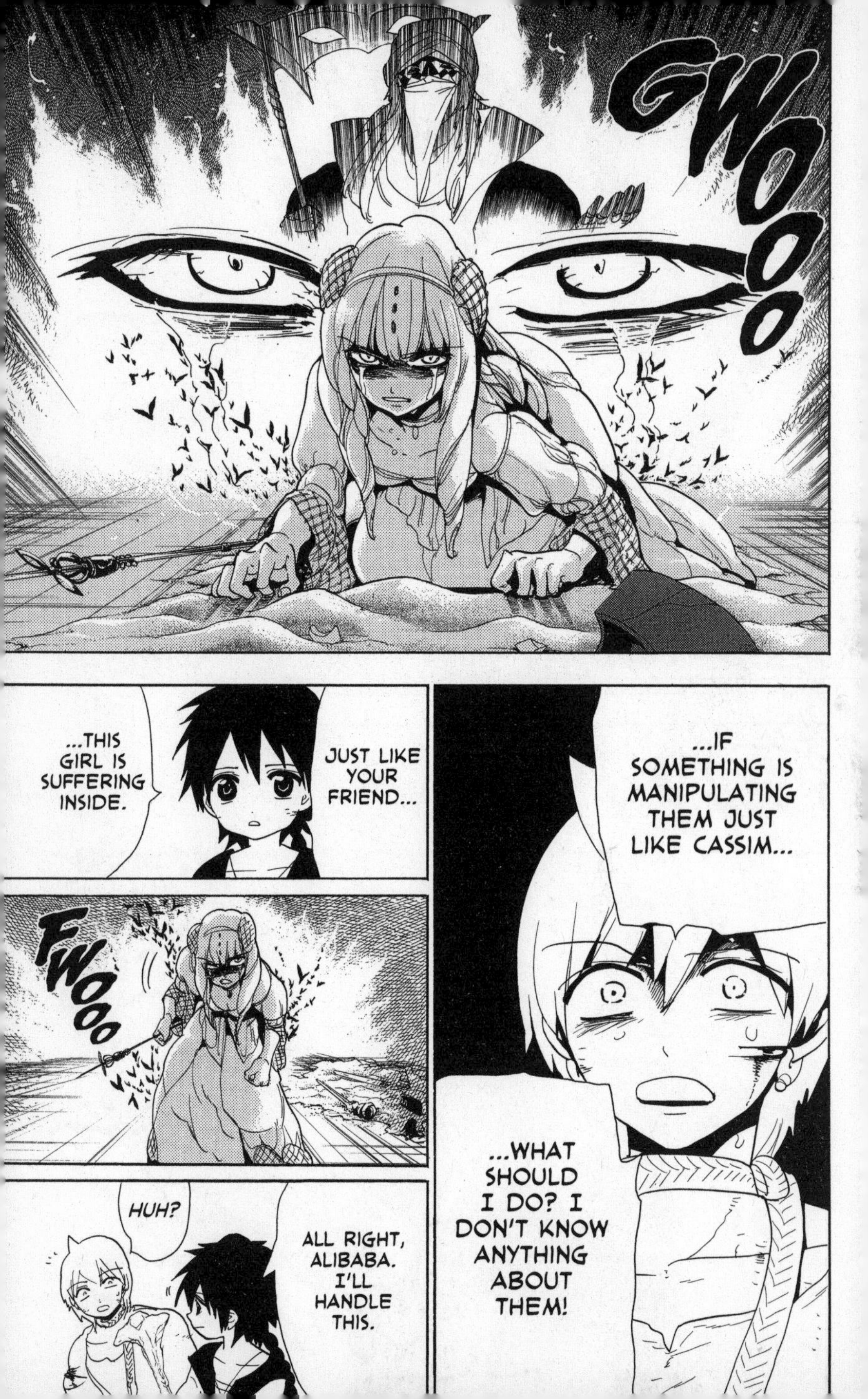
GWOOOO
...IF SOMETHING IS MANIPULATING THEM JUST LIKE CASSIM...
...WHAT SHOULD I DO? I DON'T KNOW ANYTHING ABOUT THEM!
JUST LIKE YOUR FRIEND...
...THIS GIRL IS SUFFERING INSIDE.
FWOOO
ALL RIGHT, ALIBABA. I'LL HANDLE THIS.
HUH?

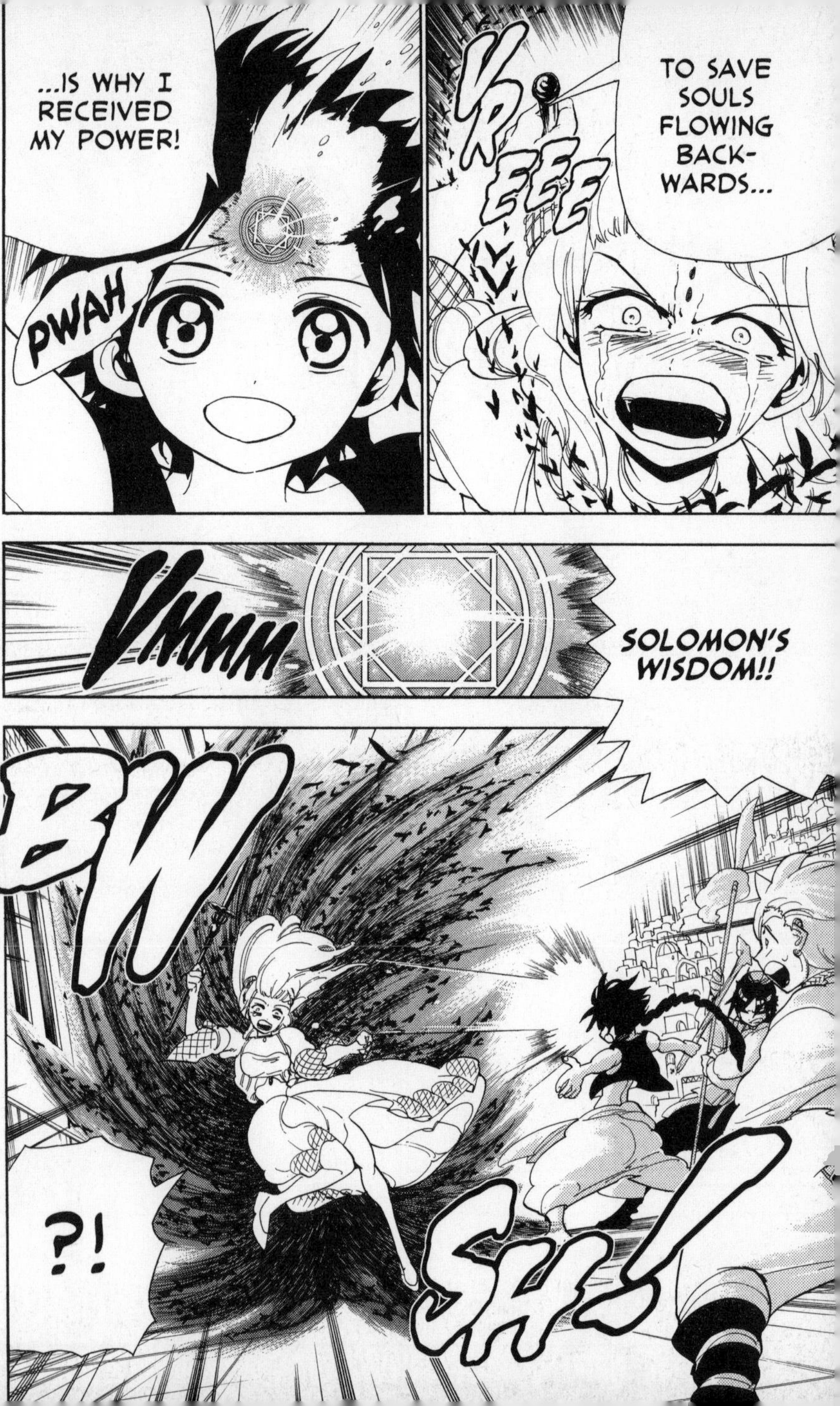
TO SAVE SOULS FLOWING BACK-WARDS...
VREEE
...IS WHY I RECEIVED MY POWER!
PWAH
VMMMM
SOLOMON'S WISDOM!!
BW
SH!
?!

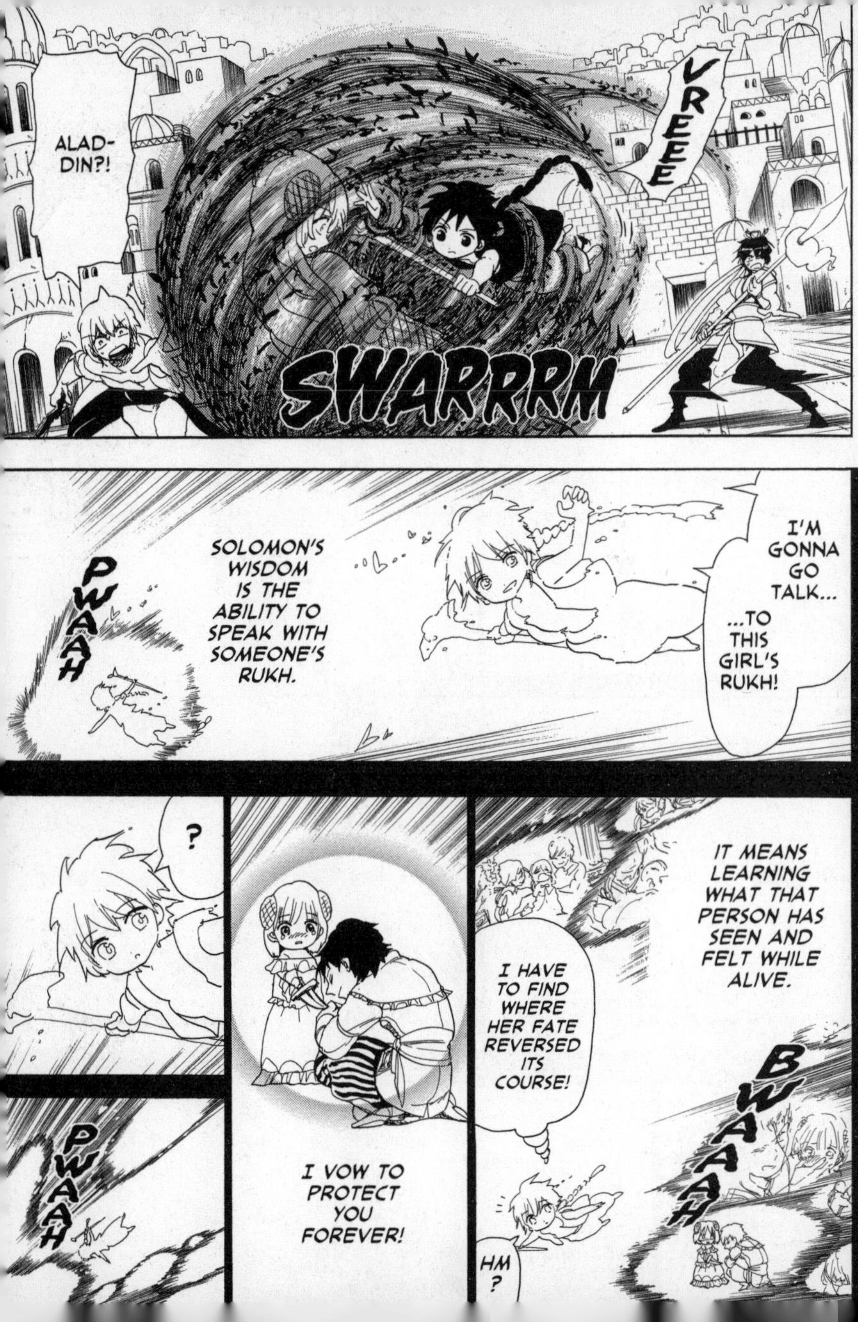
VREEE
ALAD-DIN?!
SWARRRM
I'M GONNA GO TALK...
...TO THIS GIRL'S RUKH!
SOLOMON'S WISDOM IS THE ABILITY TO SPEAK WITH SOMEONE'S RUKH.
PWAAH
IT MEANS LEARNING WHAT THAT PERSON HAS SEEN AND FELT WHILE ALIVE.
I HAVE TO FIND WHERE HER FATE REVERSED ITS COURSE!
BWAAAH
HM?
I VOW TO PROTECT YOU FOREVER!
?
PWAAH

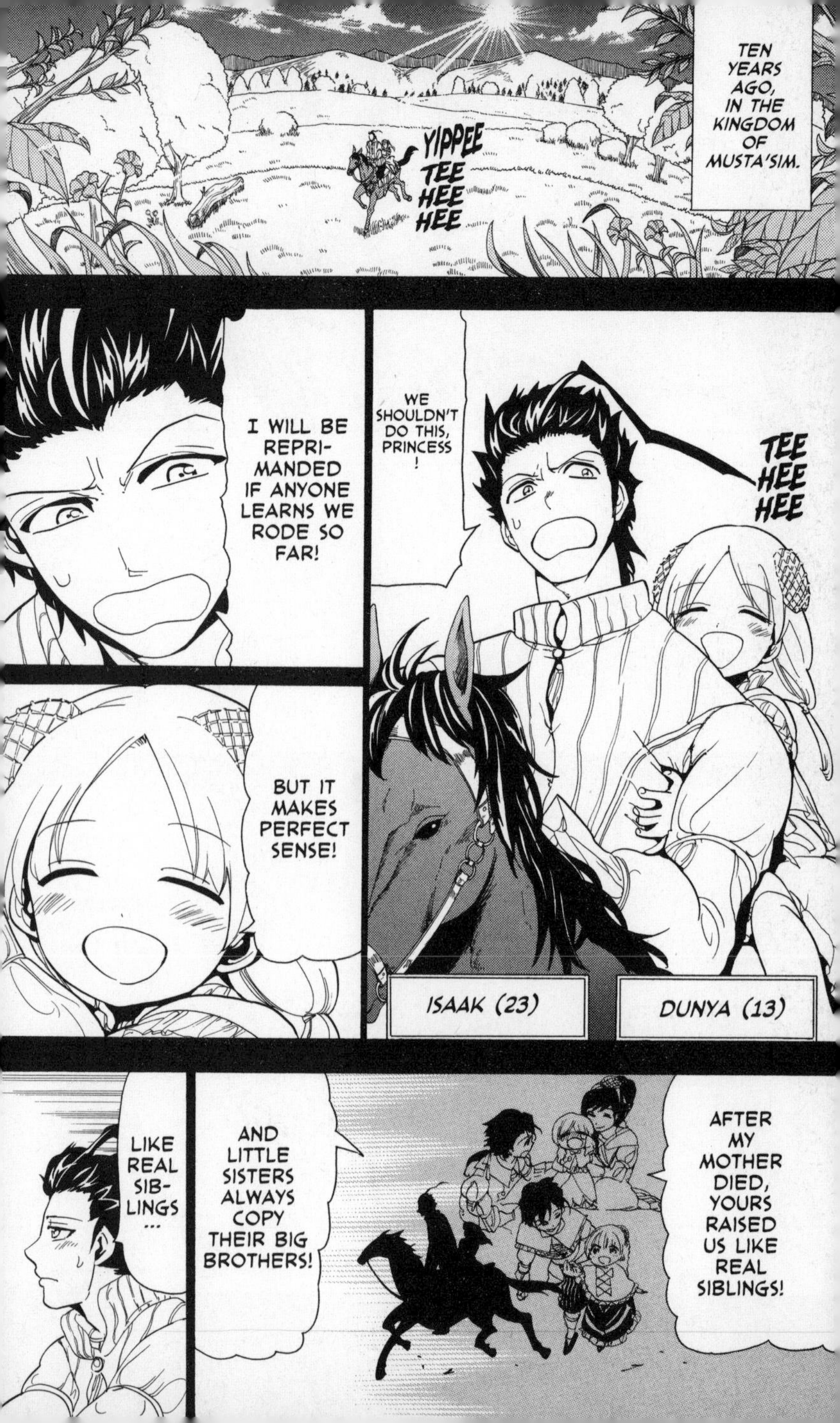
TEN YEARS AGO, IN THE KINGDOM OF MUSTA'SIM.
YIPPEE TEE HEE HEE
WE SHOULDN'T DO THIS, PRINCESS!
TEE HEE HEE
DUNYA (13)
ISAAK (23)
I WILL BE REPRIMANDED IF ANYONE LEARNS WE RODE SO FAR!
BUT IT MAKES PERFECT SENSE!
AFTER MY MOTHER DIED, YOURS RAISED US LIKE REAL SIBLINGS!
AND LITTLE SISTERS ALWAYS COPY THEIR BIG BROTHERS!
LIKE REAL SIBLINGS...

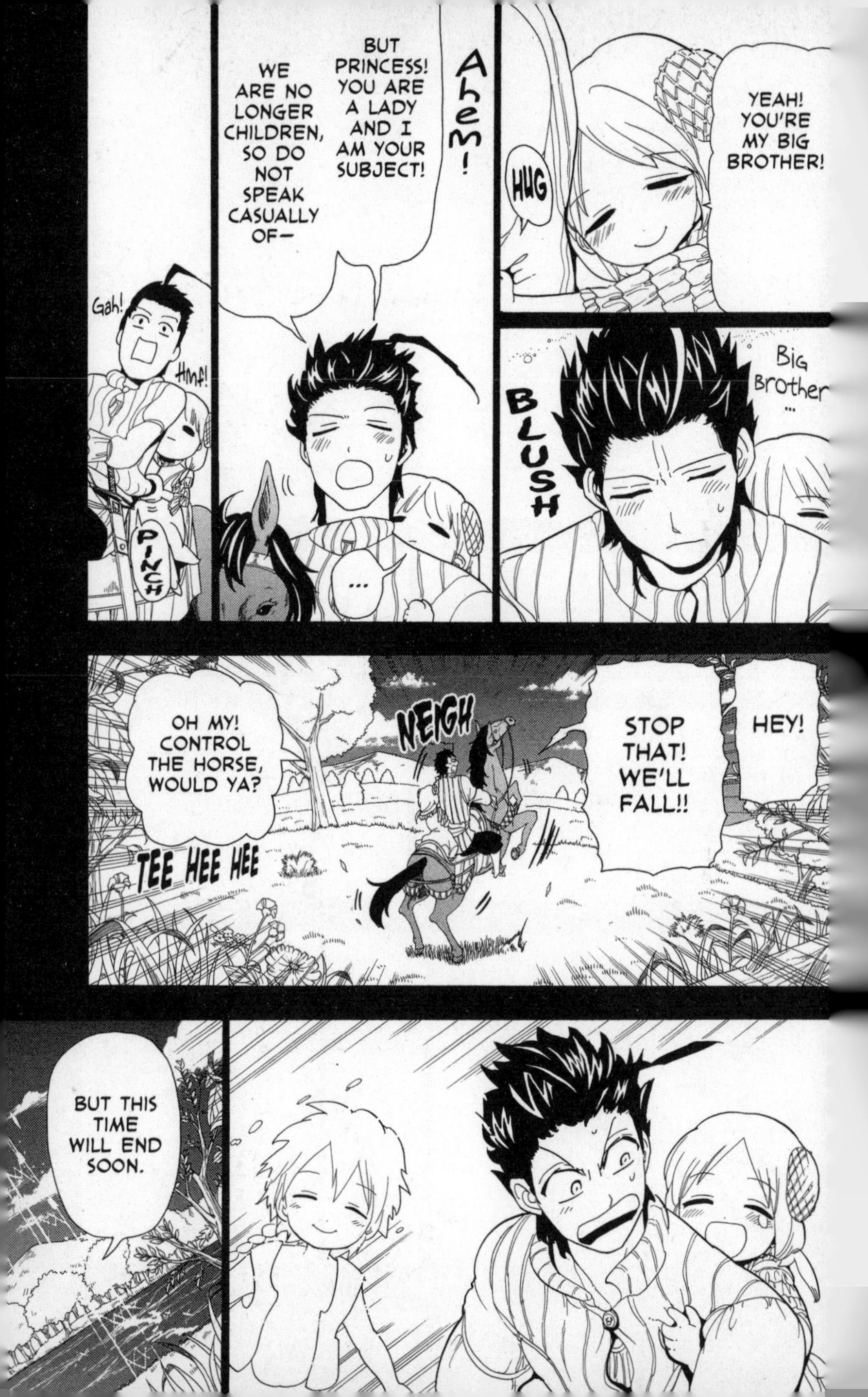
YEAH! YOU'RE MY BIG BROTHER!
HUG
Big Brother...
BLUSH
Ahem!
BUT PRINCESS! YOU ARE A LADY AND I AM YOUR SUBJECT!
WE ARE NO LONGER CHILDREN, SO DO NOT SPEAK CASUALLY OF—
...
Gah!
Hmf!
PINCH
HEY!
STOP THAT! WE'LL FALL!!
NEIGH
OH MY! CONTROL THE HORSE, WOULD YA?
TEE HEE HEE
BUT THIS TIME WILL END SOON.

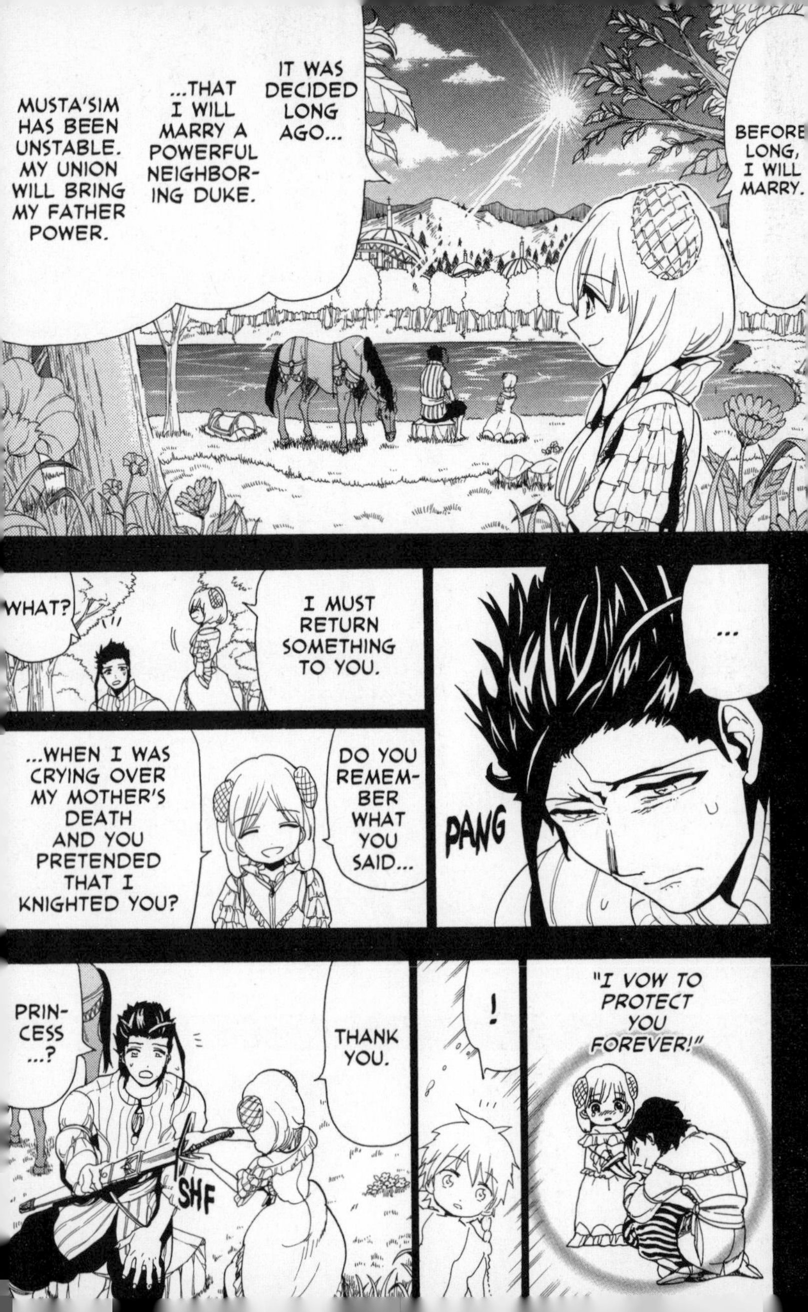
BEFORE LONG, I WILL MARRY.
IT WAS DECIDED LONG AGO...
...THAT I WILL MARRY A POWERFUL NEIGHBOR-ING DUKE.
MUSTA'SIM HAS BEEN UNSTABLE. MY UNION WILL BRING MY FATHER POWER.
...
PANG
I MUST RETURN SOMETHING TO YOU.
WHAT?
DO YOU REMEM-BER WHAT YOU SAID...
...WHEN I WAS CRYING OVER MY MOTHER'S DEATH AND YOU PRETENDED THAT I KNIGHTED YOU?
"I VOW TO PROTECT YOU FOREVER!"
!
THANK YOU.
PRIN-CESS ...?
SHF

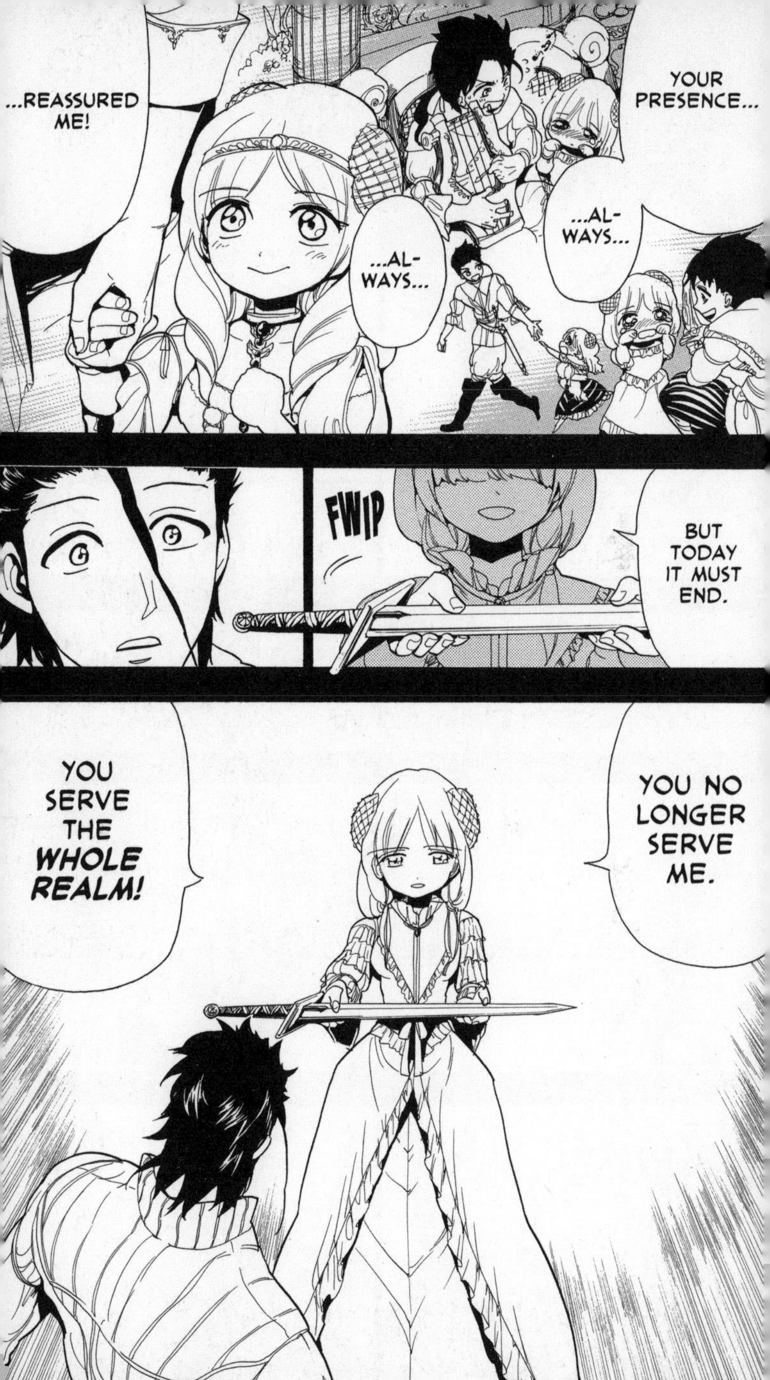
YOUR PRESENCE...
...AL-WAYS...
...AL-WAYS...
...REASSURED ME!
FWIP
BUT TODAY IT MUST END.
YOU NO LONGER SERVE ME.
YOU SERVE THE WHOLE REALM!

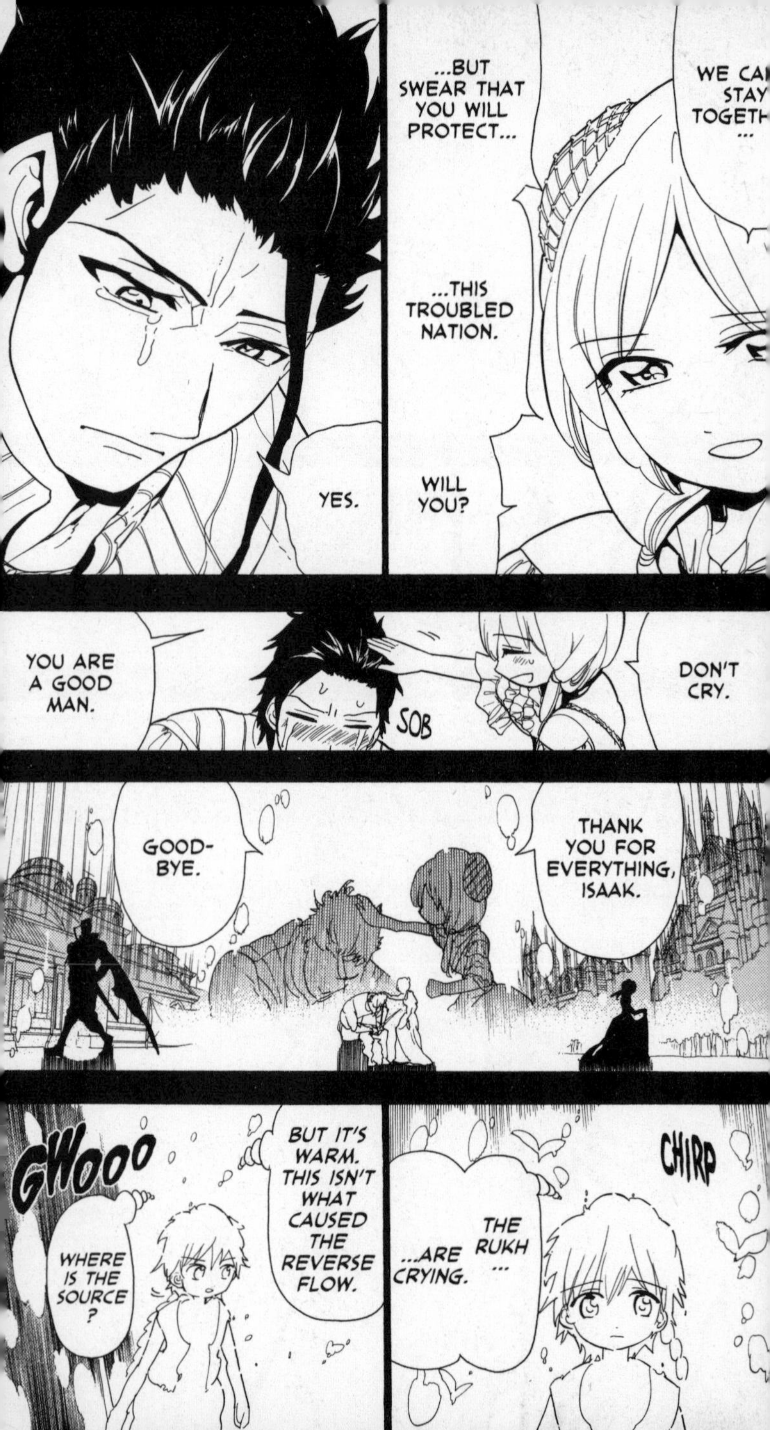
WE CA STAY TOGETH ...
...BUT SWEAR THAT YOU WILL PROTECT...
...THIS TROUBLED NATION.
WILL YOU?
YES.
DON'T CRY.
SOB
YOU ARE A GOOD MAN.
THANK YOU FOR EVERYTHING, ISAAK.
GOOD-BYE.
CHIRP
THE RUKH ...
...ARE CRYING.
BUT IT'S WARM. THIS ISN'T WHAT CAUSED THE REVERSE FLOW.
GWOOO
WHERE IS THE SOURCE ?

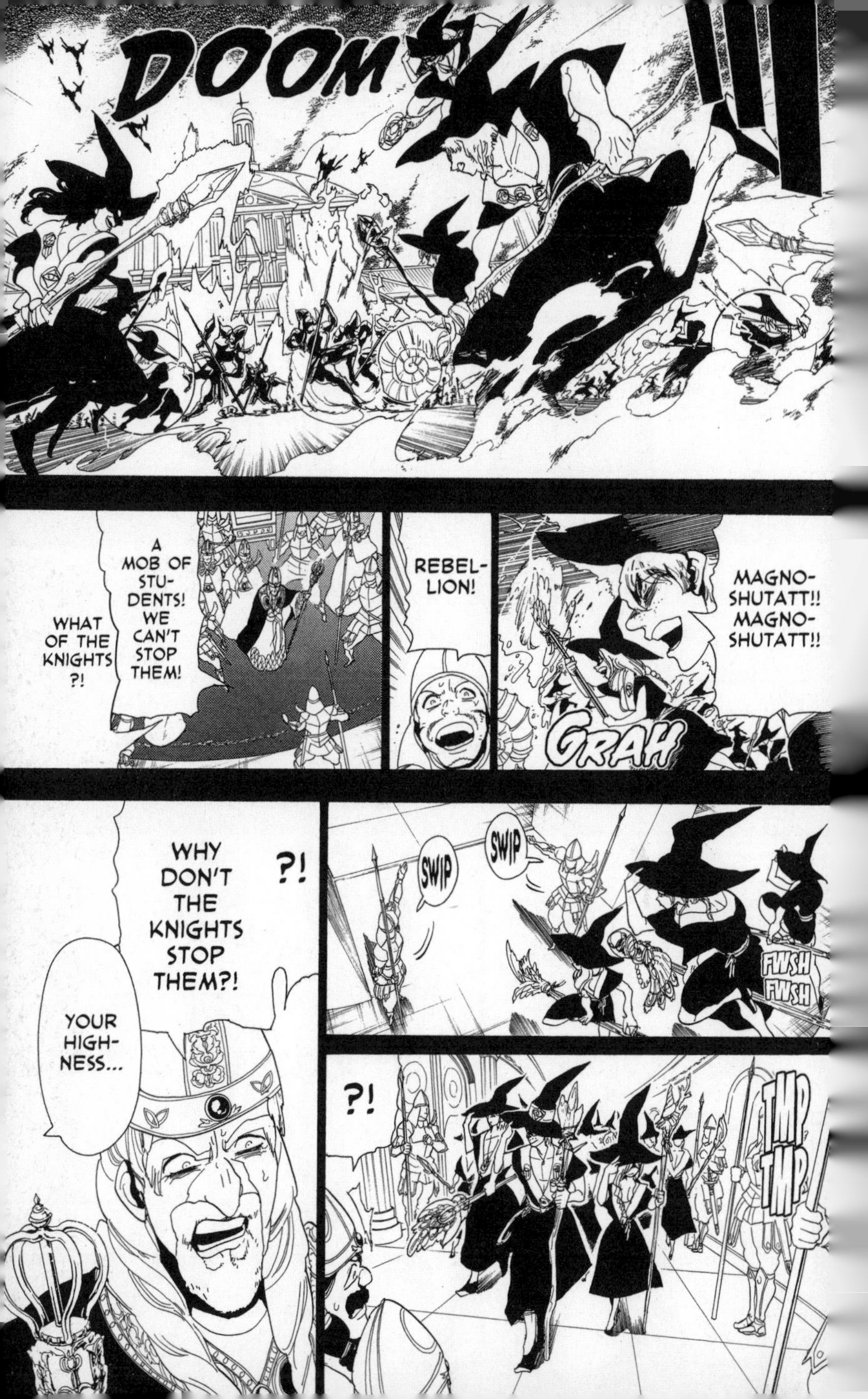
DOOM
MAGNO-SHUTATT!! MAGNO-SHUTATT!!
GRAH
REBEL-LION!
A MOB OF STU-DENTS! WE CAN'T STOP THEM!
WHAT OF THE KNIGHTS?!
SWIP
SWIP
FWSH FWSH
TMP TMP
?!
?!
WHY DON'T THE KNIGHTS STOP THEM?!
YOUR HIGH-NESS...

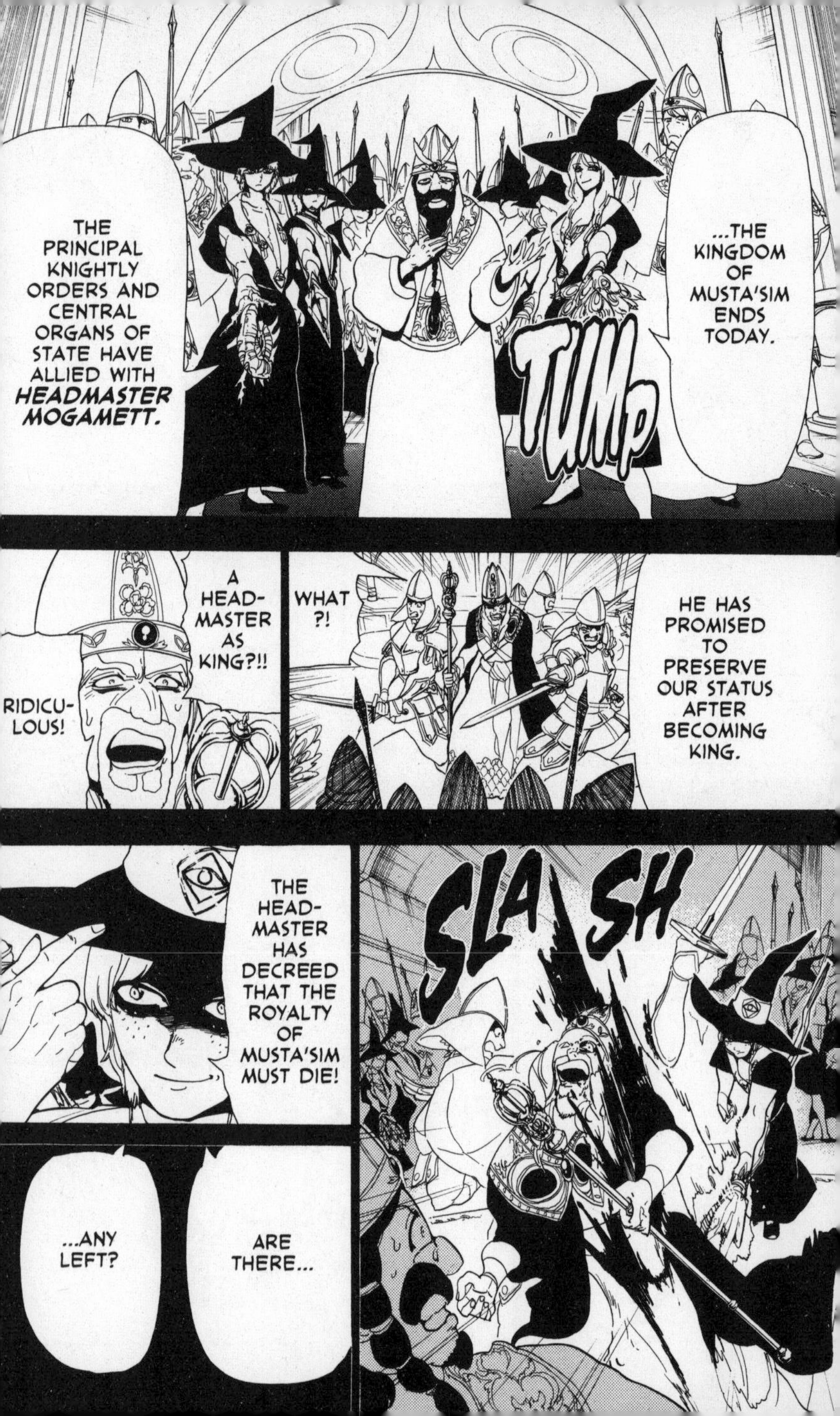
...THE KINGDOM OF MUSTA'SIM ENDS TODAY.
TUMP
THE PRINCIPAL KNIGHTLY ORDERS AND CENTRAL ORGANS OF STATE HAVE ALLIED WITH *HEADMASTER MOGAMETT.*
HE HAS PROMISED TO PRESERVE OUR STATUS AFTER BECOMING KING.
WHAT?!
A HEAD-MASTER AS KING?!!
RIDICU-LOUS!
SLASH
THE HEAD-MASTER HAS DECREED THAT THE ROYALTY OF MUSTA'SIM MUST DIE!
ARE THERE...
...ANY LEFT?

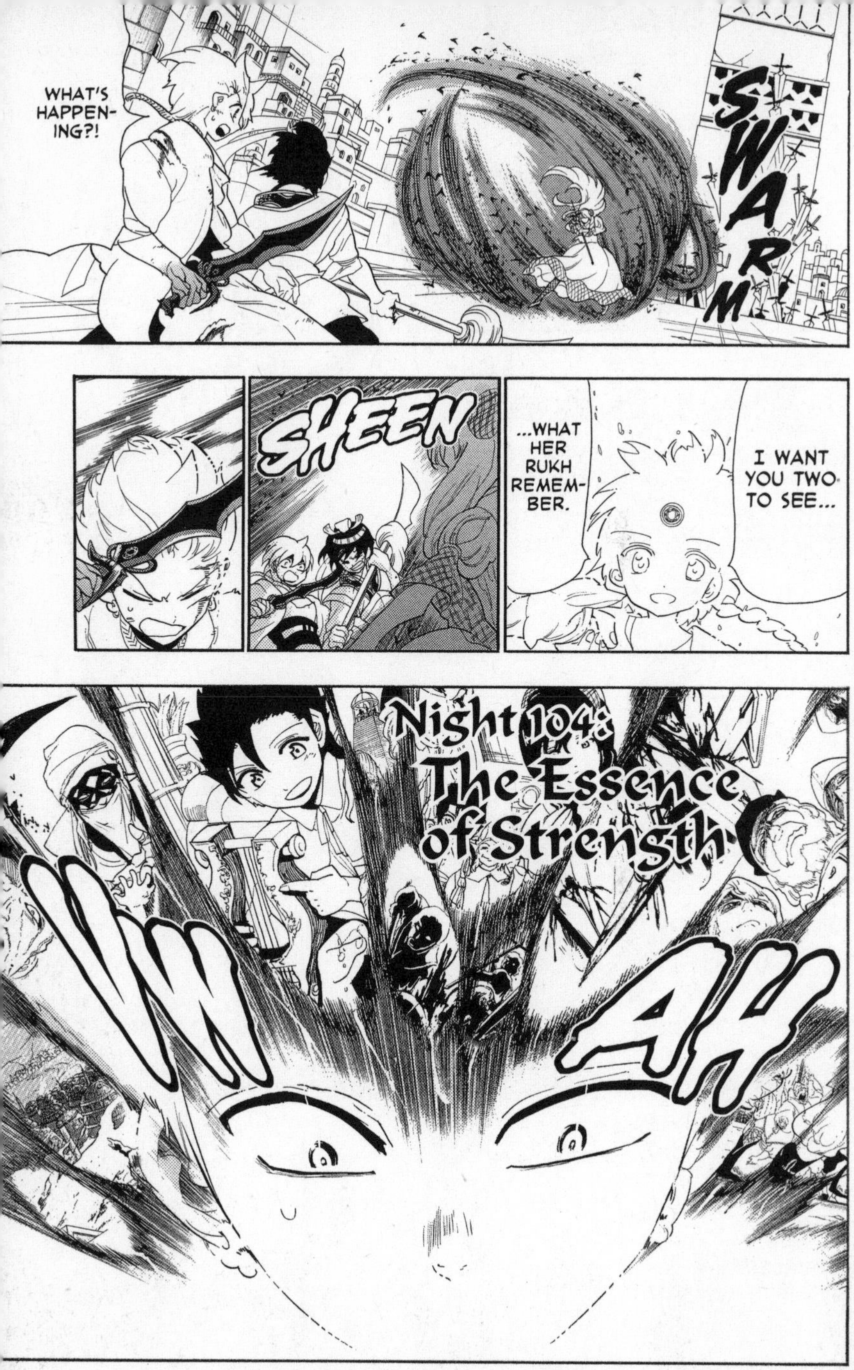
SWARM
WHAT'S HAPPENING?!
I WANT YOU TWO TO SEE...
...WHAT HER RUKH REMEMBER.
SHEEN
Night 104: The Essence of Strength
WAH

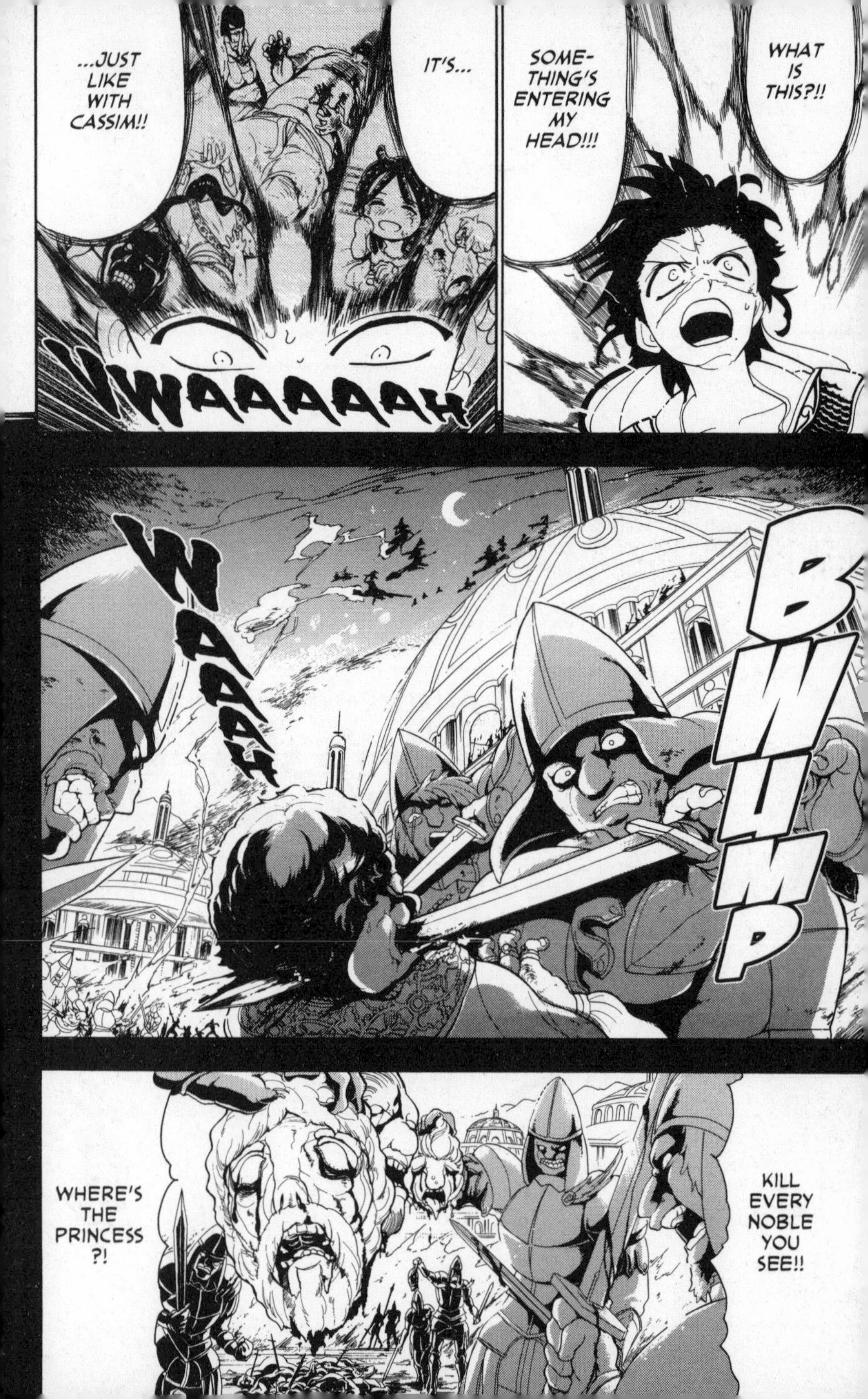
WHAT IS THIS?!!
SOME-THING'S ENTERING MY HEAD!!!
IT'S...
...JUST LIKE WITH CASSIM!!
WAAAAAAH
BWUMP
WAAAAH
KILL EVERY NOBLE YOU SEE!!
WHERE'S THE PRINCESS?!

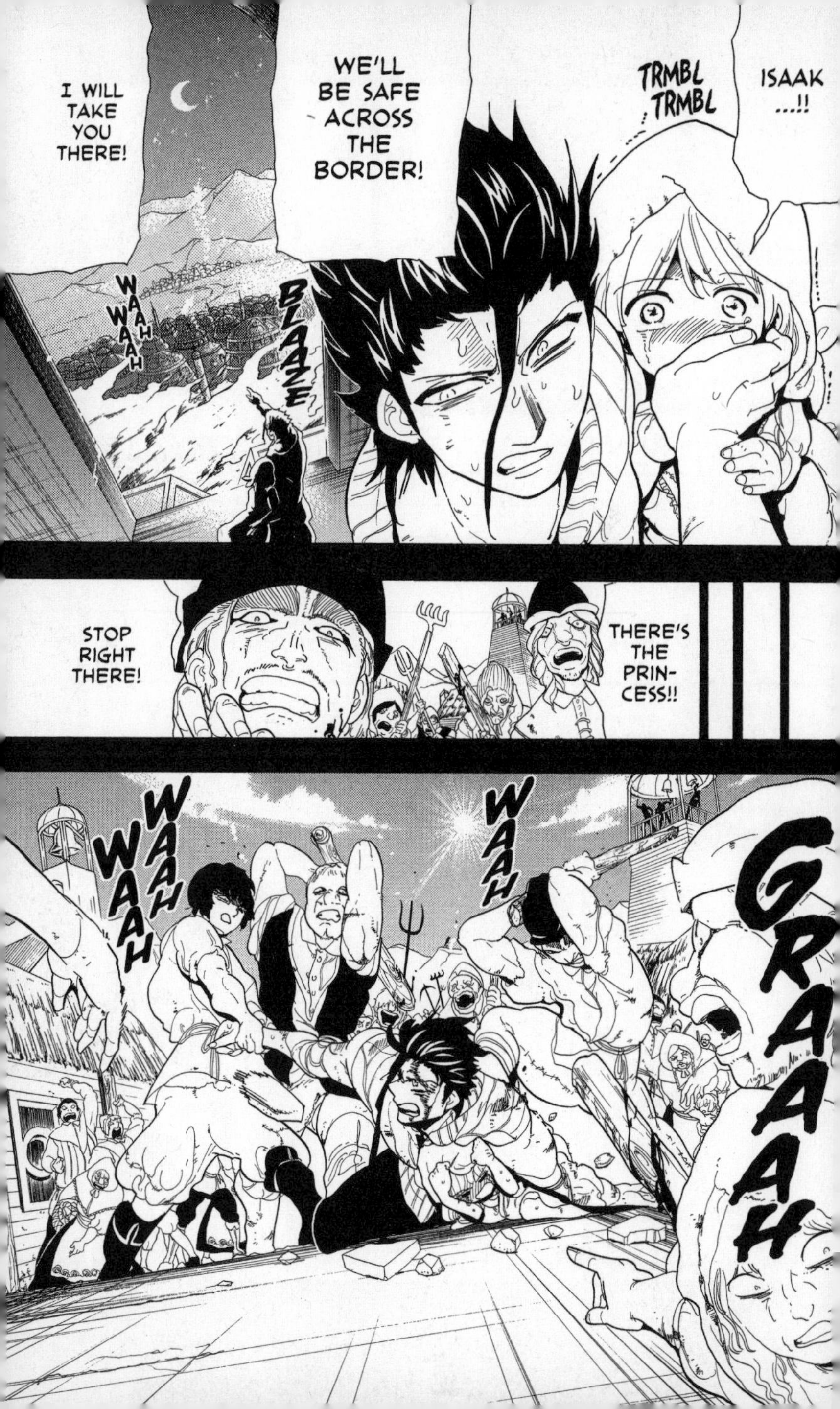
ISAAK ...!!
TRMBL TRMBL
WE'LL BE SAFE ACROSS THE BORDER!
I WILL TAKE YOU THERE!
BLAAZE
WAAH WAAH
THERE'S THE PRIN-CESS!!
STOP RIGHT THERE!
GRAAAAH
WAAH
WAAH WAAH

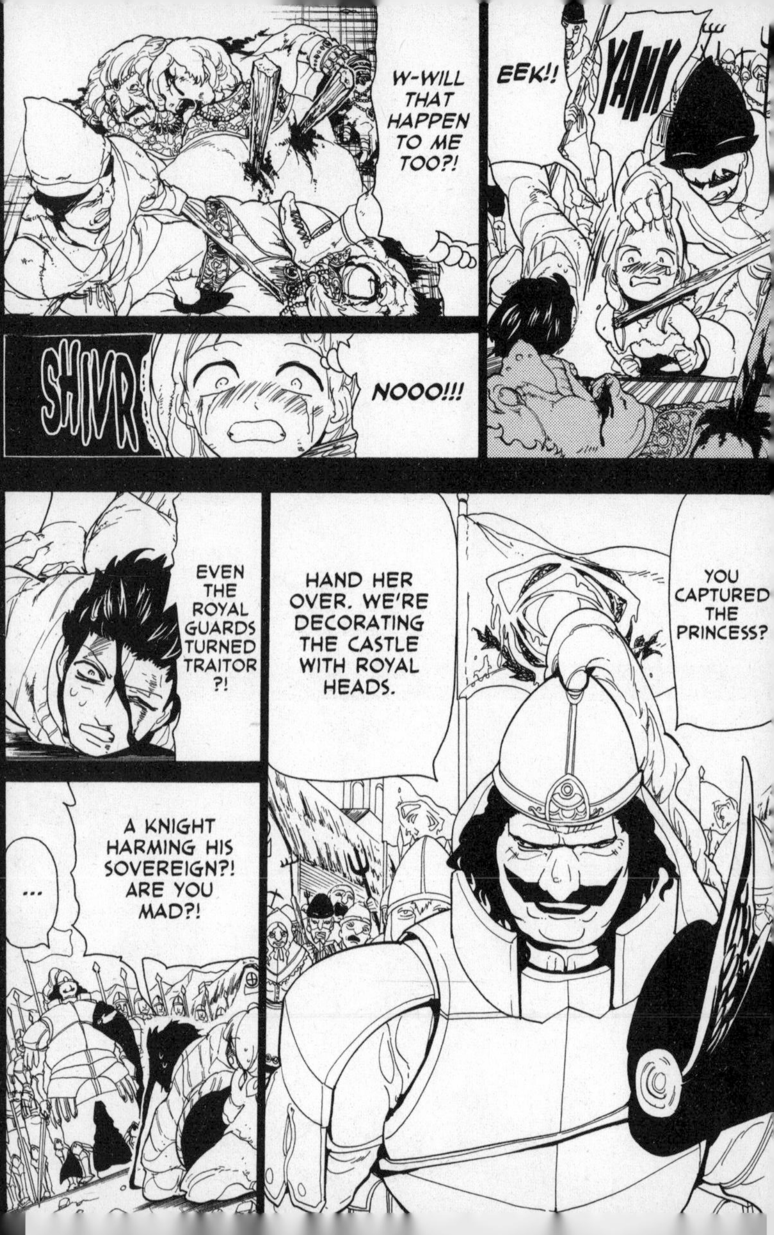
EEK!!
YANK
W-WILL THAT HAPPEN TO ME TOO?!
NOOO!!!
SHIVR
YOU CAPTURED THE PRINCESS?
HAND HER OVER. WE'RE DECORATING THE CASTLE WITH ROYAL HEADS.
EVEN THE ROYAL GUARDS TURNED TRAITOR?!
A KNIGHT HARMING HIS SOVEREIGN?! ARE YOU MAD?!
...

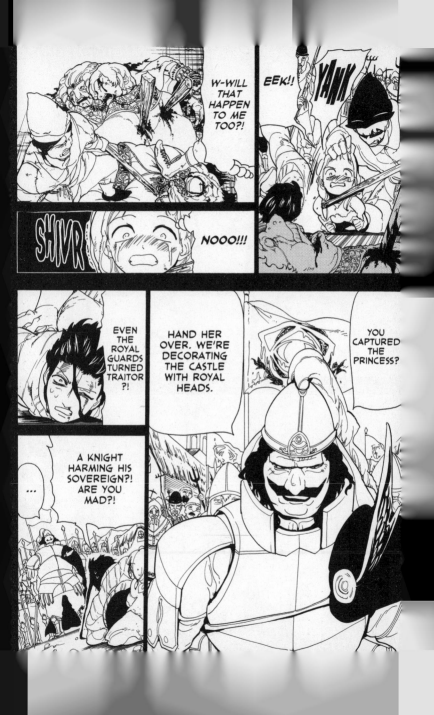

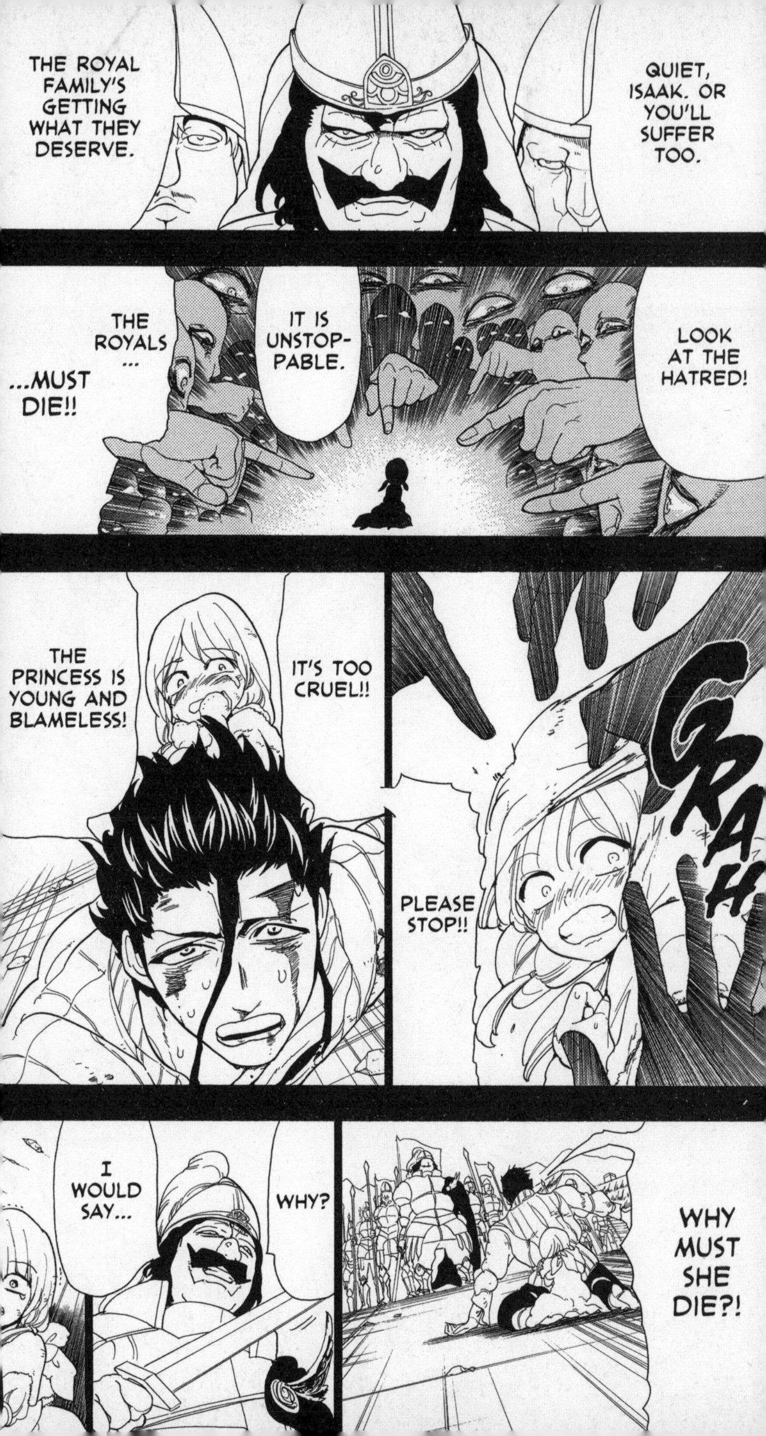
QUIET, ISAAK. OR YOU'LL SUFFER TOO.
THE ROYAL FAMILY'S GETTING WHAT THEY DESERVE.
LOOK AT THE HATRED!
IT IS UNSTOP-PABLE.
THE ROYALS ...
...MUST DIE!!
GRAH
PLEASE STOP!!
IT'S TOO CRUEL!!
THE PRINCESS IS YOUNG AND BLAMELESS!
WHY MUST SHE DIE?!
WHY?
I WOULD SAY...

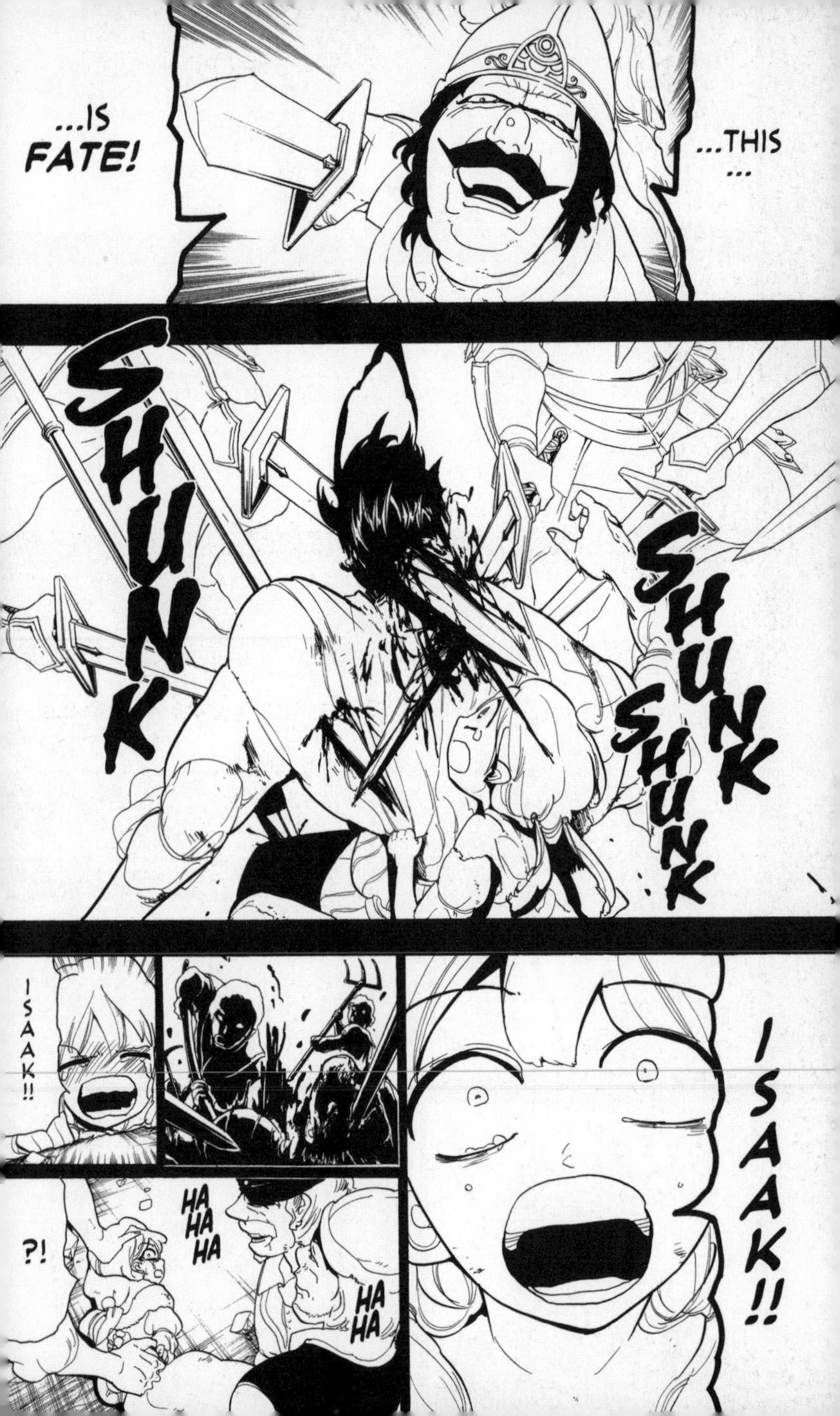
...THIS ...
...IS FATE!
SHUNK SHUNK
SHUNK
ISAAK!!
ISAAK!!
?!
HA HA HA
HA HA

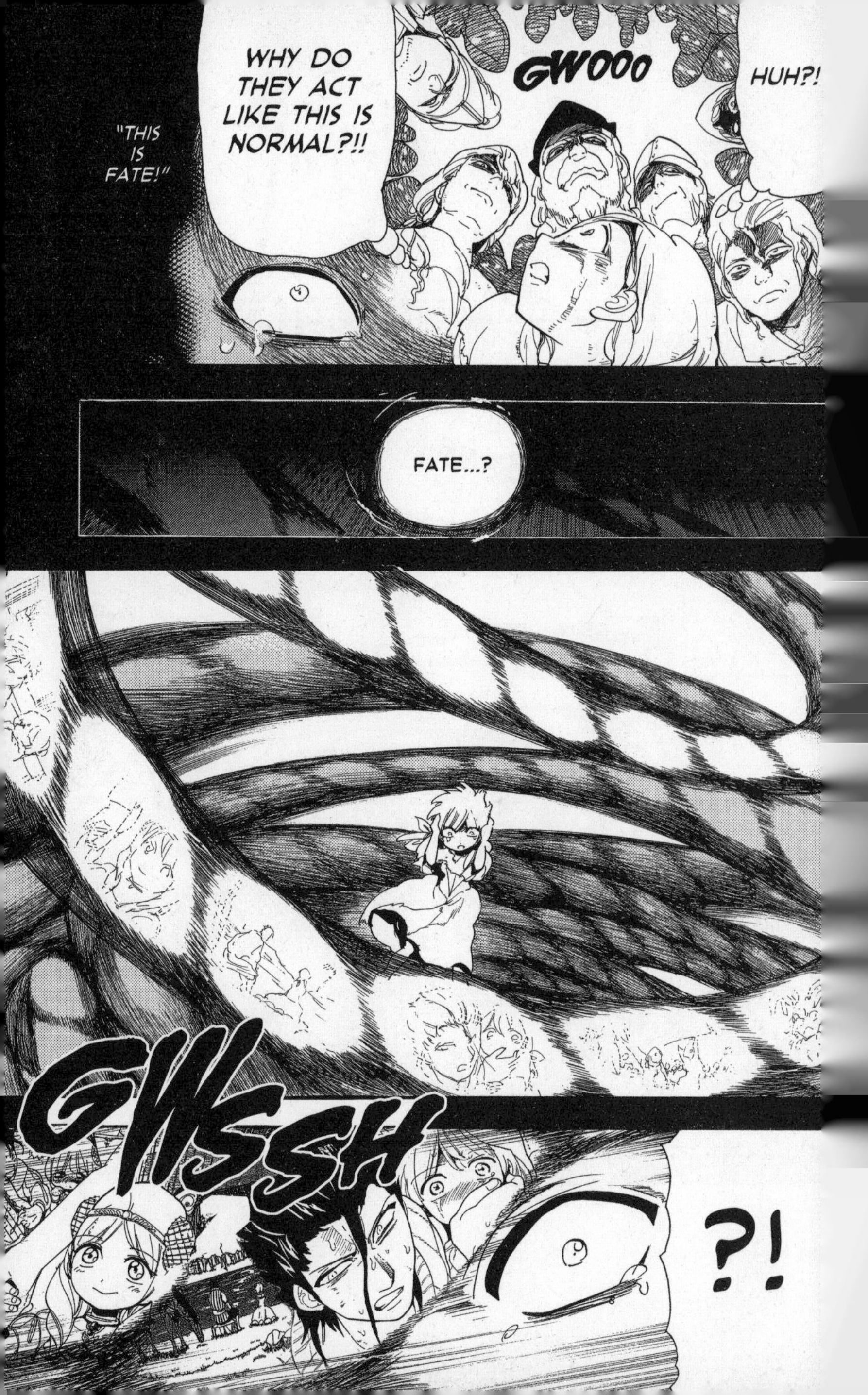
HUH?!
GWOOO
WHY DO THEY ACT LIKE THIS IS NORMAL?!!
"THIS IS FATE!"
FATE...?
GWSSH
?!

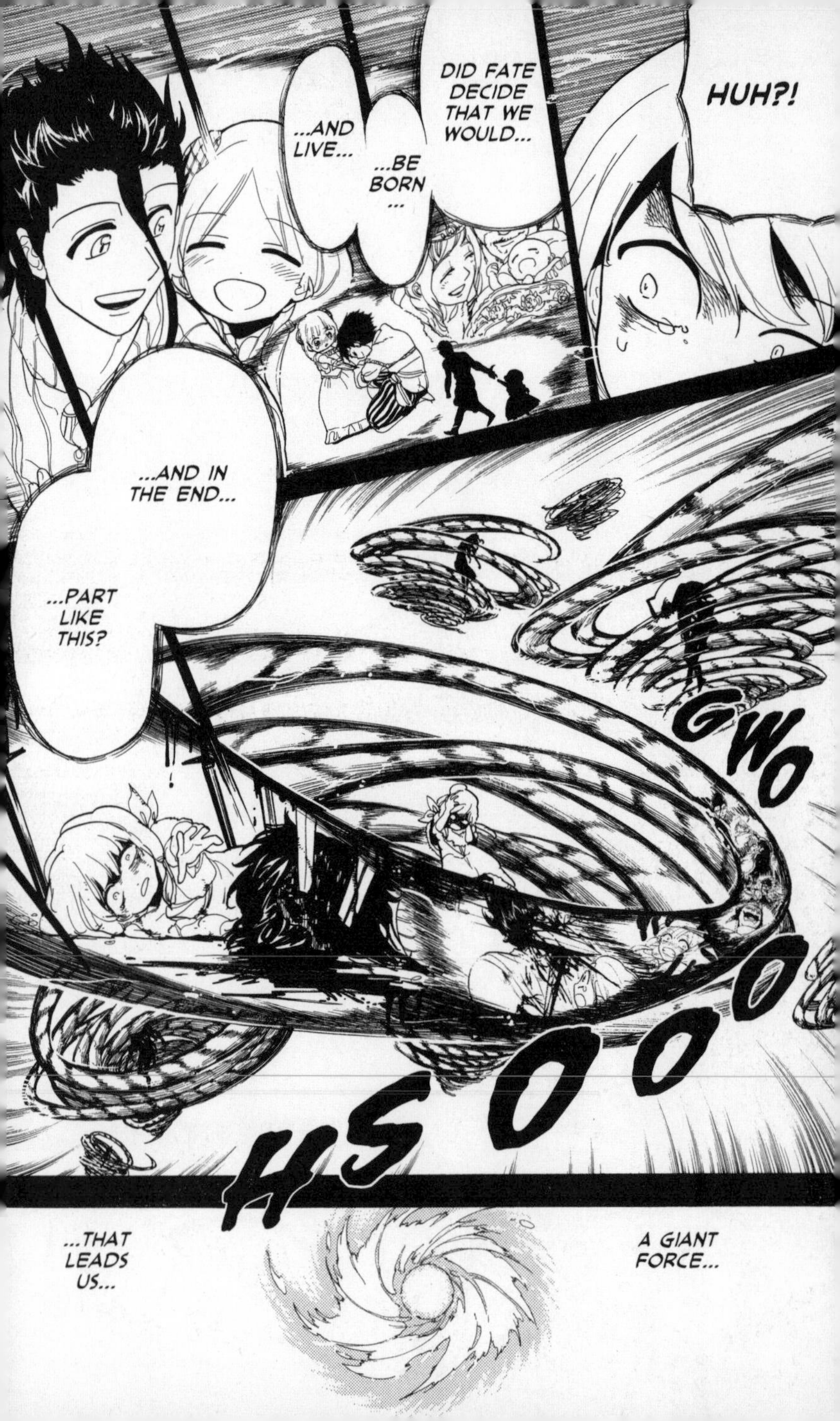
HUH?!
DID FATE DECIDE THAT WE WOULD...
...BE BORN...
...AND LIVE...
...AND IN THE END...
...PART LIKE THIS?
GWO
HSOOOO
!
A GIANT FORCE...
...THAT LEADS US...

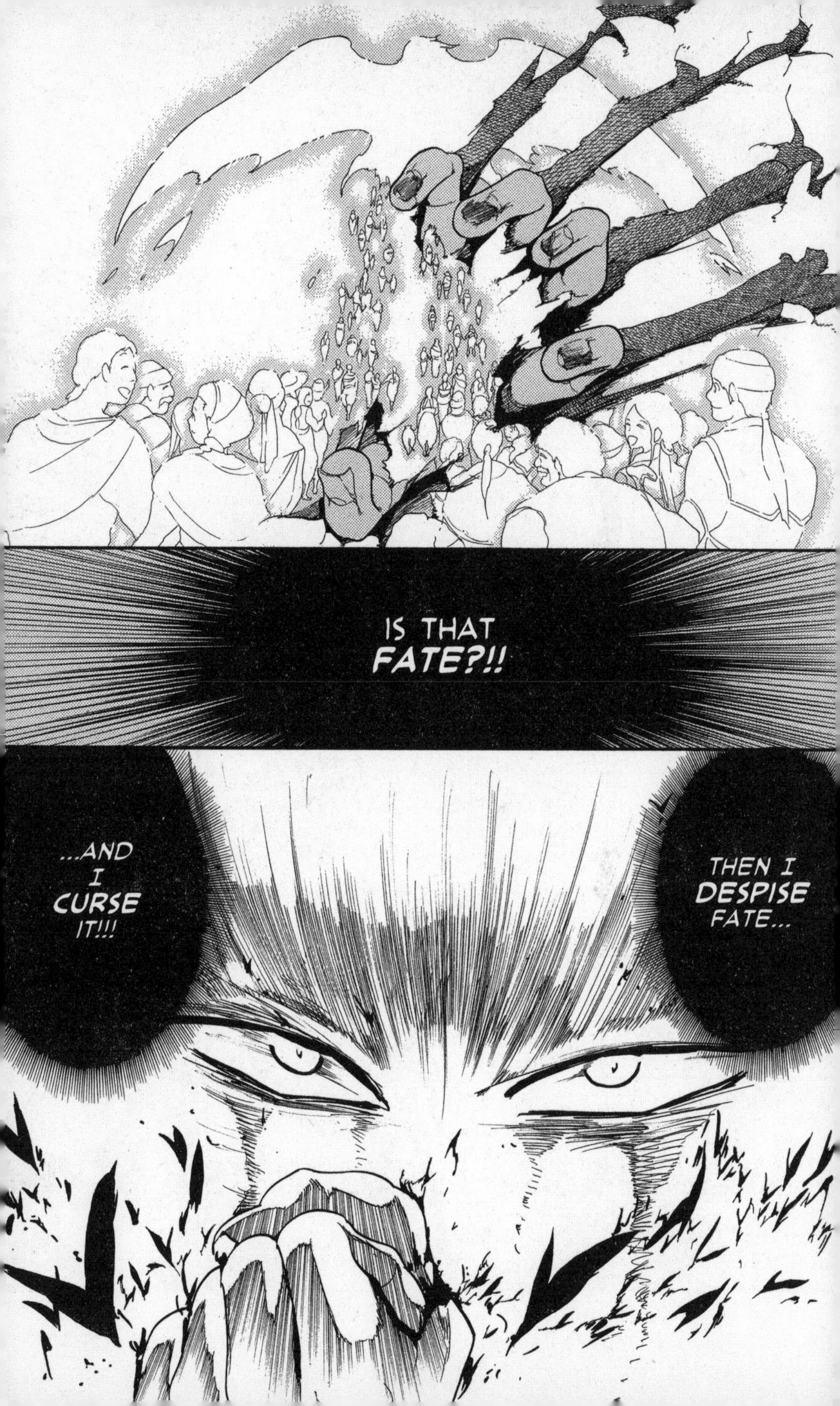
IS THAT FATE?!!
THEN I DESPISE FATE...
...AND I CURSE IT!!!

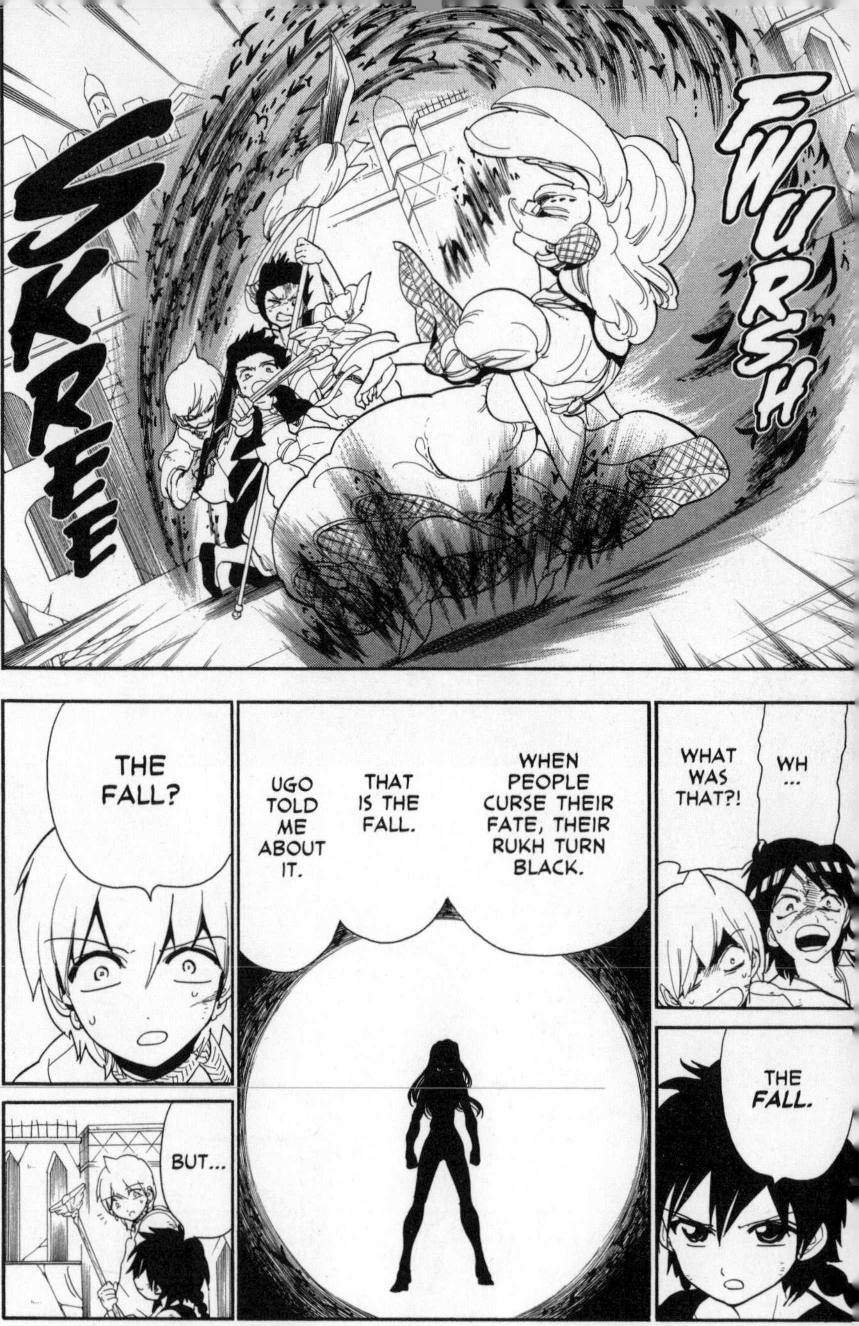
FWURSH
SKREE
WH...
WHAT WAS THAT?!
THE FALL.
WHEN PEOPLE CURSE THEIR FATE, THEIR RUKH TURN BLACK.
THAT IS THE FALL.
UGO TOLD ME ABOUT IT.
THE FALL?
BUT...

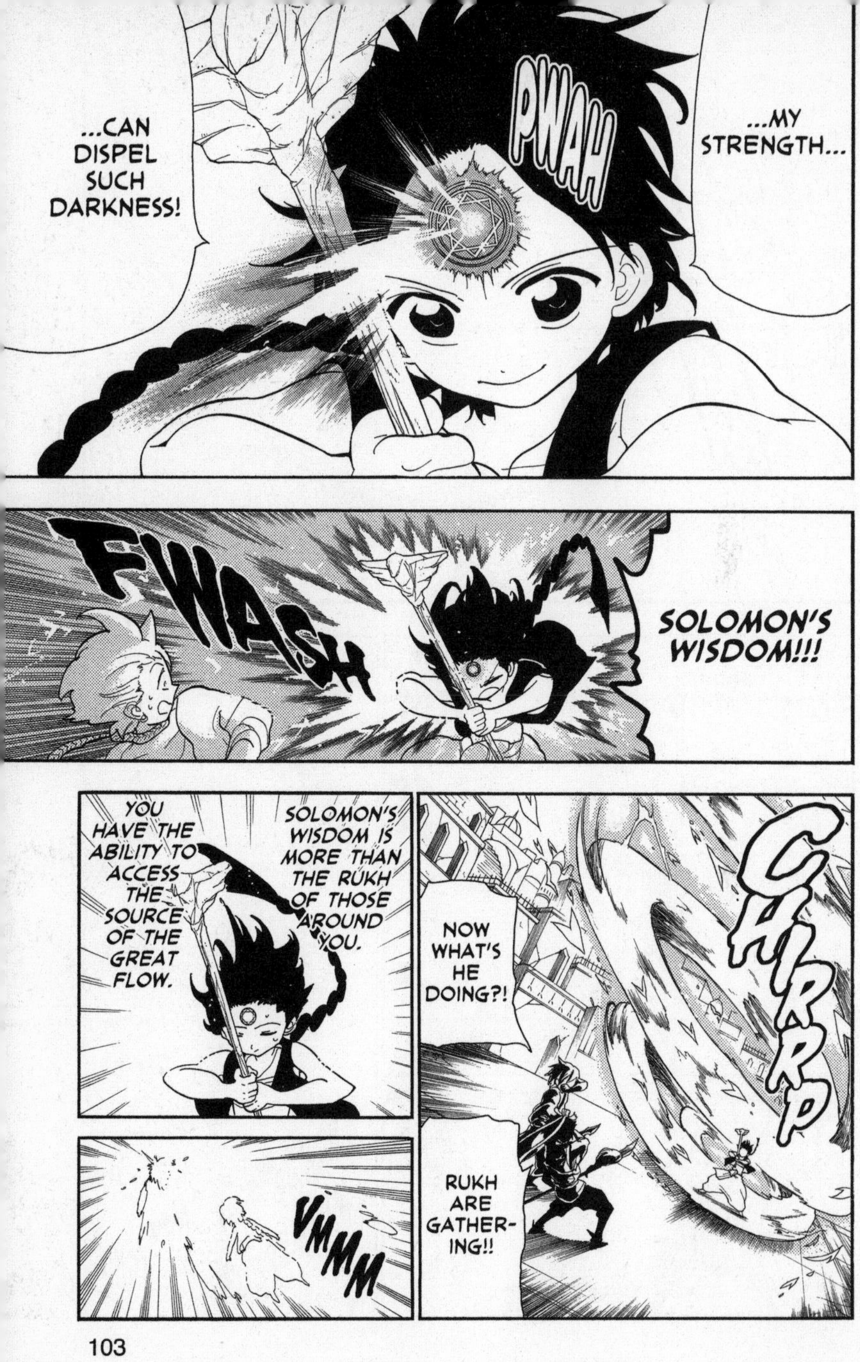
...MY STRENGTH...
PWAH
...CAN DISPEL SUCH DARKNESS!
SOLOMON'S WISDOM!!!
FWASH
CHIRP
NOW WHAT'S HE DOING?!
RUKH ARE GATHERING!!
SOLOMON'S WISDOM IS MORE THAN THE RUKH OF THOSE AROUND YOU.
YOU HAVE THE ABILITY TO ACCESS THE SOURCE OF THE GREAT FLOW.
VMMM

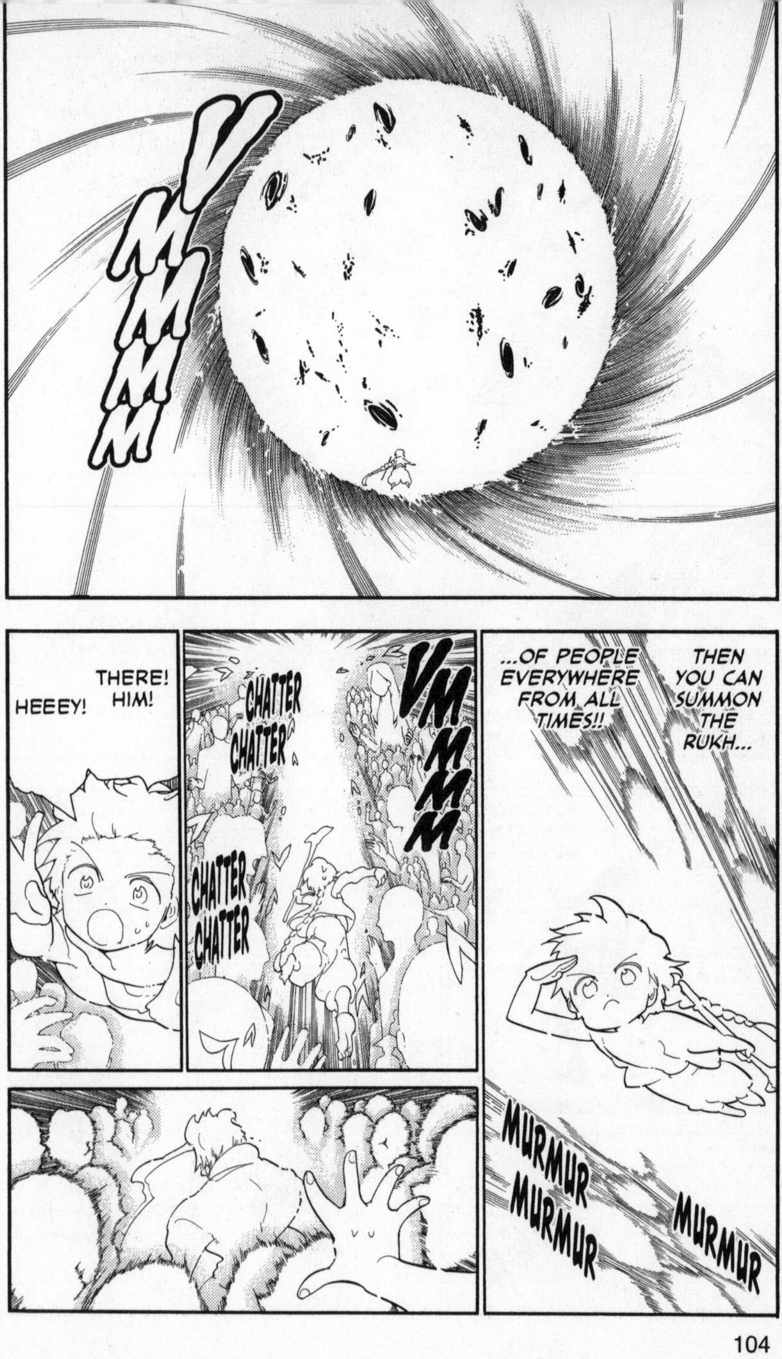
VMMMM
THEN YOU CAN SUMMON THE RUKH...
...OF PEOPLE EVERYWHERE FROM ALL TIMES!!
MURMUR
MURMUR
MURMUR
MURMUR
VMMMMM
CHATTER CHATTER
CHATTER CHATTER
THERE! HIM!
HEEEY!

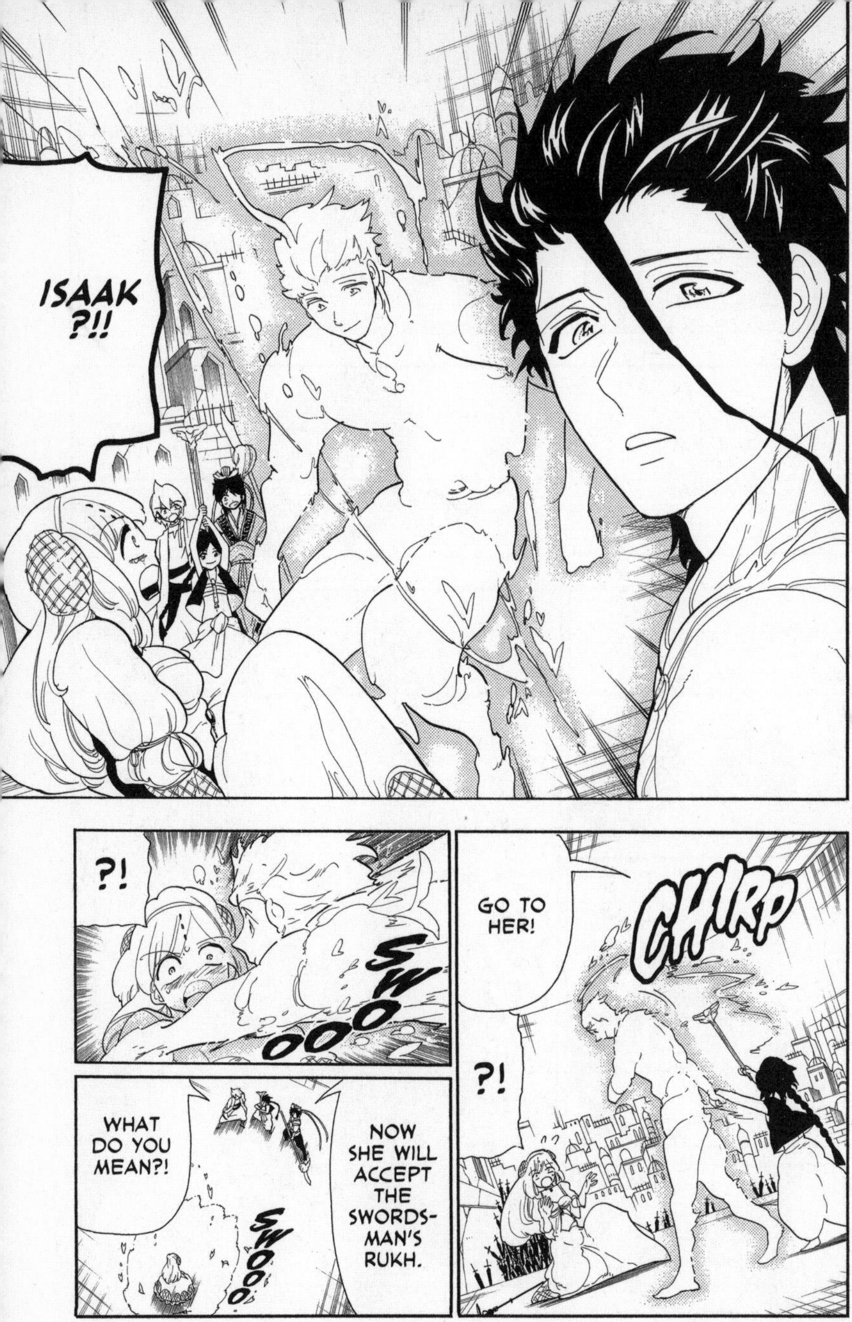
ISAAK ?!!
GO TO HER!
CHIRP
?!
?!
SWOOOOO
NOW SHE WILL ACCEPT THE SWORDS-MAN'S RUKH.
SWOOO
WHAT DO YOU MEAN?!

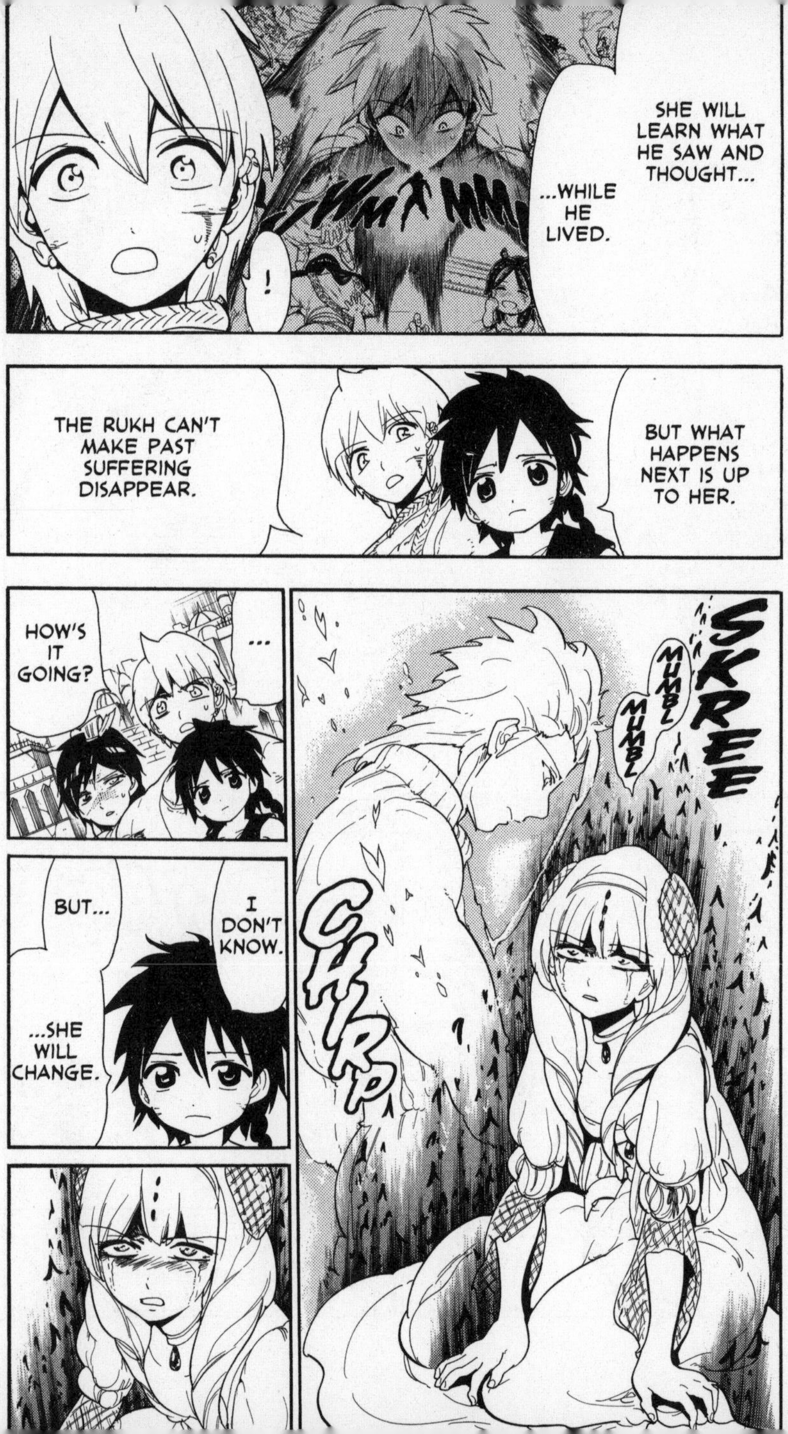
SHE WILL LEARN WHAT HE SAW AND THOUGHT...
...WHILE HE LIVED.
!
BUT WHAT HAPPENS NEXT IS UP TO HER.
THE RUKH CAN'T MAKE PAST SUFFERING DISAPPEAR.
SKREE
MUMBL MUMBL
CHIRP
HOW'S IT GOING?
...
I DON'T KNOW.
BUT...
...SHE WILL CHANGE.
...

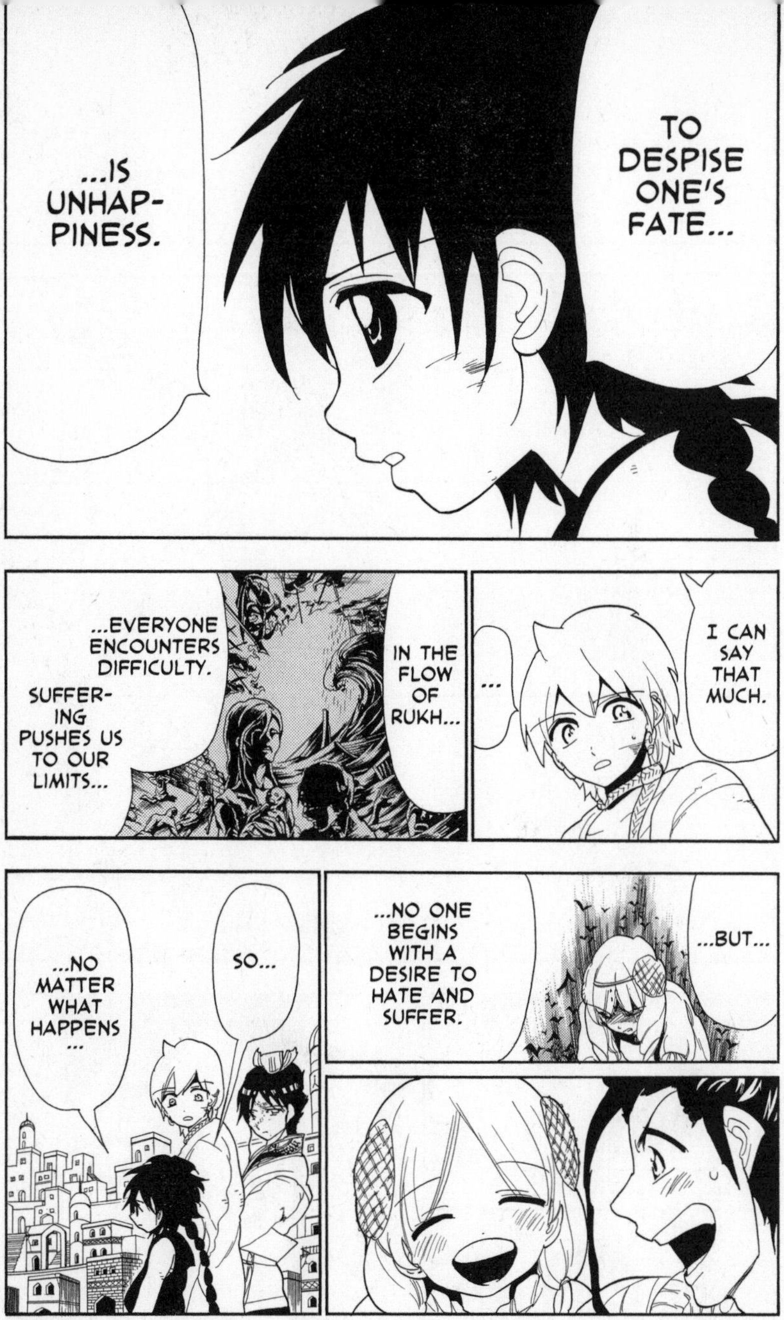
TO DESPISE ONE'S FATE...
...IS UNHAPPINESS.
I CAN SAY THAT MUCH.
...
IN THE FLOW OF RUKH...
...EVERYONE ENCOUNTERS DIFFICULTY.
SUFFERING PUSHES US TO OUR LIMITS...
...BUT...
...NO ONE BEGINS WITH A DESIRE TO HATE AND SUFFER.
SO...
...NO MATTER WHAT HAPPENS...

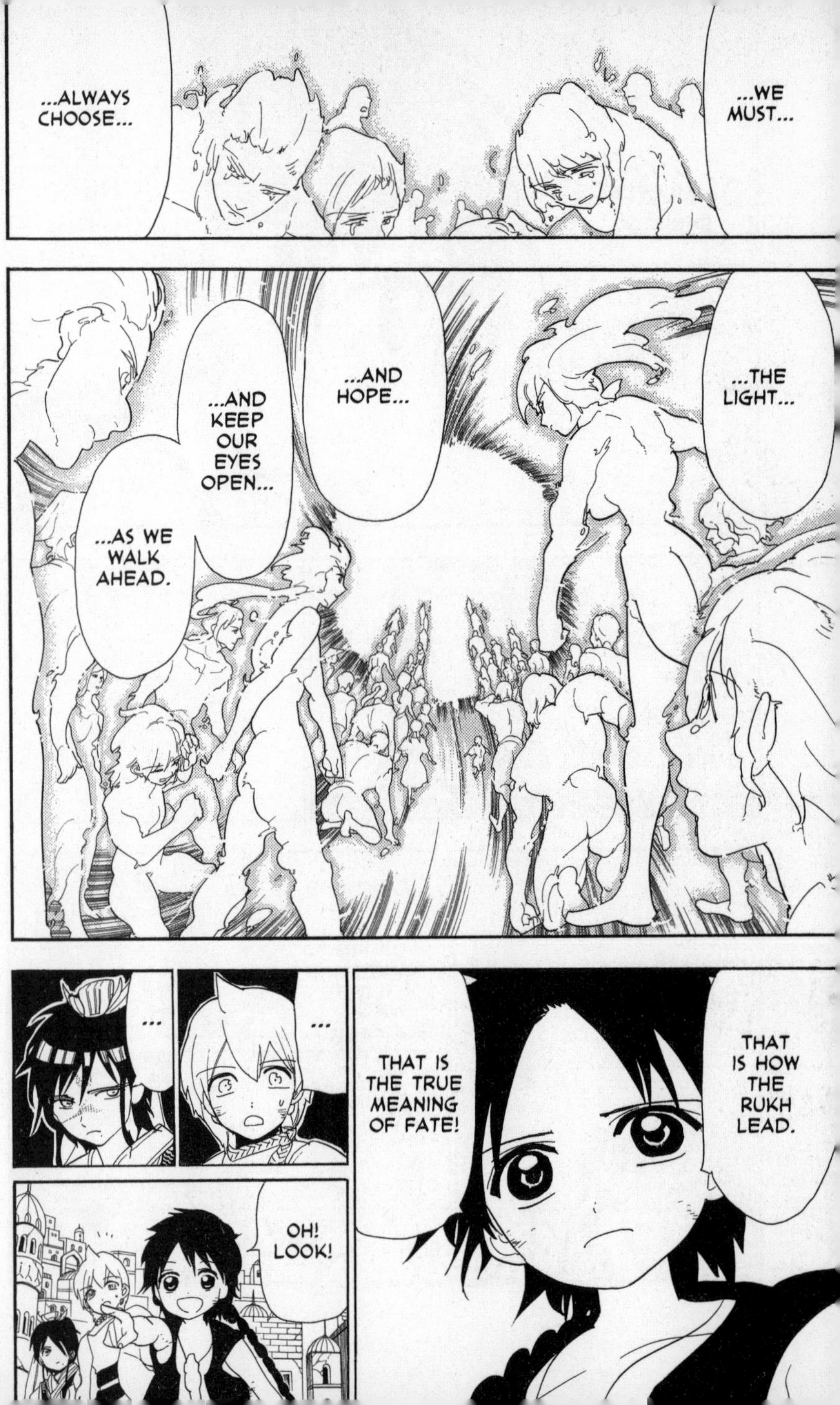
...WE MUST...
...ALWAYS CHOOSE...
...THE LIGHT...
...AND HOPE...
...AND KEEP OUR EYES OPEN...
...AS WE WALK AHEAD.
THAT IS HOW THE RUKH LEAD.
THAT IS THE TRUE MEANING OF FATE!
...
...
OH! LOOK!

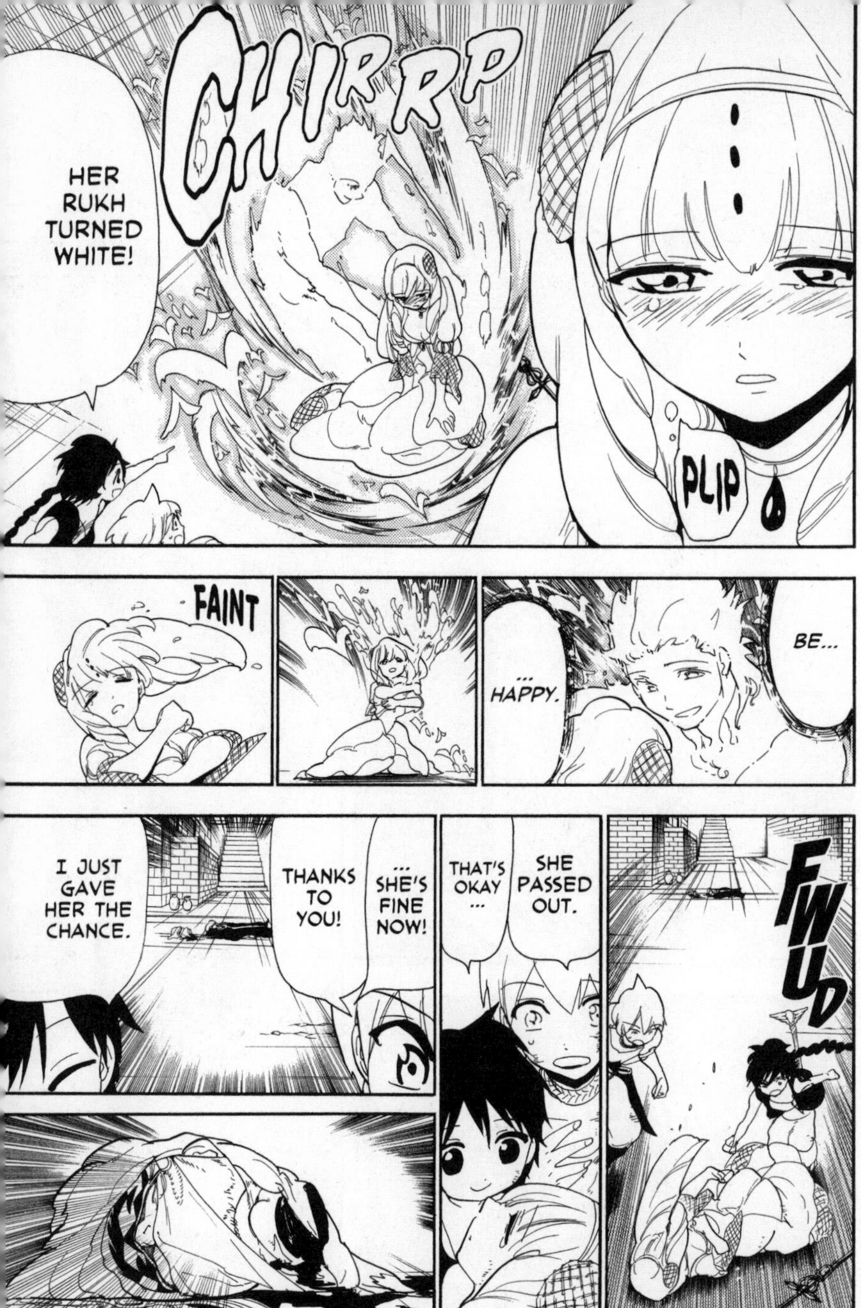

...
PLIP
CHIRRP
HER RUKH TURNED WHITE!
BE...
... HAPPY.
FAINT
FWUD
SHE PASSED OUT.
THAT'S OKAY ...
... SHE'S FINE NOW!
THANKS TO YOU!
I JUST GAVE HER THE CHANCE.

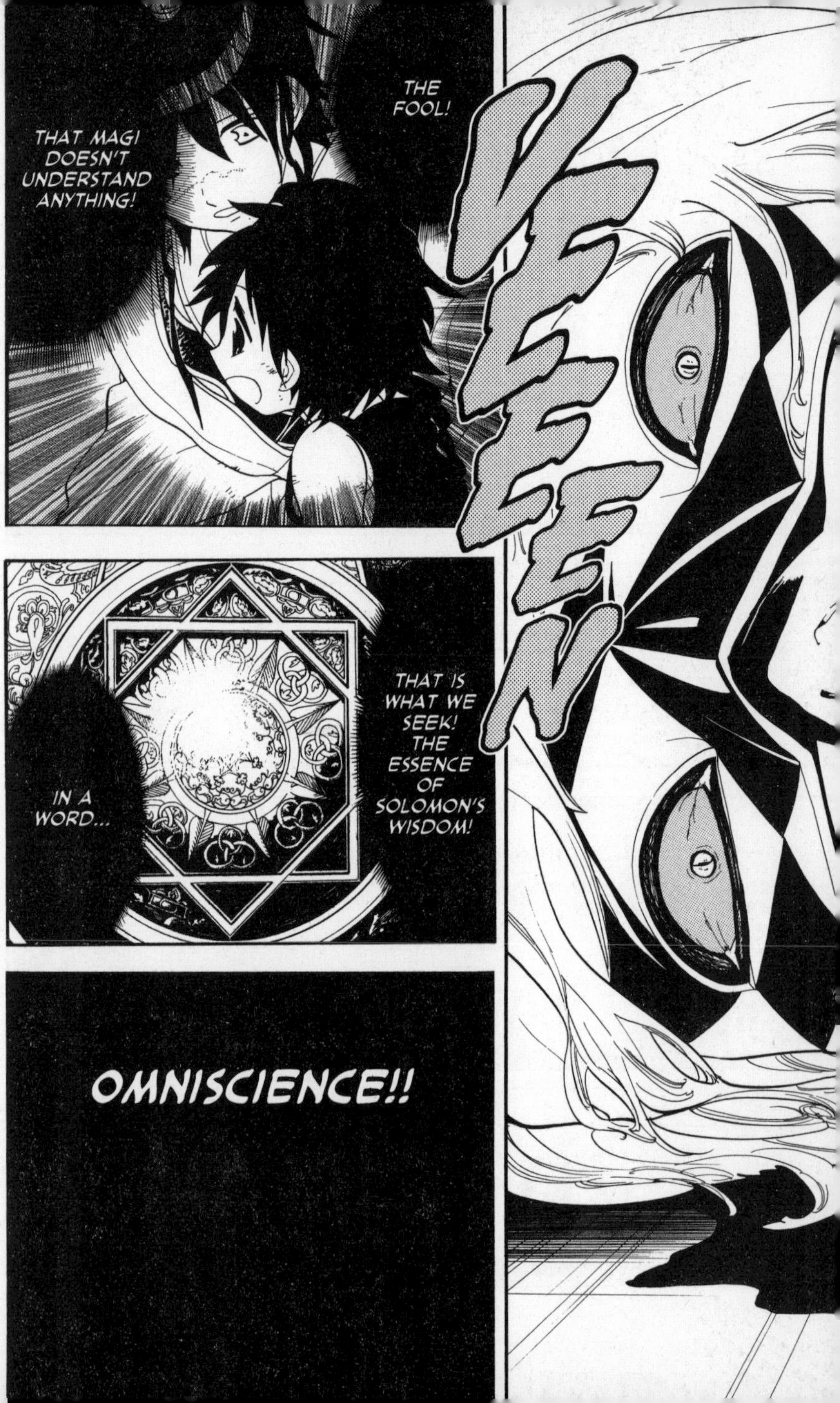
THE FOOL!
THAT MAGI DOESN'T UNDERSTAND ANYTHING!
THAT IS WHAT WE SEEK! THE ESSENCE OF SOLOMON'S WISDOM!
IN A WORD...
OMNISCIENCE!!

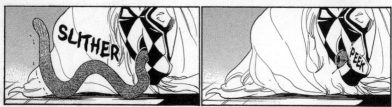

SLITHER

PEEK

SLITHER

HISS!

Night 105:
Dungeon Capturer

SLITHER

SLITHER

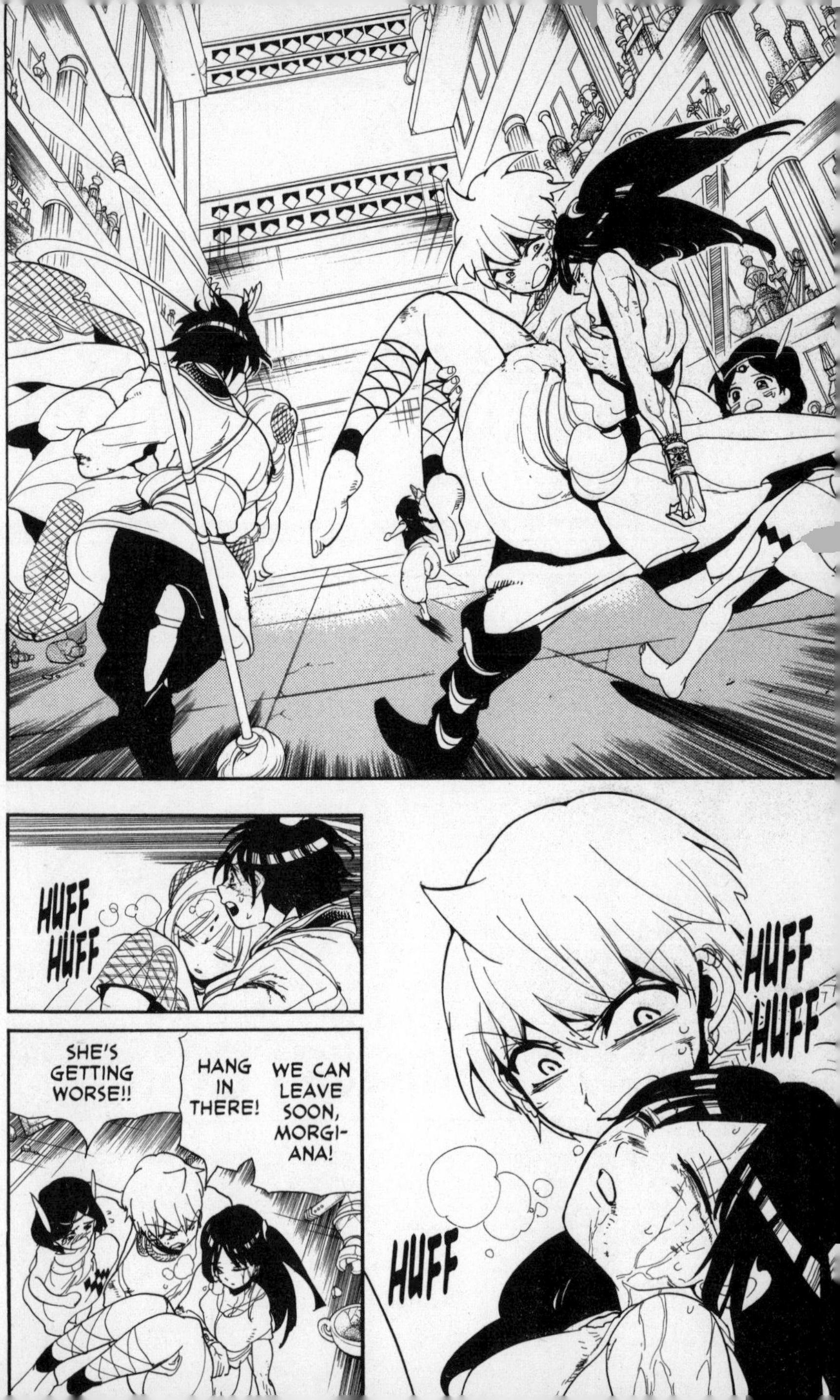
HUFF HUFF
HUFF
HUFF HUFF
WE CAN LEAVE SOON, MORGI-ANA!
HANG IN THERE!
SHE'S GETTING WORSE!!

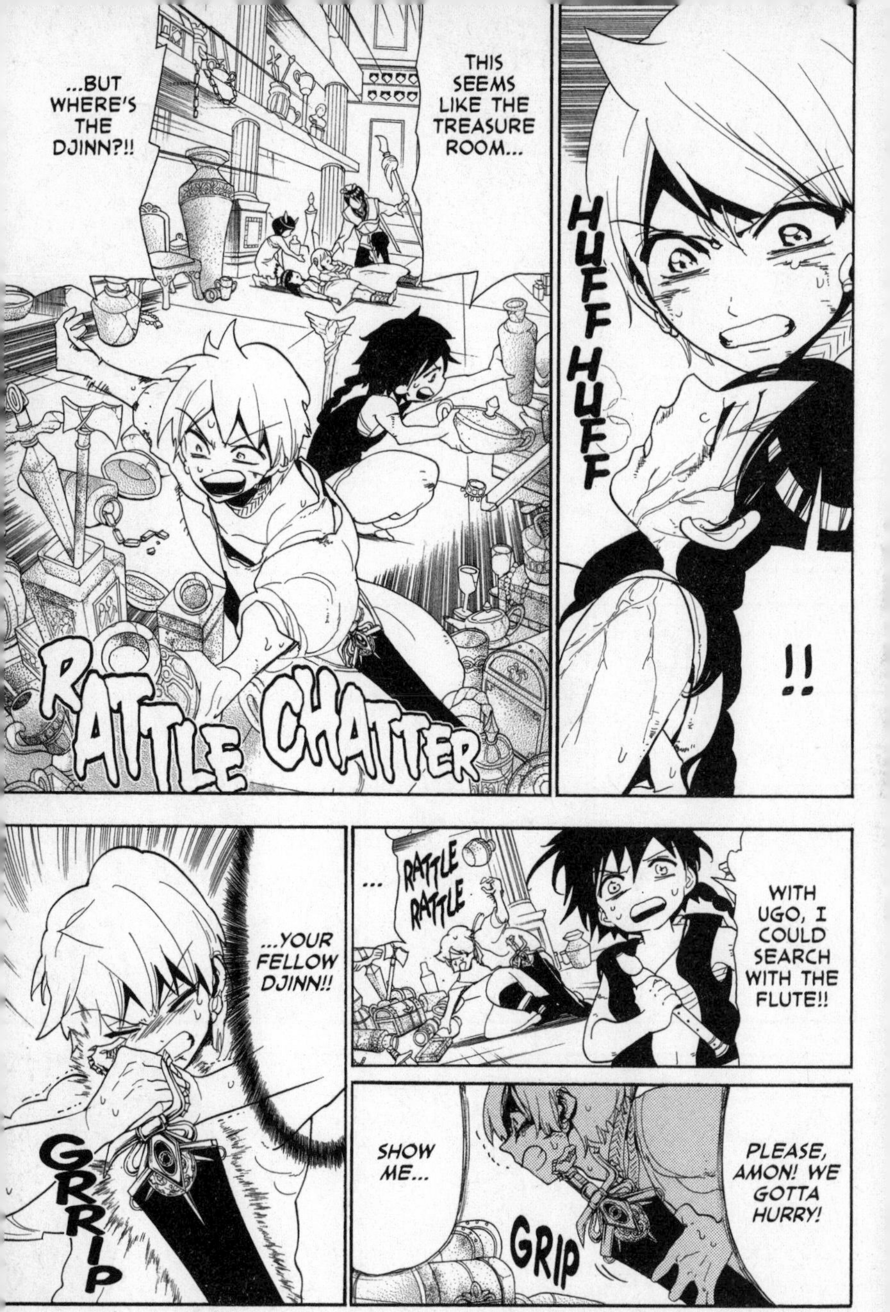
HUFF HUFF
!!
THIS SEEMS LIKE THE TREASURE ROOM...
...BUT WHERE'S THE DJINN?!!
RATTLE CHATTER
WITH UGO, I COULD SEARCH WITH THE FLUTE!!
RATTLE RATTLE
...
PLEASE, AMON! WE GOTTA HURRY!
SHOW ME...
GRIP
...YOUR FELLOW DJINN!!
GRRIP

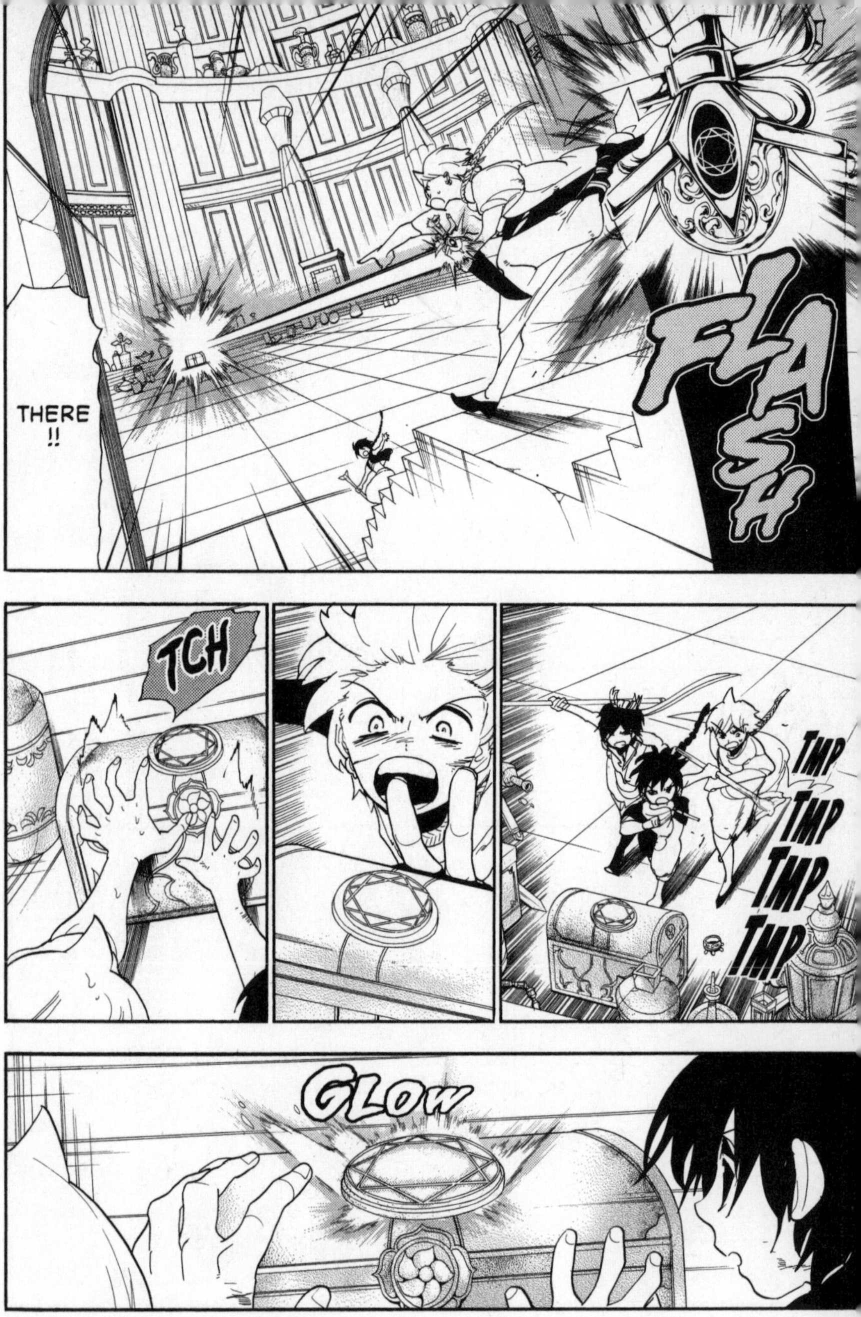
FLASH
THERE !!
TMP TMP TMP TMP TMP
TCH
GLOW

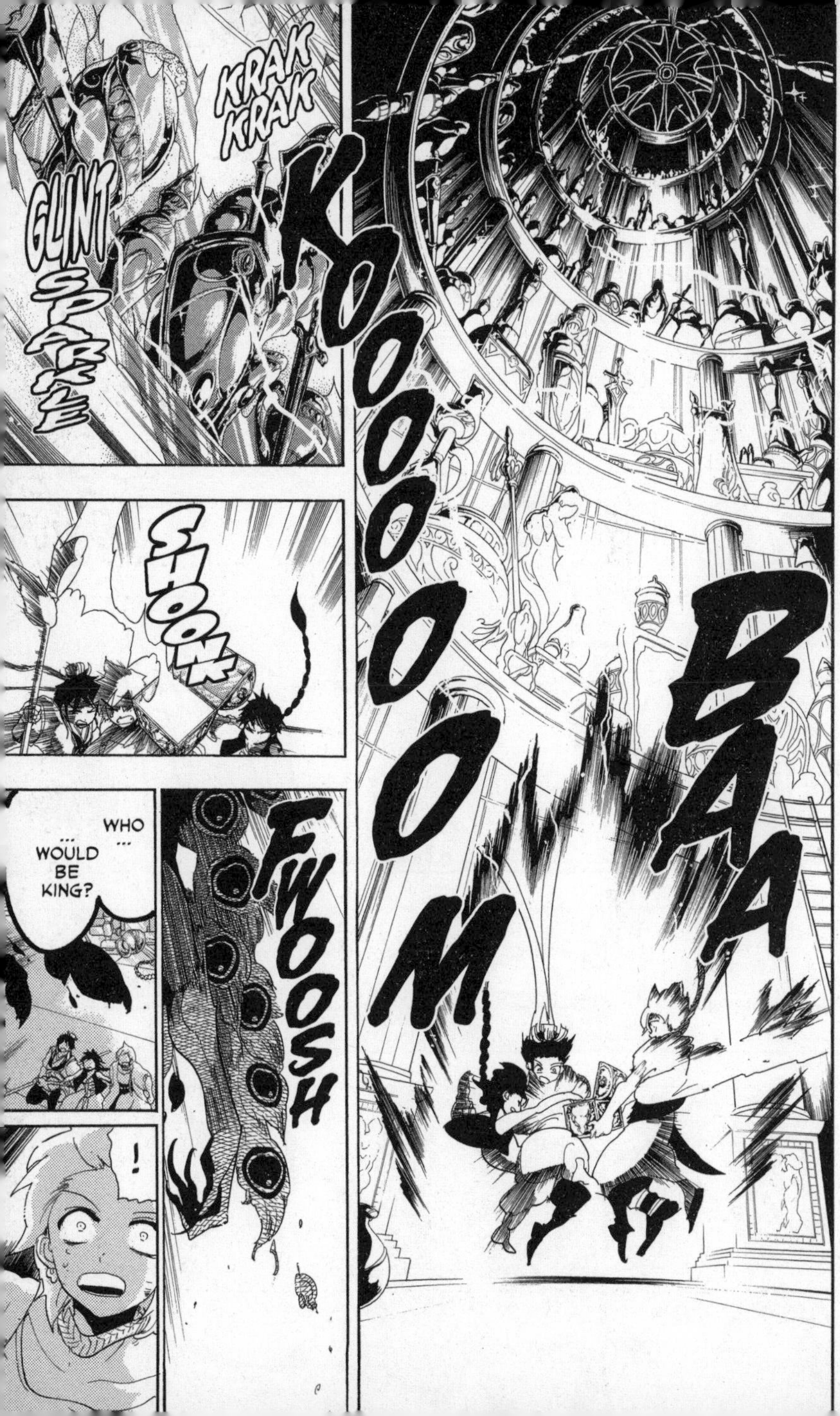
BAA
KOOOOOM
KRAK KRAK
GLINT
SPARKLE
SHOONK
FWOOSH
WHO ... WOULD BE KING?
!

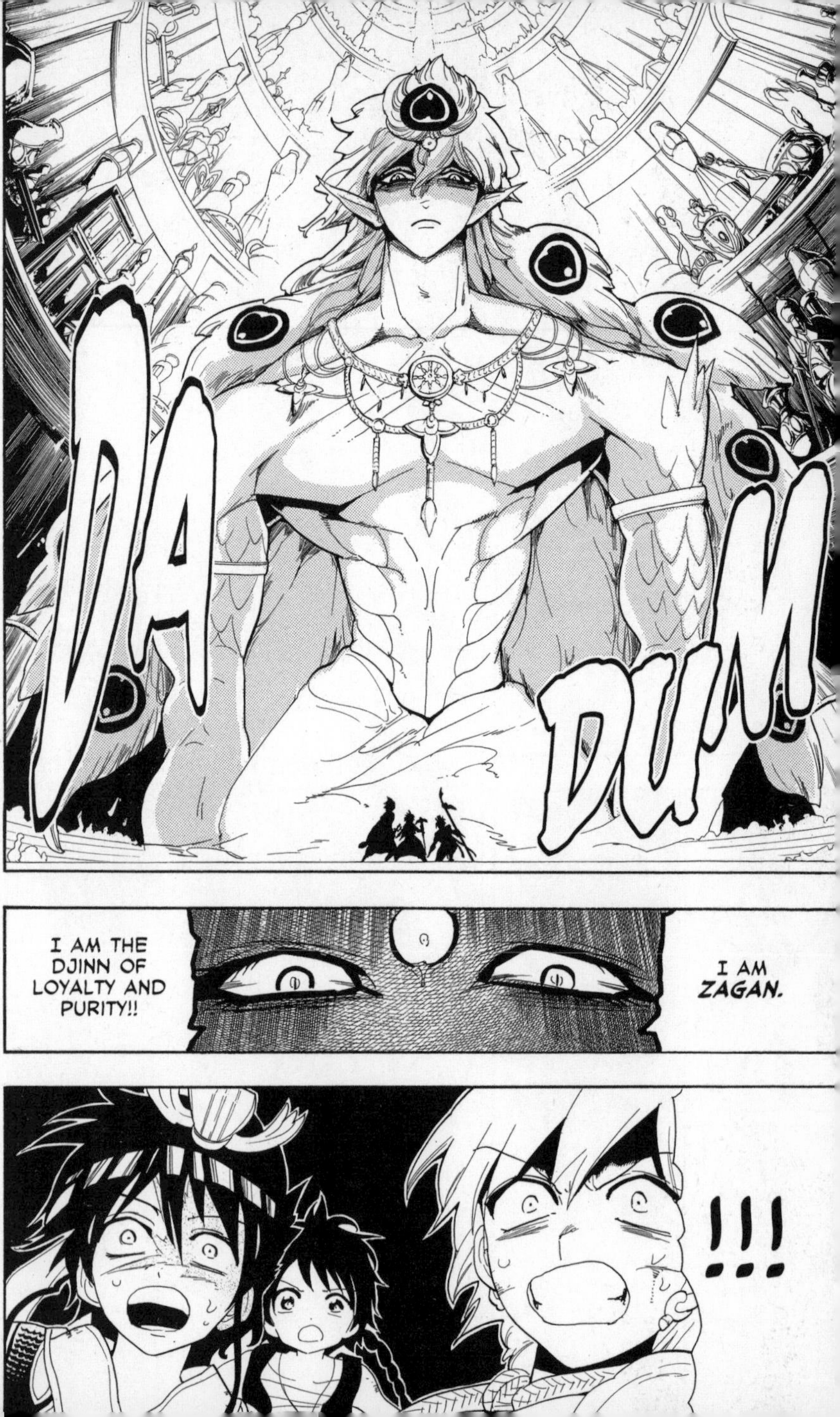
DA DUM
I AM ZAGAN.
I AM THE DJINN OF LOYALTY AND PURITY!!
!!!

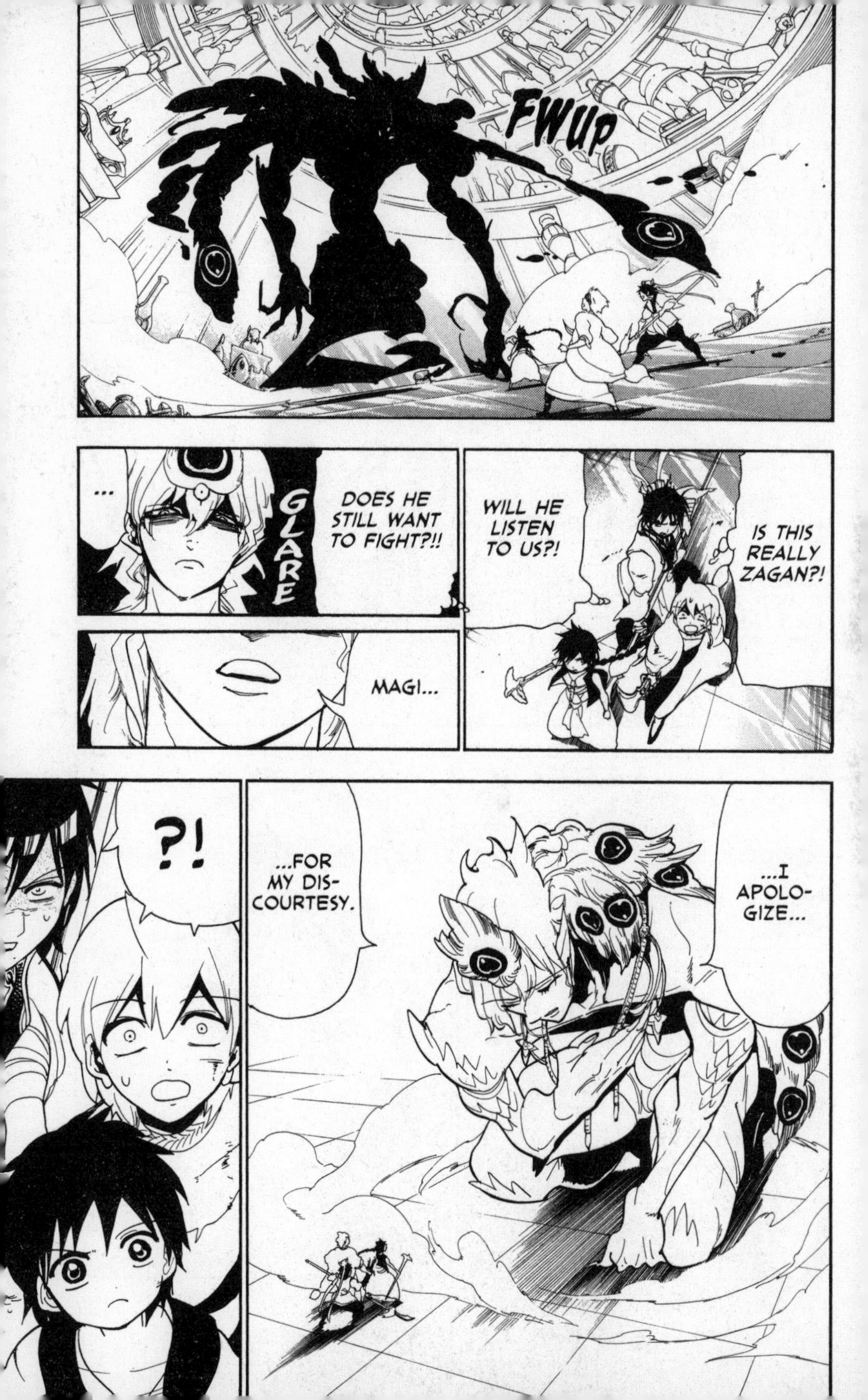
FWUP
IS THIS REALLY ZAGAN?!
WILL HE LISTEN TO US?!
...
DOES HE STILL WANT TO FIGHT?!!
GLARE
...
MAGI...
...I APOLOGIZE...
...FOR MY DIS-COURTESY.
?!

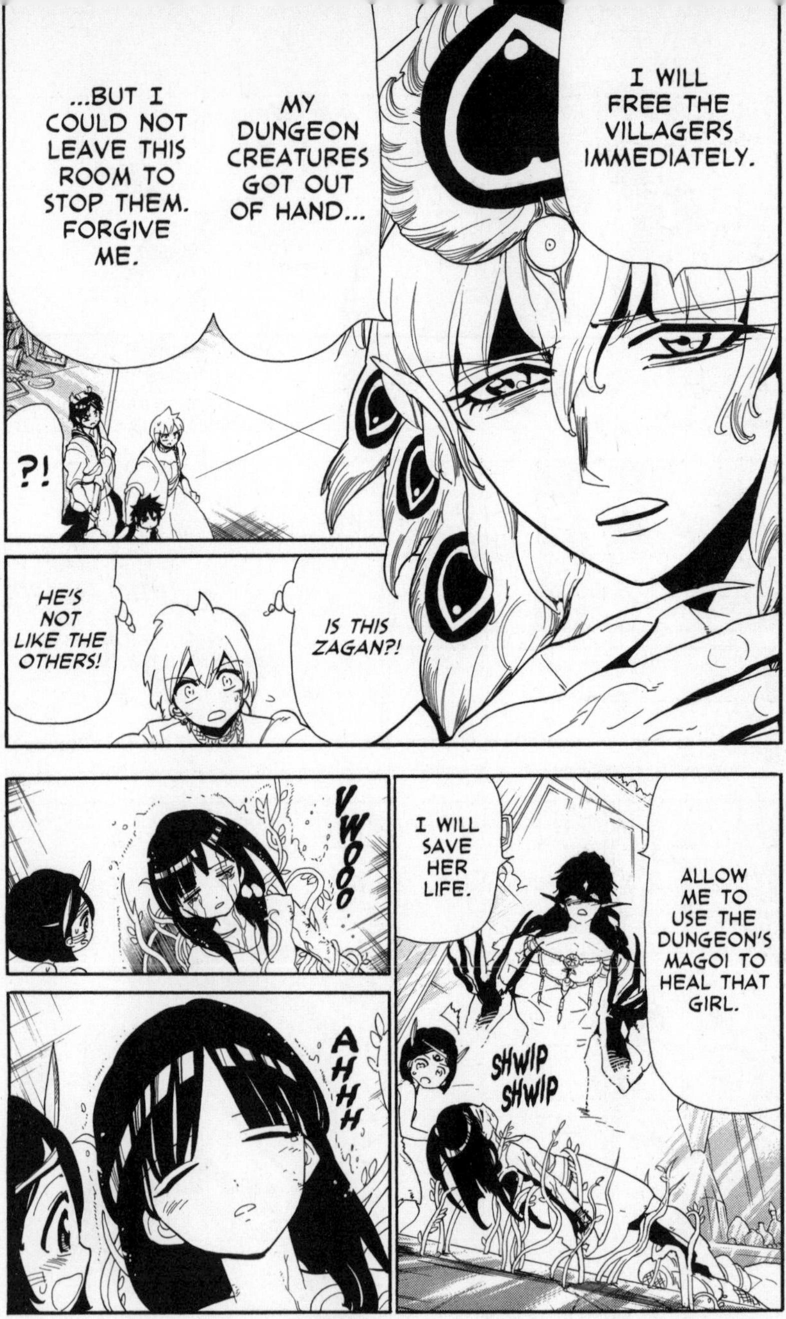
I WILL FREE THE VILLAGERS IMMEDIATELY.
MY DUNGEON CREATURES GOT OUT OF HAND...
...BUT I COULD NOT LEAVE THIS ROOM TO STOP THEM. FORGIVE ME.
?!
IS THIS ZAGAN?!
HE'S NOT LIKE THE OTHERS!
ALLOW ME TO USE THE DUNGEON'S MAGOI TO HEAL THAT GIRL.
I WILL SAVE HER LIFE.
SHWIP SHWIP
VWOOOO
AHHH

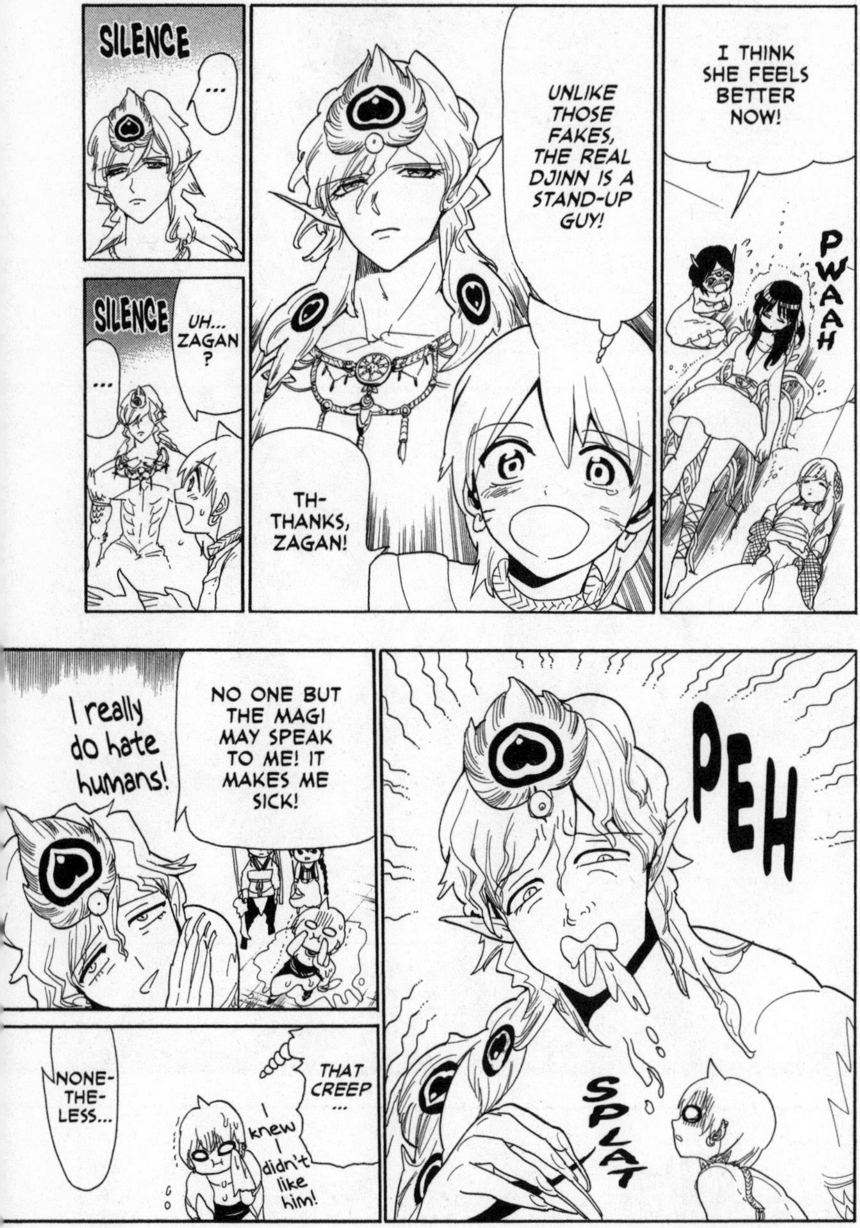
I THINK SHE FEELS BETTER NOW!
PWAAH
UNLIKE THOSE FAKES, THE REAL DJINN IS A STAND-UP GUY!
TH- THANKS, ZAGAN!
SILENCE
...
SILENCE
UH... ZAGAN?
...
PEH
SPLAT
NO ONE BUT THE MAGI MAY SPEAK TO ME! IT MAKES ME SICK!
I really do hate humans!
THAT CREEP...
I knew I didn't like him!
NONE-THE-LESS...

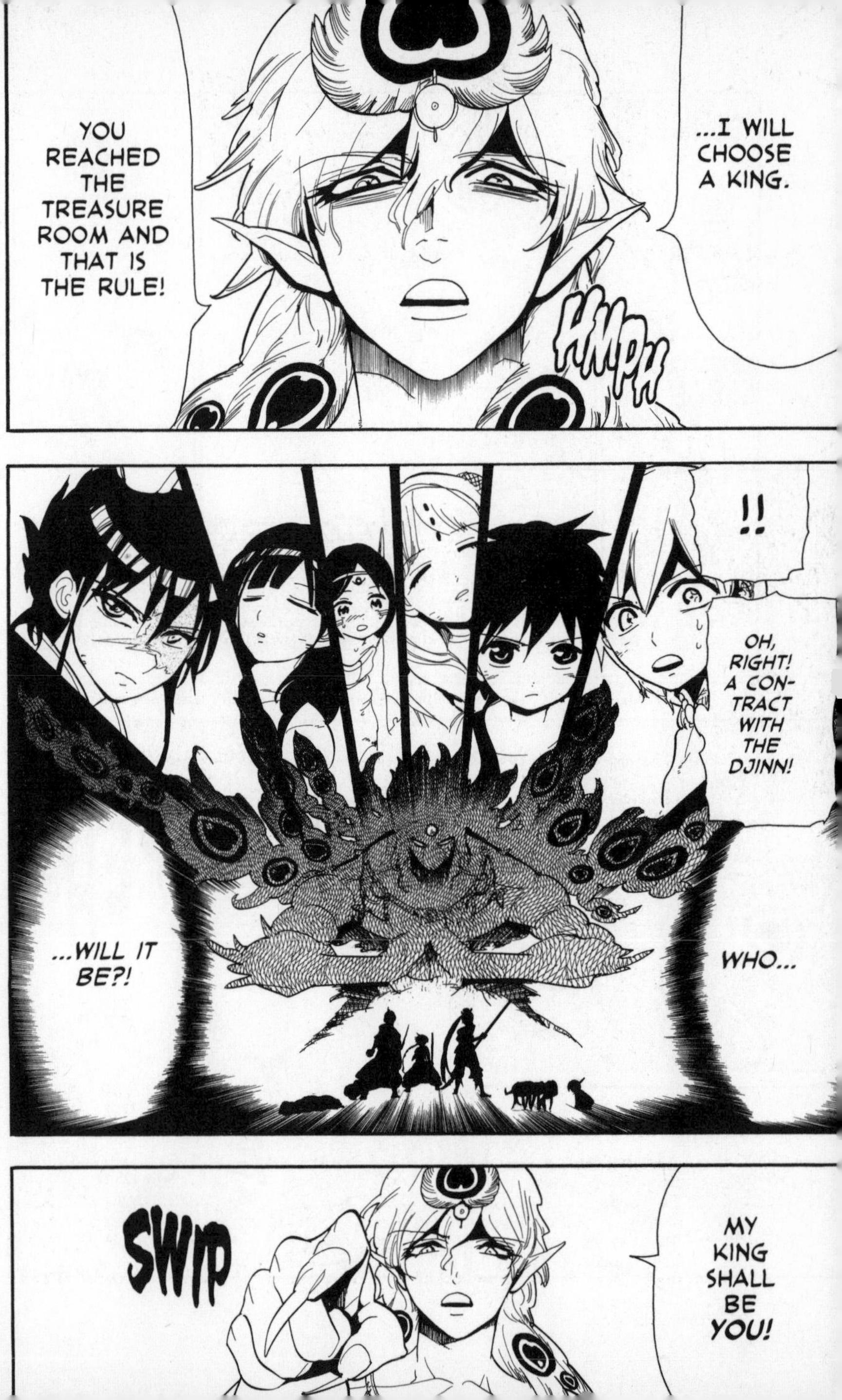
...I WILL CHOOSE A KING.
HMPH
YOU REACHED THE TREASURE ROOM AND THAT IS THE RULE!
!!
OH, RIGHT! A CONTRACT WITH THE DJINN!
WHO...
...WILL IT BE?!
MY KING SHALL BE YOU!
SWIP

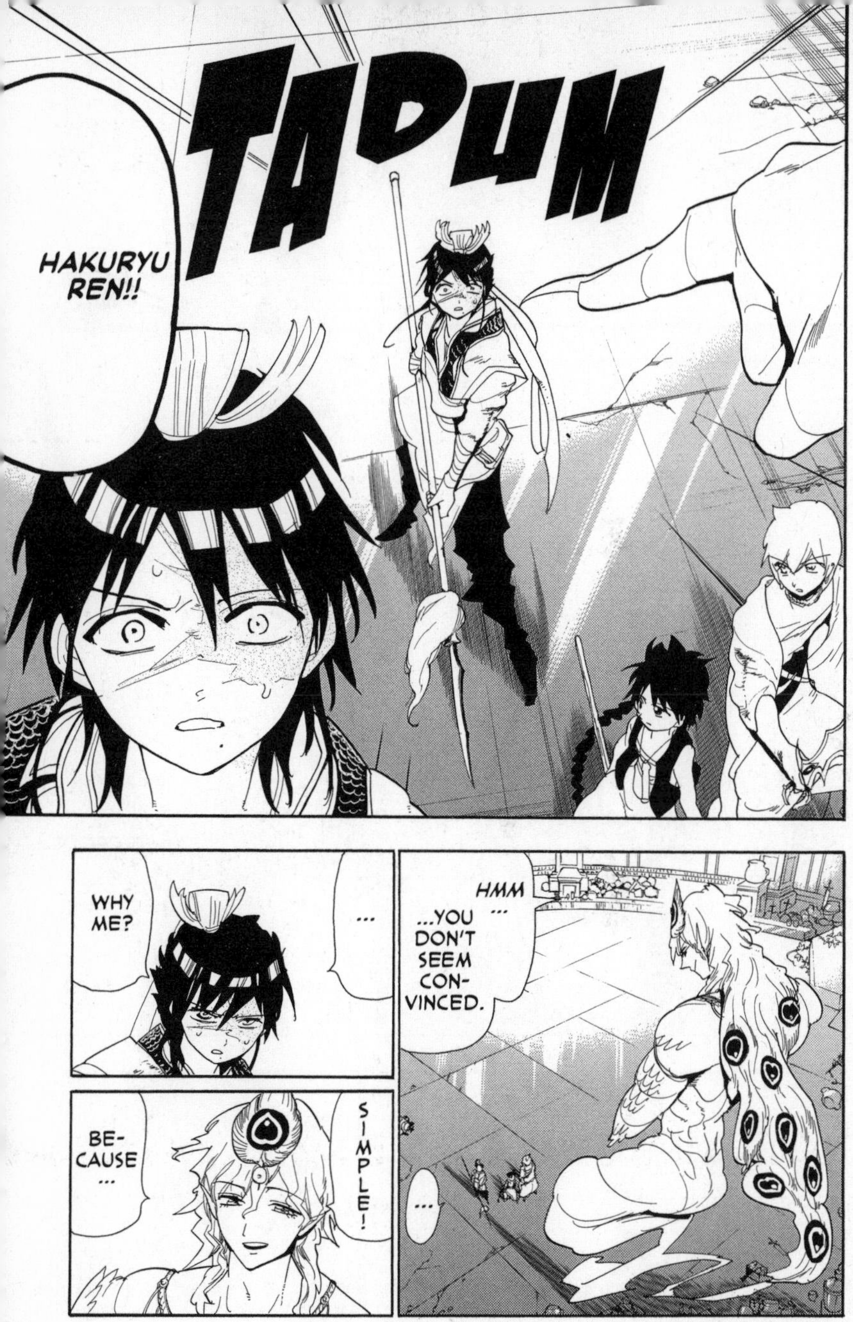
TADUM
HAKURYU REN!!
HMM ...
...YOU DON'T SEEM CON-VINCED.
...
...
WHY ME?
SIMPLE!
BE-CAUSE ...

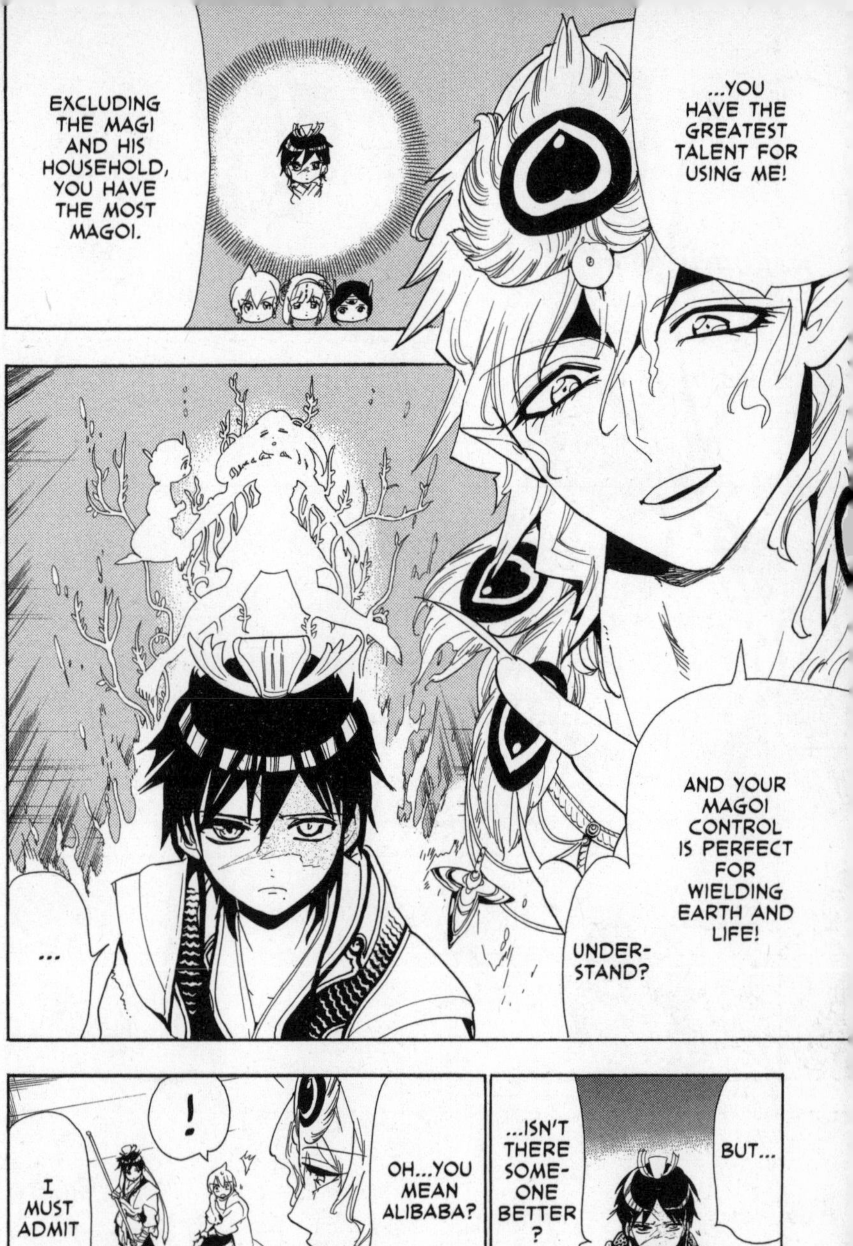
...YOU HAVE THE GREATEST TALENT FOR USING ME!
EXCLUDING THE MAGI AND HIS HOUSEHOLD, YOU HAVE THE MOST MAGOI.
AND YOUR MAGOI CONTROL IS PERFECT FOR WIELDING EARTH AND LIFE!
UNDER-STAND?
...
BUT...
...ISN'T THERE SOME-ONE BETTER?
OH...YOU MEAN ALIBABA?
!
I MUST ADMIT...

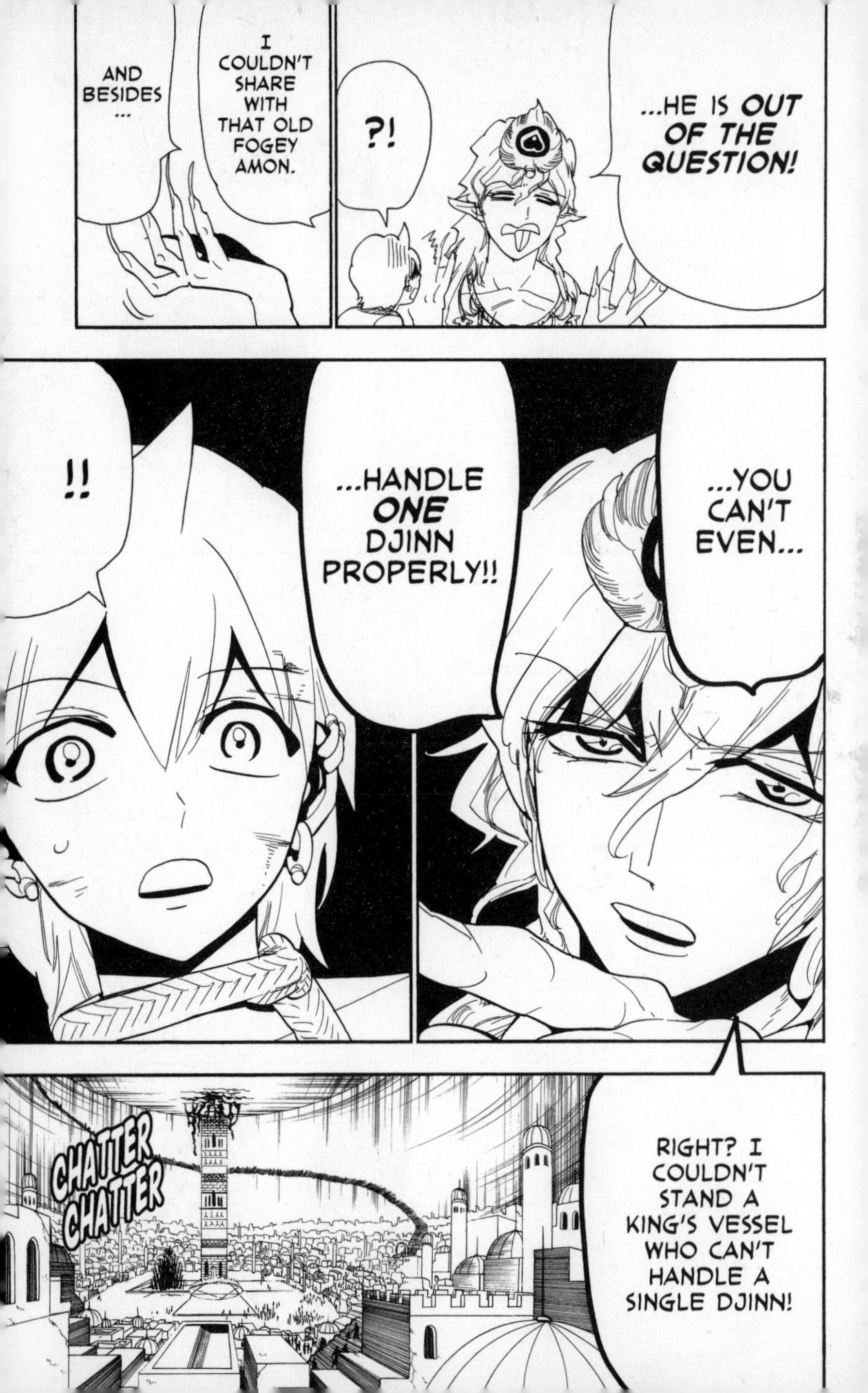
...HE IS OUT OF THE QUESTION!
?!
I COULDN'T SHARE WITH THAT OLD FOGEY AMON.
AND BESIDES...
...YOU CAN'T EVEN...
...HANDLE ONE DJINN PROPERLY!!
!!
RIGHT? I COULDN'T STAND A KING'S VESSEL WHO CAN'T HANDLE A SINGLE DJINN!
CHATTER CHATTER

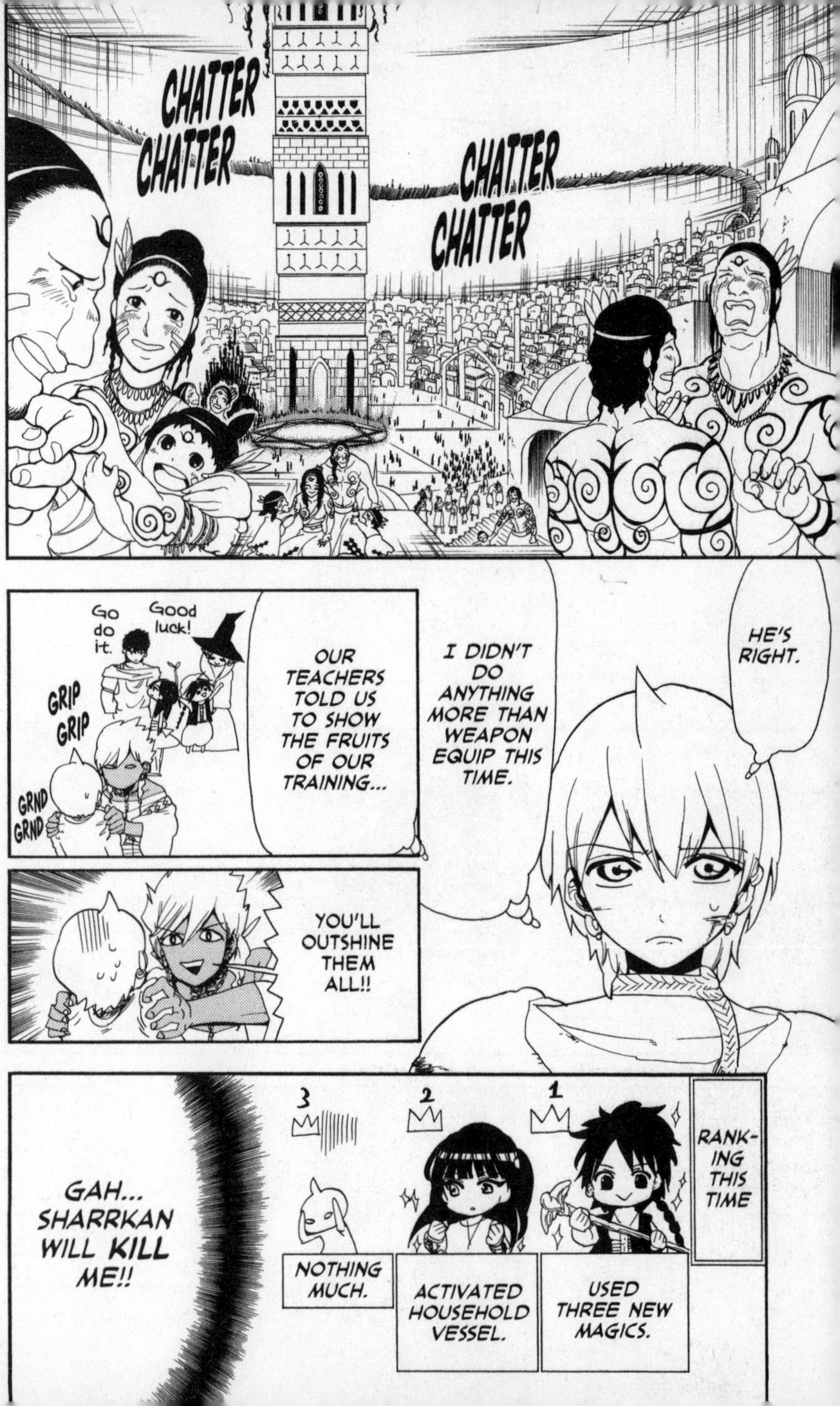
CHATTER CHATTER
CHATTER CHATTER
HE'S RIGHT.
I DIDN'T DO ANYTHING MORE THAN WEAPON EQUIP THIS TIME.
OUR TEACHERS TOLD US TO SHOW THE FRUITS OF OUR TRAINING...
Good luck!
Go do it.
GRIP GRIP
GRND GRND
YOU'LL OUTSHINE THEM ALL!!
RANKING THIS TIME
1
USED THREE NEW MAGICS.
2
ACTIVATED HOUSEHOLD VESSEL.
3
NOTHING MUCH.
GAH... SHARRKAN WILL KILL ME!!

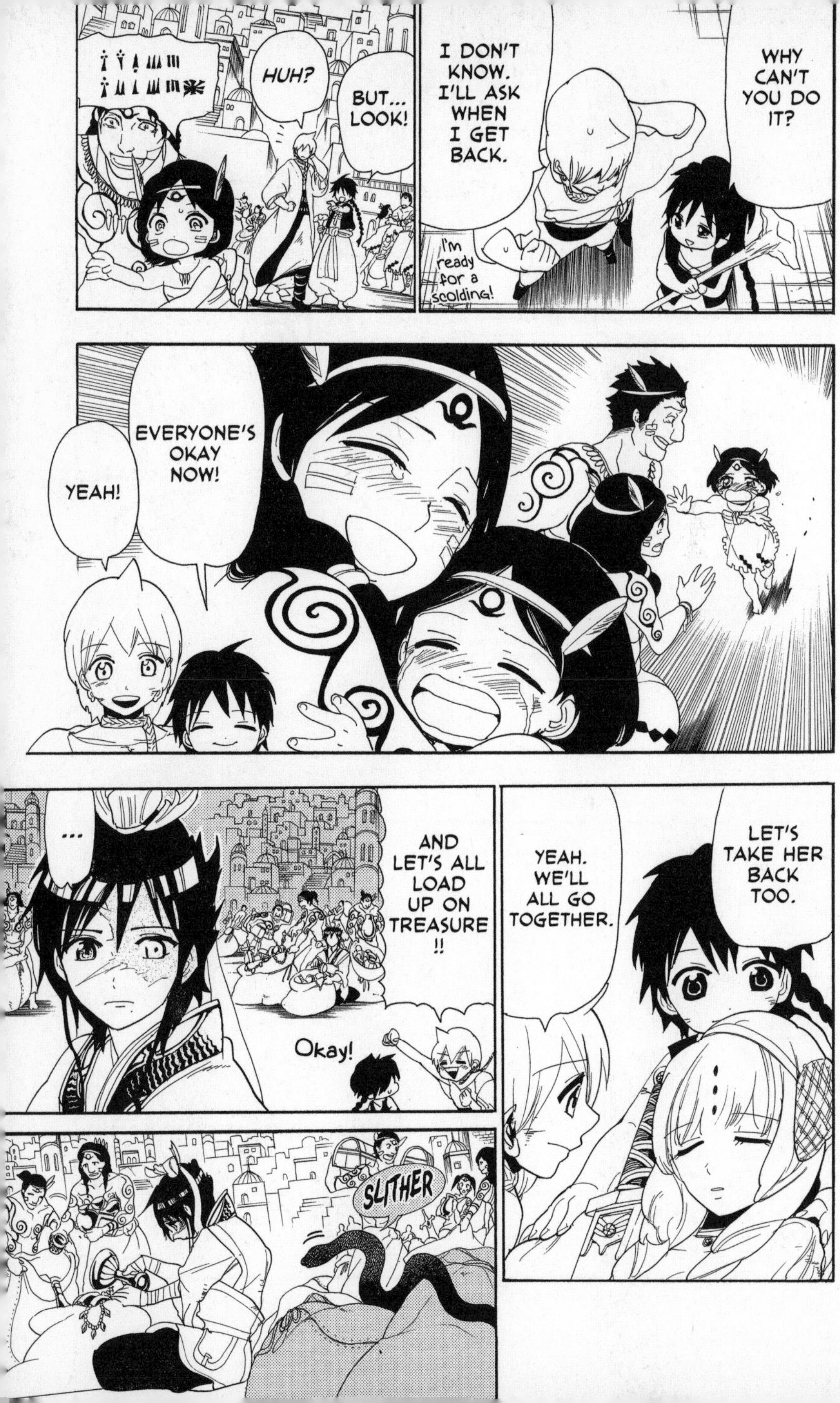
WHY CAN'T YOU DO IT?
I DON'T KNOW. I'LL ASK WHEN I GET BACK.
I'm ready for a scolding!
BUT... LOOK!
HUH?
EVERYONE'S OKAY NOW!
YEAH!
LET'S TAKE HER BACK TOO.
YEAH. WE'LL ALL GO TOGETHER.
AND LET'S ALL LOAD UP ON TREASURE!!
Okay!
...
SLITHER

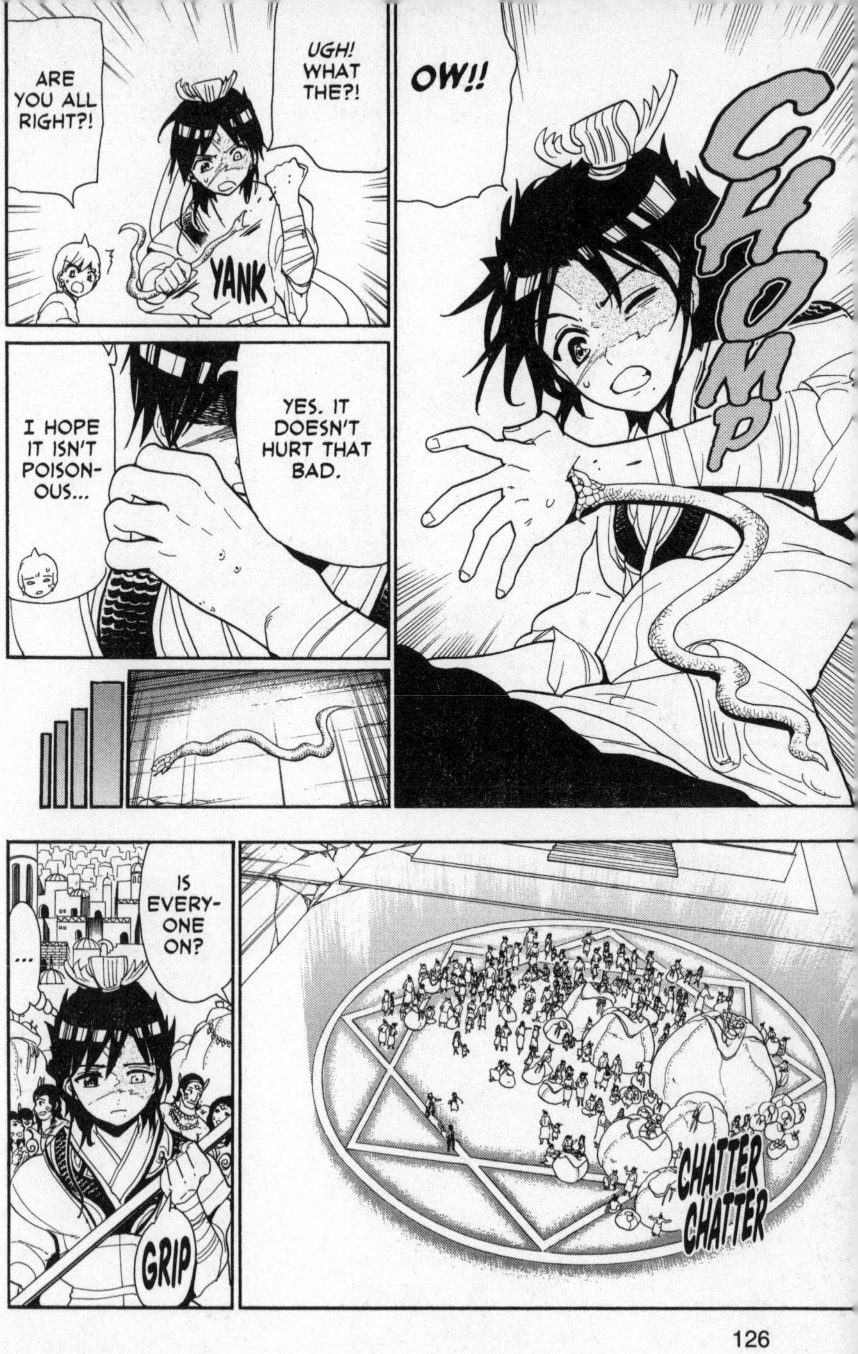
OW!!
CHOMP
UGH! WHAT THE?!
ARE YOU ALL RIGHT?!
YANK
YES. IT DOESN'T HURT THAT BAD.
I HOPE IT ISN'T POISON-OUS...
CHATTER CHATTER
IS EVERY-ONE ON?
...
GRIP

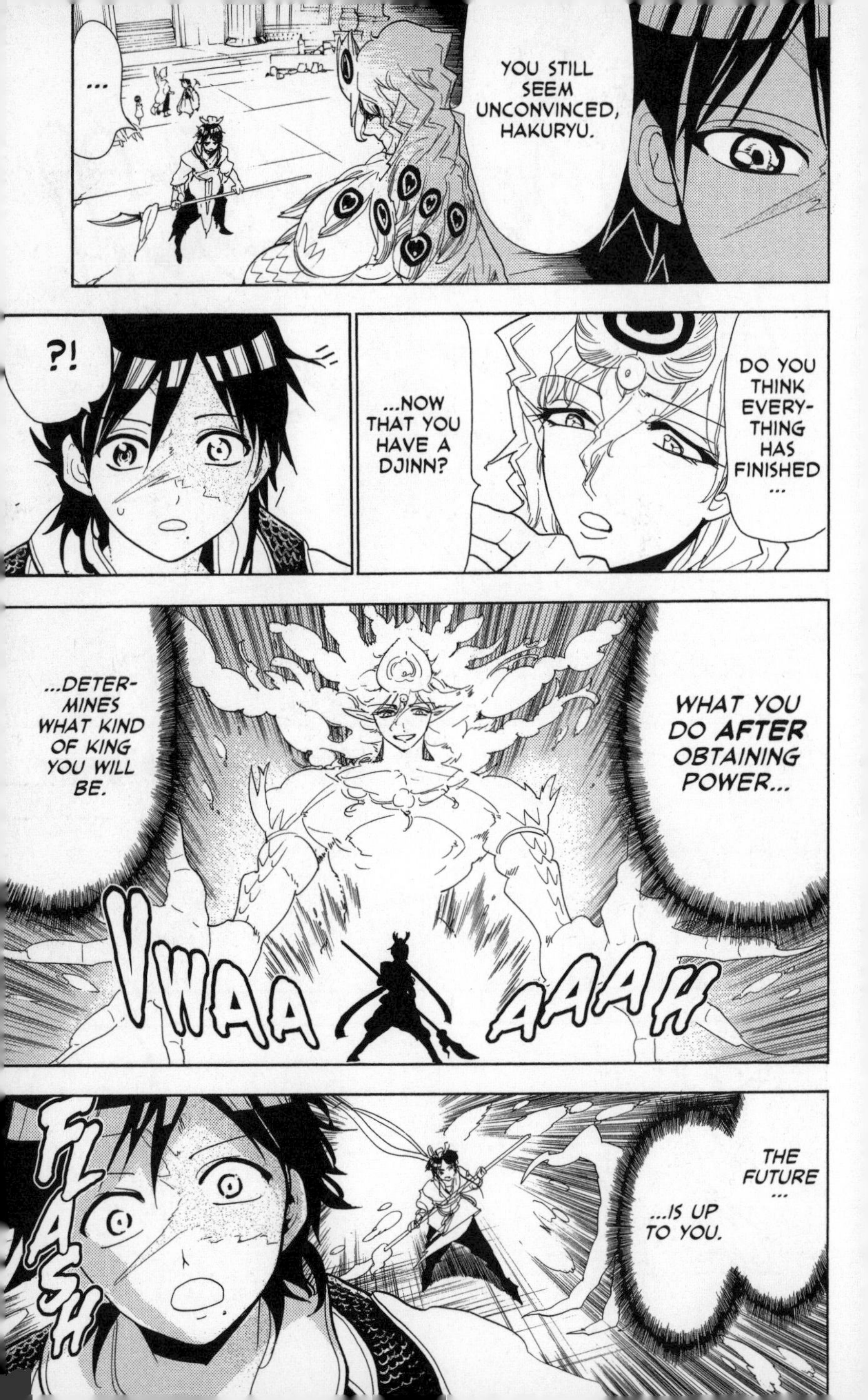
YOU STILL SEEM UNCONVINCED, HAKURYU.
...
DO YOU THINK EVERY-THING HAS FINISHED...
...NOW THAT YOU HAVE A DJINN?
?!
WHAT YOU DO AFTER OBTAINING POWER...
...DETER-MINES WHAT KIND OF KING YOU WILL BE.
VWAA AAAH
THE FUTURE...
...IS UP TO YOU.
FLASH

VREEEEEN

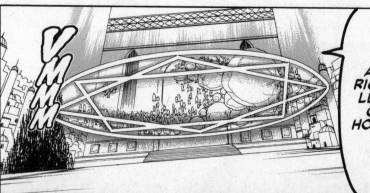

ALL RIGHT! LET'S GO HOME!!

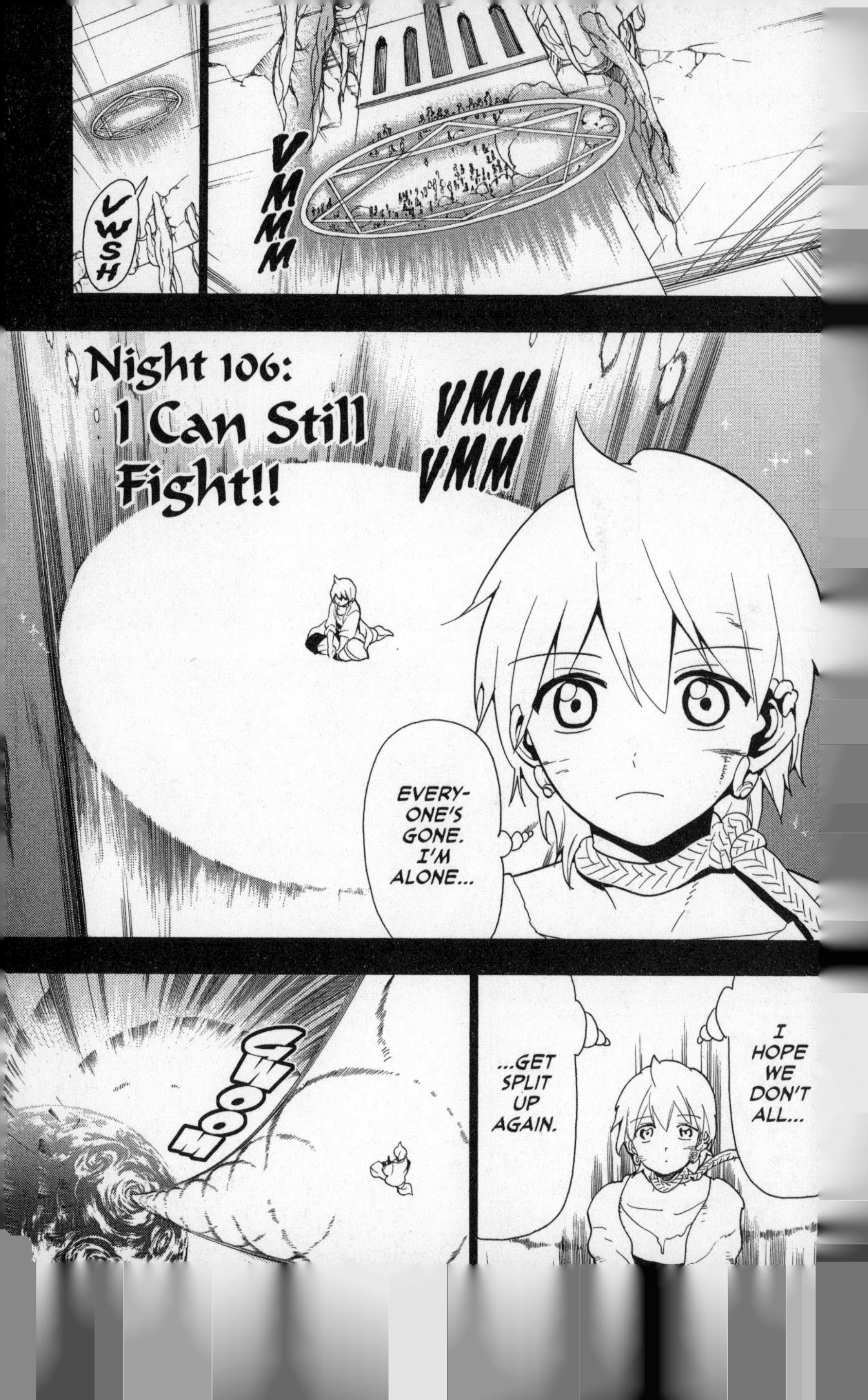
VMMM
VWSH
Night 106: I Can Still Fight!!
VMM VMM
EVERY-ONE'S GONE. I'M ALONE...
I HOPE WE DON'T ALL...
...GET SPLIT UP AGAIN.
GWOOM

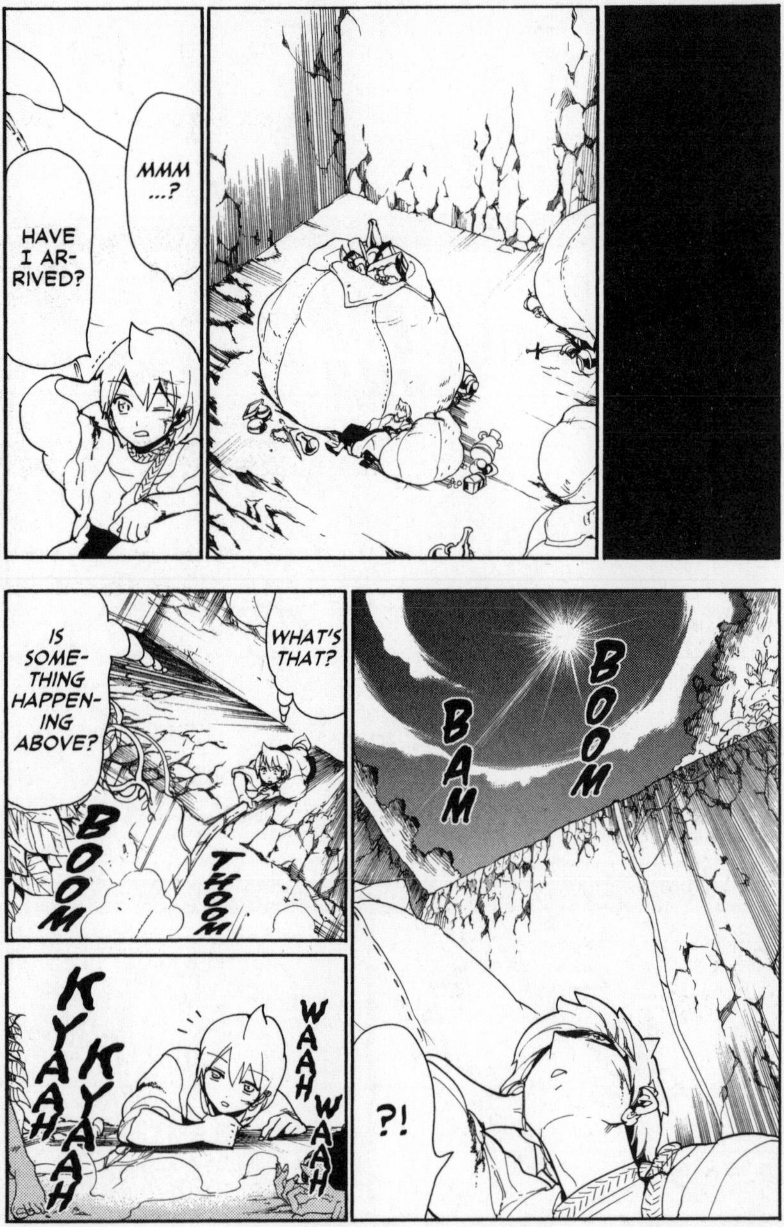
MMM ...?
HAVE I AR- RIVED?
BOOM
BAM
?!
WHAT'S THAT?
IS SOME- THING HAPPEN- ING ABOVE?
THOOM
BOOM
WAAH
WAAH
KYAAH
KYAAH

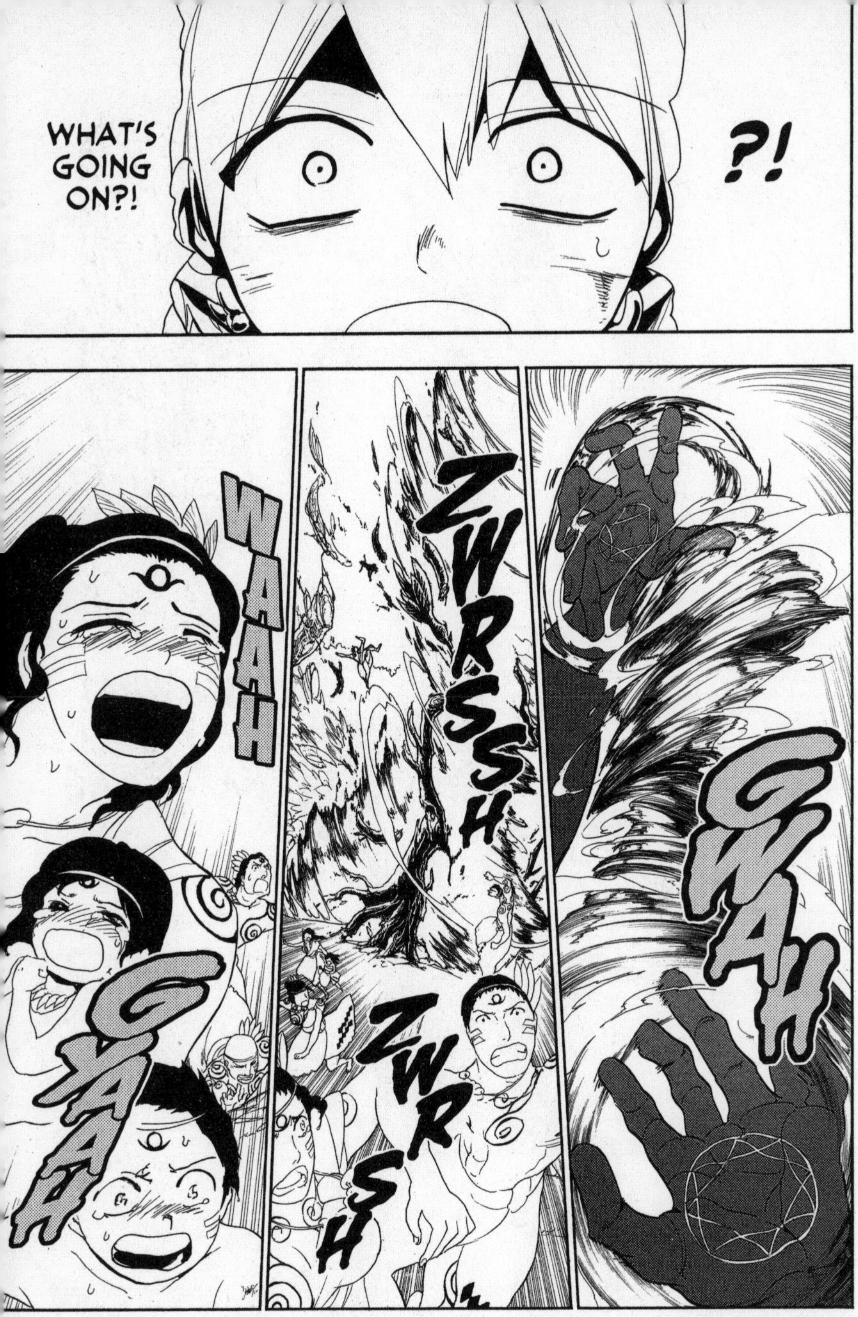
?!
WHAT'S GOING ON?!
GWAH
ZWRSSH
ZWRSH
WAAH
GYAAAH

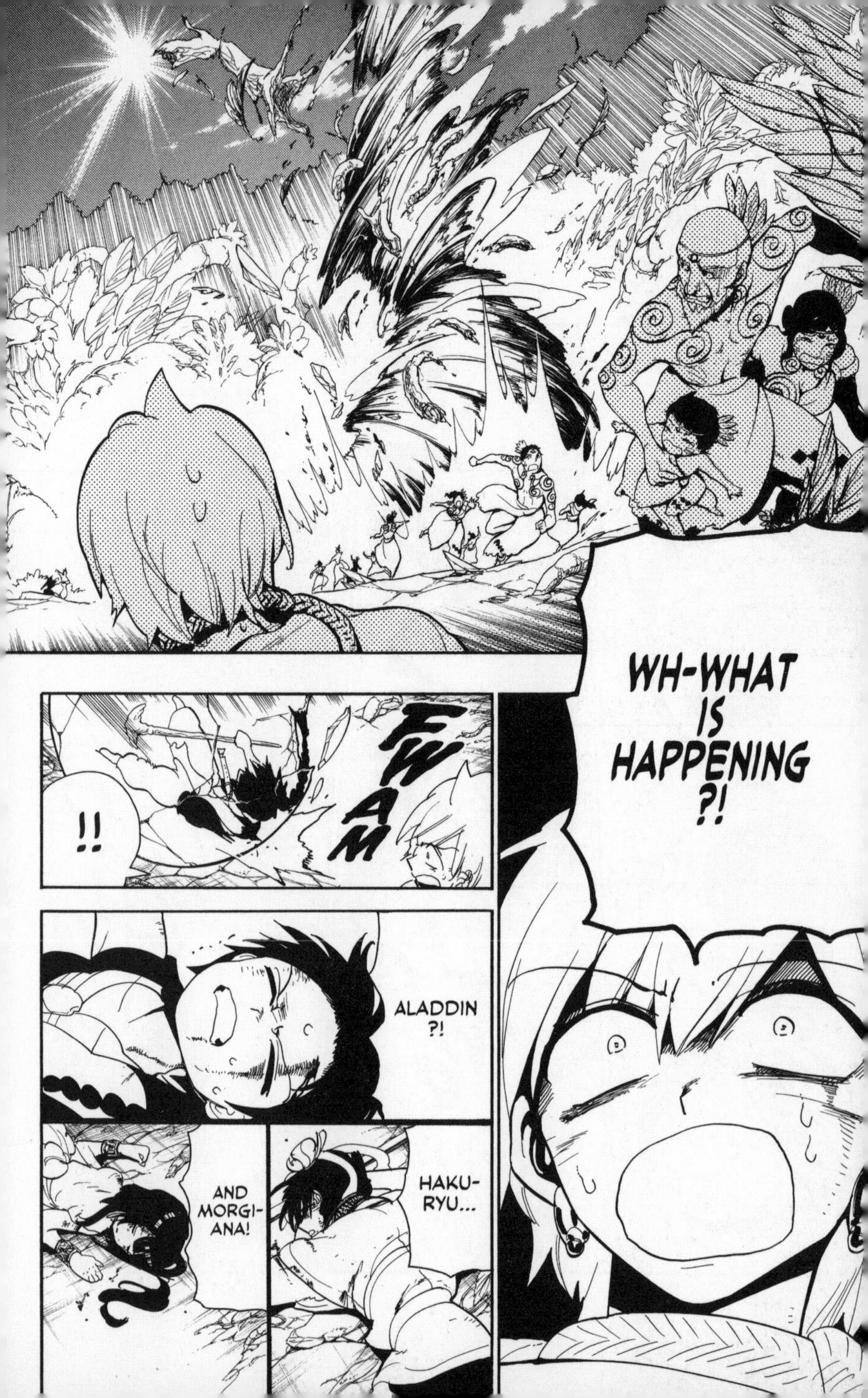
WH-WHAT IS HAPPENING?!
FWAM
!!
ALADDIN?!
HAKU-RYU...
AND MORGI-ANA!

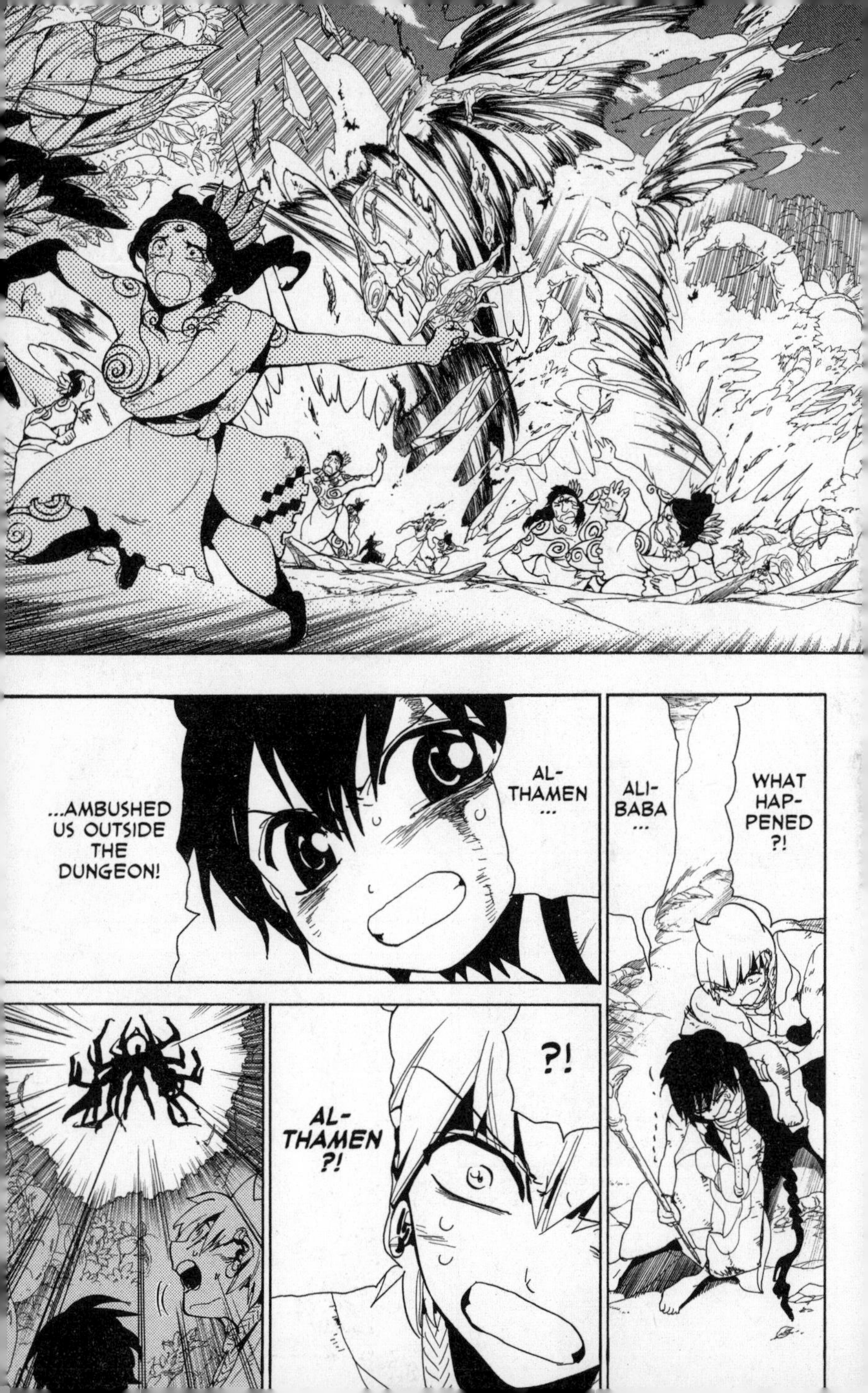
WHAT HAPPENED?!
ALIBABA...
ALTHAMEN...
...AMBUSHED US OUTSIDE THE DUNGEON!
?!
ALTHAMEN?!

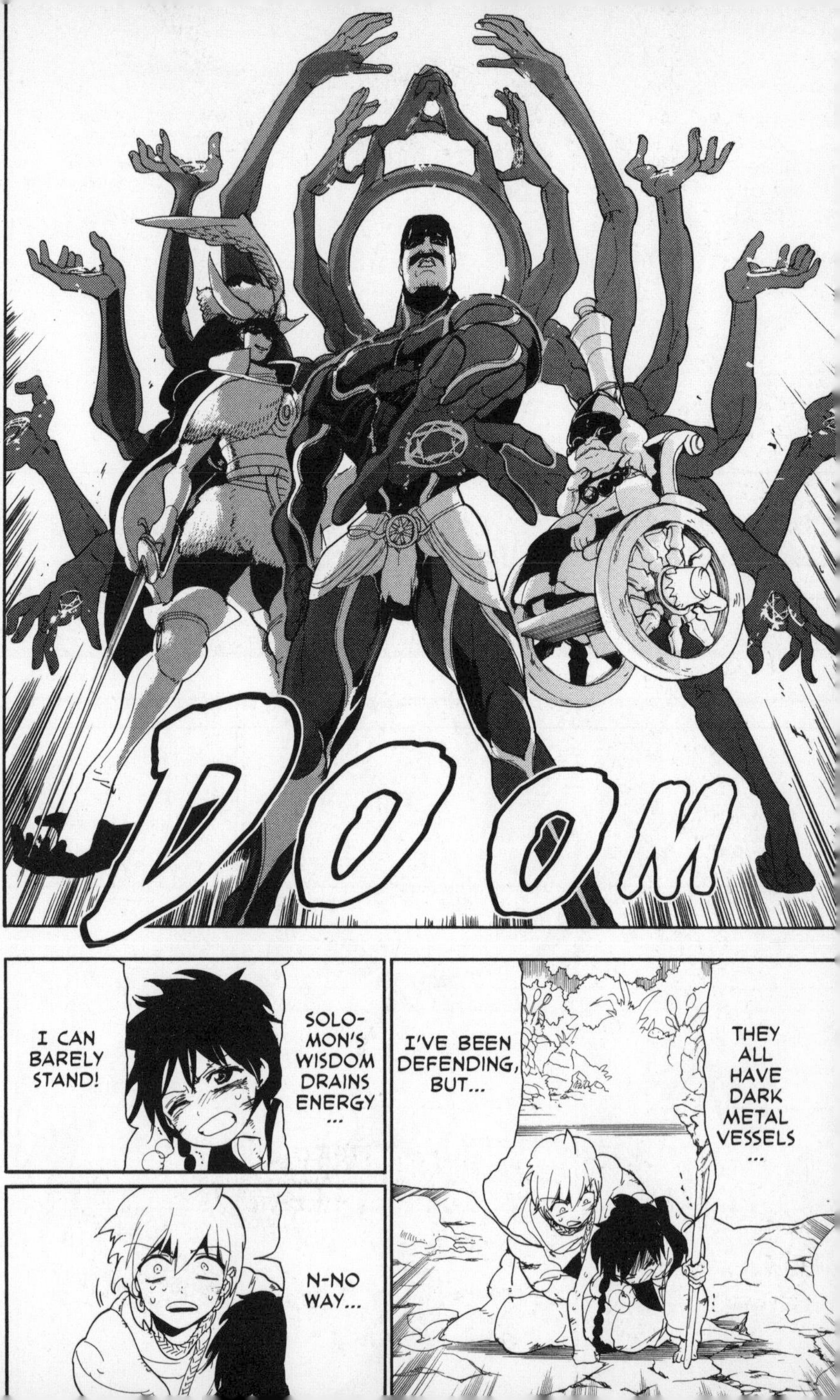
DOOM
THEY ALL HAVE DARK METAL VESSELS...
I'VE BEEN DEFENDING, BUT...
SOLO-MON'S WISDOM DRAINS ENERGY...
I CAN BARELY STAND!
N-NO WAY...

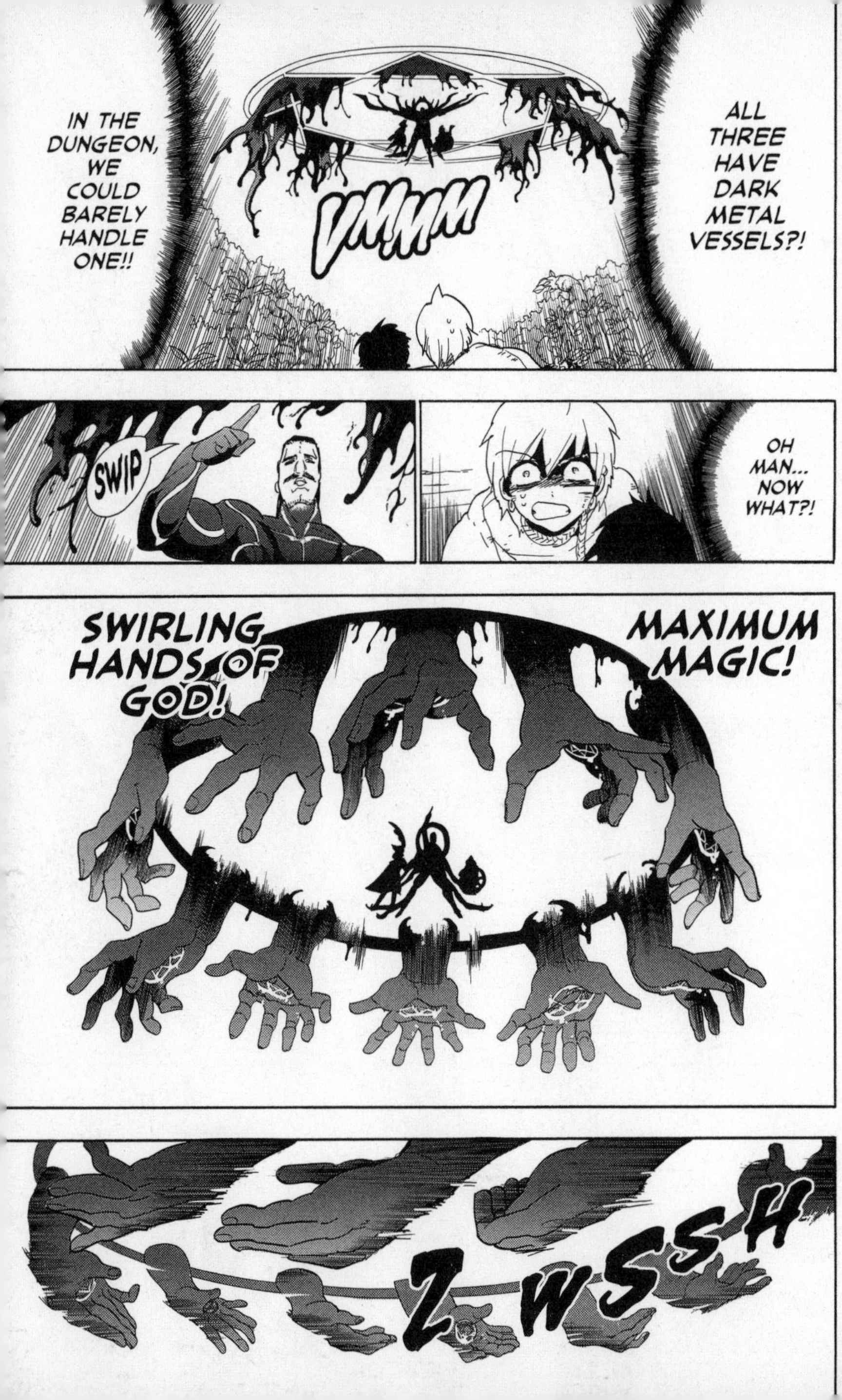
ALL THREE HAVE DARK METAL VESSELS?!
IN THE DUNGEON, WE COULD BARELY HANDLE ONE!!
VMMM
OH MAN... NOW WHAT?!
SWIP
MAXIMUM MAGIC!
SWIRLING HANDS OF GOD!
ZWSSH

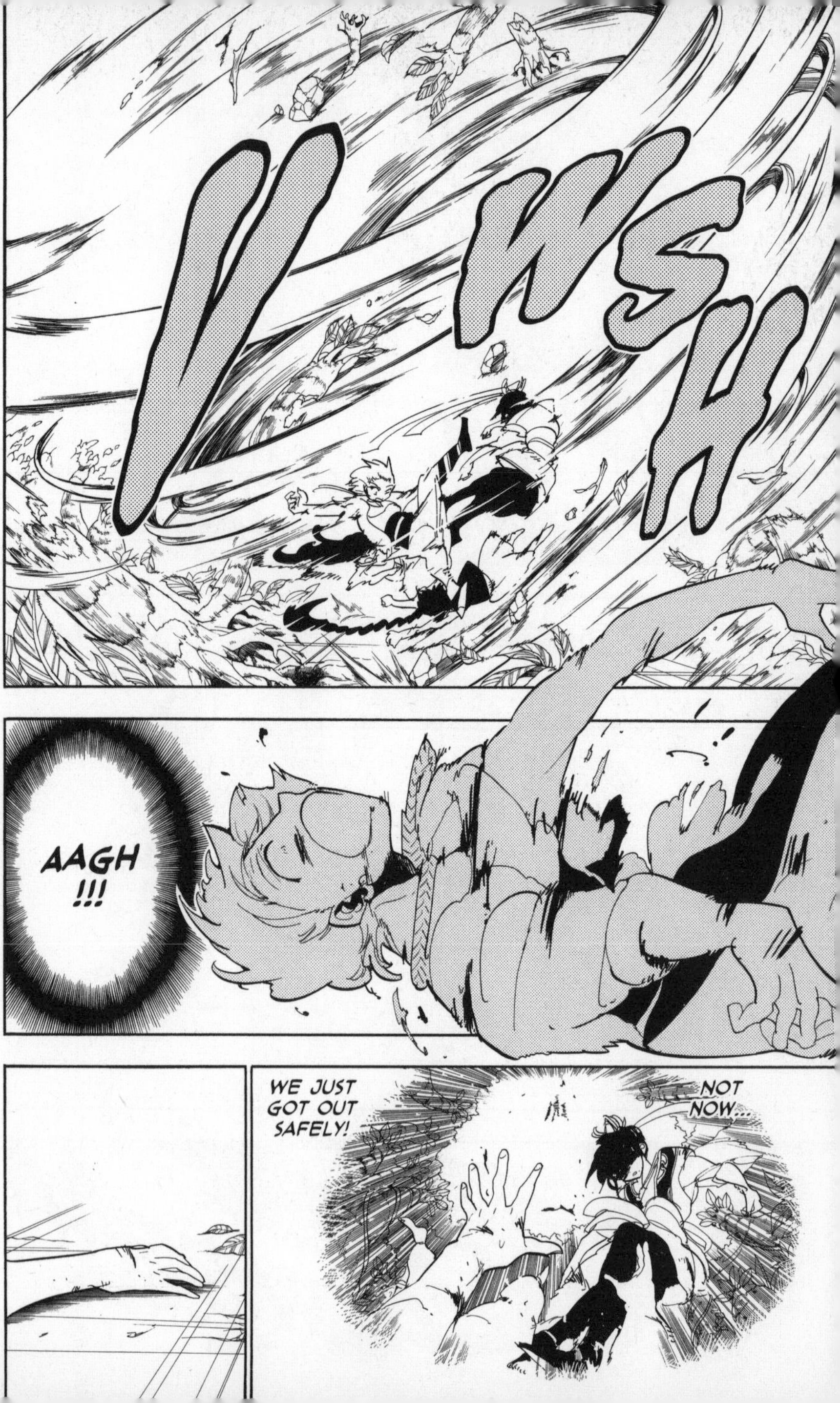
AAGH !!!
NOT NOW...
WE JUST GOT OUT SAFELY!

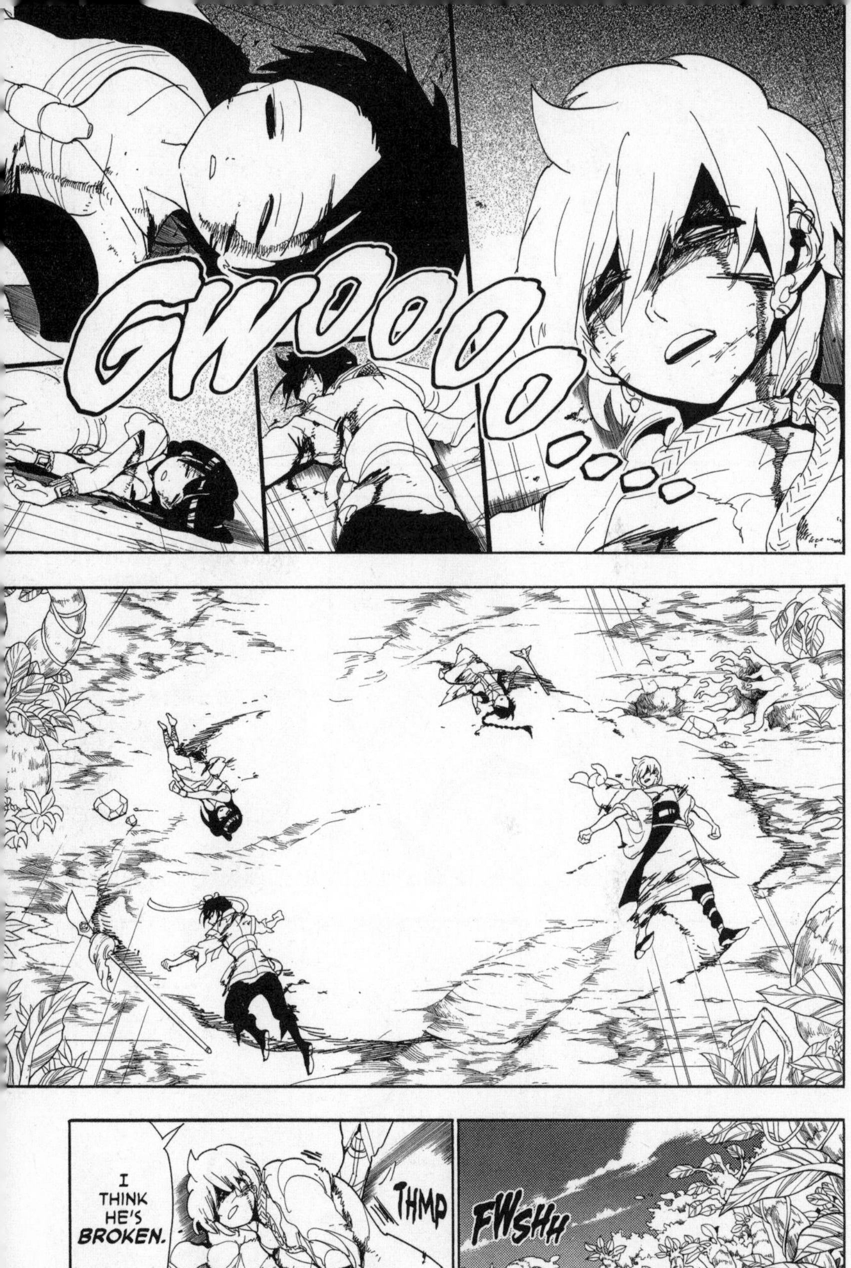
GWOOOOO.....
FWSHH
THMP
I THINK HE'S BROKEN.

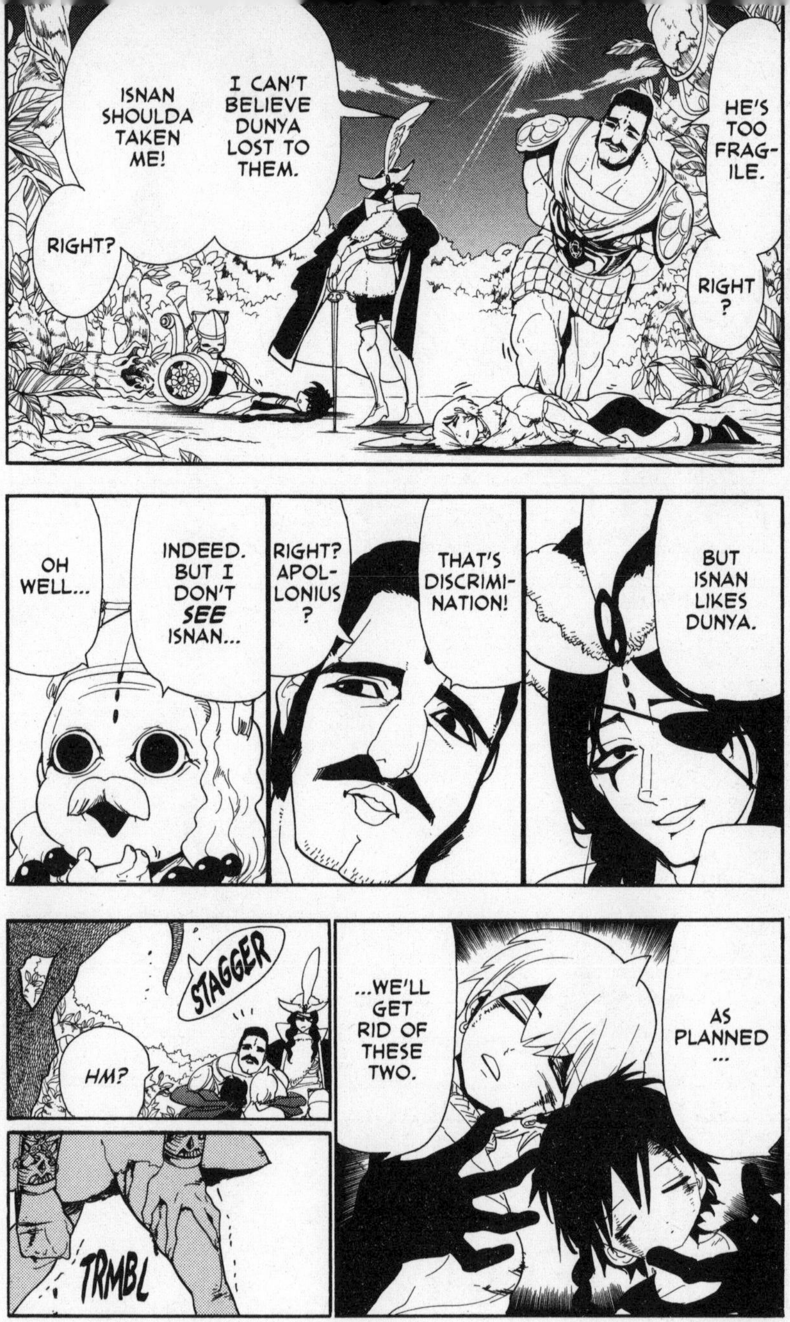
HE'S TOO FRAG-ILE.
RIGHT?
I CAN'T BELIEVE DUNYA LOST TO THEM.
ISNAN SHOULDA TAKEN ME!
RIGHT?
BUT ISNAN LIKES DUNYA.
THAT'S DISCRIMI-NATION!
RIGHT? APOL-LONIUS?
INDEED. BUT I DON'T *SEE* ISNAN...
OH WELL...
AS PLANNED...
...WE'LL GET RID OF THESE TWO.
STAGGER
HM?
TRMBL

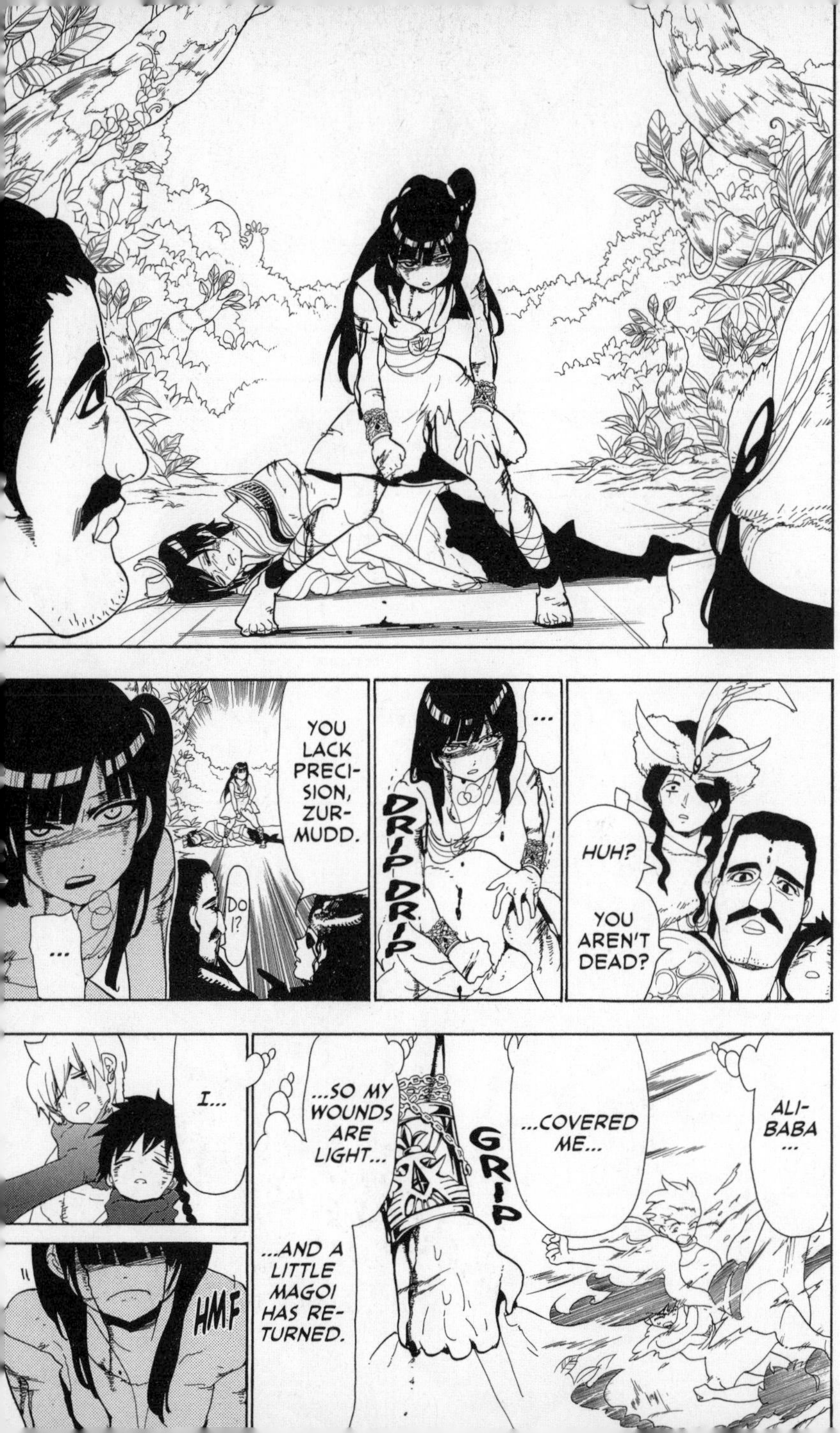
HUH?
YOU AREN'T DEAD?
...
DRIP DRIP DRIP
YOU LACK PRECISION, ZURMUDD.
DO I?
...
ALIBABA...
...COVERED ME...
GRIP
...SO MY WOUNDS ARE LIGHT...
...AND A LITTLE MAGOI HAS RETURNED.
I...
HMF

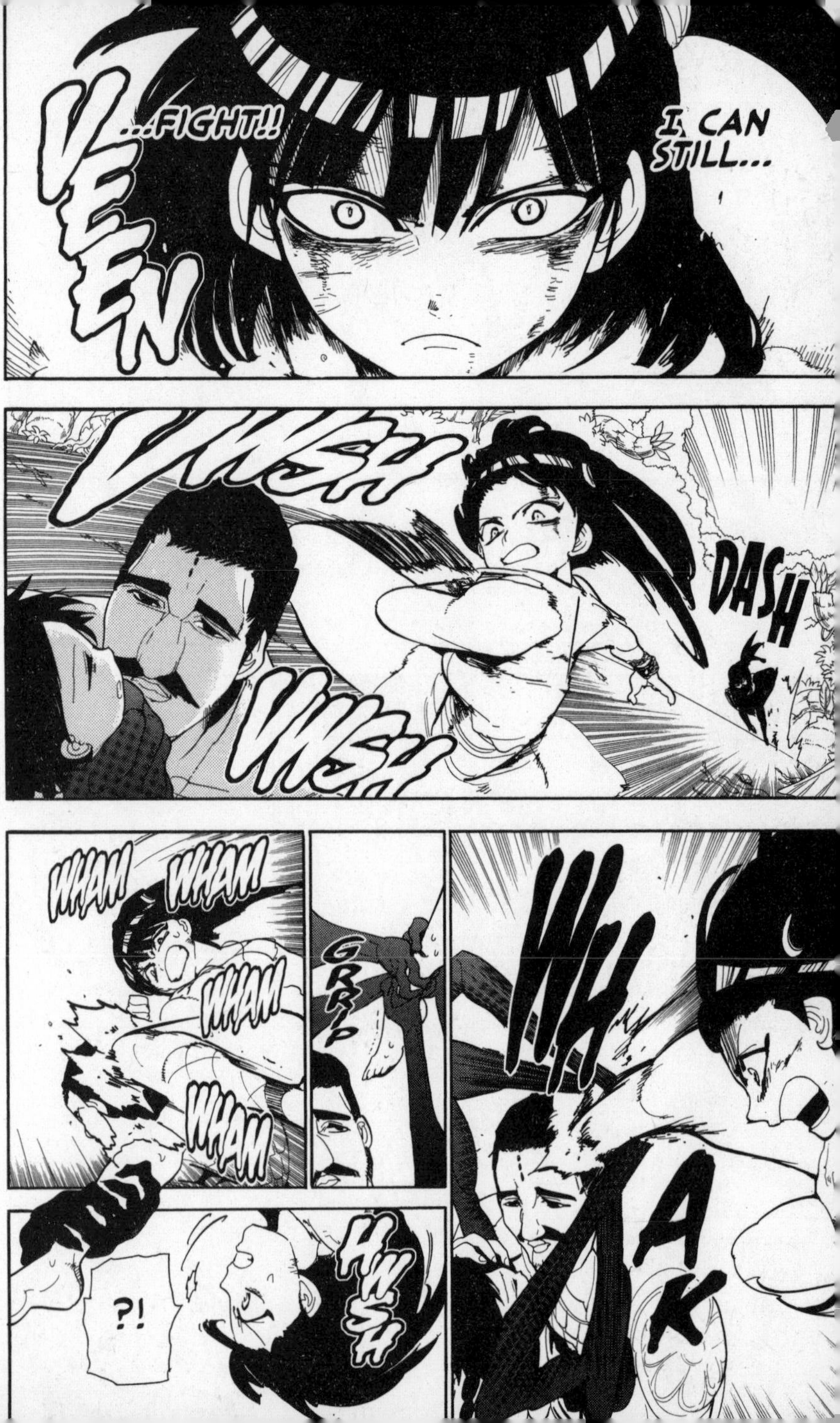

I CAN STILL...
...FIGHT!!
VEEN
DASH
VWSH
VWSH
WHAK
GRRIP
WHAM
WHAM
WHAM
WHAM
HWSH
?!

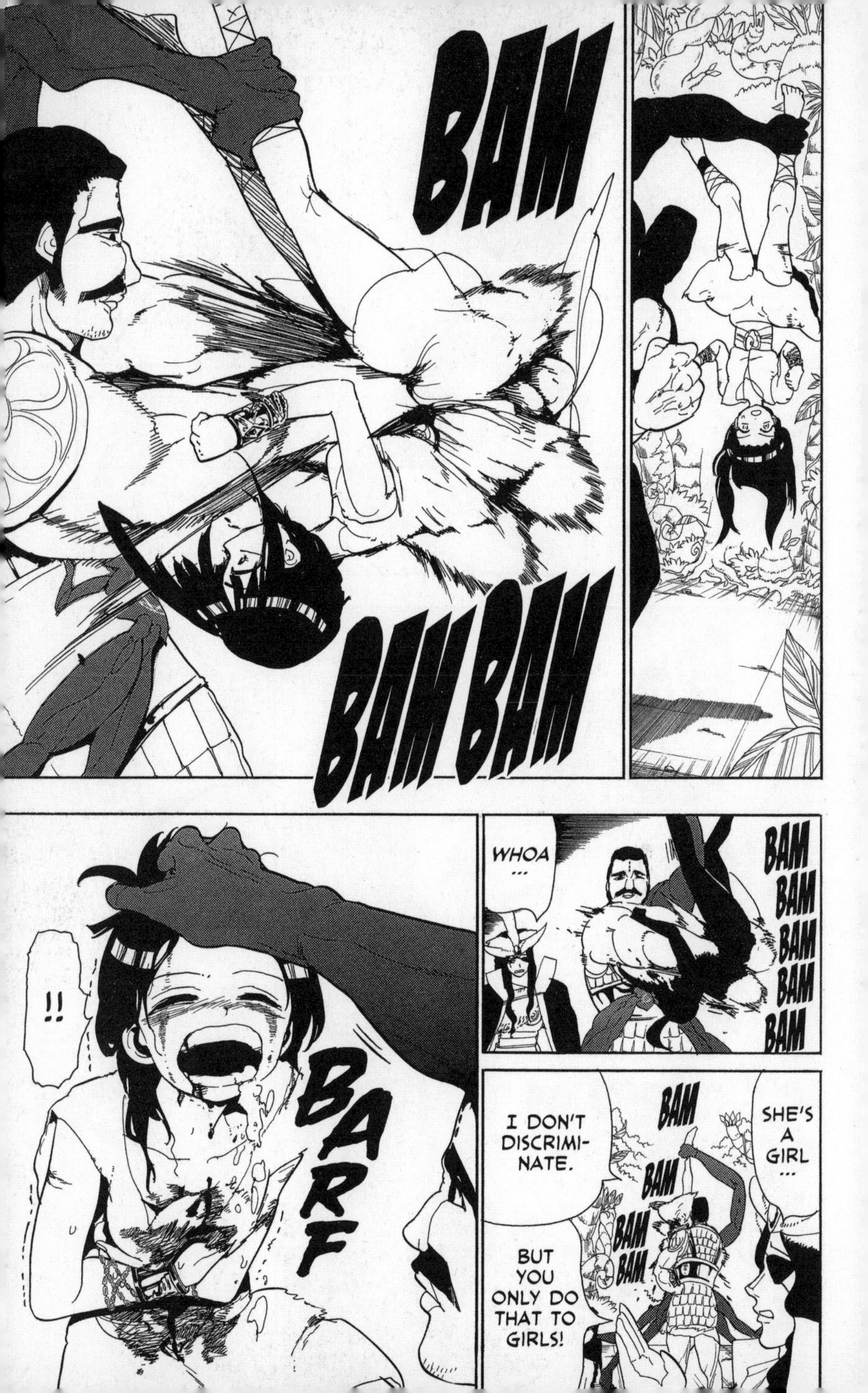
BAM
BAM BAM
WHOA...
BAM BAM BAM BAM BAM BAM
SHE'S A GIRL...
BAM
I DON'T DISCRIMINATE.
BAM BAM BAM
BUT YOU ONLY DO THAT TO GIRLS!
!!
BARF

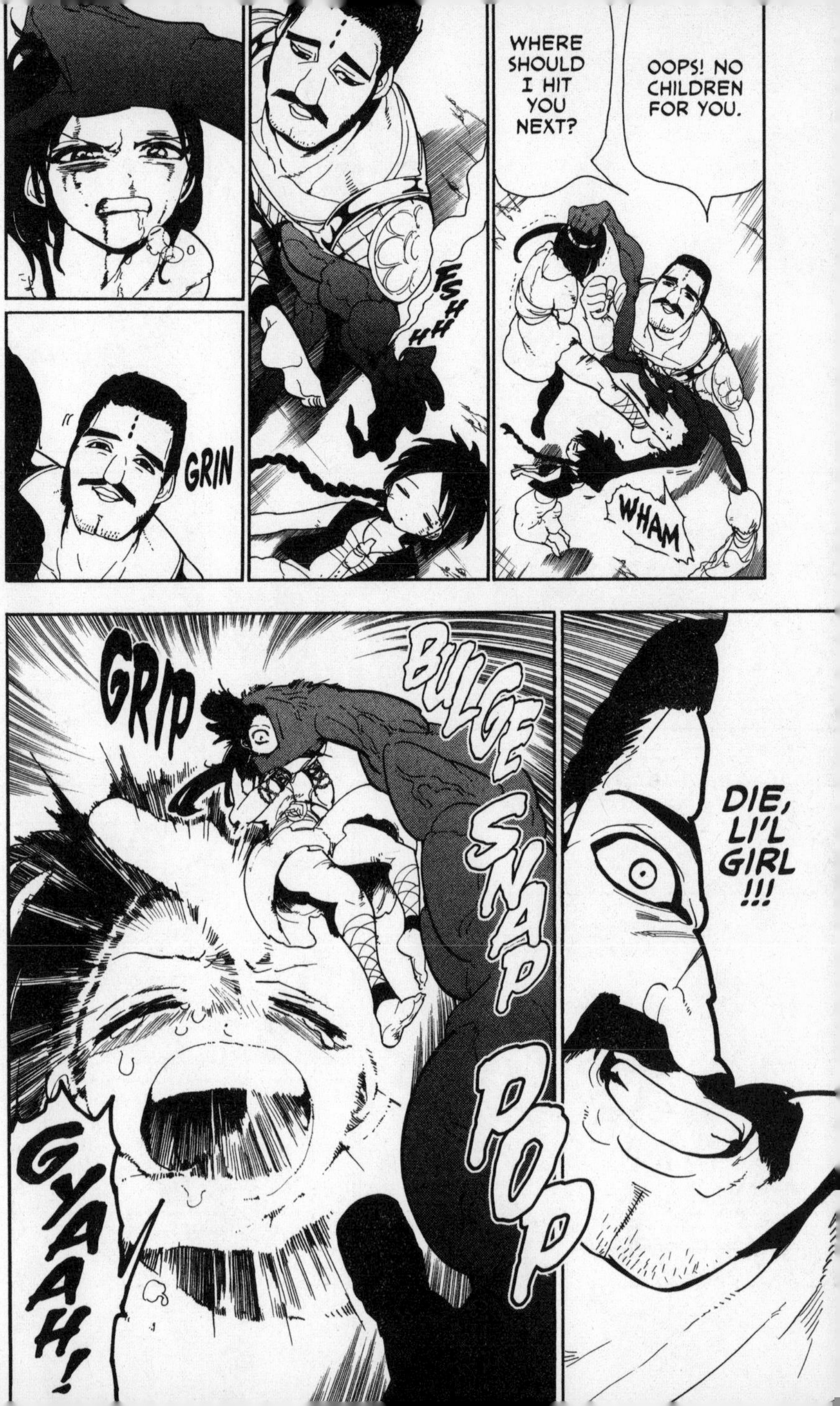
OOPS! NO CHILDREN FOR YOU.
WHERE SHOULD I HIT YOU NEXT?
WHAM
FSHHH
GRIN
DIE, LI'L GIRL!!!
BULGE
GRIP
SNAP
POP
GYAAH!

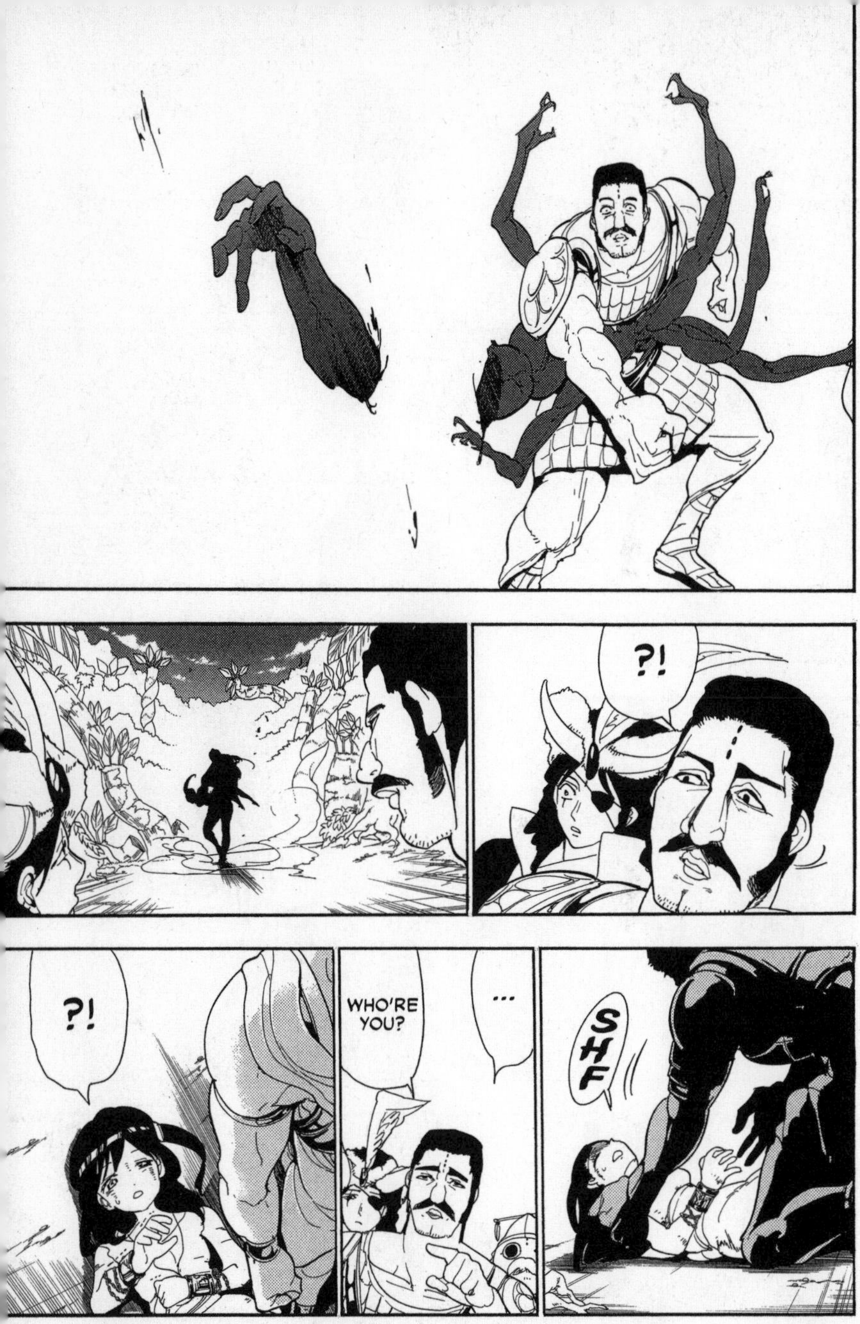
?!
SHF
...
WHO'RE YOU?
?!

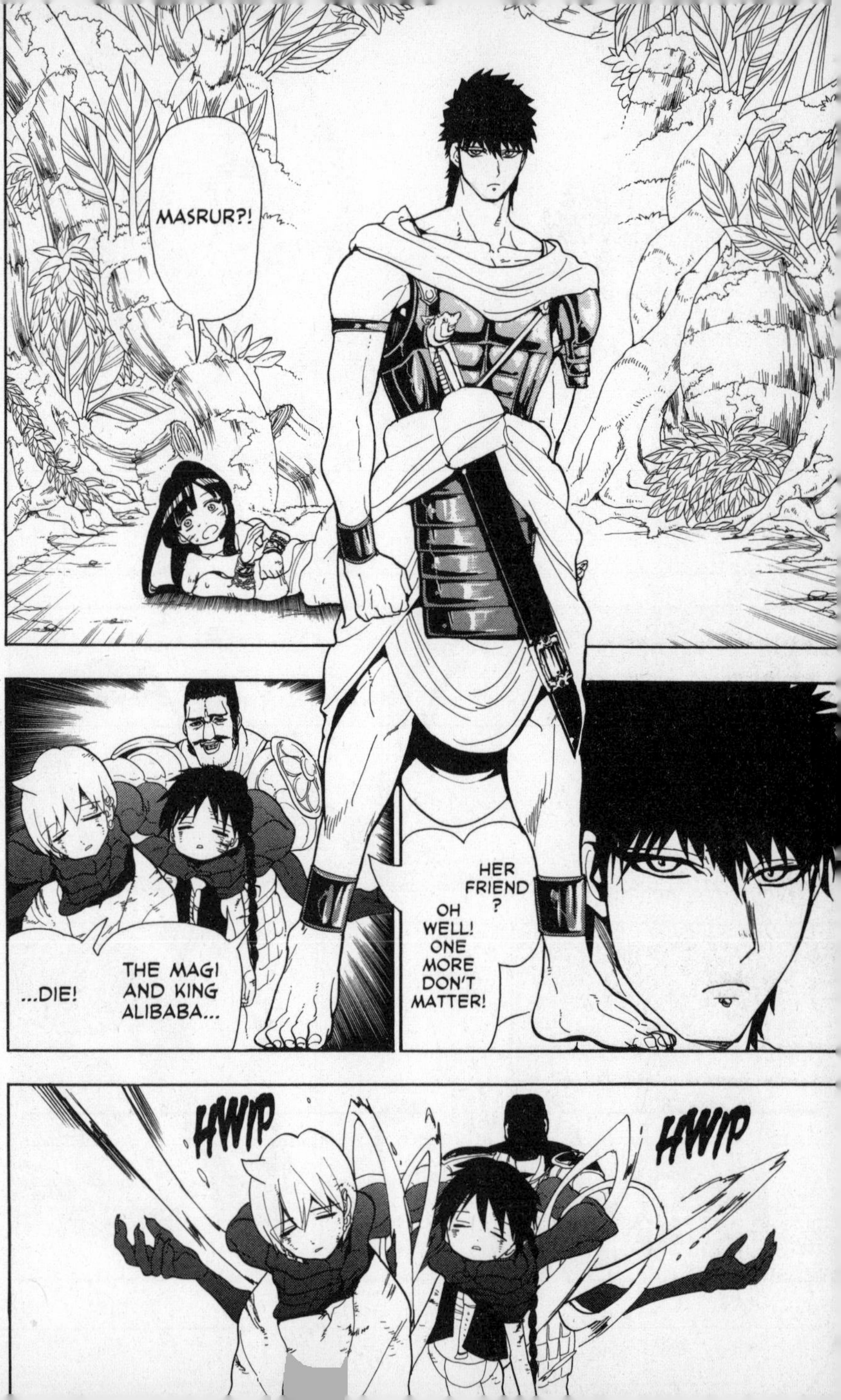
MASRUR?!
HER FRIEND?
OH WELL! ONE MORE DON'T MATTER!
THE MAGI AND KING ALIBABA...
...DIE!
HWIP
HWIP

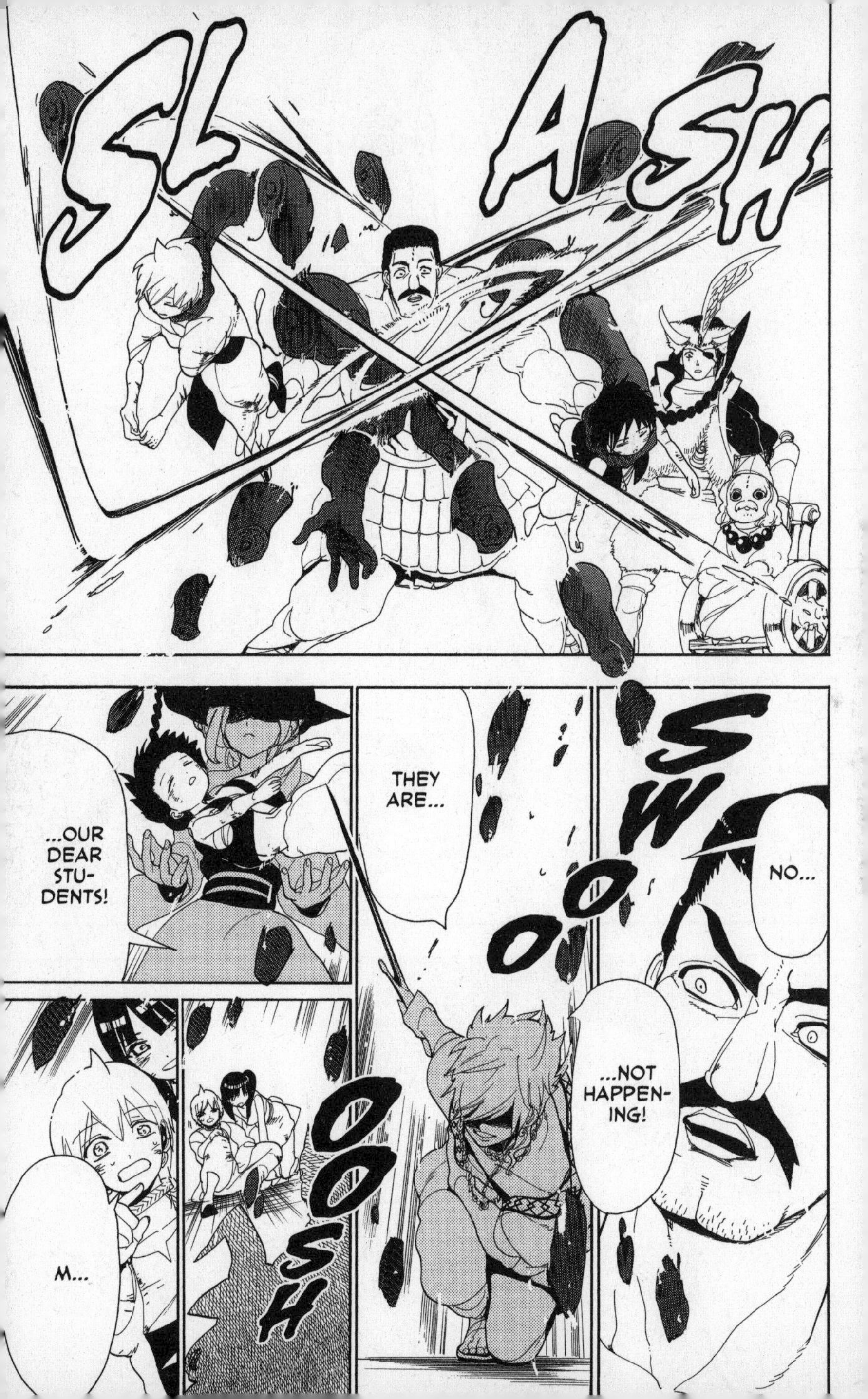
SLASH
SWOOOO
NO...
...NOT HAPPENING!
THEY ARE...
OOOSH
...OUR DEAR STUDENTS!
M...

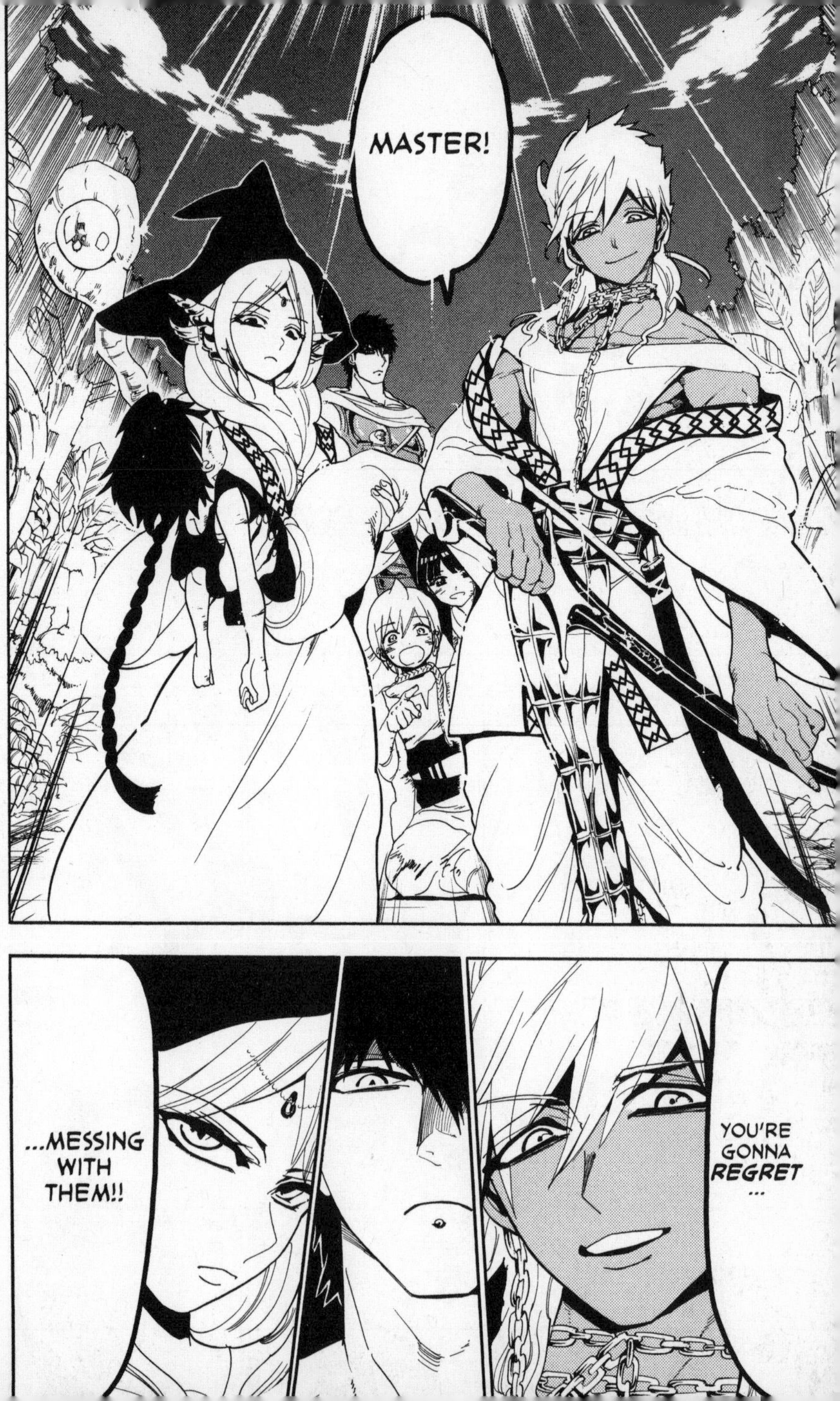
MASTER!
YOU'RE GONNA REGRET ...
...MESSING WITH THEM!!

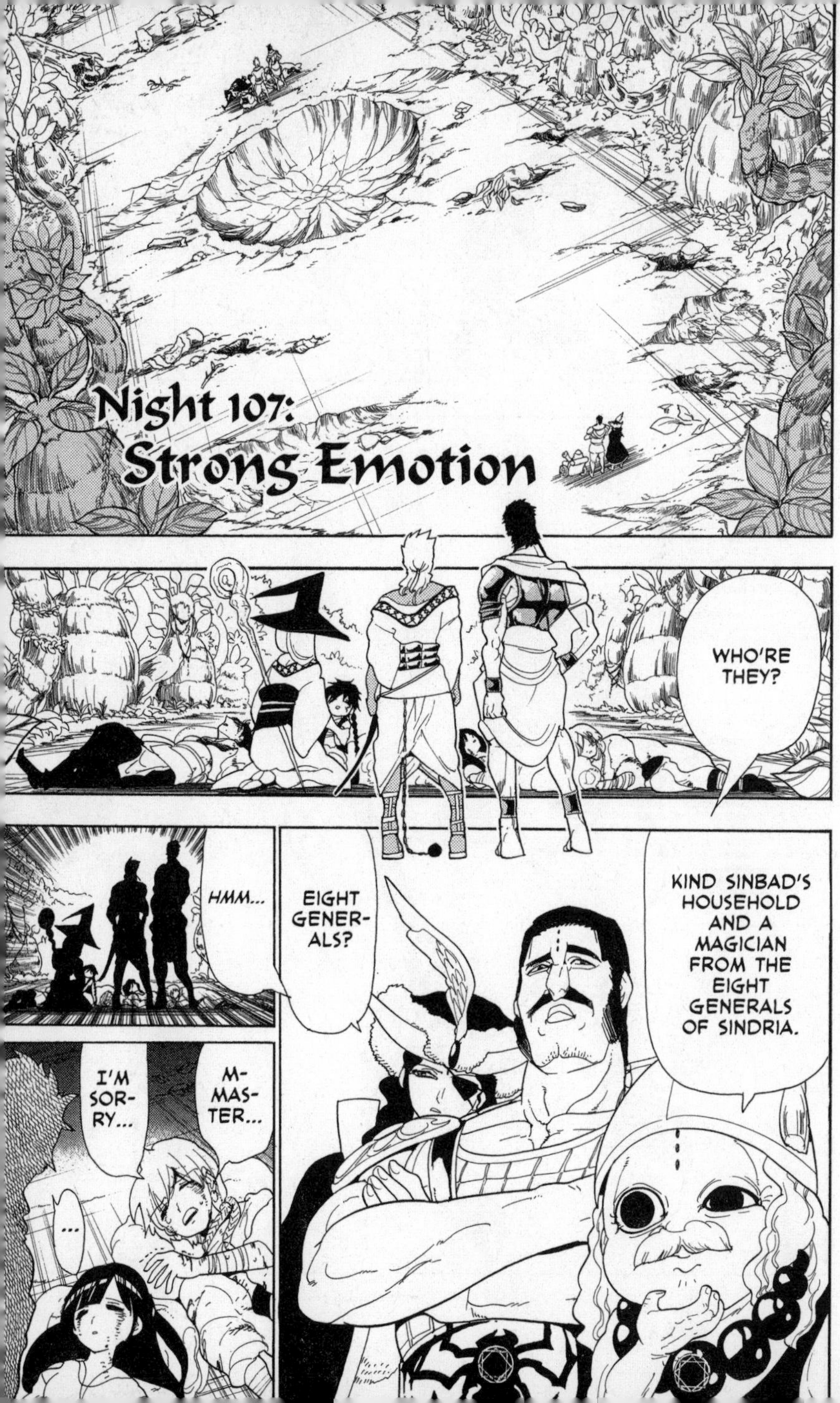
Night 107: Strong Emotion
WHO'RE THEY?
KIND SINBAD'S HOUSEHOLD AND A MAGICIAN FROM THE EIGHT GENERALS OF SINDRIA.
EIGHT GENERALS?
HMM...
M-MASTER...
I'M SORRY...
...

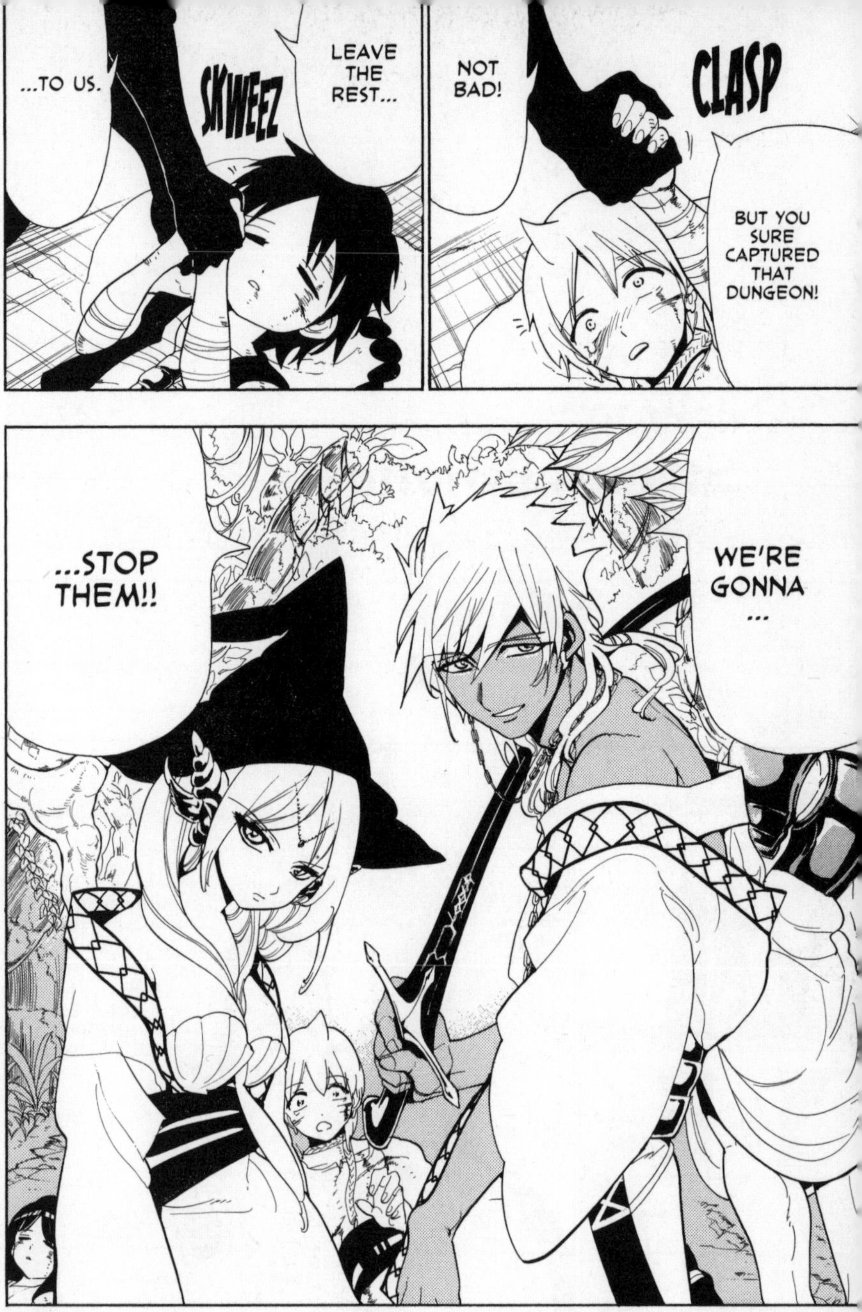
CLASP
NOT BAD!
BUT YOU SURE CAPTURED THAT DUNGEON!
LEAVE THE REST...
SKWEEZ
...TO US.
WE'RE GONNA ...
...STOP THEM!!

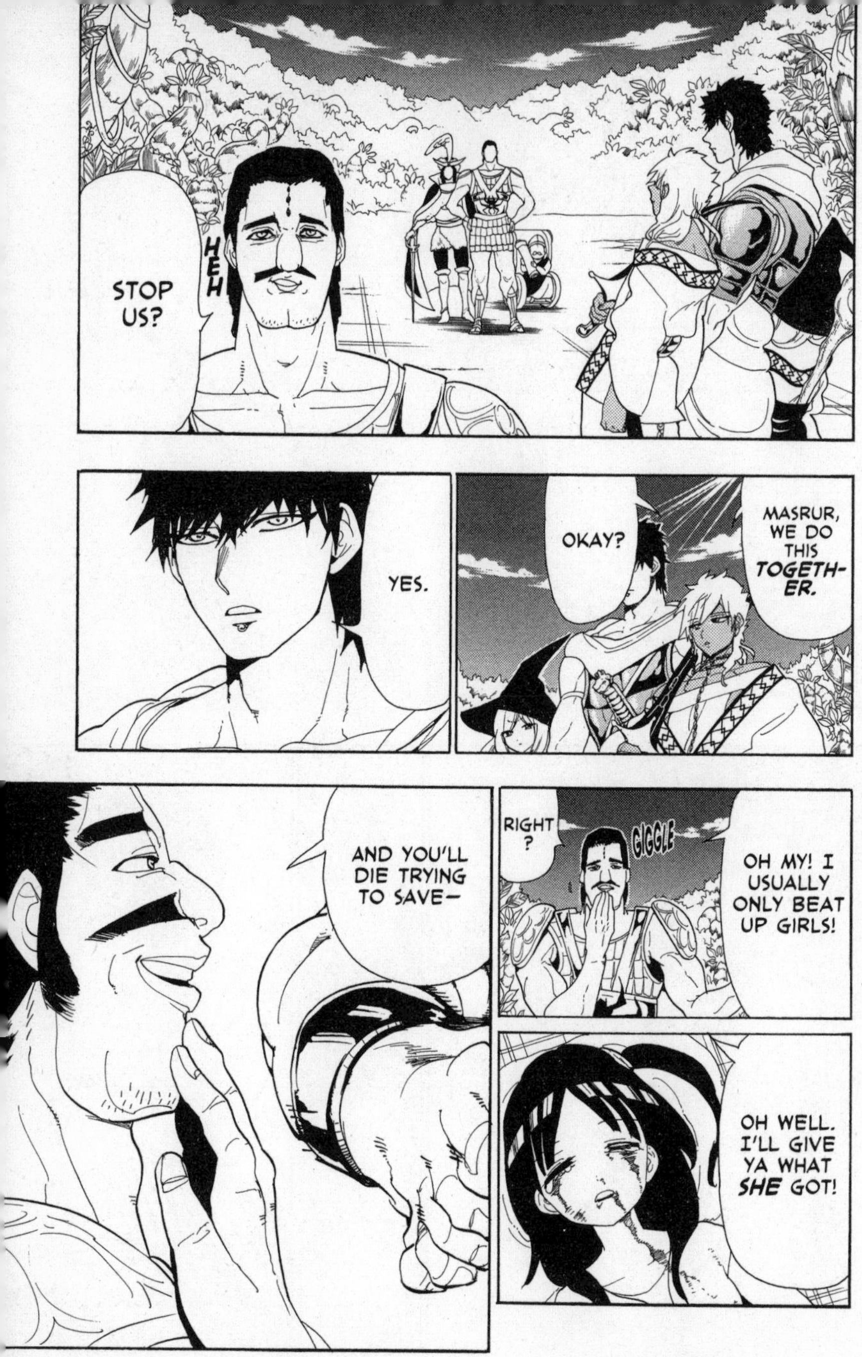
HEH
STOP US?
MASRUR, WE DO THIS *TOGETHER.*
OKAY?
YES.
OH MY! I USUALLY ONLY BEAT UP GIRLS!
GIGGLE
RIGHT?
OH WELL. I'LL GIVE YA WHAT *SHE* GOT!
AND YOU'LL DIE TRYING TO SAVE—

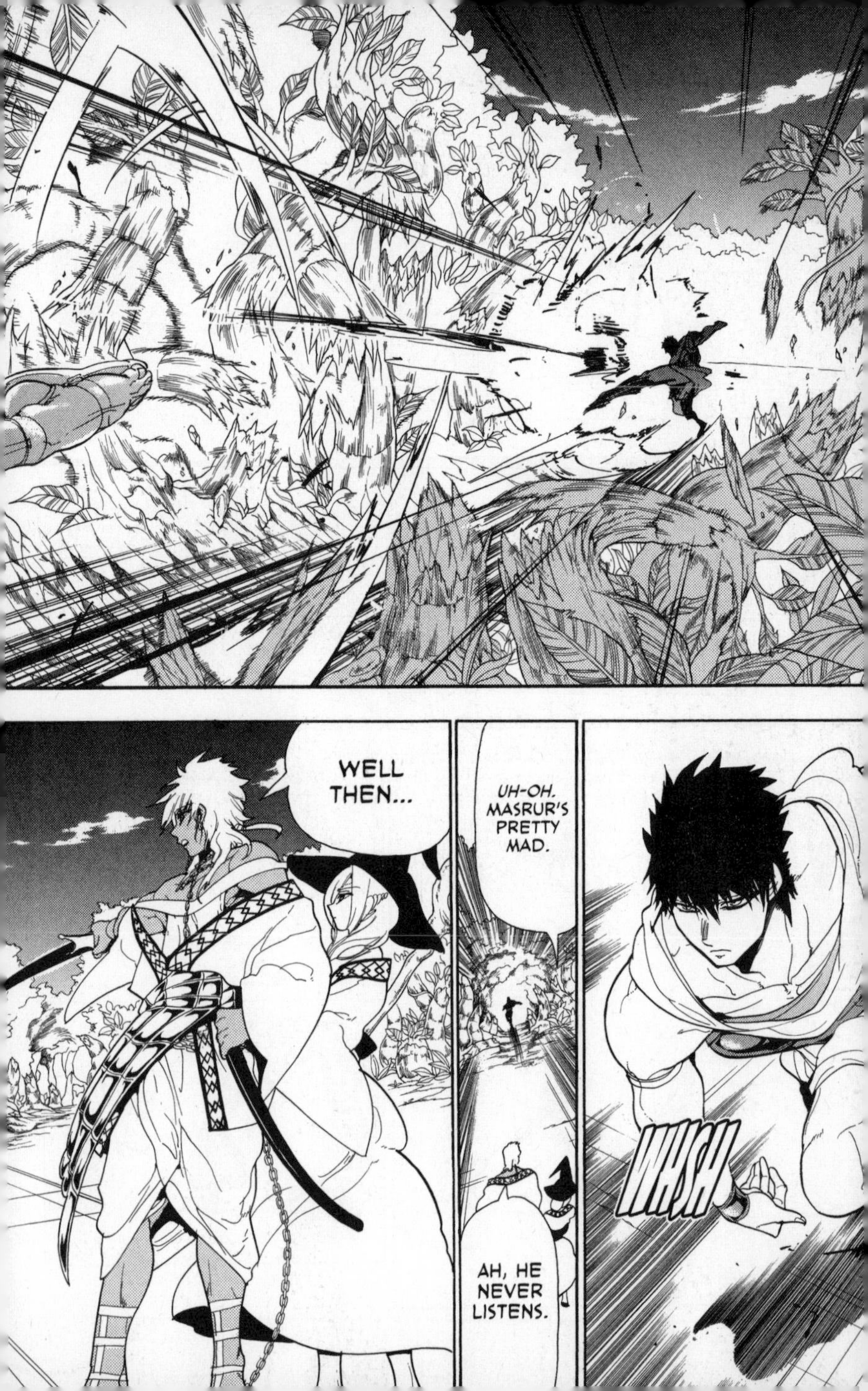
WHSH
UH-OH. MASRUR'S PRETTY MAD.
AH, HE NEVER LISTENS.
WELL THEN...

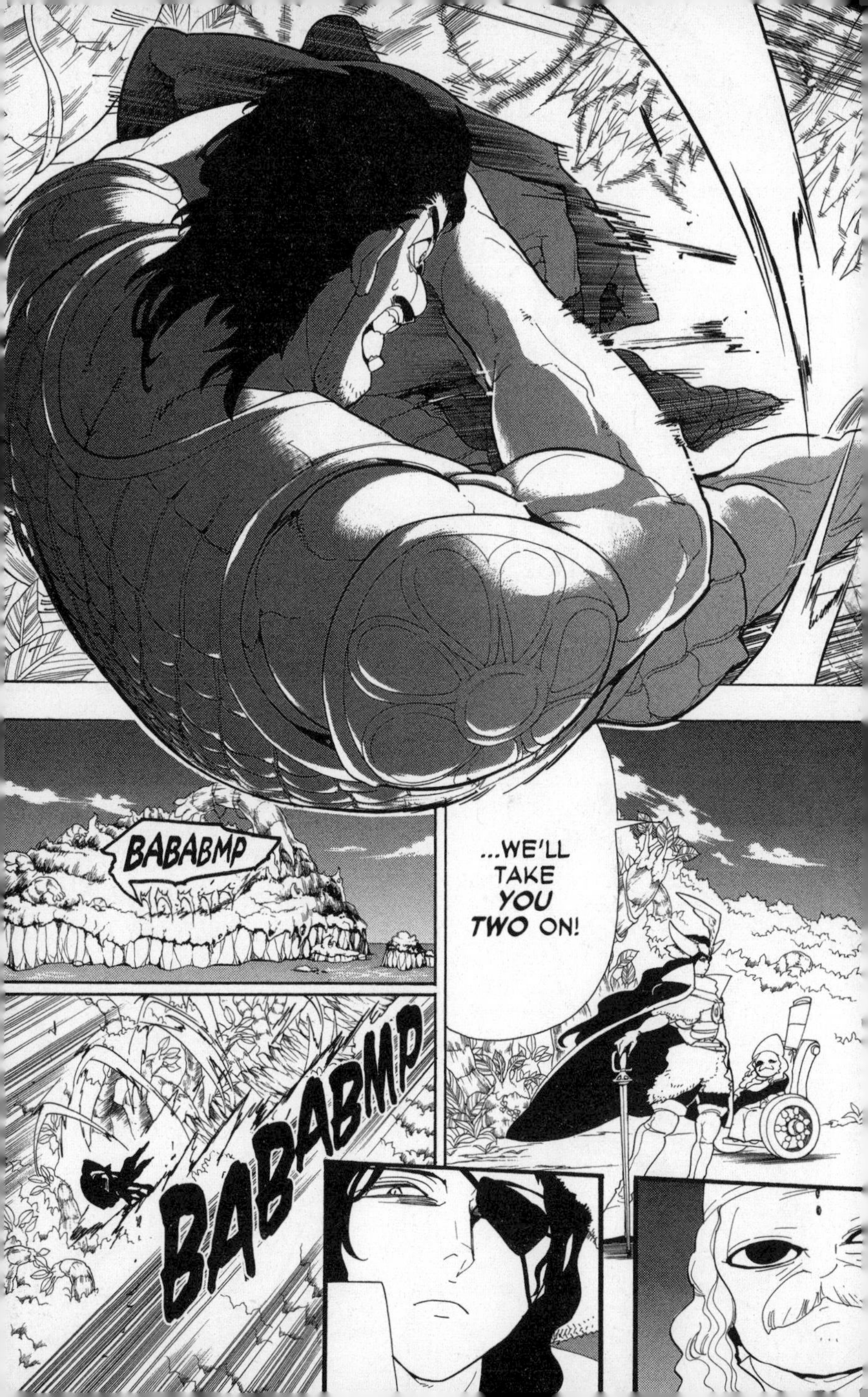
...WE'LL TAKE YOU TWO ON!
BABABMP
BABABMP

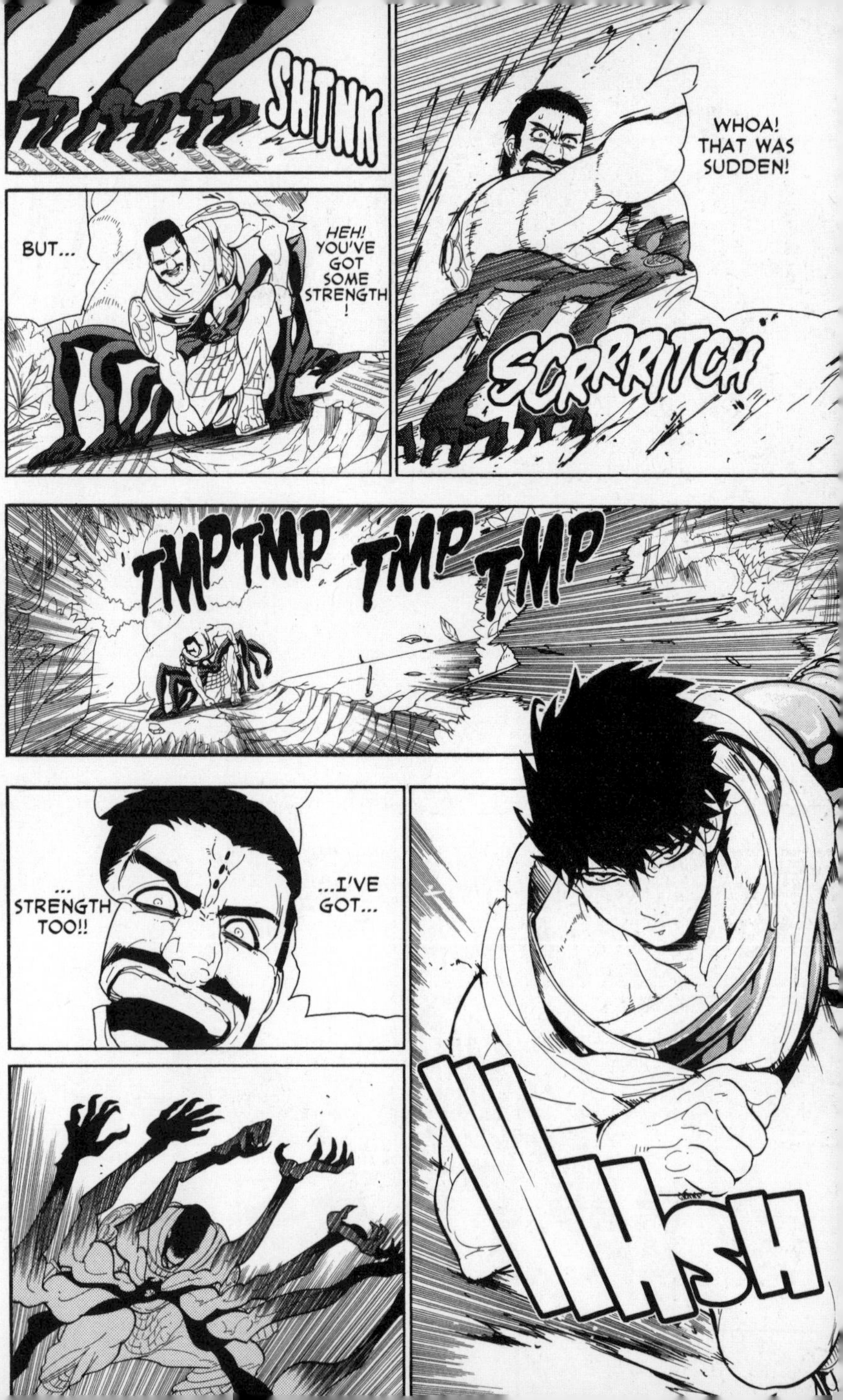
WHOA! THAT WAS SUDDEN!
SCRRITCH
SHTNK
HEH! YOU'VE GOT SOME STRENGTH!
BUT...
TMP TMP TMP TMP
WHSH
...I'VE GOT...
... STRENGTH TOO!!

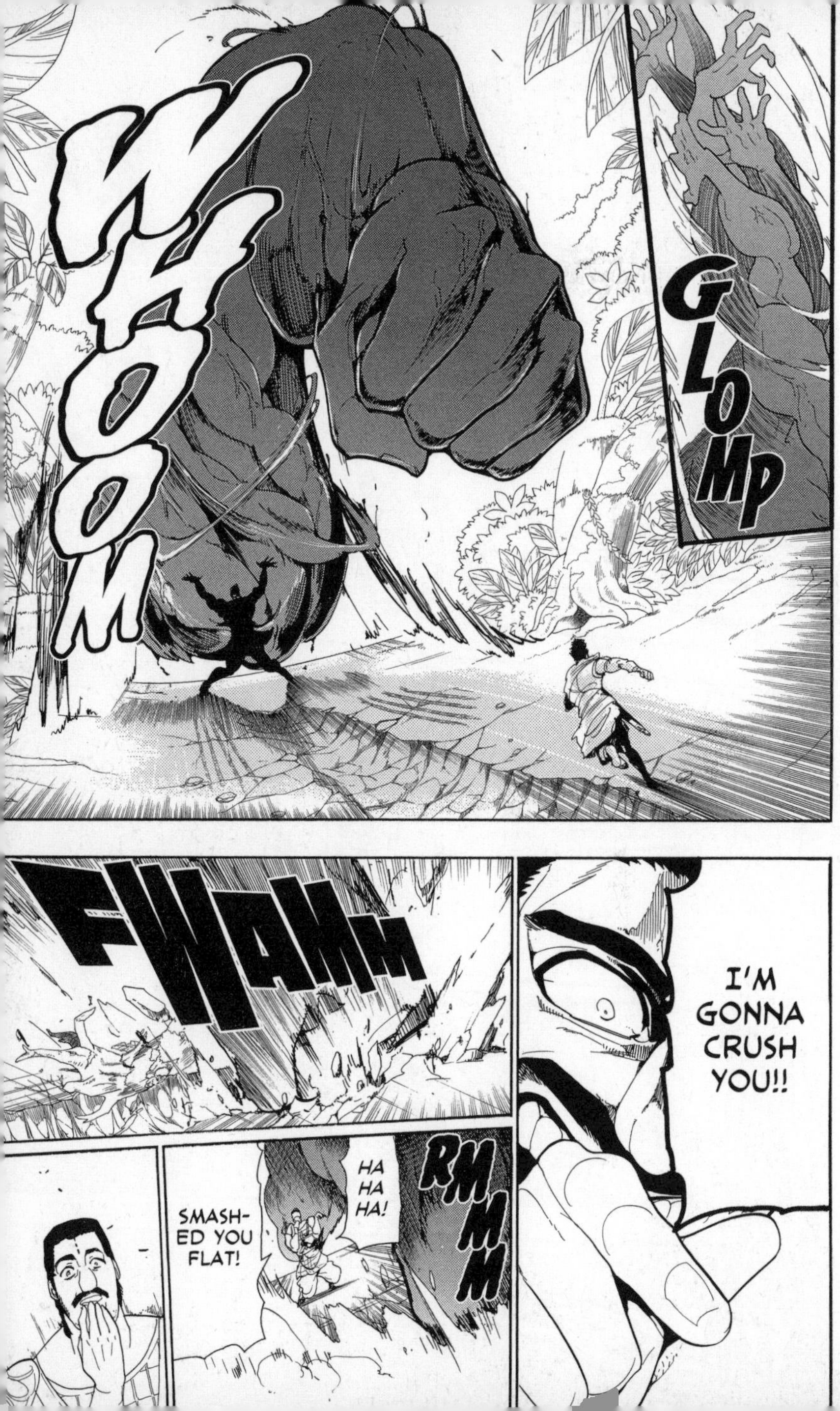
GLOMP
WHOOM
I'M GONNA CRUSH YOU!!
FWAMM
RMMM
HA HA HA!
SMASHED YOU FLAT!

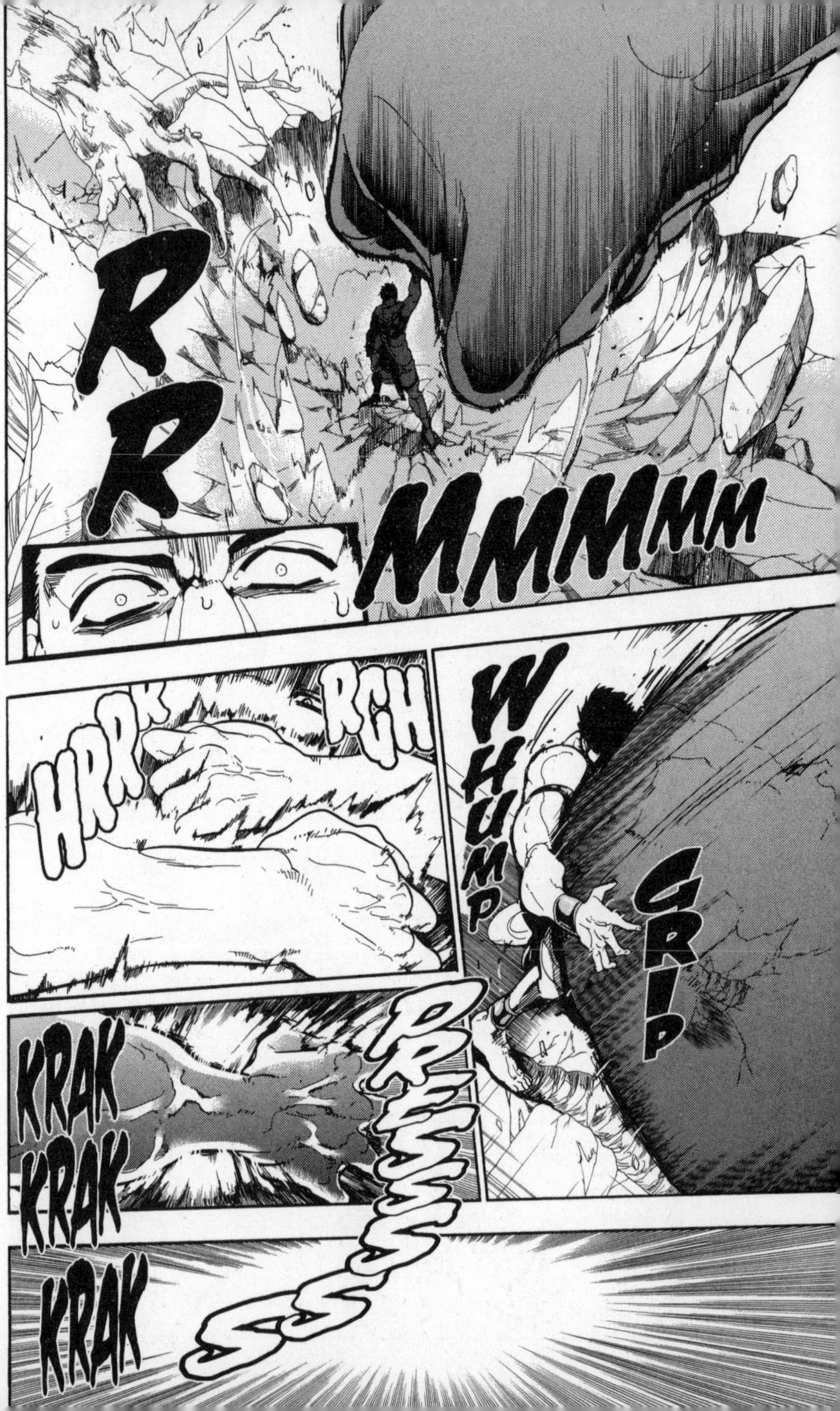
RR
MMMMMM
WHUMP
GRIP
HRRK
RCH
DRMMMMSSS
KRAK KRAK KRAK

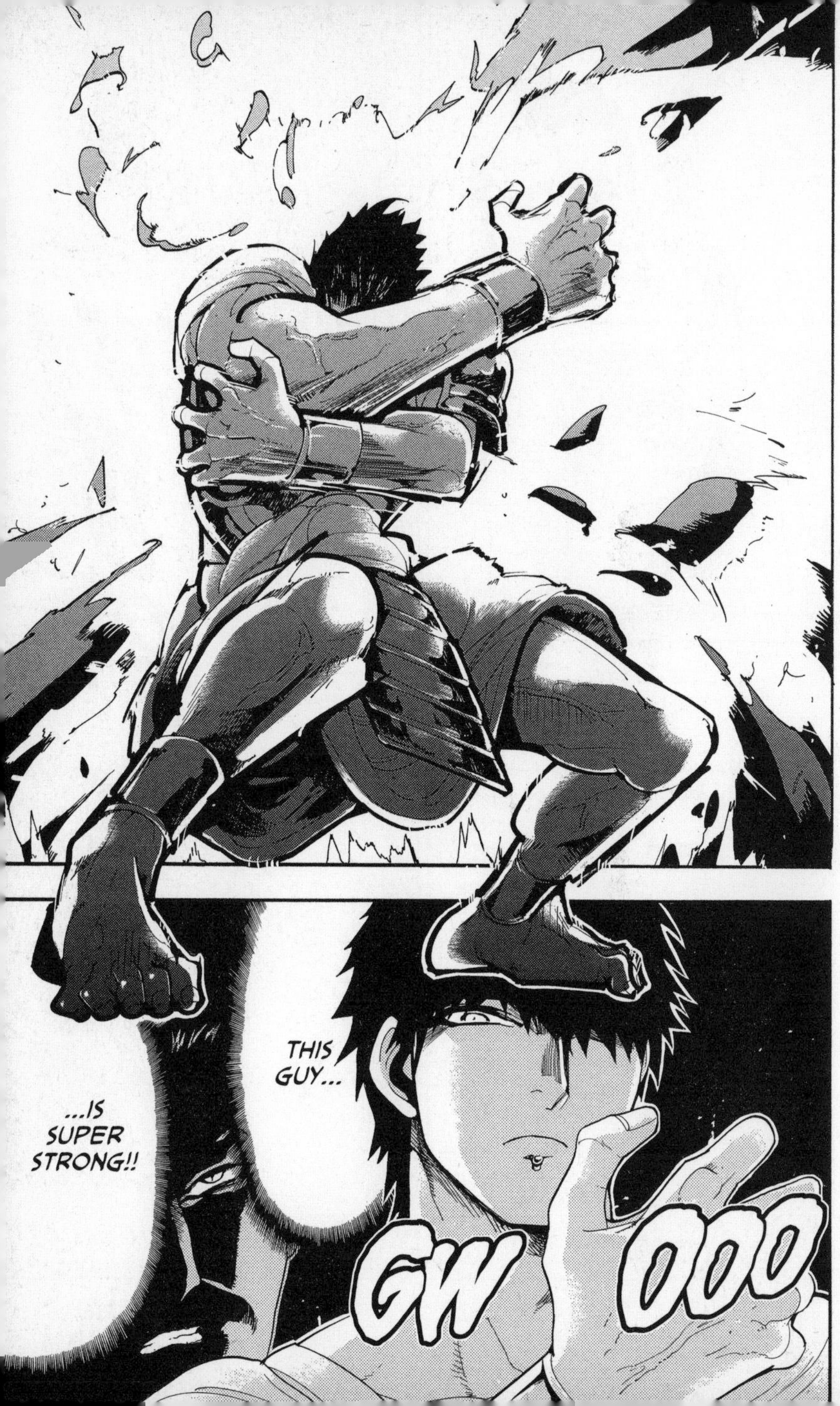
THIS GUY...
...IS SUPER STRONG!!
GWOOO

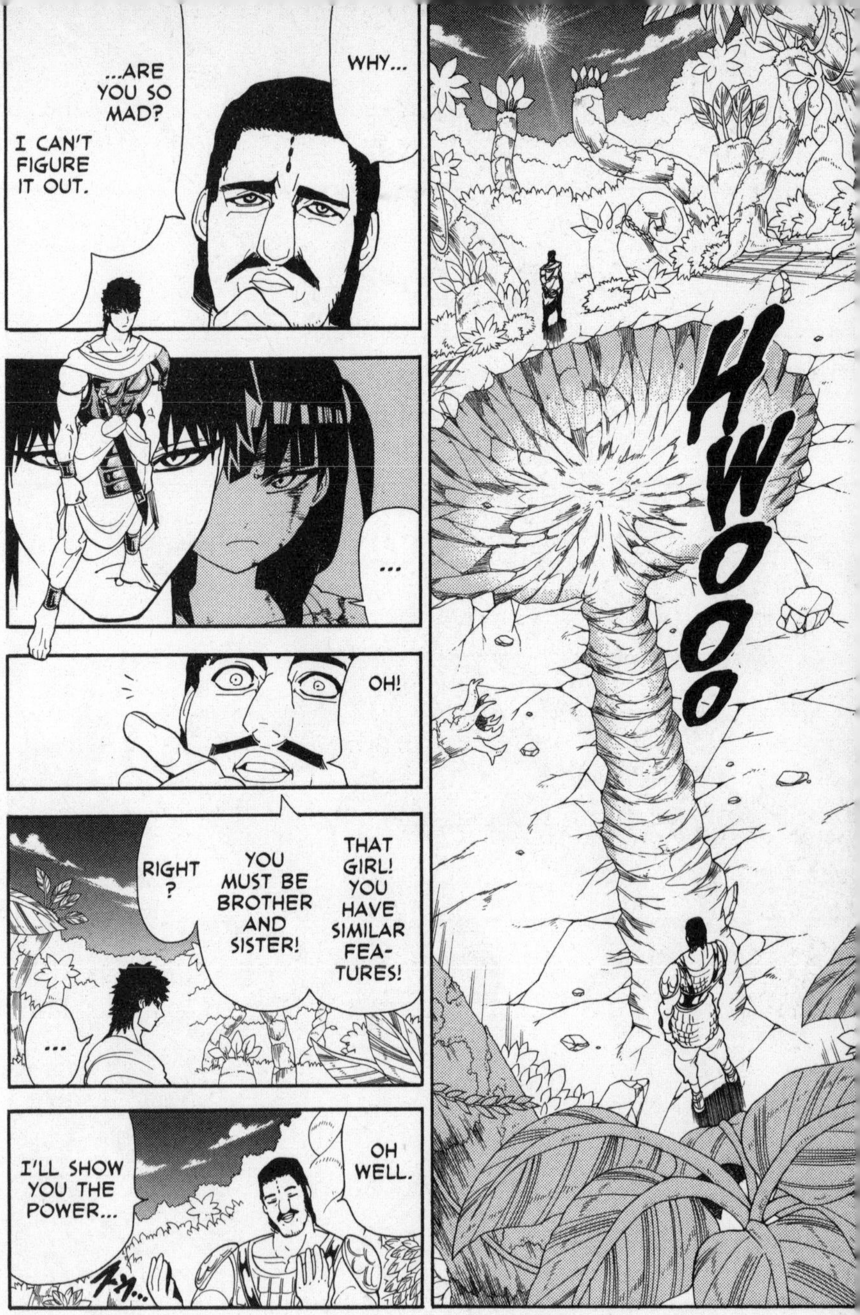
HWOOOO
WHY...
...ARE YOU SO MAD?
I CAN'T FIGURE IT OUT.
...
OH!
THAT GIRL! YOU HAVE SIMILAR FEA-TURES!
YOU MUST BE BROTHER AND SISTER!
RIGHT?
...
OH WELL.
I'LL SHOW YOU THE POWER...

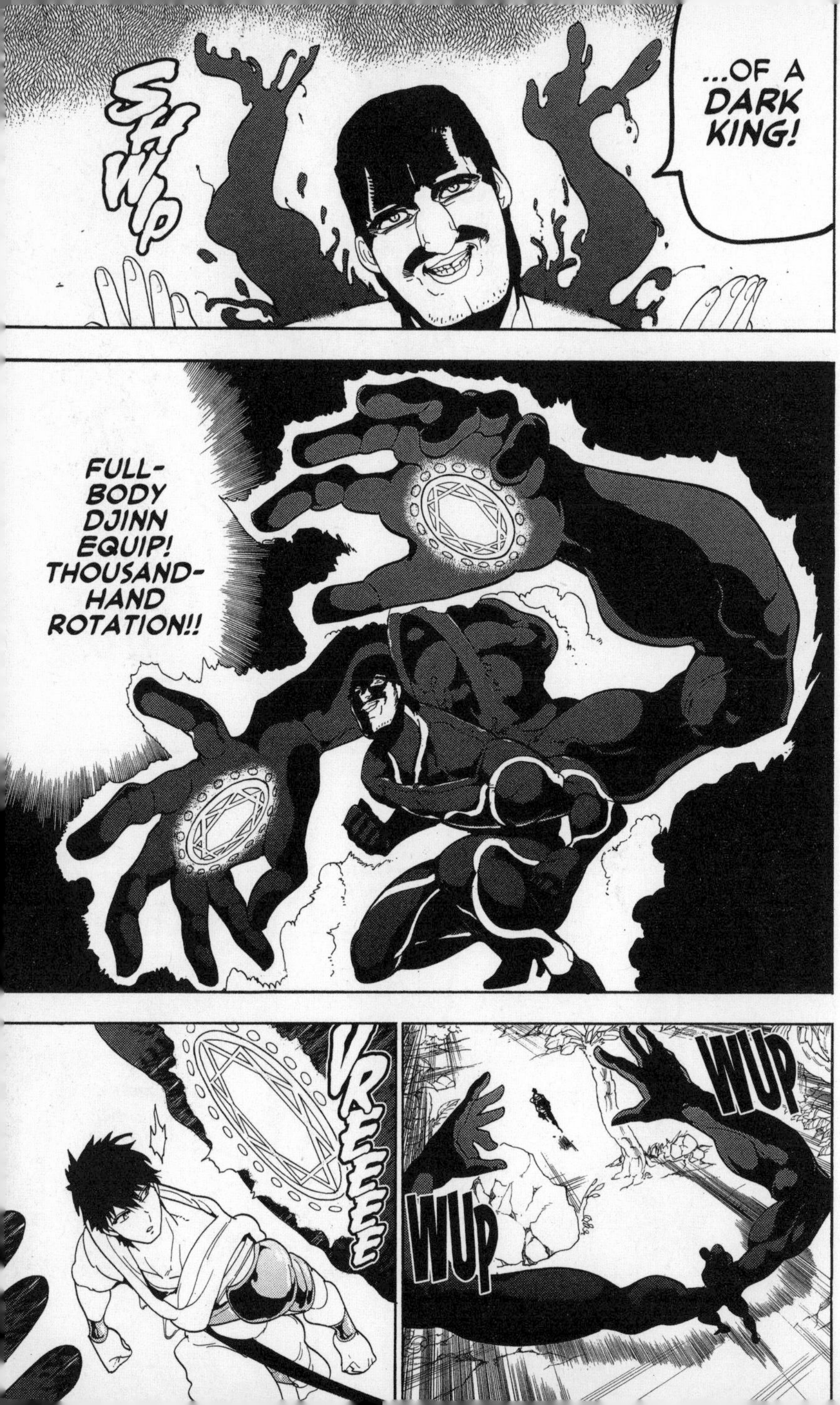
...OF A DARK KING!
SHWIP
FULL-BODY DJINN EQUIP! THOUSAND-HAND ROTATION!!
WUP
WUP
VREEEEE

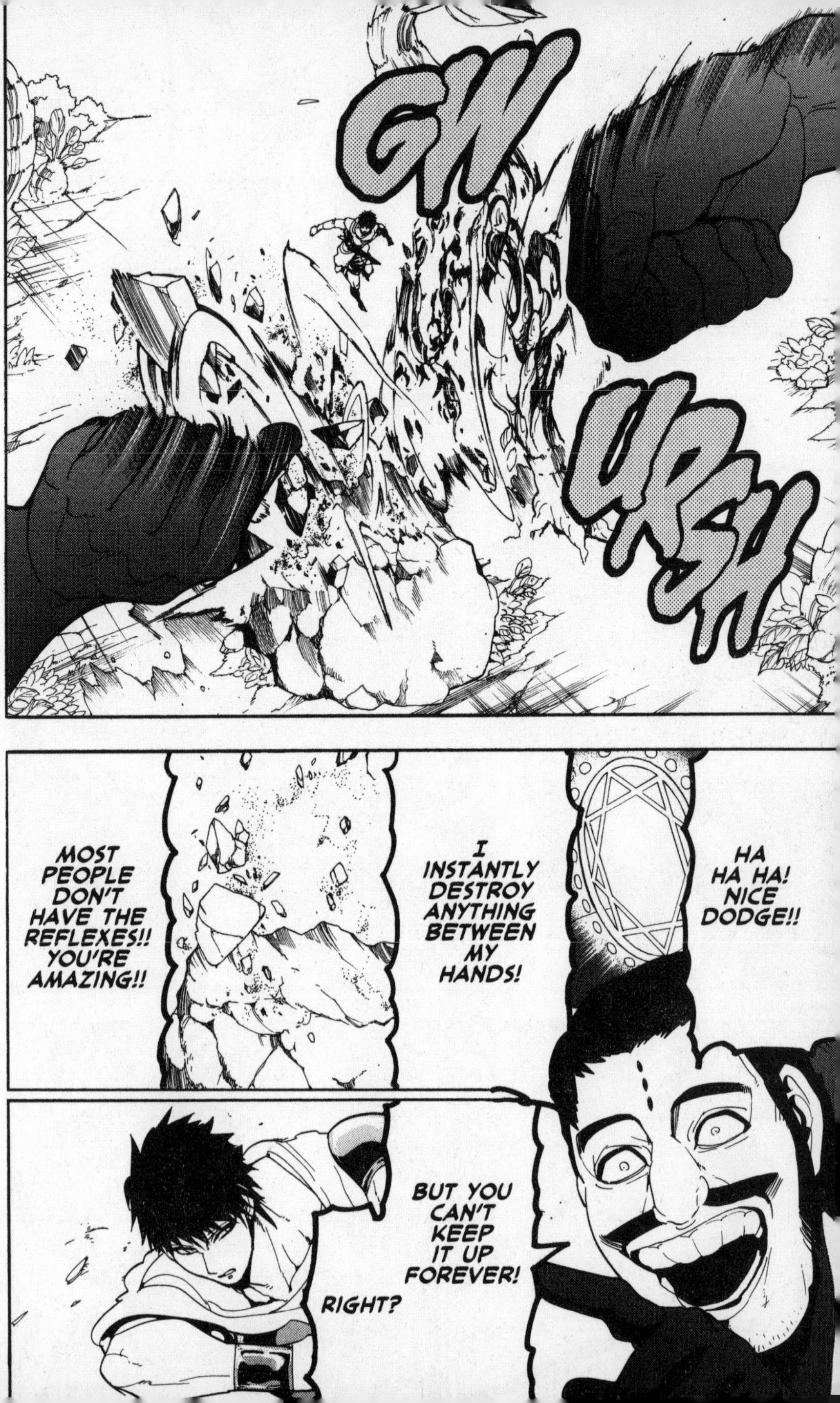
GH
URSH
HA HA HA! NICE DODGE!!
I INSTANTLY DESTROY ANYTHING BETWEEN MY HANDS!
MOST PEOPLE DON'T HAVE THE REFLEXES!! YOU'RE AMAZING!!
BUT YOU CAN'T KEEP IT UP FOREVER!
RIGHT?

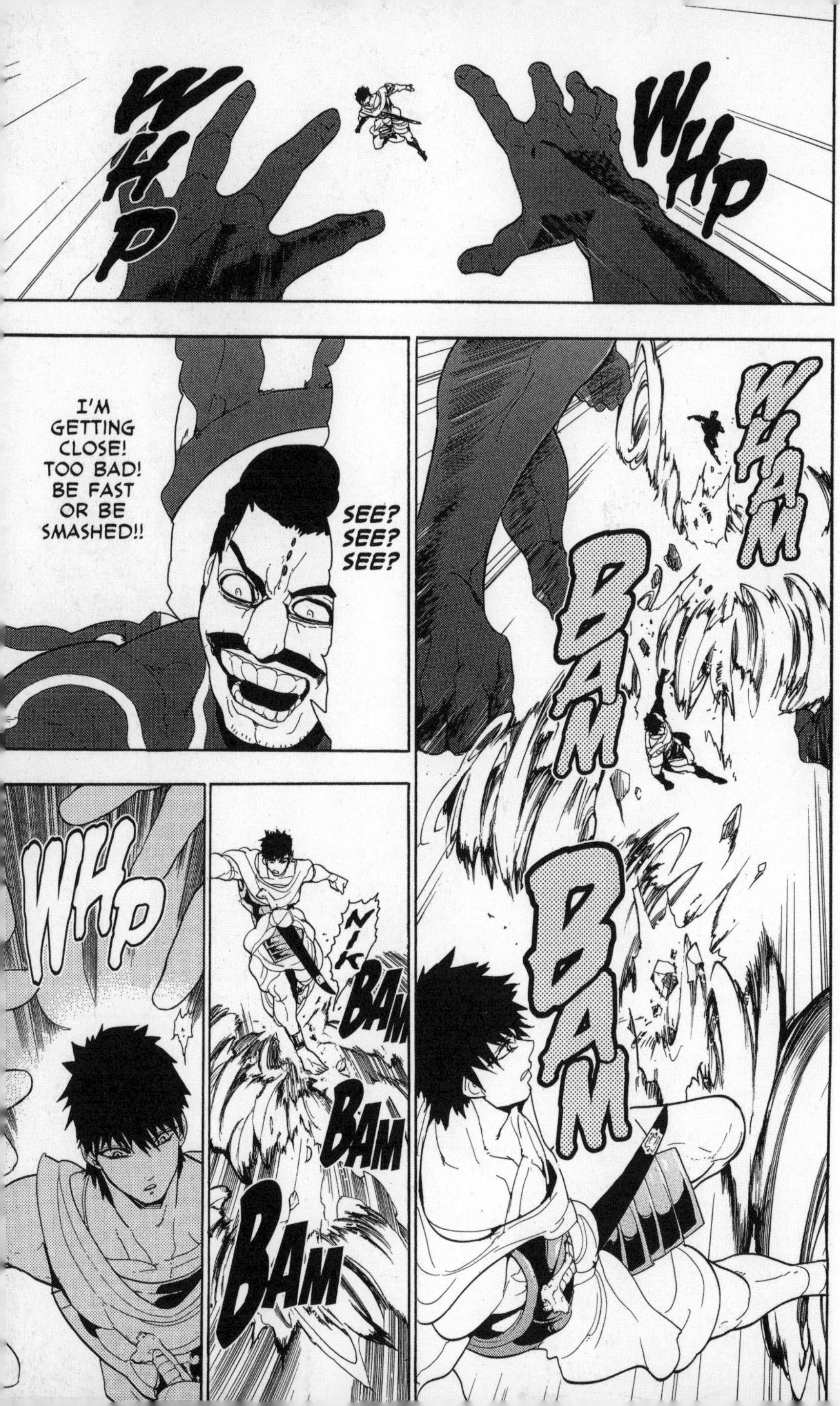
WHP
WHP
WHAM
BAM
BAM
SEE? SEE? SEE?
I'M GETTING CLOSE! TOO BAD! BE FAST OR BE SMASHED!!
NIK
BAM
BAM
BAM
WHP

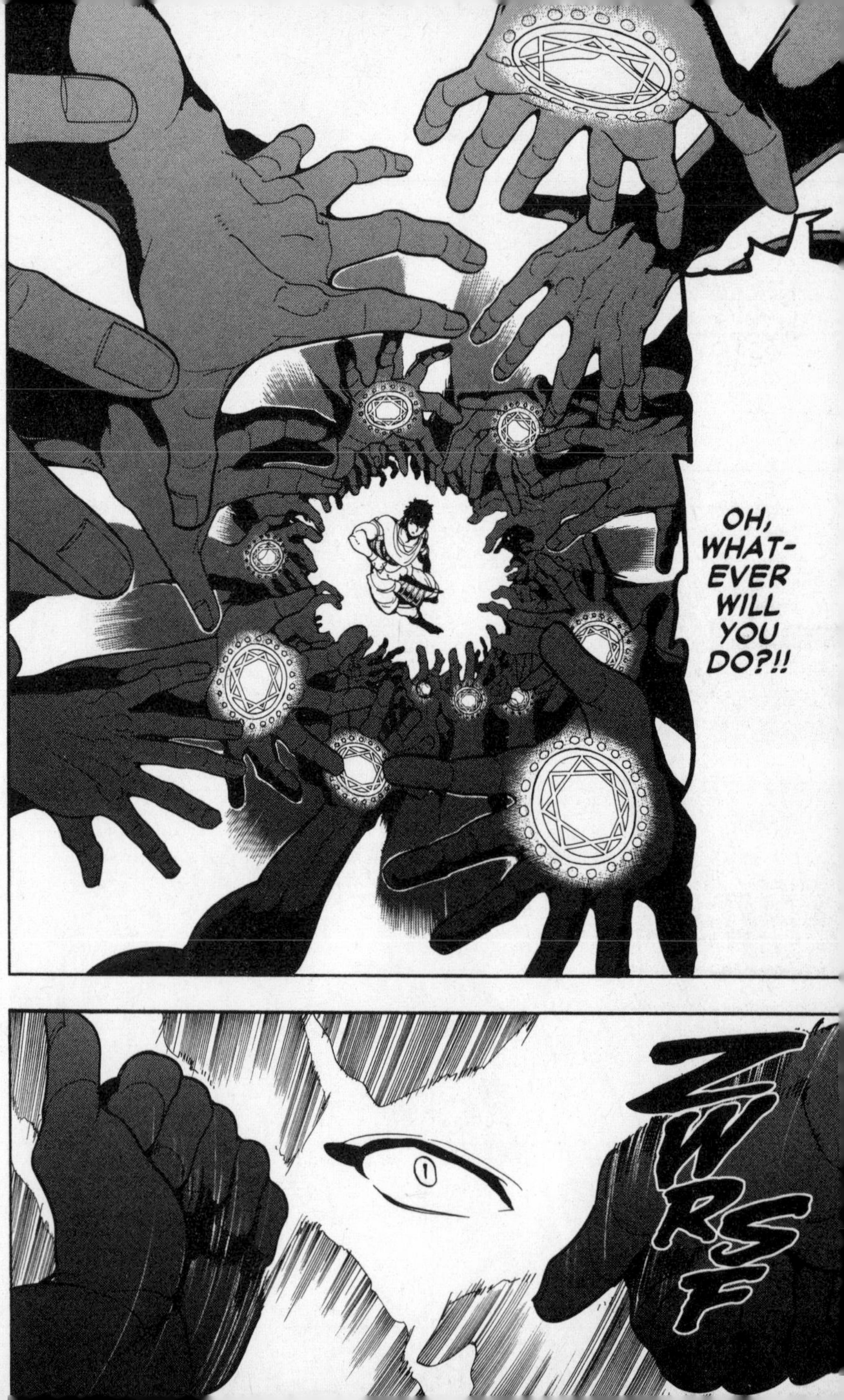

OH, WHAT-EVER WILL YOU DO?!!
WRSF

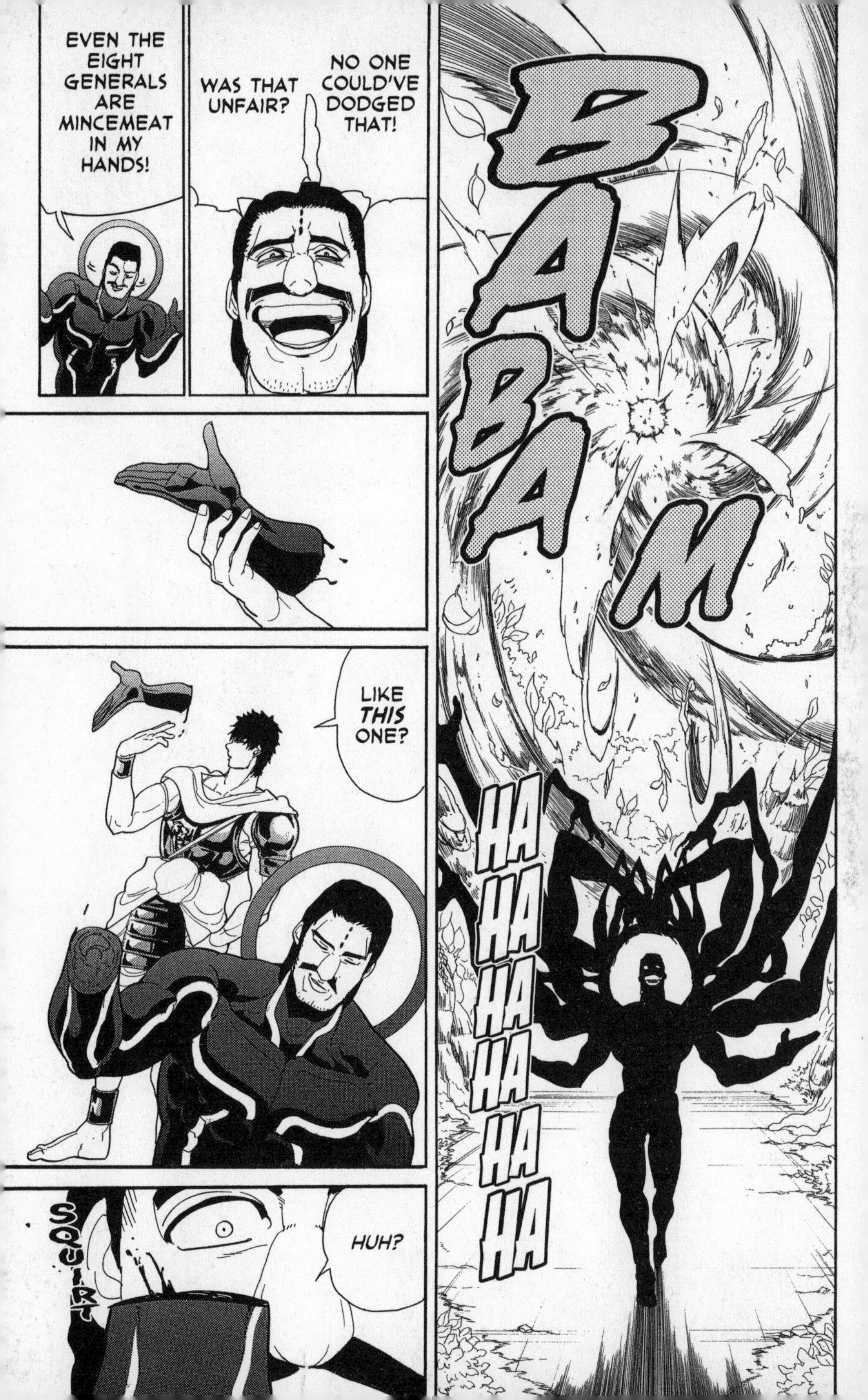
BABAM
HA HA HA HA HA HA HA HA HA
NO ONE COULD'VE DODGED THAT!
WAS THAT UNFAIR?
EVEN THE EIGHT GENERALS ARE MINCEMEAT IN MY HANDS!
LIKE *THIS* ONE?
SQUIRT
HUH?

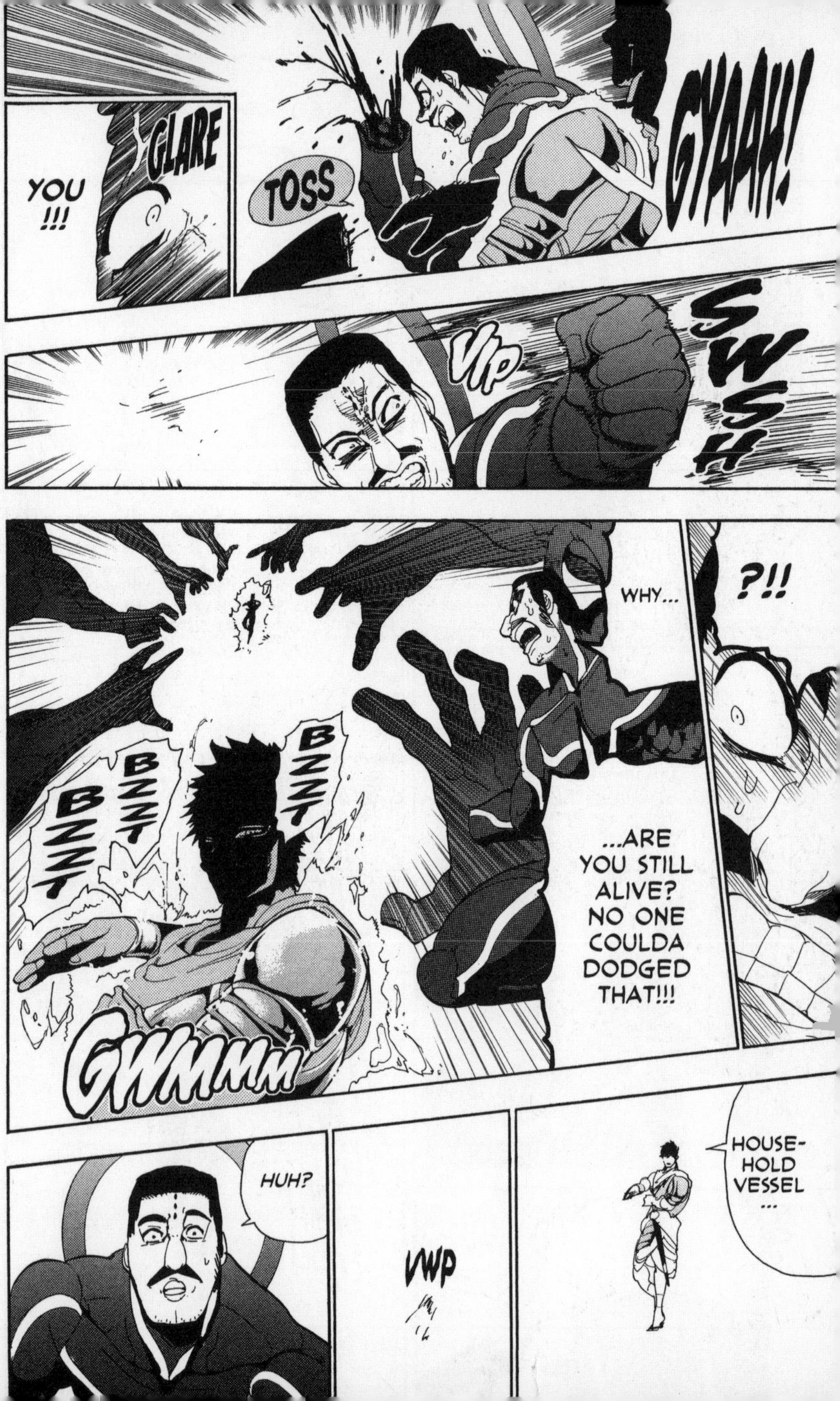
GYAAH!!
TOSS
GLARE
YOU !!!
SWSH
VIP
?!!
WHY...
...ARE YOU STILL ALIVE? NO ONE COULDA DODGED THAT!!!
BZZT
BZZT
BZZT
GWMMM
HOUSE-HOLD VESSEL ...
VWP
HUH?

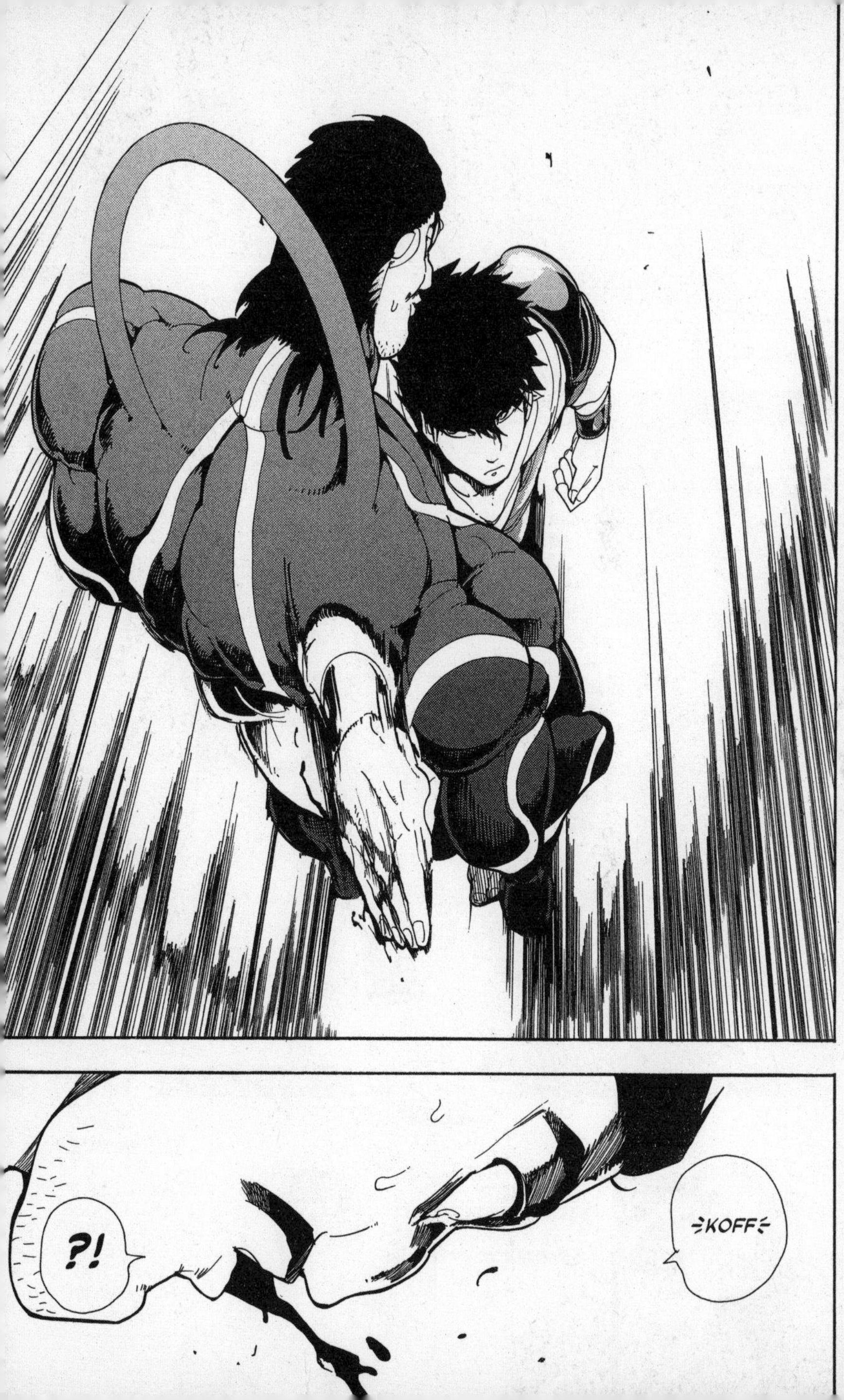
KOFF
?!

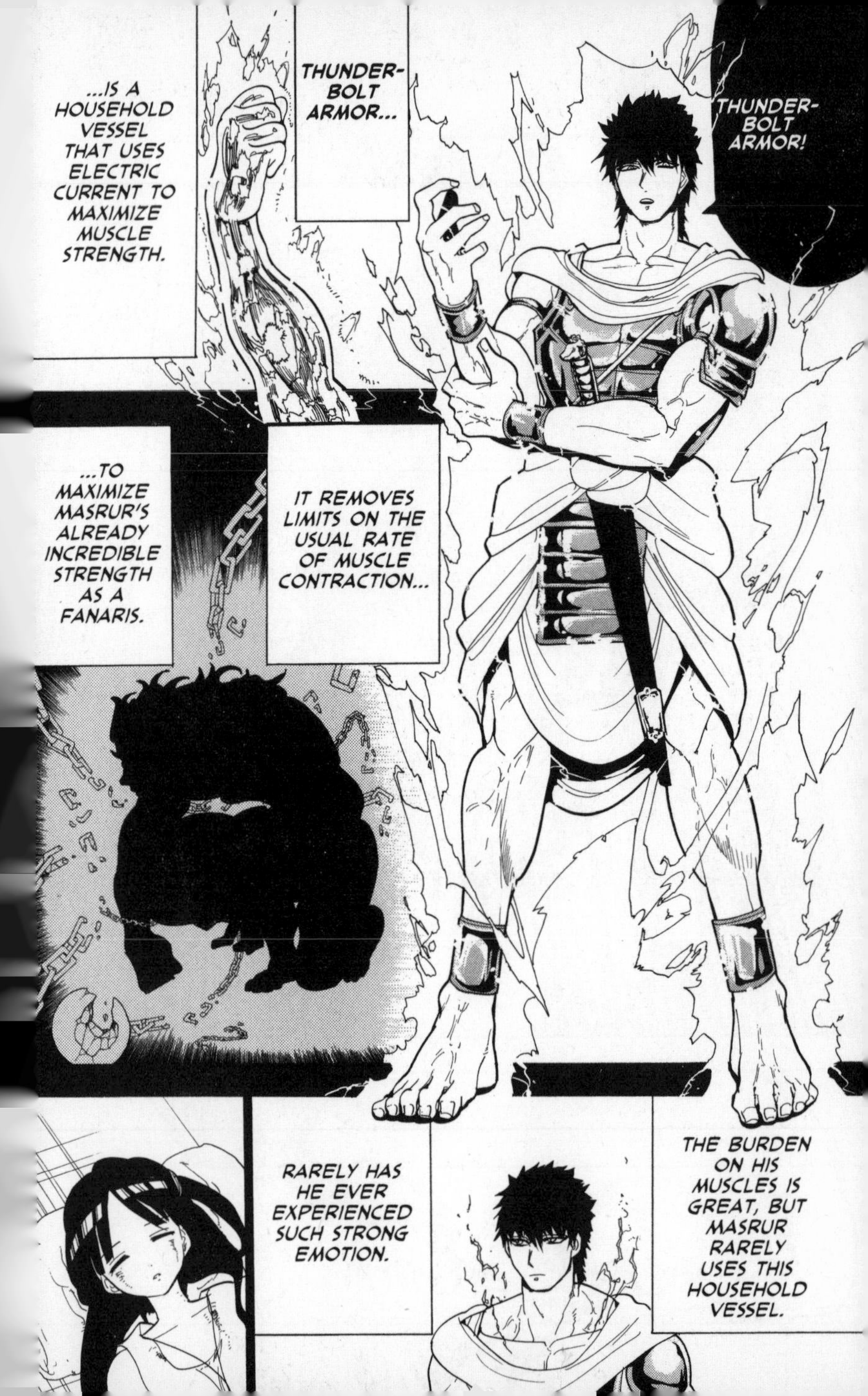

THUNDERBOLT ARMOR!
THUNDERBOLT ARMOR...
...IS A HOUSEHOLD VESSEL THAT USES ELECTRIC CURRENT TO MAXIMIZE MUSCLE STRENGTH.
IT REMOVES LIMITS ON THE USUAL RATE OF MUSCLE CONTRACTION...
...TO MAXIMIZE MASRUR'S ALREADY INCREDIBLE STRENGTH AS A FANARIS.
THE BURDEN ON HIS MUSCLES IS GREAT, BUT MASRUR RARELY USES THIS HOUSEHOLD VESSEL.
RARELY HAS HE EVER EXPERIENCED SUCH STRONG EMOTION.

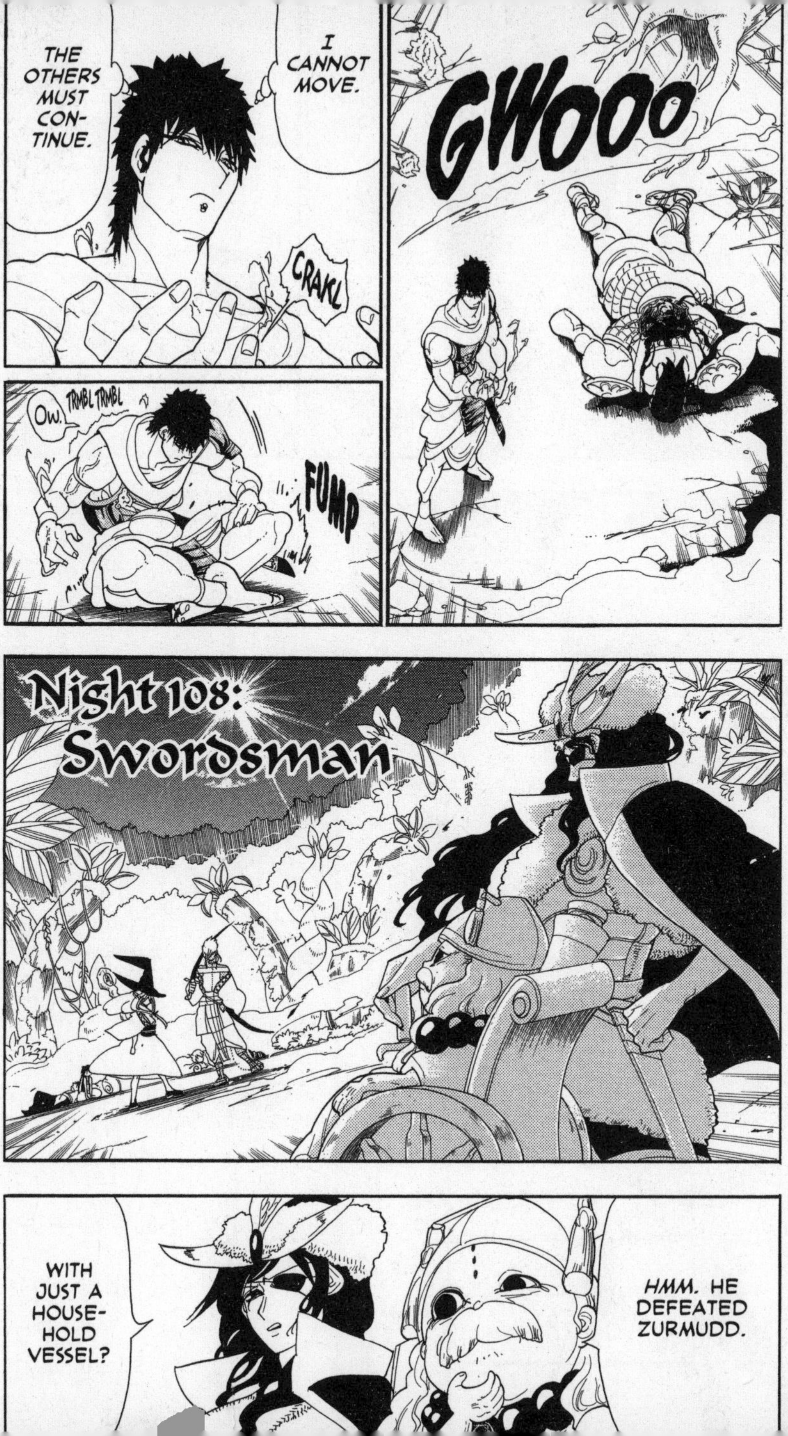
GWOOO
I CANNOT MOVE.
THE OTHERS MUST CONTINUE.
CRAKL
TRMBL TRMBL
Ow.
FUMP
Night 108: Swordsman
HMM. HE DEFEATED ZURMUDD.
WITH JUST A HOUSEHOLD VESSEL?

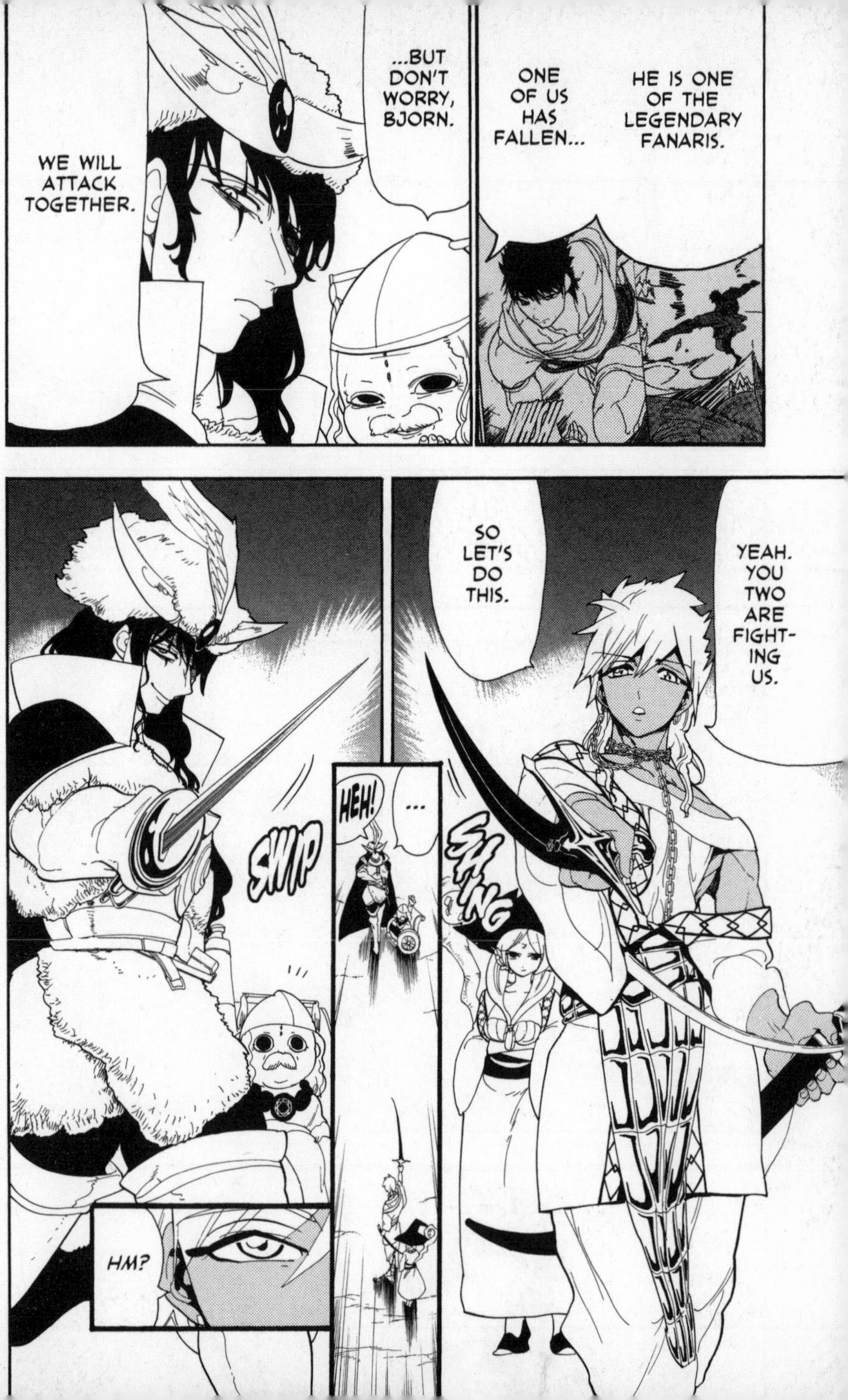
HE IS ONE OF THE LEGENDARY FANARIS.
ONE OF US HAS FALLEN...
...BUT DON'T WORRY, BJORN.
WE WILL ATTACK TOGETHER.
YEAH. YOU TWO ARE FIGHT-ING US.
SO LET'S DO THIS.
SHING
...
HEH!
SWIP
HM?

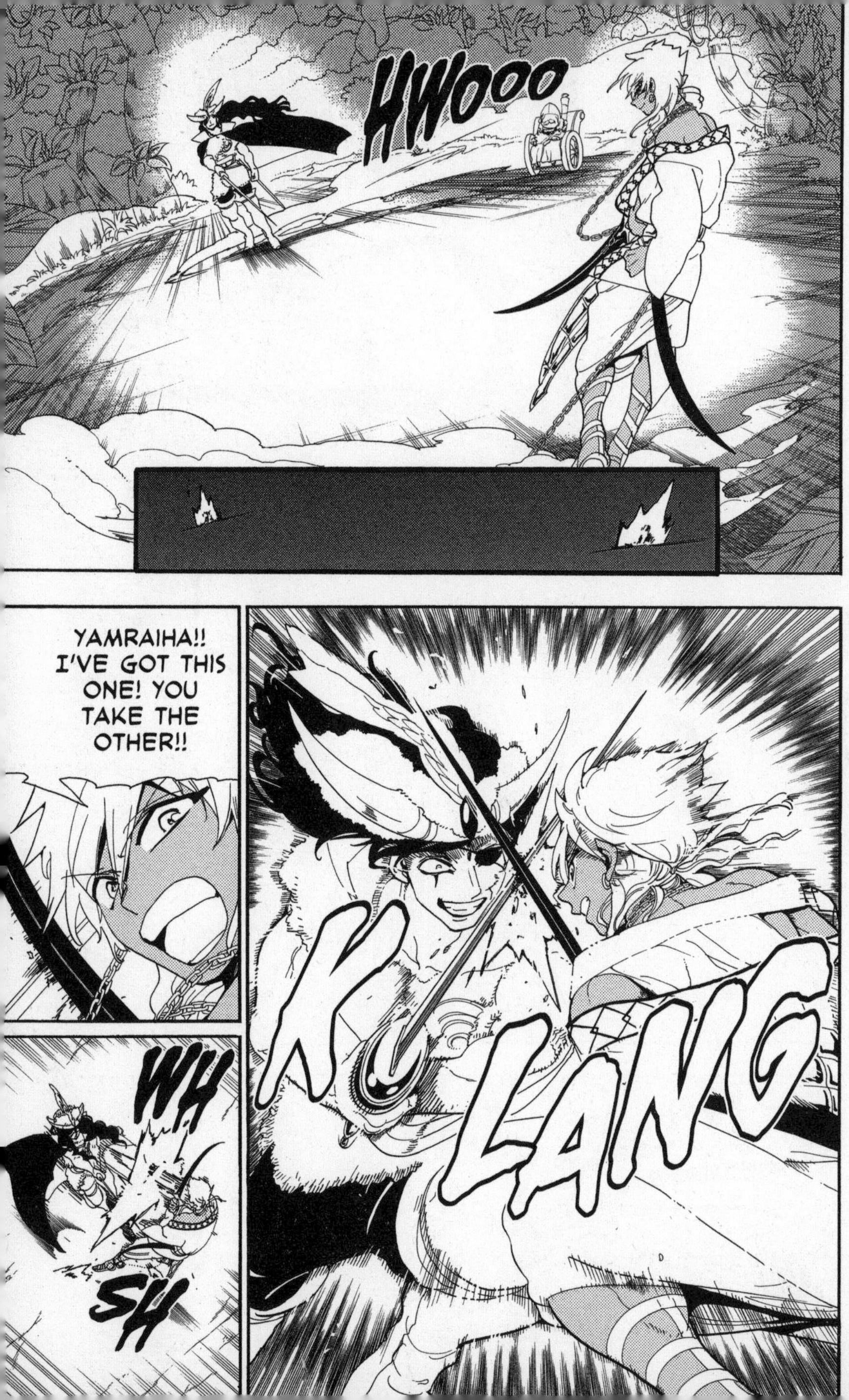
HWOOO
KLANG
YAMRAIHA!! I'VE GOT THIS ONE! YOU TAKE THE OTHER!!
WHSH

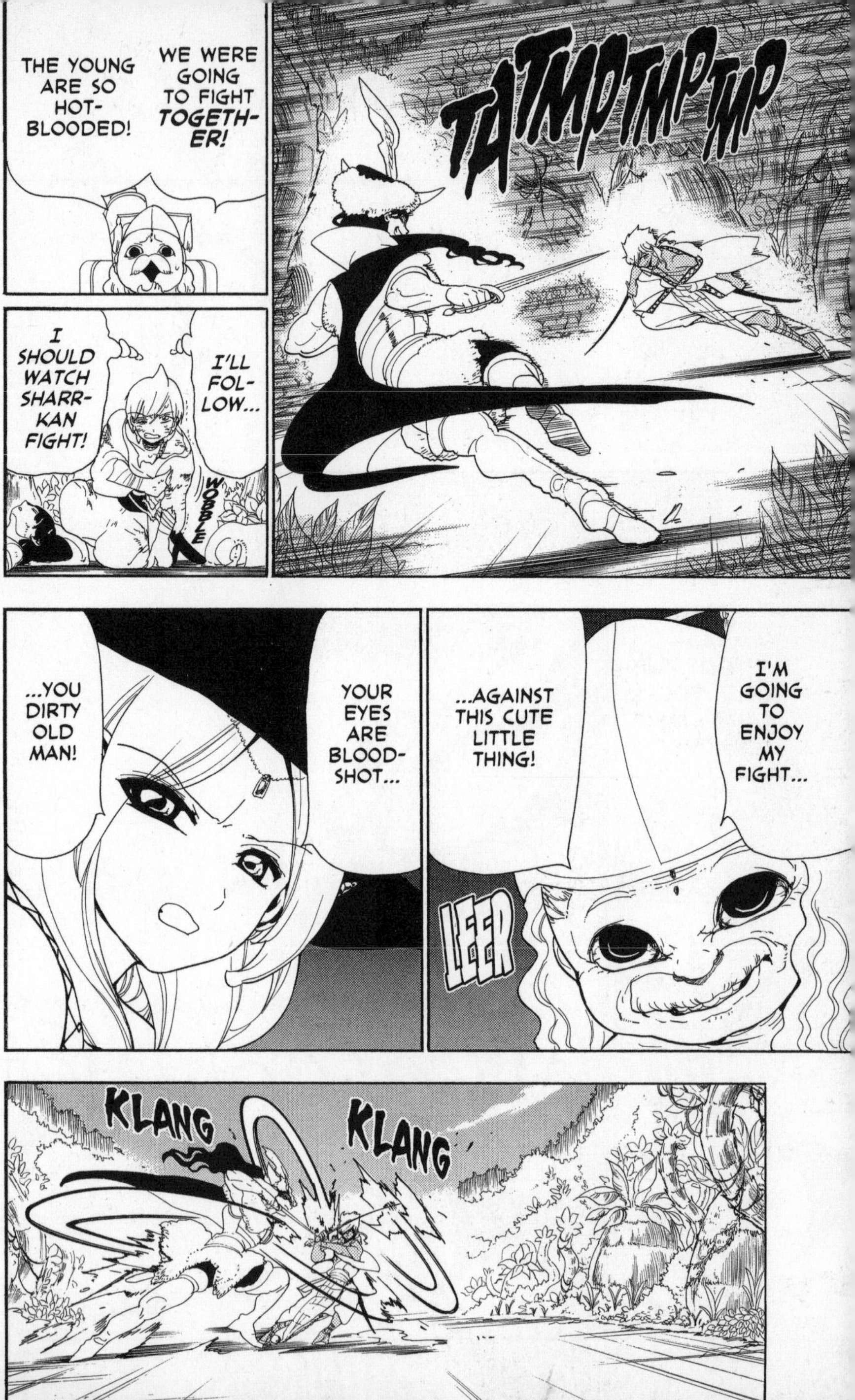
TATMPTMPTMPTMP
WE WERE GOING TO FIGHT TOGETHER!
THE YOUNG ARE SO HOT-BLOODED!
I'LL FOLLOW...
WOBBLE
I SHOULD WATCH SHARRKAN FIGHT!
I'M GOING TO ENJOY MY FIGHT...
...AGAINST THIS CUTE LITTLE THING!
LEER
YOUR EYES ARE BLOODSHOT...
...YOU DIRTY OLD MAN!
KLANG
KLANG

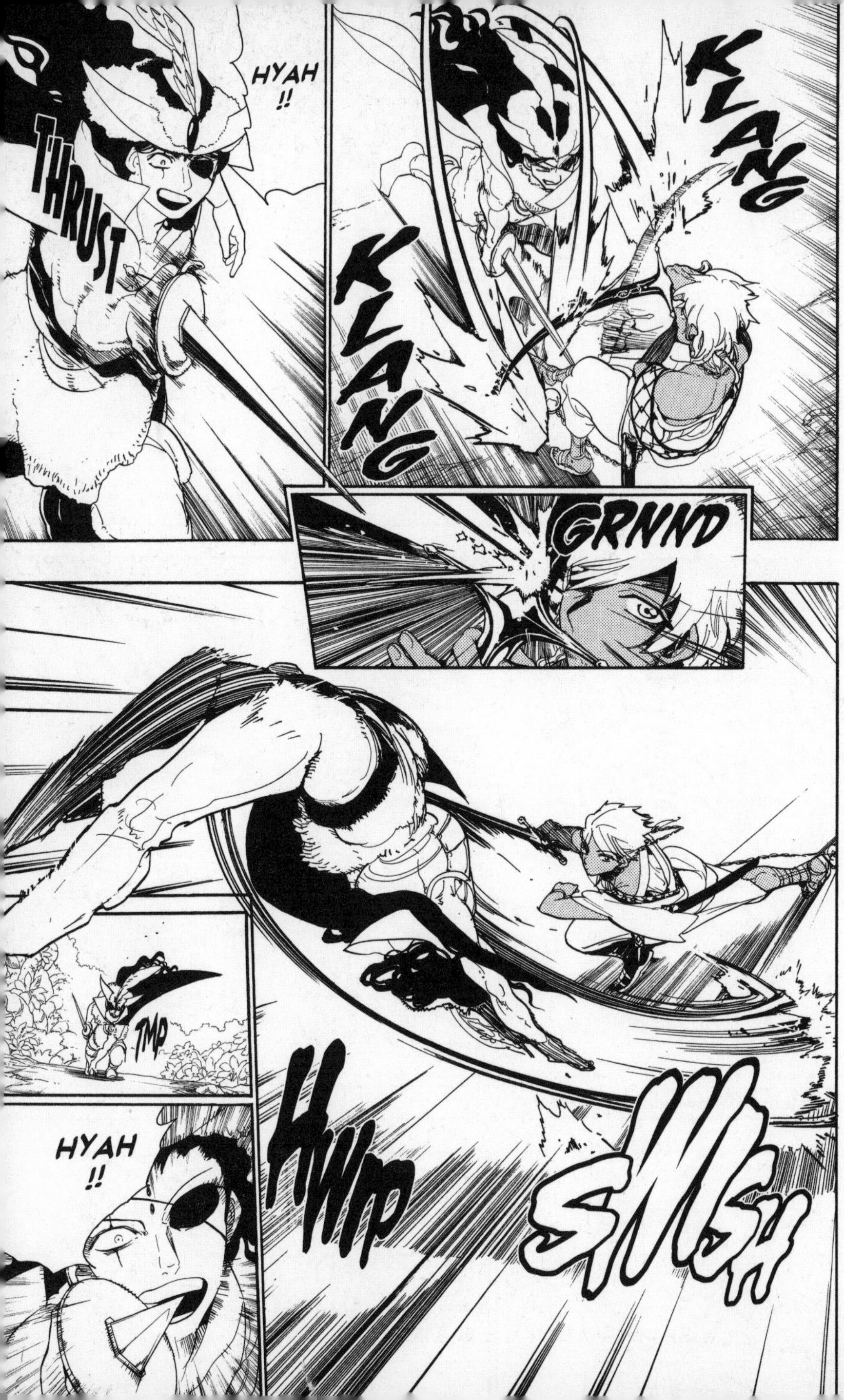
KLANG
KLANG
HYAH !!
THRUST
GRNND
SWISH
HWIP
TMP
HYAH !!

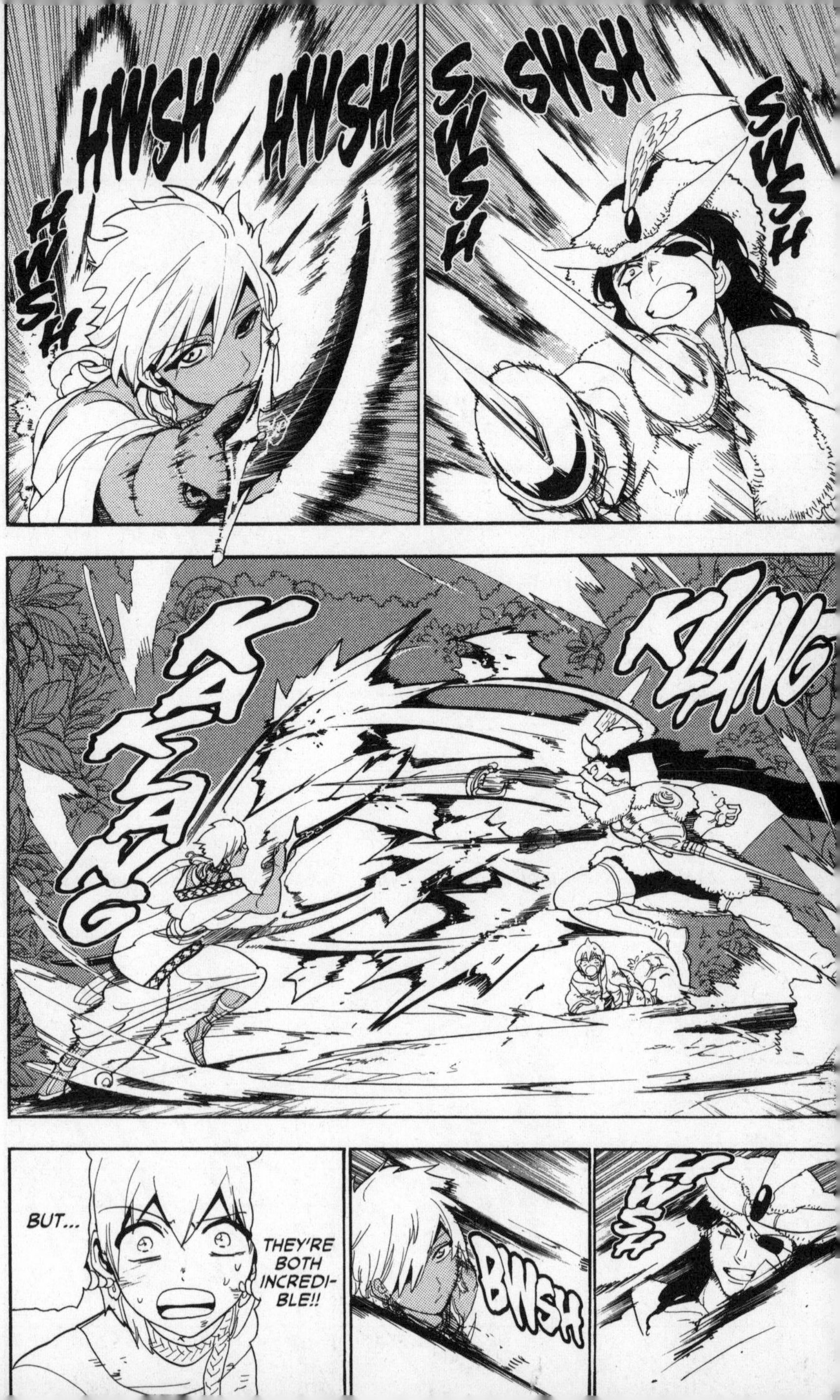
SWSH
SWSH
SWSH
HWSH
HWSH
HWSH
KLANG
KAKLANG
HWSH
BWSH
BUT...
THEY'RE BOTH INCREDIBLE!!

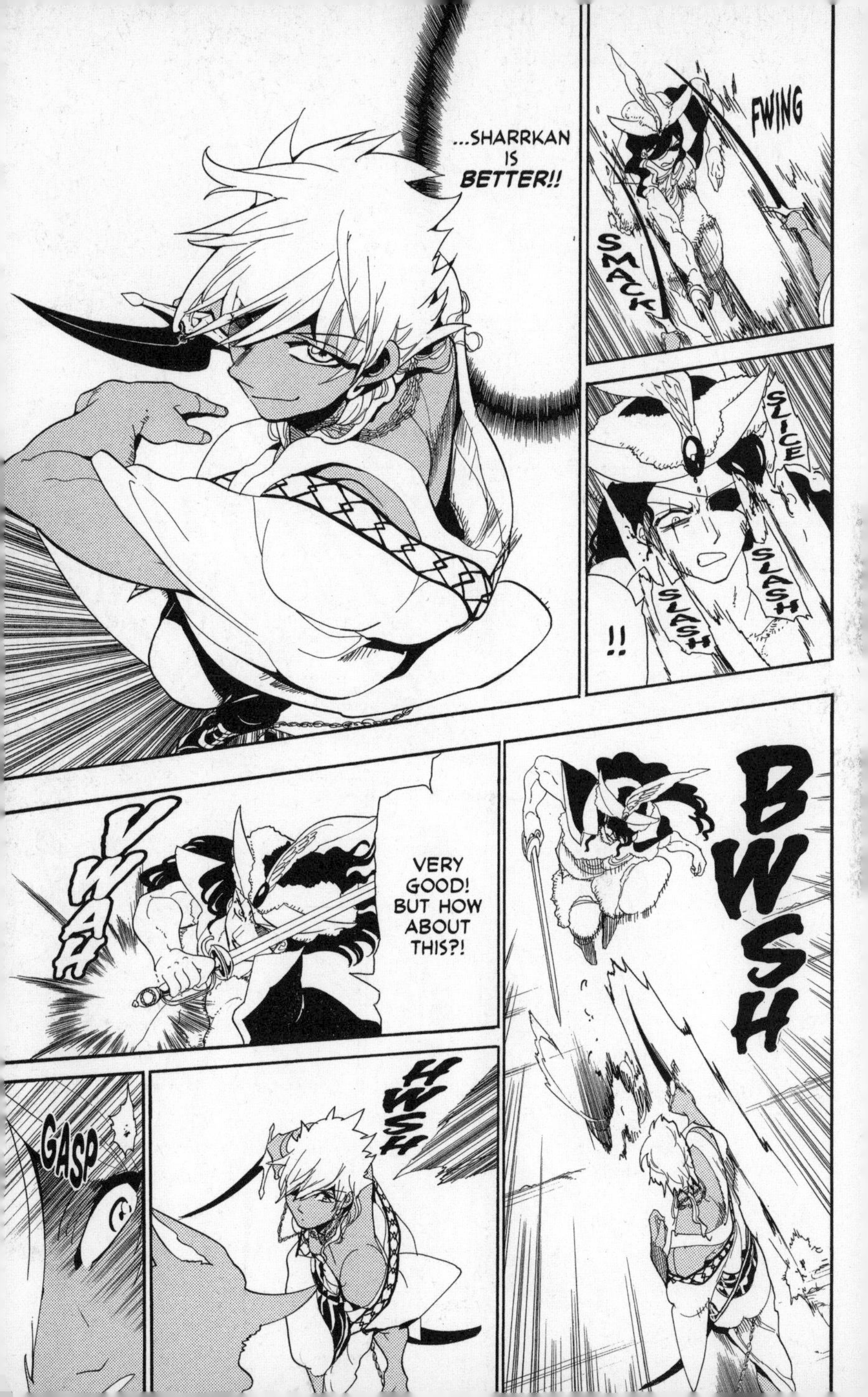
FWING
SMACK
SLICE
SLASH
SLASH
!!
...SHARRKAN IS *BETTER!!*
BWSH
VWAA
VERY GOOD! BUT HOW ABOUT THIS?!
HWSH
GASP

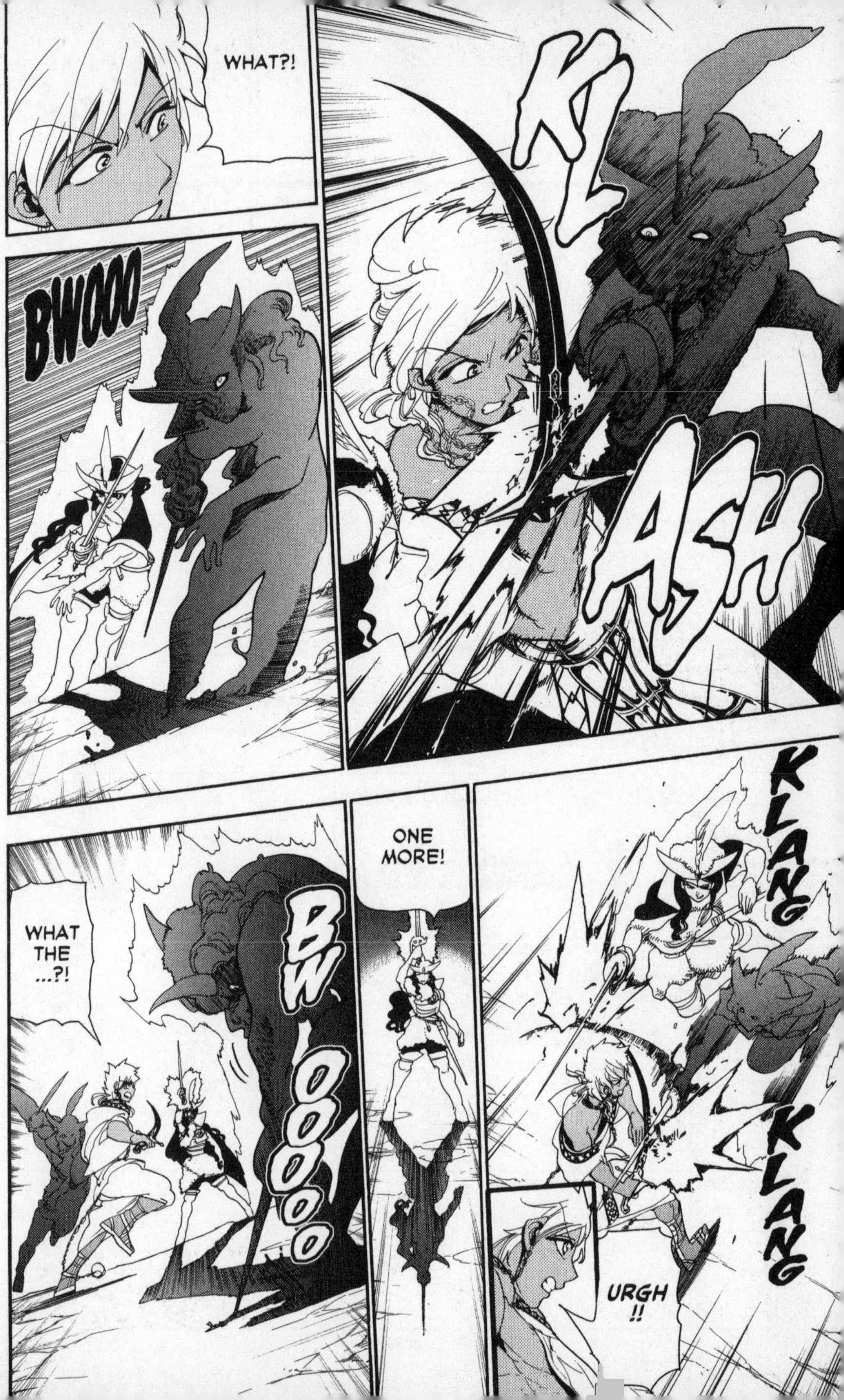
KL
ASH
WHAT?!
BWOOO
KLANG
KLANG
URGH!!
ONE MORE!
BW
OOOOOO
WHAT THE ...?!

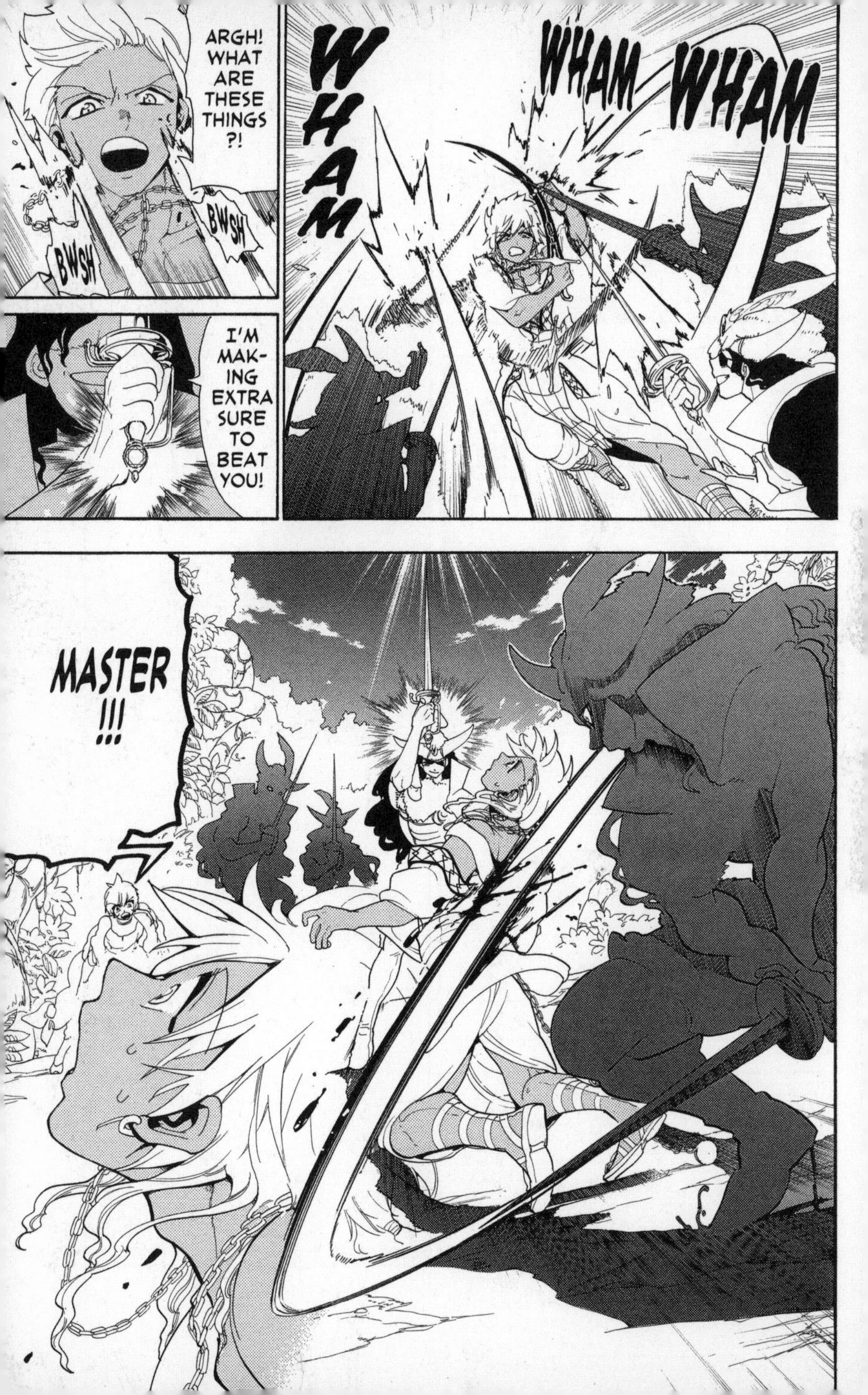
WHAM WHAM
WHAM
ARGH! WHAT ARE THESE THINGS?!
BWSH
BWSH
I'M MAK-ING EXTRA SURE TO BEAT YOU!
MASTER!!!

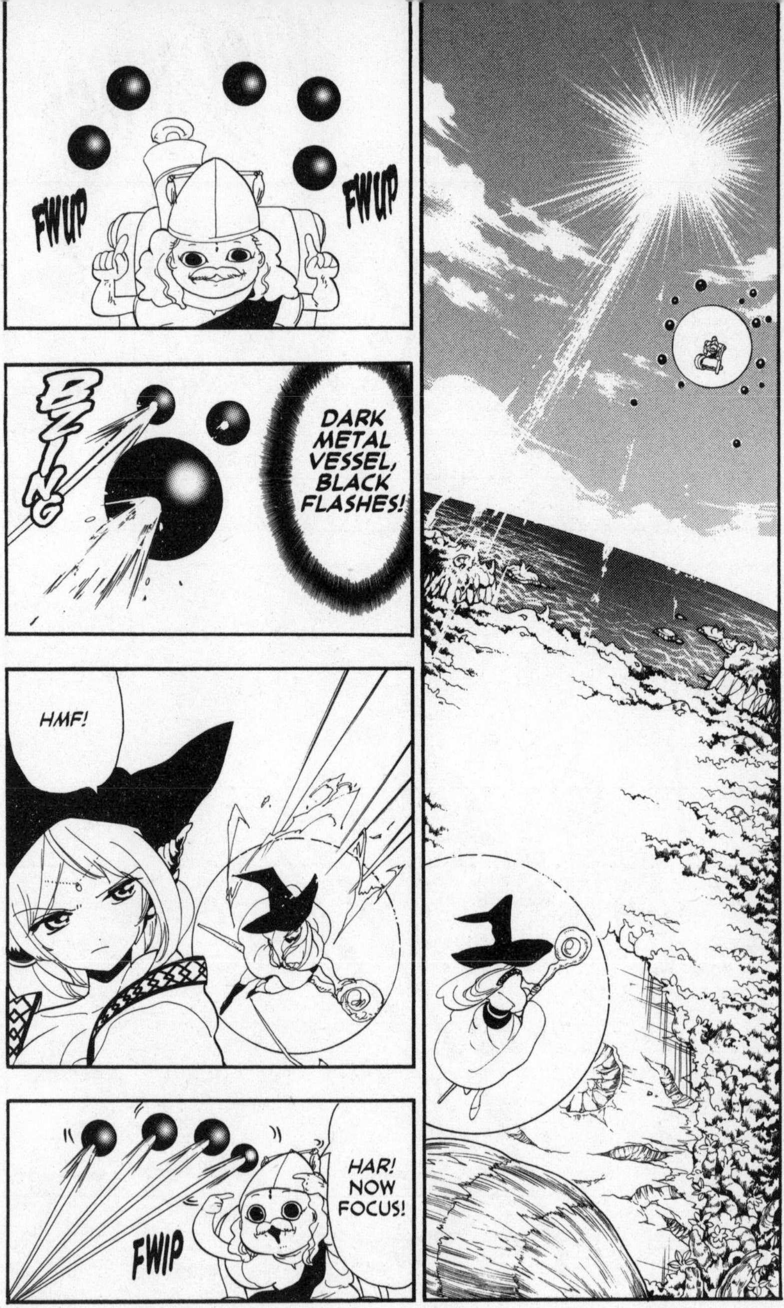
FWUP
FWUP
DARK METAL VESSEL, BLACK FLASHES!
BZING
HMF!
HAR! NOW FOCUS!
FWIP

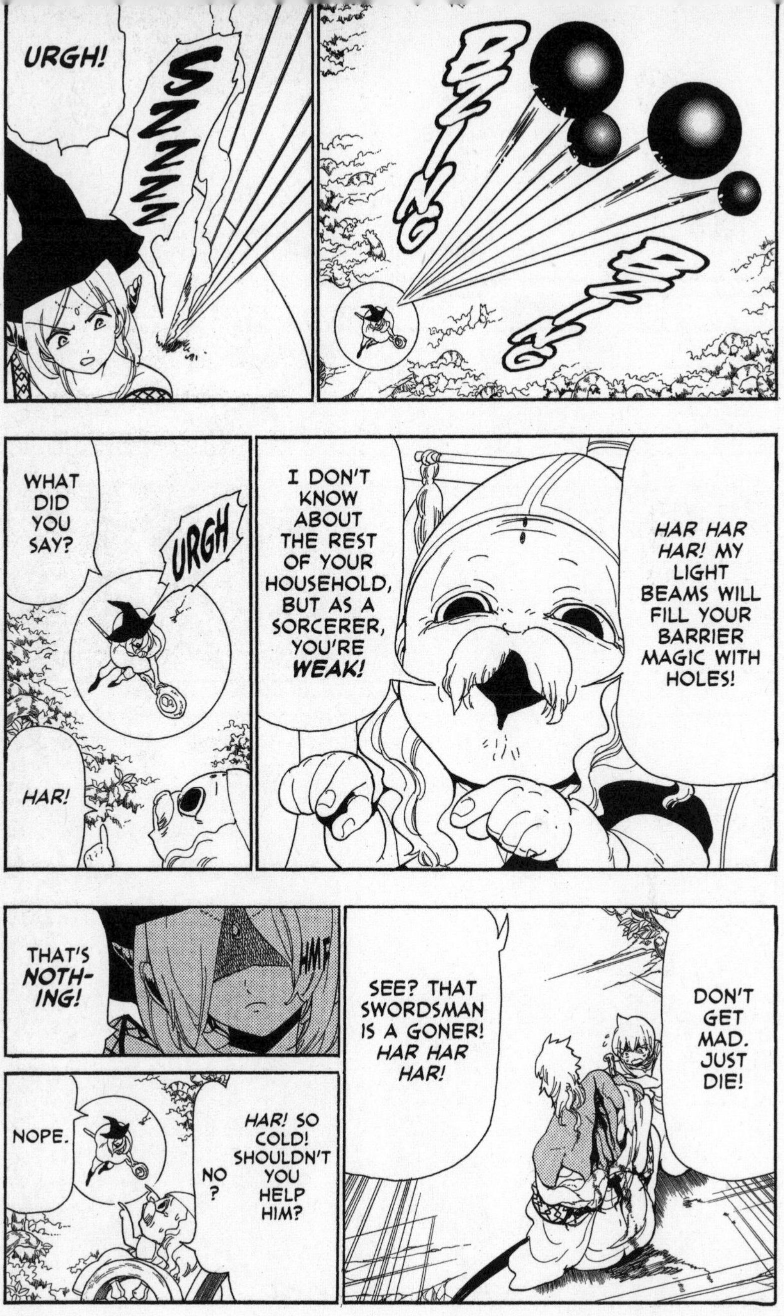
BZING
BZING
URGH!
SZZZZZ
HAR HAR HAR! MY LIGHT BEAMS WILL FILL YOUR BARRIER MAGIC WITH HOLES!
I DON'T KNOW ABOUT THE REST OF YOUR HOUSEHOLD, BUT AS A SORCERER, YOU'RE WEAK!
WHAT DID YOU SAY?
URGH
HAR!
DON'T GET MAD. JUST DIE!
SEE? THAT SWORDSMAN IS A GONER! HAR HAR HAR!
HMF
THAT'S NOTHING!
HAR! SO COLD! SHOULDN'T YOU HELP HIM?
NO?
NOPE.

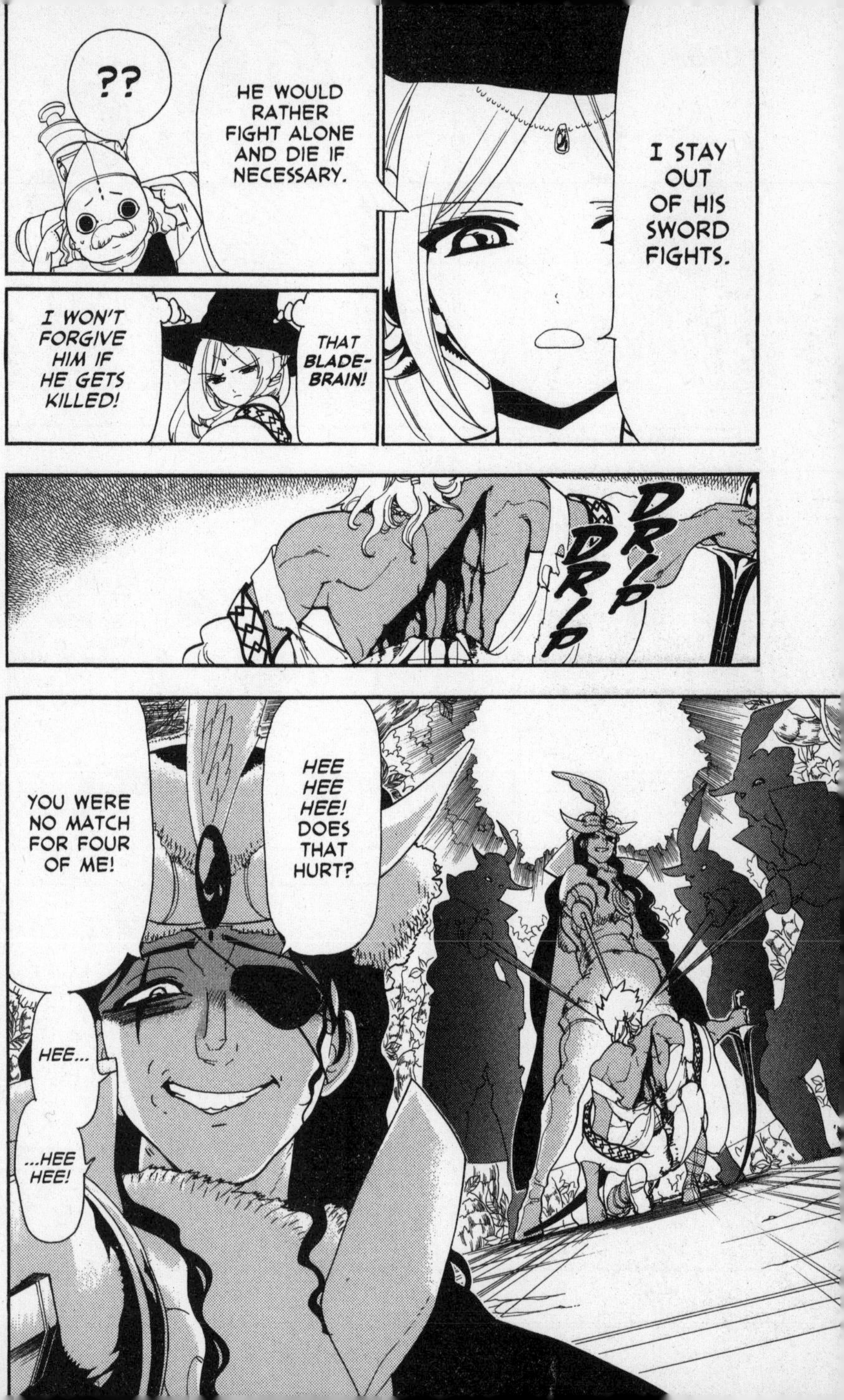
I STAY OUT OF HIS SWORD FIGHTS.
HE WOULD RATHER FIGHT ALONE AND DIE IF NECESSARY.
??
THAT BLADE-BRAIN!
I WON'T FORGIVE HIM IF HE GETS KILLED!
DRIP DRIP DRIP
HEE HEE HEE! DOES THAT HURT?
YOU WERE NO MATCH FOR FOUR OF ME!
HEE...
...HEE HEE!

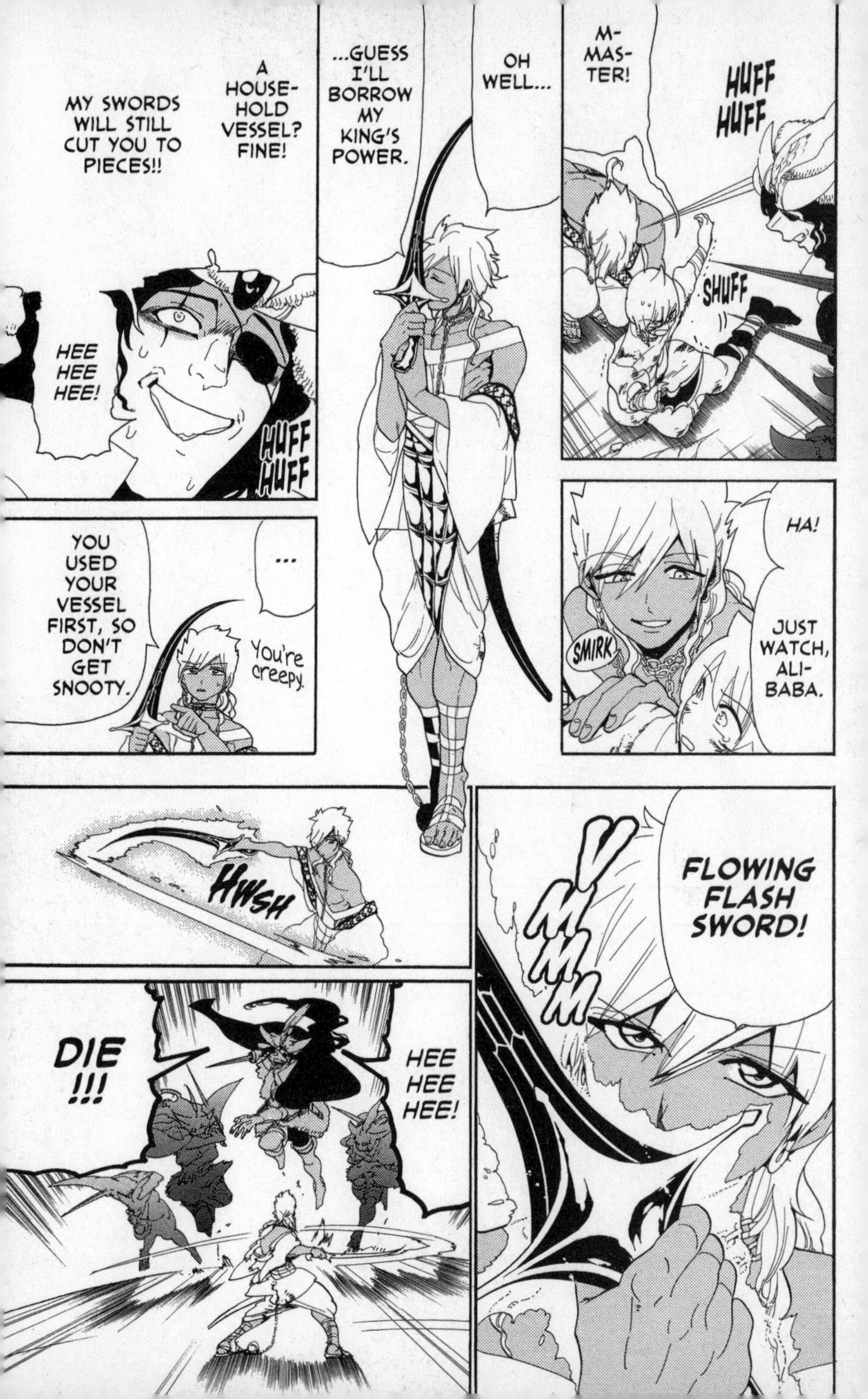
M-MASTER!
HUFF HUFF
SHUFF
HA!
JUST WATCH, ALI-BABA.
SMIRK
OH WELL...
...GUESS I'LL BORROW MY KING'S POWER.
A HOUSEHOLD VESSEL? FINE!
MY SWORDS WILL STILL CUT YOU TO PIECES!!
HEE HEE HEE!
HUFF HUFF
...
YOU USED YOUR VESSEL FIRST, SO DON'T GET SNOOTY.
You're creepy.
FLOWING FLASH SWORD!
VMMM
HWSH
HEE HEE HEE!
DIE!!!

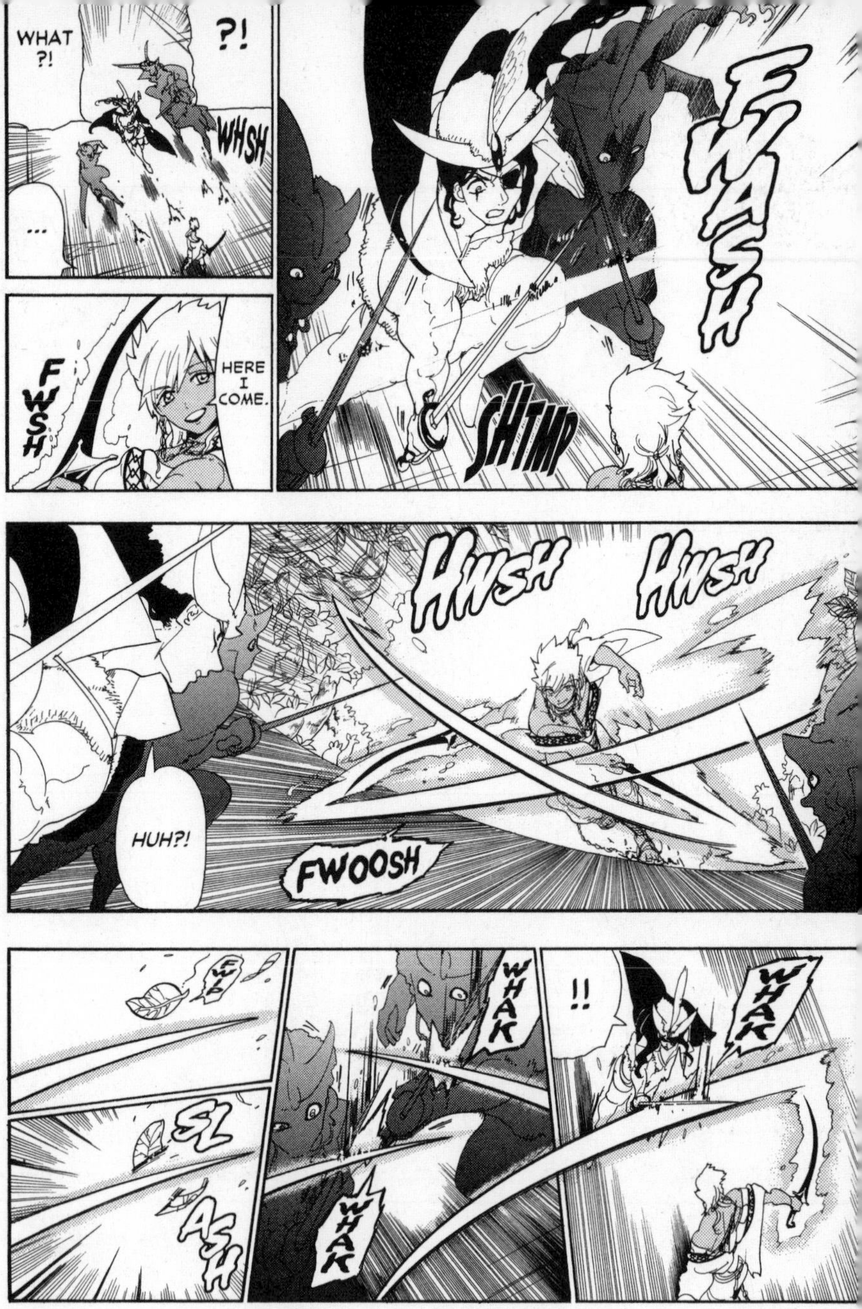
FWASH
SHTMP
?!
WHAT ?!
WHSH
...
HERE I COME.
FWSH
HWSH
HWSH
FWOOSH
HUH?!
WHAK
!!
WHAK
WHAK
FWIP
SL
ASH

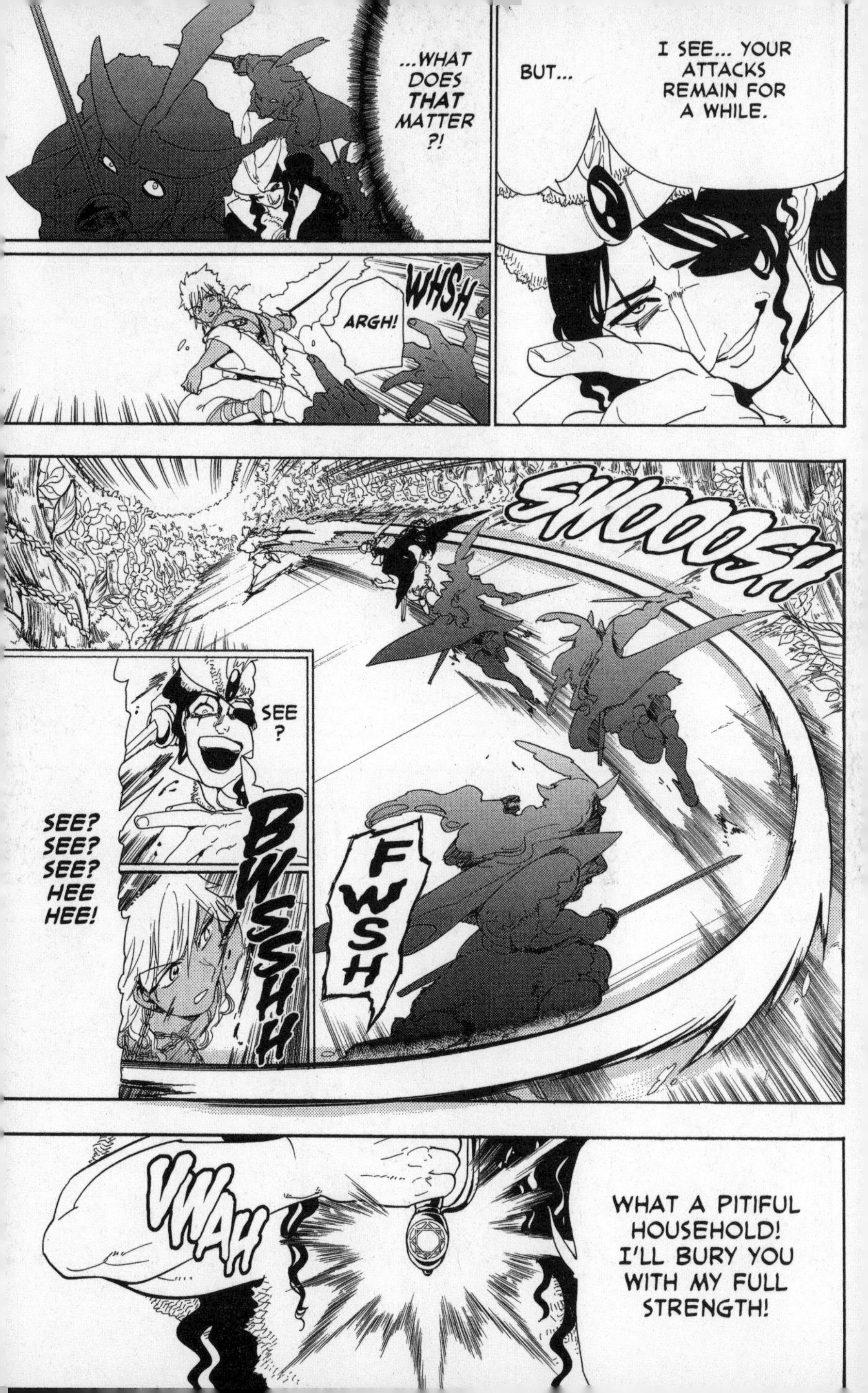
I SEE... YOUR ATTACKS REMAIN FOR A WHILE.
BUT...
...WHAT DOES THAT MATTER?!
WHSH
ARGH!
SWOOOSH
FWSH
SEE?
SEE? SEE? SEE? HEE HEE!
BWSSHH
WHAT A PITIFUL HOUSEHOLD! I'LL BURY YOU WITH MY FULL STRENGTH!
VWAH

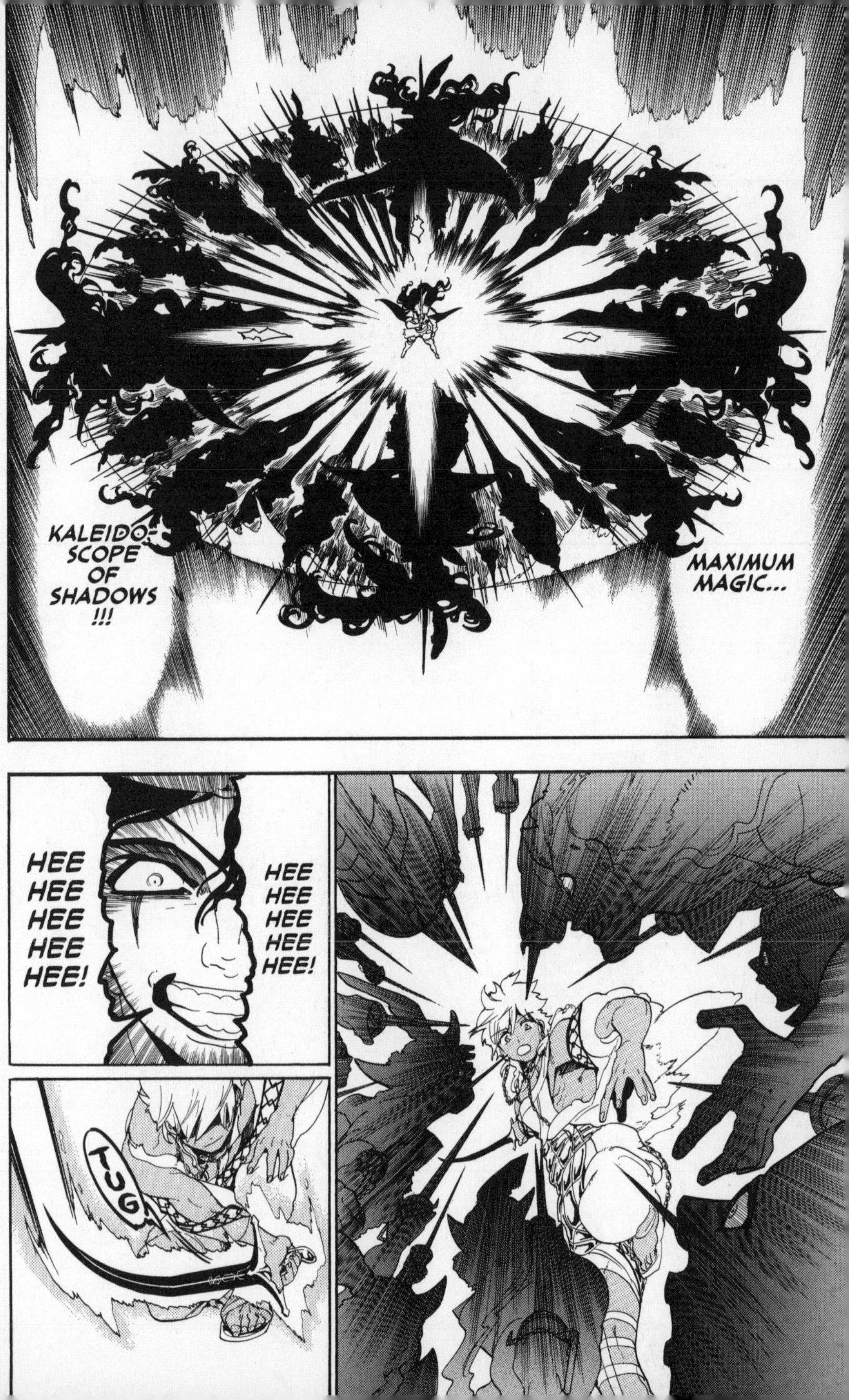
MAXIMUM MAGIC...
KALEIDO-SCOPE OF SHADOWS!!!
HEE HEE HEE HEE HEE!
HEE HEE HEE HEE HEE!
TUG

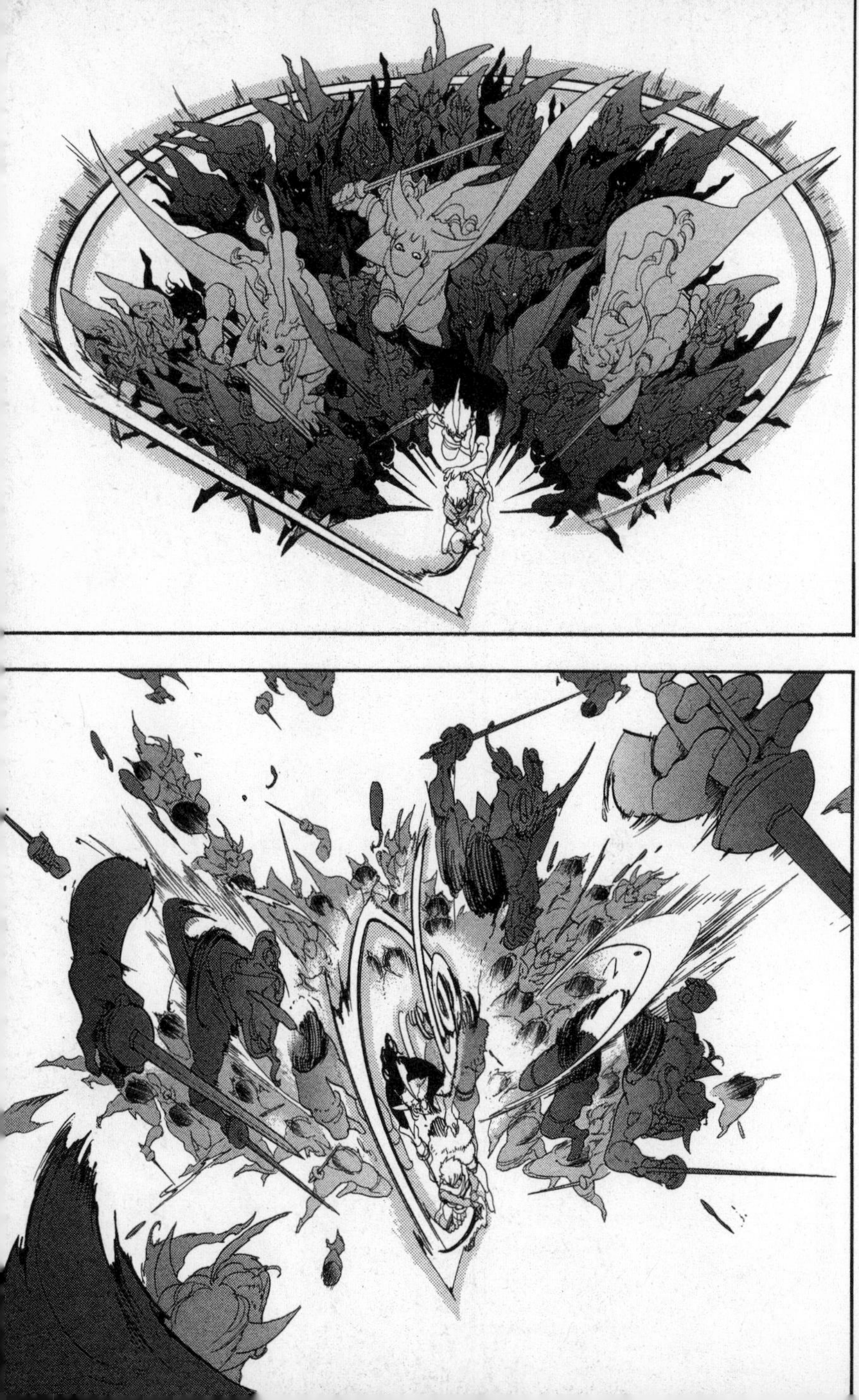

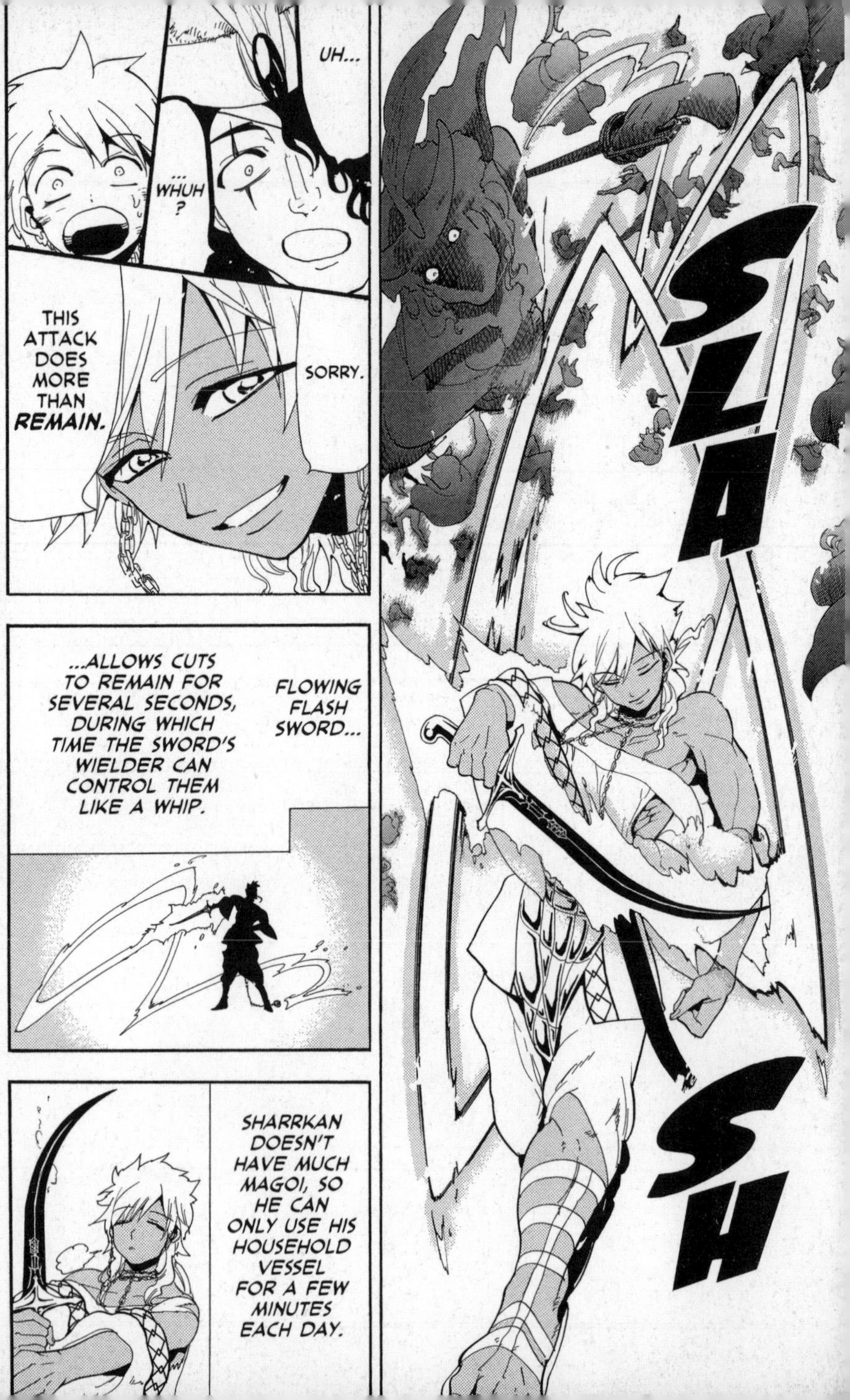

SLASH
UH...
...WHUH?
SORRY.
THIS ATTACK DOES MORE THAN *REMAIN.*
FLOWING FLASH SWORD...
...ALLOWS CUTS TO REMAIN FOR SEVERAL SECONDS, DURING WHICH TIME THE SWORD'S WIELDER CAN CONTROL THEM LIKE A WHIP.
SHARRKAN DOESN'T HAVE MUCH MAGOI, SO HE CAN ONLY USE HIS HOUSEHOLD VESSEL FOR A FEW MINUTES EACH DAY.

The labyrinth of magic
MAGI マギ
11

Staff

■ Story & Art

Shinobu Ohtaka

■ Regular Assistants

Akira Sugito

Tanimoto

Makoto Akui

Yoshihumi Otera

Hiro Maizima

■ Editor
Kazuaki Ishibashi

■ Sales & Promotion
Shinichirou Todaka

Atsushi Chiku

■ Designer
Yasuo Shimura + Bay Bridge Studio

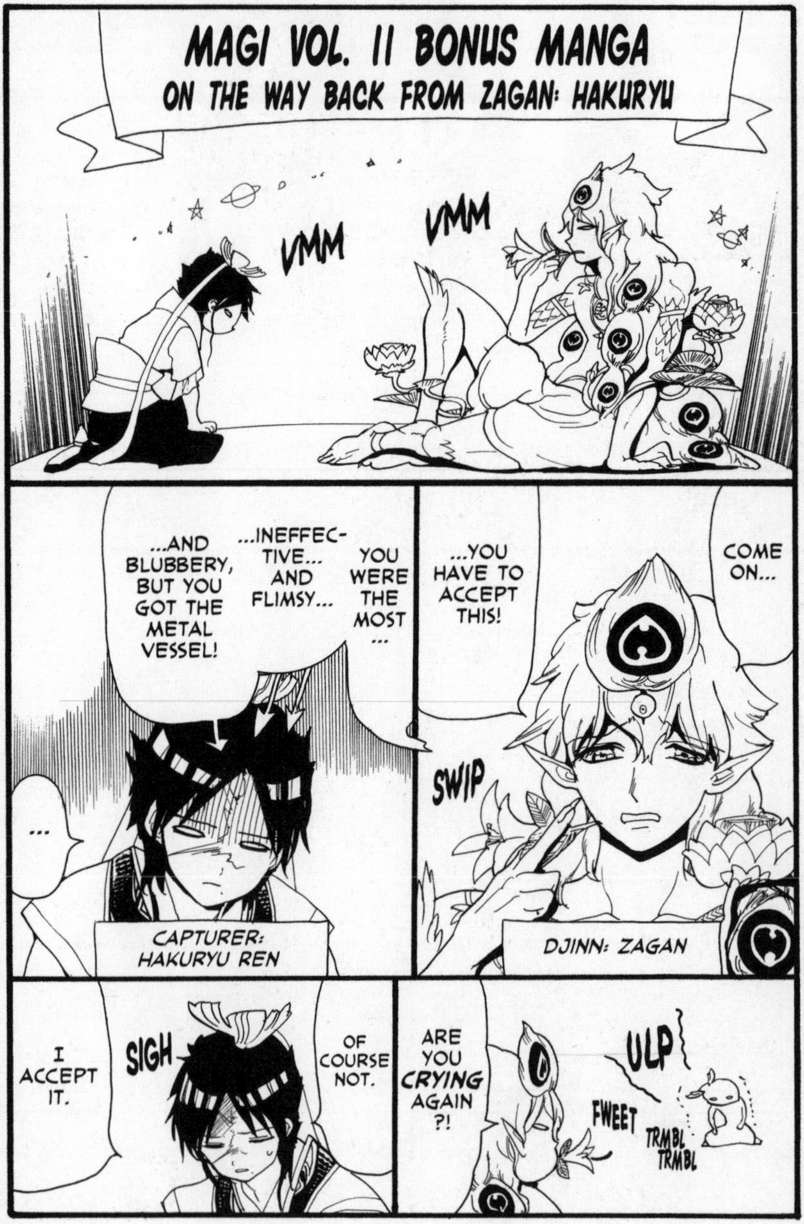
MAGI VOL. 11 BONUS MANGA
ON THE WAY BACK FROM ZAGAN: HAKURYU
VMM
VMM
COME ON...
...YOU HAVE TO ACCEPT THIS!
SWIP
DJINN: ZAGAN
YOU WERE THE MOST ...
...INEFFEC-TIVE... AND FLIMSY...
...AND BLUBBERY, BUT YOU GOT THE METAL VESSEL!
...
CAPTURER: HAKURYU REN
ARE YOU CRYING AGAIN ?!
ULP
FWEET
TRMBL TRMBL
OF COURSE NOT.
SIGH
I ACCEPT IT.

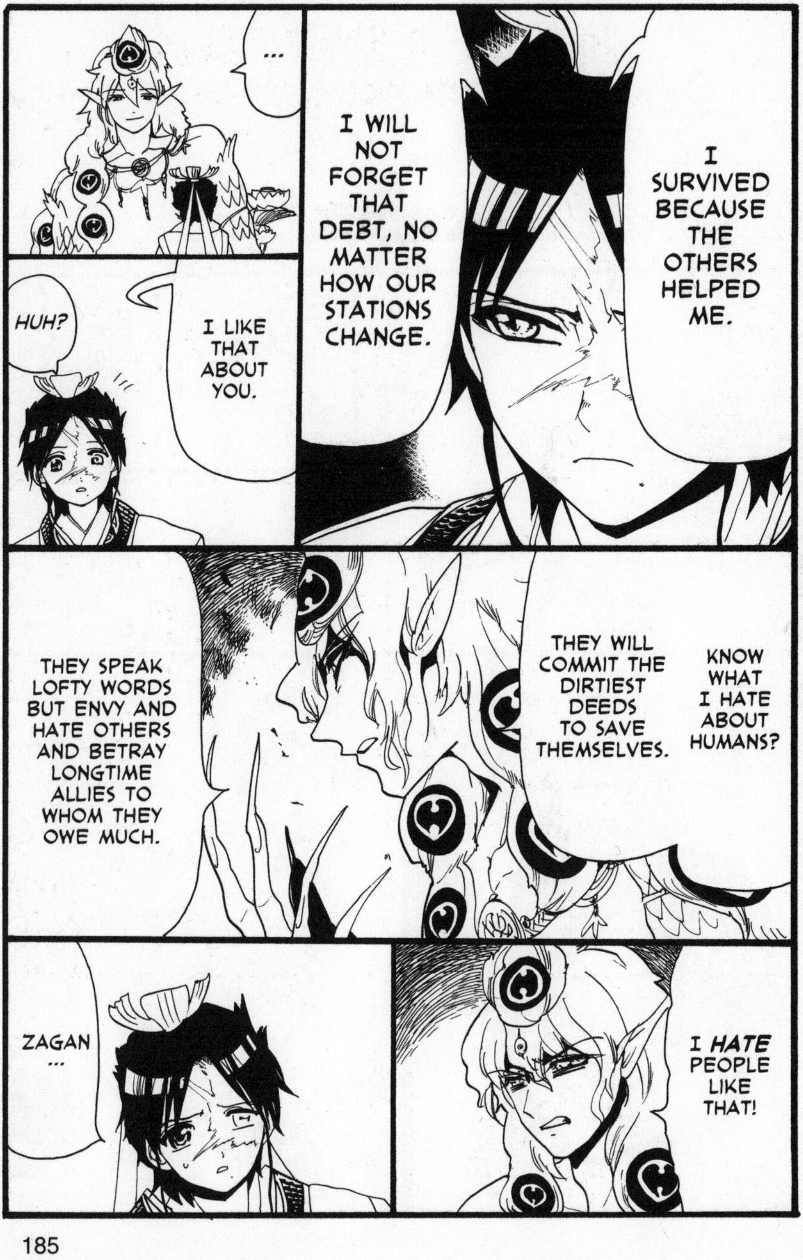
I SURVIVED BECAUSE THE OTHERS HELPED ME.
I WILL NOT FORGET THAT DEBT, NO MATTER HOW OUR STATIONS CHANGE.
...
I LIKE THAT ABOUT YOU.
HUH?
KNOW WHAT I HATE ABOUT HUMANS?
THEY WILL COMMIT THE DIRTIEST DEEDS TO SAVE THEMSELVES.
THEY SPEAK LOFTY WORDS BUT ENVY AND HATE OTHERS AND BETRAY LONGTIME ALLIES TO WHOM THEY OWE MUCH.
I *HATE* PEOPLE LIKE THAT!
ZAGAN ...

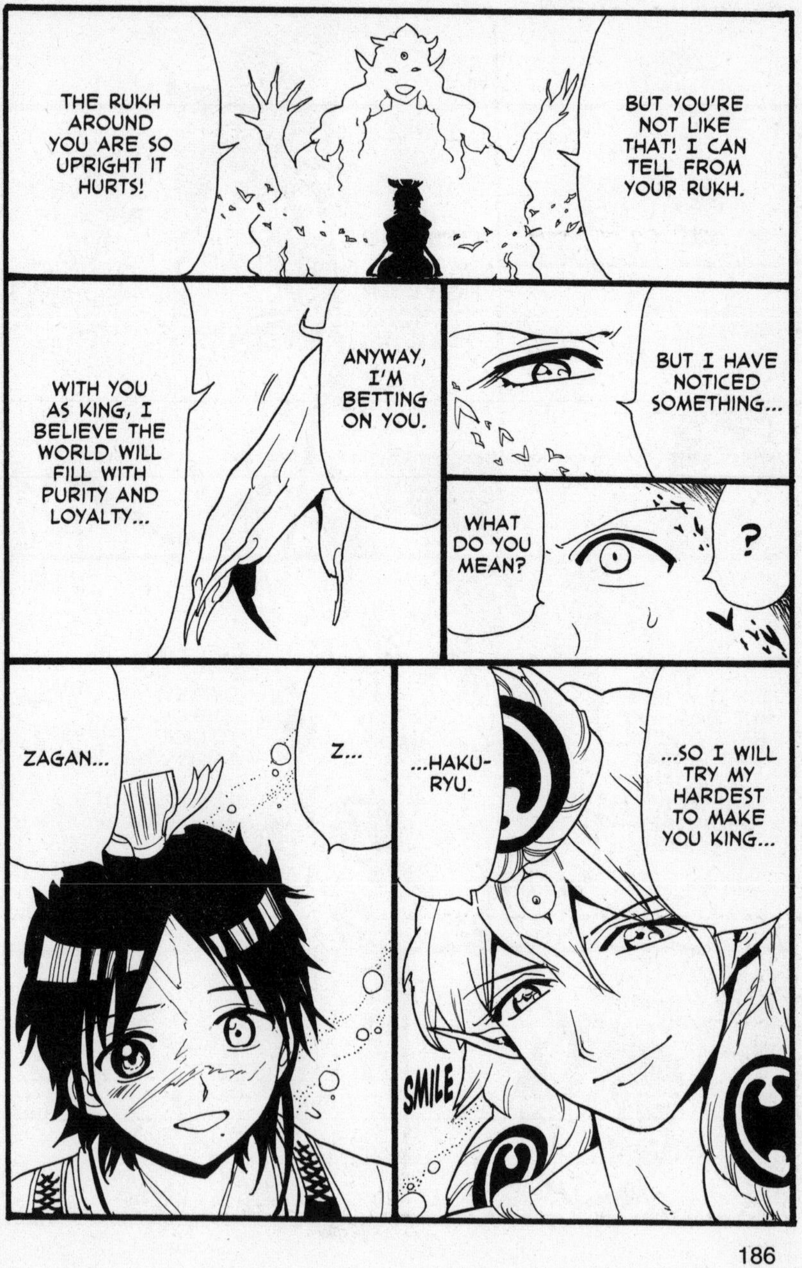
BUT YOU'RE NOT LIKE THAT! I CAN TELL FROM YOUR RUKH.
THE RUKH AROUND YOU ARE SO UPRIGHT IT HURTS!
BUT I HAVE NOTICED SOMETHING...
?
WHAT DO YOU MEAN?
ANYWAY, I'M BETTING ON YOU.
WITH YOU AS KING, I BELIEVE THE WORLD WILL FILL WITH PURITY AND LOYALTY...
...SO I WILL TRY MY HARDEST TO MAKE YOU KING...
...HAKU-RYU.
SMILE
Z...
ZAGAN...

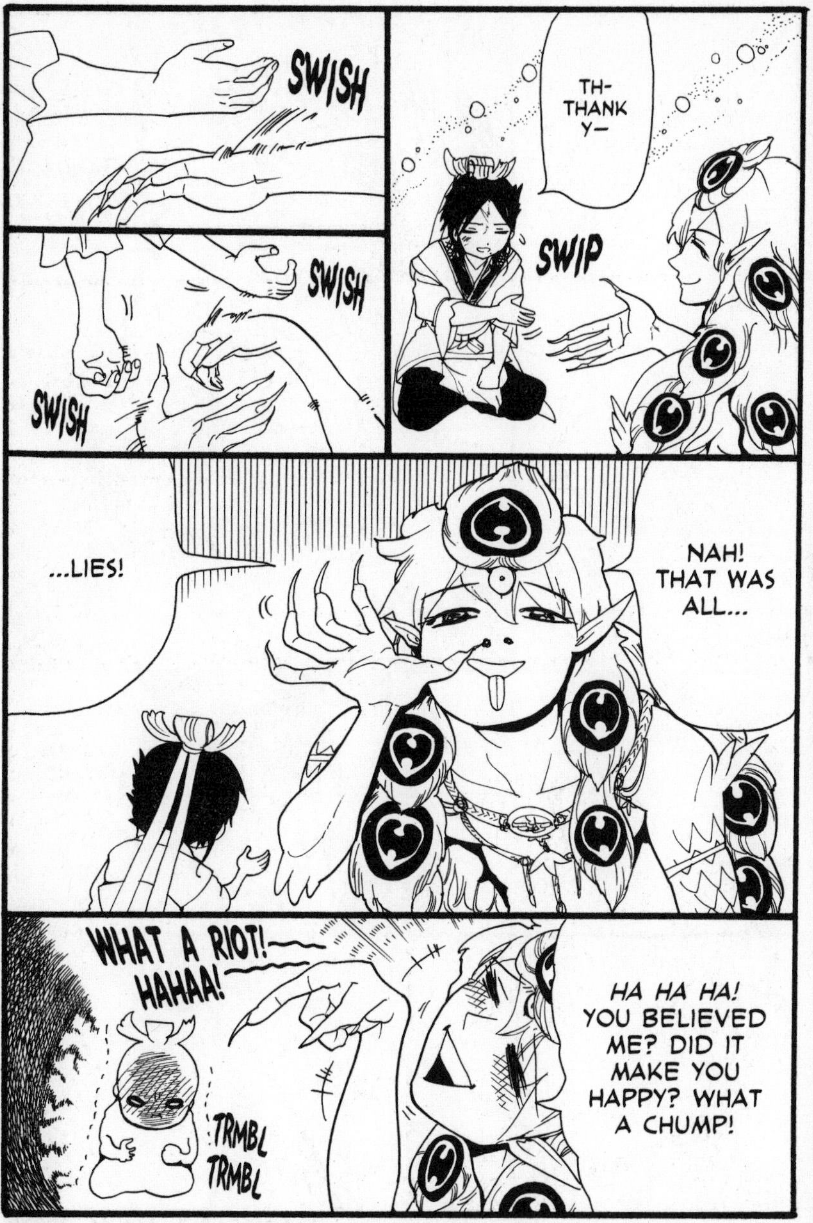
TH- THANK Y—
SWIP
SWISH
SWISH
SWISH
NAH! THAT WAS ALL...
...LIES!
HA HA HA! YOU BELIEVED ME? DID IT MAKE YOU HAPPY? WHAT A CHUMP!
WHAT A RIOT! HAHAA!
TRMBL TRMBL

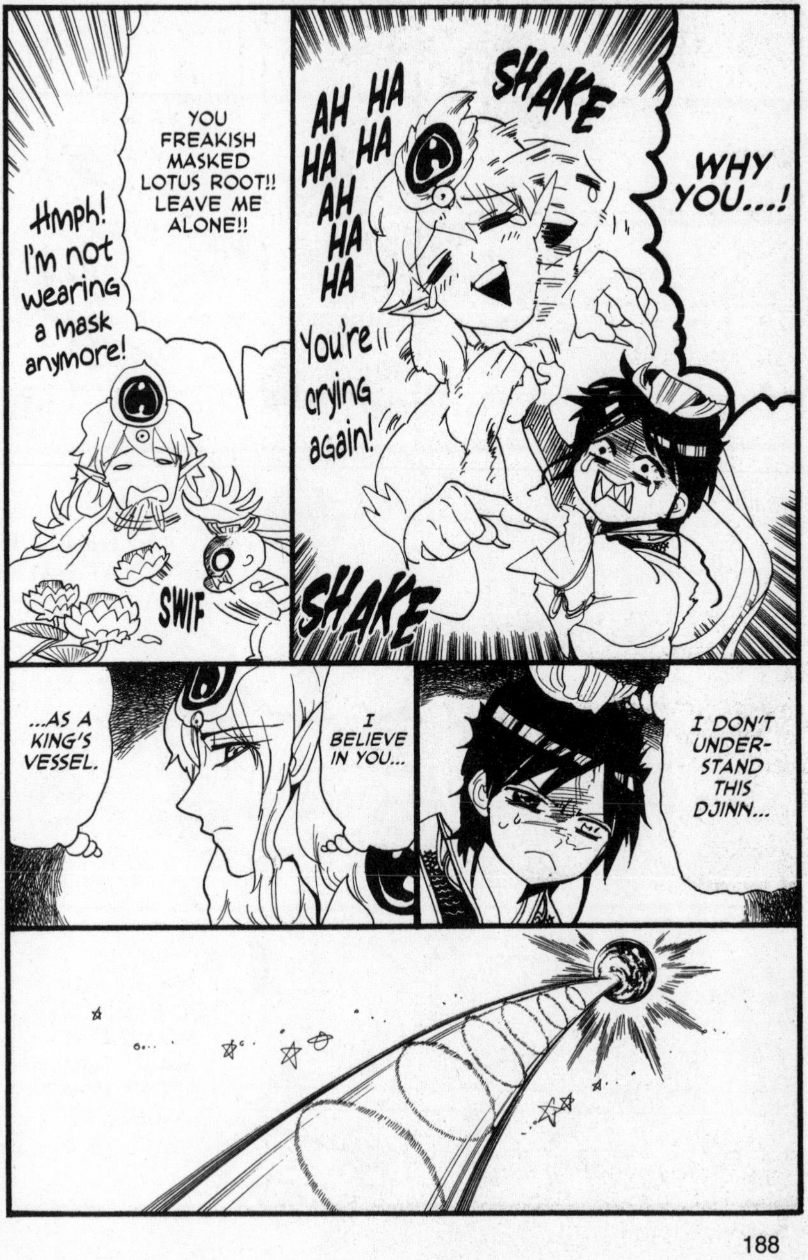
WHY YOU...!
SHAKE
AH HA HA HA AH HA HA HA
You're crying again!
SHAKE
YOU FREAKISH MASKED LOTUS ROOT!! LEAVE ME ALONE!!
Hmph! I'm not wearing a mask anymore!
SWIF
I DON'T UNDER-STAND THIS DJINN...
I BELIEVE IN YOU...
...AS A KING'S VESSEL.

On the Way Back from Zagan: Morgiana

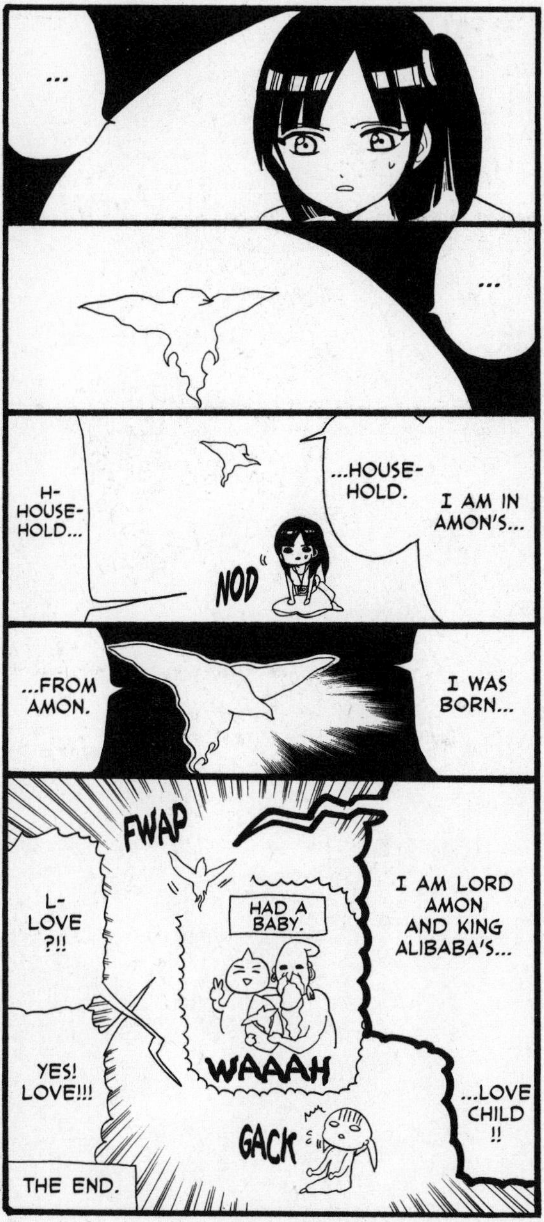
...
...
I AM IN AMON'S...
...HOUSE-HOLD.
H-HOUSE-HOLD...
NOD
I WAS BORN...
...FROM AMON.
I AM LORD AMON AND KING ALIBABA'S...
FWAP
L-LOVE?!!
HAD A BABY.
...LOVE CHILD!!
WAAAH
YES! LOVE!!!
GACK
THE END.

**SHINOBU
OHTAKA**

*Please enjoy
Volume 11!*

MAGI

Volume 11

Shonen Sunday Edition

Story and Art by
SHINOBU OHTAKA

MAGI Vol.11
by Shinobu OHTAKA
© 2009 Shinobu OHTAKA
All rights reserved.
Original Japanese edition published by SHOGAKUKAN.
English translation rights in the United States of America, Canada, the United Kingdom,
Ireland, Australia and New Zealand arranged with SHOGAKUKAN.

Translation & English Adaptation ◆ John Werry

Touch-up Art & Lettering ◆ Stephen Dutro

Editor ◆ Mike Montesa

The stories, characters and incidents mentioned in this publication are entirely fictional.

No portion of this book may be reproduced or transmitted in any form or
by any means without written permission from the copyright holders.

Printed in the U.S.A.

Published by VIZ Media, LLC
P.O. Box 77010
San Francisco, CA 94107

10 9 8 7 6 5 4 3 2 1
First printing, April 2015

PARENTAL ADVISORY
MAGI is rated T for Teen.
This volume contains
suggestive themes.
ratings.viz.com

WWW.SHONENSUNDAY.COM

www.viz.com

You're reading the
WRONG WAY

◆◇◆◇◆◇◆◇◆◇◆◇◆◇◆◇◆◇◆◇◆◇◆◇◆◇◆◇◆◇◆◇◆◇◆

MAGI reads from right to left, starting in the upper-right corner. Japanese is read from **right** to **left**, meaning that action, sound effects, and word-balloon order are completely reversed from English order.

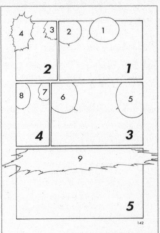